THE FIRST AMERICAN
CONSTITUTIONS

The Institute of Early American
History and Culture
is sponsored jointly by
The College of William and Mary in Virginia
and The Colonial Williamsburg Foundation.

THE FIRST AMERICAN CONSTITUTIONS

Republican Ideology and the Making of the
State Constitutions in the Revolutionary Era

WILLI PAUL ADAMS
Translated by Rita and Robert Kimber

With a Foreword by Richard B. Morris

Published for the
Institute of Early American History and Culture
Williamsburg, Virginia

by The University of North Carolina Press
Chapel Hill

Translation and revision of
Republikanische Verfassung und bürgerliche Freiheit
© 1973 by Hermann Luchterhand Verlag, Darmstadt und Neuwied

© 1980 The University of North Carolina Press
All rights reserved
Manufactured in the United States of America
Library of Congress Catalog Card Number 79-10887
ISBN 0-8078-1388-5

Library of Congress Cataloging in Publication Data

Adams, Willi Paul, 1940–
The first American constitutions.

Translation and revision of Republikanische Verfassung
und bürgerliche Freiheit.
Bibliography: p.
Includes index.
1. United States—Constitutional history.
2. Civil rights—United States.   3. United States
—History.   4. State rights.   I. Institute of Early American
History and Culture, Williamsburg, Va.   II. Title.
JK31.A2413   342'.73'029   79-10887
ISBN 0-8078-1388-5

To Angela, again

FOREWORD

During the bicentennial year 1976, the American Historical Association sponsored an international contest for the best scholarly book or manuscript on the Era of the American Revolution written in a language other than English and completed since July 1, 1969. The award consisted of underwriting the cost of the translation and publication of the prize book, along with the underwriting of the travel expenses incurred by the author in order to re-check sources and documents in the United States preparatory to the publication of the manuscript. After examining thirty-one entries, ranging from Arabic and Sinhalese to Japanese and Serbo-Croatian, a jury of distinguished historians chose this work by Dr. Willi Paul Adams, entitled in its original German version, *Republikanische Verfassung und bürgerliche Freiheit: Die Verfassungen und politischen Ideen der amerikanischen Revolution*.

Of the rich variety of topics in American constitutional history, the development of the constitutional structure of the nation and the several states prior to the Federal Convention of 1787 has received less attention in depth than the heroic subject deserves. Dr. Adams essays to repair this omission, and, while some of the ground he traverses has been traveled by others, perhaps nowhere else will one find so incisive and illuminating an analysis of such innovative concepts as constitutionalism, republicanism, and federalism, of "mixed government" and other basic constitutional principles that set the American Revolution apart from those that followed.

Dr. Adams's treatment of the concept of "constituent power" may be cited as one of numerous examples of the penetrating critiques afforded by this study. As the author sees it, America invented "not only the thing but the name for it." Believing that the moral foundations of government rest upon the consent of the governed, the author shows how the attachment of a substantial body of the people to the cause of independence provided the underpinnings for the concept of constituent power. Adams discerns the roots of a people's government in the early Revolutionary machinery, the elaborate Patriot infrastructure, linking artisans and mechanics. In New England, he finds the church, the town meeting, the county conventions, and the provincial council and assembly joining forces to recruit a broad-based support for revolution. Outside the formal political structure, he might have added the militia as well. Tracing step-by-step the mechanism by which the delegates to the First and Second Continental Congresses were selected, and stressing extralegal methods of registering the public's will, responsive in no small part to the necessities of the Revolutionary situation, Dr. Adams points to the result—a continental-wide Revolutionary machinery, both on the national and the state level. From these Revolutionary steps emerged a system of dual sovereignty, with the Congress exercising external authority and the states a limited or internal sovereignty, the latter bolstered by Article II of the Articles of Confederation, a crucial provision adopted with little debate.

A logical extension of the notion that government rested upon the consent of the governed was the acceptance and incorporation in this dual constitutional structure of the doctrine of resort to "first principles," embracing the right to amend or change a constitution, a subject of great relevance to Americans today.

Dr. Adams brings ripe scholarship to the task of tracing the somewhat divergent paths taken by "democracy" and "republicanism" during the post-Revolutionary years, points to the plebiscitary element in the state constitutions, particularly in New England, where from the outset instructions to representatives were taken for granted, and demonstrates how pragmatic rather than doctrinaire principles determined constitutional and legal ideas on such subjects as office holding, slavery, and religious toleration.

The author does not regard the Constitution that supplanted the Articles as representing a counterrevolution or restoration, differing in that respect from antifederalist historians writing in the populist tradition. A king was not restored; the British Cabinet system not adopted; but instead, political institutions were instituted incorporating principles of division of powers and checks and balances, principles thoroughly grounded in the state constitutional experience in the Revolutionary and Confederation years.

Dr. Adams is, admittedly, hardly the first to demonstrate the interaction of European and primarily English radical thought on American constitutional ideology. What gives special distinction to his analysis is the perspective of a European scholar that he brings to bear on the subject. Dr. Adams is an admirer of the American constitutional achievements, but his admiration is tempered by consciousness of occasional wrong turnings, as he views them. With authority he informs us about what was innovative in theory and practice in the

American experience and wherein lay the debt to European legal and political theory. Above all, his book attests to the soundness of the constitutional ideas of the Founding Fathers, and serves to explain why the free republic they had created would prove durable.

Richard B. Morris

CONTENTS

Preface

Recent interpretations of the intellectual history of the American
Revolution set out, following the model of Perry Miller's brilliant
reconstruction of the Puritan mind, to recreate one composite Revolutionary American mind. In doing so, they encountered the great
temptation of the American historian of the Revolutionary period, the
temptation to serve the national need for a founding ideology or, in
Hannah Arendt's terminology, a founding mythology.[2] The ideological origins and consequences of the American Revolution are of singular significance for American national history because they are an
integral part of the making of the nation and its form of government,
and as such are part of the foundations of national identity and of the
legitimacy of the present political system. The authors of the relevant
studies probably never set out consciously to perform this service for
their nation in time for its bicentennial jubilee. But the celebrating
American public of 1976 could easily read their interpretations as
providing a "revolutionary" heritage, the essence of which was national consensus, not radical dissent, civil disobedience, violence,
and civil war.

The great weakness—and ultimate disservice to the nation—of
this view is its neglect of the dynamic role of dissent within the
patriotic and republican fold. When the advocates of independence
began to make use of their new freedom to reorganize the political

1. "Interessen (materielle und ideelle), nicht: Ideen beherrschen unmittelbar
das Handeln der Menschen. Aber die 'Weltbilder', welche durch 'Ideen'
geschaffen wurden, haben sehr oft als Weichensteller die Bahnen bestimmt,
in denen die Dynamik der Interessen das Handeln fortbewegte." Max Weber,
Gesammelte Aufsätze zur Religionssoziologie (Tübingen, 1920–1921), I, 252, my
translation.
2. Hannah Arendt, *On Revolution* (London, 1963), chap. 5.

process, it soon became evident that the guiding values of eighteenth-century American republican government, popular sovereignty, liberty, equality, and property, did not only function as unifying calls to action. They also divided Americans into more or less radical, more or less compromising, republicans. Some republicans proved to be more republican than others.

The making of the first state constitutions forced politically active citizens to take certain positions because they posed a series of questions that demanded unequivocal answers. A member of a provincial congress about to vote on the suffrage clause in a draft constitution had to decide whether he and his constituents wanted as property qualifications for electors of senators a freehold worth one hundred pounds sterling, forty pounds sterling, or no freehold qualification at all. He had to decide whether he wanted the governor to be elected by the house of representatives, by the senate—if he favored a two-chamber legislature at all—or by the voters, and what qualification these voters should have to meet; how powerful he wanted the republican governor to be in order to be effective and hold his own in the balance between the three branches; whether he wanted judges to serve for seven years or for life; whether the sovereignty of the people allowed life tenure of public officials; how the equality of all men was to be reconciled with the continued existence of slavery; whether property must not be protected against majority decisions; who or what was to be represented in the legislative assemblies, adult white men, the land they owned, or the corporation called town, parish, or county that sent them, regardless of the size of its population and territory; whether it was fair or not for the more densely populated coastal areas to dominate the hinterland; how much power the states would have to transfer to the Continental Congress to enable it to function as the federation's government vis-à-vis the European powers. Rhetoric, antimonarchical or antiaristocratic, did not do to answer these questions, and not surprisingly, patriotic republicans differed in how they responded.

European interpreters tend to overlook the differences among American republicans and often believe they have grasped the essential characteristic of the American Revolution when they state that it was a "bourgeois" and yet not a French type of revolution, or when, in order not to use a holy word in vain, they call it a colonial war for independence. This Europe-centered view shares the weakness of the consensus-oriented patriotic view in that it suggests harmony and solidarity where the contemporaries experienced struggle and conflict.

In order to avoid isolating ideas from action and to escape the danger of grand-scale homogenization, the following interpretation of the political ideas of the American Revolution focuses on the concrete issues that arose when, from 1774 on, rebelling colonists discarded the institutions of colonial government and substituted their own. The establishment of new institutions, or the confirmation of old ones, forced the revolutionaries to relate their political and social ideas to their actions and interests in specific situations. The result, it is hoped, will contribute to a history of political mentality as well as to the history of constitutional government and democracy.

The introductory chapter sketches the state of the constitutional and ideological conflict in 1774. The following three chapters describe the organizational questions posed by the disintegration of the colonial regime, especially the making of the state constitutions between 1776 and 1780. Chapter four refutes the assumption that republican government and democratic government meant two quite different things in the language of the founding generation. Chapter five explains the contemporary distinction between a well-intentioned but emotional profession of "principles" and the proven exigencies of "forms" of government. In chapters six through twelve, the debate concerning basic concepts of the American variant of republican government is analyzed, progressing from popular sovereignty to liberty, equality, property, the common good, representation, and the separation and balance of powers, to the development of a federal form of government that came to be the key to American success in nation building.

My interest in the intellectual history of the American Revolution was first aroused by the seminars that Gerald Stourzh gave between 1964 and 1969 as the first professor of American history at the John F. Kennedy Institute of North American Studies of the Free University of Berlin. Ever since, he has guided and advised me beyond the duties of a thesis advisor. I am grateful to him. Hans R. Guggisberg and Ernst Fraenkel read the thesis version. Wilhelm Bleek was very helpful with extended criticism at the stage of turning the thesis into a book. The library staff of the Kennedy Institute, under the competent directorship of Hans Kolligs, greatly aided my research. In the United States, Edmund S. Morgan and Staughton Lynd advised me during a first research trip in 1965/66 that was financed by the Deutsche

Gesellschaft für Amerikastudien and the Deutscher Akademischer Austauschdienst. Gordon S. Wood helped me find my way in his field. In 1972, the Deutsche Forschungsgemeinschaft made possible a stay as research fellow at the Charles Warren Center for Studies in American History of Harvard University, where I enjoyed all the advantages that this extremely useful institution offers in facilitating communication with resident experts, in my case with Bernard Bailyn and Oscar Handlin, and with the co-fellows, in my case especially with Stephen S. Webb and Henry D. Shapiro; the latter gave a major portion of the manuscript of the translation the benefit of his critical talents. In New York, Richard B. Morris and Ene Sirvet were helpful with items in the John Jay papers.

The English language edition was made possible by the American Historical Association's Bicentennial Award of 1976. The committee was headed by the association's president, Richard B. Morris. Aubrey C. Land, also on the committee, gave an incisive piece of advice for the English edition based on his close analysis of the German text. As a foreign scholar who has disproportionately profited from the international spirit of the A.H.A., I can only acknowledge in gratitude the importance of translating more of the work of students of American history around the world.

Anyone who takes the trouble to compare the German with the English edition should not fault Rita and Robert Kimber's excellent translation for discrepancies. Whole sentences, paragraphs, and sections were rewritten, omitted, or added, following the advice of my editors, whose self-effacing service to scholarship I learned to admire; I wish present-day publishers of historical monographs in Germany had even one Norman Fiering and one Cynthia Carter.

My most unsparing critic and unfailing supporter was Angela Meurer Adams.

Despite all the debts I incurred, Karl Popper was right when he said, "No book can ever be finished. While working on it we learn just enough to find it immature the moment we turn away from it."

THE FIRST AMERICAN
CONSTITUTIONS

Introduction

The people would be united in what they would easily see to be a constitutional opposition to tyranny. You know there is a charm in the word "constitutional."

Samuel Adams to Joseph Warren, September 24, 1774

The First American Constitutions

The enlightened monarch of Prussia spent the evening of his birthday in 1784 at the Berlin Academy of Sciences at a lecture arranged in his honor. The topic befitted the occasion: "On Forms of Government, and Which Is the Best?" The speaker, one of Frederick's ministers, commented on a most recent development: "Our century," he said in French, "by the birth of the American Republic has provided us with a new phenomenon." But, he maintained, this did not disprove his conviction that the time for republican government was "definitely over." The new state owed its existence to nothing more than a series of mistakes by the British government and to the political and commercial rivalry between Britain and France. "We will have to wait at least half a century," he insisted, "before we know whether and how this new republic, this confederated body, will consolidate the form of its government; at this time its existence does not prove anything in favor of the republican form."[1] The new phenomenon that prompted these comments and others like them in Europe had been conveniently defined by a set of public documents that were translated into several European languages and published along with other news

1. Ewald Friedrich Graf von Hertzberg, *Huit dissertations qui M. le Comte de Hertzberg, Ministre d'Etat, Membre et actuellement Curateur de l'Académie de Berlin, a lues dans les assemblées publiques de l'Académie Royale des Sciences et Belles Lettres de Berlin, Tenue pour l'anniversaire du Roi Frédéric II dans les Années 1780–1787* (Berlin, 1787), 147. For other reactions in the German-speaking part of Europe to the establishment of republican government in North America, see Horst Dippel, *Germany and the American Revolution, 1770–1800: A Sociohistorical Investigation of Late Eighteenth-Century Political Thinking*, trans. Bernhard A. Uhlendorf (Chapel Hill, N.C., 1977), 170–171.

3

about the war in North America.[2] For the European observer of two hundred years later as well as for his American contemporaries, these first American constitutions have lost their primacy of place to the Constitution of 1787/1788. Bicentennial patriotic rhetoric has often fused the Declaration of Independence and the Constitution into one all-engulfing Revolutionary act. Yet the Constitution was not adopted in 1776. Before that happened twelve critical years later, its authors and supporters, as well as its critics, had often looked back on the diverse constitutions of the first hour. The result of the deliberations of 1787 was not an adaptation of the British constitution, as some Americans had wished and as the European philosophes in their admiration of British liberties may even have expected. Instead, the president's office, with its brief four-year term, was basically modeled on that of a state governor, not on that of a monarch; a federal senator was to have more in common with a state senator than with a lord; and the separation of the three branches of the federal government was to take a shape unknown in Britain. Essentially, the basic structure of the Federal Constitution of 1787 was that of certain of the existing state constitutions writ large.

An attempt to reconstruct the political and social thought of the founders during the Revolution can hardly begin, therefore, with what we know of the proceedings of the Federal Convention in Philadelphia in 1787, or with the defense of its work in *The Federalist*. On the other hand, in the Declaration of Independence we find only a pithy statement of beliefs; legally speaking, it was an irrelevant credo that could not in itself give the vote to any white man or freedom to any black. Before credos could become matters of practice, political leaders in each state had to formulate the rules of the political process in state constitutions and in key laws. Similarly, relations between the states, and in particular the states' desire for individual autonomy, are revealed better in the Articles of Confederation than in the "Unanimous Declaration of the Thirteen United States of America." And the diversity in political thinking among those who favored independence was nowhere expressed more clearly than in the public debate that accompanied the drafting and adoption of the first constitutions.

2. Robert R. Palmer has found that in France the American state constitutions were published at least five times between 1776 and 1786. *The Age of the Democratic Revolution: A Political History of Europe and America, 1760–1800* (Princeton, N.J., 1959–1964), I, 263–282.

Four of these constitutional documents predated the Declaration of Independence. On January 6, 1776, six months before the Declaration, the colony of New Hampshire adopted the first written constitution ever drawn up by an English colony without consultation with or the approval of the crown or Parliament.[3] It was the intention of the ratifying body, a provincial congress convened in violation of existing British law and made up of delegates from towns everywhere in the colony, that this constitution be in effect only until the conflict with England was resolved. In South Carolina a provincial congress adopted a similar constitution on March 26, 1776. This instrument, too, was meant to be in force only until agreement with England could be reached. On July 2, 1776, the provincial congress of New Jersey ratified the last of these provisional constitutions.

Earlier, the provincial congress of Virginia, officially entitled the Convention of Delegates of the Counties and Corporations in the Colony of Virginia, had been the first body to separate a bill of rights from the text of the constitution itself. On June 12, 1776, the Virginia congress endorsed a declaration of rights, which has since taken its place in history as the Virginia bill of rights. Virginia's constitution was ratified on June 29, 1776. Within a year after the Declaration of Independence the provincial congresses of Delaware (September 11, 1776), Pennsylvania (September 28, 1776), Maryland (November 8, 1776), North Carolina (December 14, 1776), Georgia (February 4, 1777), and New York (April 20, 1777) went on to ratify constitutions.

In Massachusetts the process dragged on until June 16, 1780, because the competence of the provincial congress to adopt a constitution was most sharply contested there. In March and June of 1778 an unprecedented event in the history of modern constitutionalism took place in that former colony. Almost the entire adult male population had the opportunity to vote on a constitutional draft and to suggest changes in it. This occasioned public debate on fundamental questions concerning republican constitutions that was comparable in intensity and sophistication to the debate ten years later over the draft of the new Federal Constitution. The constitution proposed in Massachusetts in 1778 was voted down by a large majority. It was not until 1780 that a convention called together specifically for the purpose of drawing up a constitution succeeded in preparing a draft that was acceptable to the majority of the town meetings.

3. References for the details of constitution making, state by state, are in chap. 3.

The two remaining states of Connecticut and Rhode Island did not adopt new constitutions until 1818 and 1842 respectively, because their royal charters of 1662 and 1663 could easily be stripped of their monarchical components and reinterpreted as republican constitutions.

The inhabitants of the area between the Hudson River valley and the Connecticut River, the territory claimed by both New York and New Hampshire that became Vermont after June 1777, established their political independence on July 8, 1777, when a convention ratified the Vermont constitution. Of all the early state constitutions this was the only one that explicitly declared slavery unconstitutional. But since the other states were more interested in peace between New York and New Hampshire than they were in a fourteenth state, Vermont was not admitted to the Union until 1791.

From October 1774 on, the thirteen colonies had coordinated their resistance against England through a council of delegates, the Continental Congress. On May 10 and May 15, 1776, after several of the colonies had already acted on their own initiative, the Congress called for a reorganization of all the colonial governments. The necessity for cooperation that the Revolutionary War imposed determined the way authority was divided between the new state governments and the Continental Congress for the next five years. A formal confederation did not come into existence until 1781, when the last of the thirteen states ratified the Articles of Confederation.

Republicanism, Federalism, and Constitutionalism

The new governmental system of 1776 was republican, federal, and constitutional.[4] None of these adjectives used alone would adequately

4. On the contemporary meaning of "republican," see chap. 4, pp. 100–117 below. Federalism is discussed further in chap. 13. Classical treatises on the development of modern constitutionalism are Carl J. Friedrich, *Constitutional Government and Democracy: Theory and Practice in Europe and America* (Boston, 1941), and Karl Loewenstein, *Political Power and the Governmental Process*, 2d ed. (Chicago, 1965). M.J.C. Vile, *Constitutionalism and the Separation of Powers* (Oxford, 1967), is a broader treatment than the title suggests. On the development of American characteristics, see Gerald Stourzh, "The American Revolution, Modern Constitutionalism, and the Protection of Human Rights," in Kenneth Thompson and Robert J. Myers, eds., *Truth and Tragedy: A Tribute to Hans J. Morgenthau* (Washington, D.C., 1977), 162–176.

describe the system. More was involved than the absence of a royal family and of an aristocracy. Republican government in America, unlike that in France, did not displace an absolute monarchy but instead arose from conflict with English constitutional government, which had long been considered exemplary, particularly in protecting civil liberties. The American situation differed from the French, too, in that the struggle for independence was carried on by a large number of already organized and nearly autonomous political entities: the towns, counties, colonial assemblies, and provincial congresses. Cooperation among them could not but produce a federated governmental structure. The new order combined republicanism with already established institutions of Anglo-American constitutionalism. Thus, a federal compromise was the result, rather than a monolith that placed all sovereignty in the central government, as was to be the case in France.

The United States is the only long-lived modern republic to emerge from the "age of democratic revolution."[5] The community of republics that Jefferson had envisaged at the beginning of the French Revolution never became a reality in a world dominated by the monarchical principle. The lack of common bonds between French and American republicans and the failure of the French Revolution can be ascribed not only to differences in the social composition of the two countries but also to the different view French republicans took of the federal and constitutional components that Americans thought crucial to their system.[6]

The most significant accomplishment of the American Revolution, apart from the military achievement of independence, was the successful establishment of republican, federal, and constitutional government in a territory so extensive by European standards that conventional wisdom considered only monarchical government suit-

5. Palmer, *Age of the Democratic Revolution*; Jacques Godechot, *France and the Atlantic Revolution of the Eighteenth Century, 1770–1799*, trans. Herbert H. Rowen (New York, 1965); critical views of Palmer's and Godechot's interpretation in Peter Amann, ed., *The Eighteenth-Century Revolution: French or Western?* (Boston, 1963).
6. Compare Hannah Arendt's observation that "the most decisive distinction" between the American and French revolutions rested on the difference between the two systems each of them overthrew, British limited monarchy on the one hand, French absolutism on the other. In each case the new system of government was partly predetermined by the system it succeeded. Arendt, *On Revolution*, 154.

able for such an empire. This accomplishment would have many consequences both for the settling of North America by Europeans and for the opposition to monarchical government in Europe in the next two centuries.

The English Constitution in the Eighteenth Century

American republicanism did not arise as a counterideology to what had preceded it. It was the product of a political life that from the first decades of colonization had evolved in close conjunction with political developments in the mother country. The experiments in self-government that began in the first settlements were no less a part of British constitutional development than the concept of parliamentary sovereignty that had been taking shape in England since 1688. But it became clear from 1764 on that if both these principles were consistently adhered to, they would prove incompatible, even though both principles derived from the same political tradition of opposition to unlimited government.

Ever since 1688 the English political system had used constitutional means to settle disputes between interest groups, that is, it had accepted some basic rules governing the division of power and the decision-making process. After the Seven Years' War, some of the colonies found their interests more at odds with those of the mother country than ever before, and this division between England and the colonies inevitably took the form of constitutional conflict. This does not mean that the constitutional quarrel over taxation in the colonies was the sole "cause" of the American Revolution. It was only one aspect of a many-faceted dispute. But the fact that this conflict expressed itself in the concepts and forms of Anglo-American constitutionalism determined to a large extent the course of developments leading to Independence and the founding of the new political order.

The Americans who advocated a system of colonial self-government within the framework of the empire and the British who insisted on parliamentary sovereignty both claimed adherence to the principles of the revolution of 1688. Although the exponents of the crown and of the parliamentary majority rejected the constitutional views of the colonists as incompatible with the English constitution, in reality the colonists were not setting up a new "republican" or "democratic" political theory in opposition to Parliament's claim to sovereignty. On the contrary, they justified their resistance to direct taxation by Parliament by referring to the rights the English constitution guaranteed to the subjects of the crown. They demanded only that the principles of 1688 be applied to the population of the colonies as well as to the mother country. The main argument in the Declaration of Independence—that if a monarch does not fulfill his obligations as a ruler, he nullifies the contract between himself and his subjects—was itself part of the constitutional theory of 1688.[7]

In the middle of the eighteenth century, the English constitution was regarded as the best model for achieving political stability and for protecting individual security from arbitrary acts of government. Ever since the last Stuart king fled England in 1688, and his daughter and son-in-law assumed the throne in 1689 at the invitation of and under the conditions dictated by members of the upper and lower houses, the monarchical component of the English constitution had not been based on legitimation by the grace of God. The coronation oath required the new monarchs to exercise their office in accordance with "the statutes in parliament agreed upon, and the laws and customs of the same."[8]

The principles of 1688 derived primarily from the recognition of three independent decision-making entities that were obliged to co-operate in the legislative process: the crown, the upper house, and the lower house. Executive power rested solely with the king, the highest judicial function with the upper house. The degree of political influence of each entity varied with the personalities that held any particular office. The crown retained the political initiative, chose ministers, and tried to increase its influence over Parliament by rewarding cooperative members with lucrative offices, by gerrymandering, and by utilizing other means of corruption. But the king could not keep a minister for any extended length of time against the will of the lower house, and neither the king nor his prime minister could take any major steps without considering the wishes of the majority in the lower house.

Over and above the limits this parliamentary system imposed on the crown, independent judges saw to it that individual legal rights were safeguarded under the common law and under Parliament's

---

7. Gerald Stourzh, "William Blackstone: Teacher of Revolution," *Jahrbuch für Amerikastudien*, XV (1970), 184–200.
8. Quoted in E. Neville Williams, *The Eighteenth-Century Constitution, 1688–1815: Documents and Commentary* (Cambridge, 1960), 3. The remainder of this summary of the Revolution Settlement is based on Williams's chap. 2.

declaration of basic human rights. The deliberations between Parliament and William and Mary were constitutionally codified in the Bill of Rights of 1689, which was officially entitled "Act Declaring the Rights and Liberties of the Subject and Settling the Succession of the Crown." The law "declared" William and Mary king and queen of England, France, Ireland, and their dominions and clearly defined the prerogatives of the crown in order to prevent the abuses of absolutism. The law established those features of English government that Enlightenment thinkers would later praise so highly. It forbade the crown to nullify a law or to refuse to carry it out, to levy taxes without the consent of Parliament, to maintain a standing army in peacetime without parliamentary consent, and to take any member of Parliament to court for statements made in parliamentary session. Parliament would no longer convene solely at the discretion of the king, but it would meet "frequently." The elections of members to the lower house would be "free." The law also prohibited the courts from setting excessively high bail or imposing cruel and unusual punishments. The Bill of Rights guaranteed Protestant citizens the right to bear arms, and it guaranteed to all citizens the right to petition the king without fear of retaliatory legal action.

Together with the Act of Toleration of 1689, the Triennial Act of 1694, the Act of Settlement of 1701, and the Septennial Act of 1716, which superseded the Triennial Act, the Bill of Rights formed the major part of the written English constitution in the eighteenth century. William Blackstone, soon to be recognized as an important commentator on the constitution, summarized in 1765 the constitutional theory concerning the division of power:

And herein indeed consists the true excellence of the English government, that all the parts of it form a mutual check upon each other. In the legislature, the people are a check upon the nobility, and the nobility a check upon the people; by the mutual privilege of rejecting what the other has resolved: while the king is a check upon both, which preserves the executive power from encroachments. And this very executive power is again checked and kept within due bounds by the two houses, through the privilege they have of enquiring into, impeaching, and punishing the conduct (not indeed of the king, which would destroy his constitutional independence; but, which is more beneficial to the public) of his evil and pernicious counsellors. Thus every branch of our civil polity supports and is supported, regulates and is regulated, by the rest: for the two houses naturally drawing in two directions of opposite interest, and the prerogative in another still different from them both, they mutually keep each other from exceeding their proper limits;

while the whole is prevented from separation, and artificially connected together by the mixed nature of the crown, which is a part of the legislative, and the sole executive magistrate. Like three distinct powers in mechanics, they jointly impel the machine of government in a direction different from what either, acting by itself, would have done; but at the same time in a direction partaking of each, and formed out of all; a direction which constitutes the true line of the liberty and happiness of the community.[9]

Authors like Acherley, Bolingbroke, Hume, and Montesquieu, whose writings both expressed and helped form the views of politically articulate Englishmen, had done their part to establish the reputation of the English constitution in antiabsolutistic circles throughout Europe.[10] In 1748 Montesquieu had written in his often quoted encomium on the English constitution that Great Britain was the only country "that has for the direct end of its constitution political liberty." He added that he was not dealing with the question of whether all English citizens were actually in possession of these famous freedoms but only meant to show that the English constitution was designed to make them possible.[11] In a period when the highest goal of all learning was the discovery of the immutable laws regulating all spheres of life, this gap between governmental theory and actual practice did not detract from the value of the theory. If the principles on which the English constitution was built corresponded to natural

9. William Blackstone, *Commentaries on the Laws of England* (Philadelphia, 1771), I, 154–155.
10. Roger Acherley, *The Britannic Constitution: or, The fundamental form of government in Britain* (London, 1727), vi; Henry Saint John, Viscount Bolingbroke, *A Dissertation upon Parties . . .* , 2d ed. (London, 1735), letter 12, 147–149; David Hume, "Of Civil Liberty," in Charles W. Hendel, ed., *David Hume's Political Essays* (Indianapolis, Ind., 1953), 104. On the increasing complacency in England about the British constitution, see Bernard Bailyn, *The Origins of American Politics* (New York, 1968), 16–23; David Lindsay Keir, *The Constitutional History of Modern Britain since 1485*, 7th ed. (London, 1964), 289–292; William Holdsworth, *A History of English Law*, 6th ed. rev. (London, 1938–   ), X, 11, 714. On the praise the British constitution received from Enlightenment thinkers, see Peter Gay, *The Enlightenment: An Interpretation* (New York, 1969), II, 555.
11. Baron de Montesquieu, *The Spirit of the Laws*, trans. Thomas Nugent (New York, 1949), I, book 11, chaps. 5 and 6, quotation p. 151. Further examples of French praise for the British constitution are in Gabriel Bonno, *La Constitution britannique devant l'opinion française de Montesquieu à Bonaparte* (Paris, 1931).

laws, then the constitution would necessarily achieve perfection at a later time.

Even those critics of English constitutional reality who were known as True Whigs, Old Whigs, Radical Whigs, or Commonwealthmen felt compelled to join the chorus of praise for the English constitution and to offer their suggestions for reform as a means of finally realizing the principles of 1688. Joseph Priestley, one of the most articulate of these critics, wrote in 1768 in his *Essay on the First Principles of Government*, which received much attention in the colonies, that the English constitution was "the best actual scheme of civil policy" and that he thoroughly agreed with its greatest admirers. In his notes to Blackstone's *Commentaries* he added that it was wrong to accuse English dissenters of being republicans. In reality they were "firm and intrepid friends of the liberties of their country, and of its constitution, as a monarchy."[12] In 1776 John Cartwright, a parliamentary reformer who remained active into the nineteenth century, based his hopes for incisive reforms on the virtues of the English constitution.[13] James Burgh, in the foreword to his three-volume compilation of reform writings, protested against allegations that he favored a republic: "The present form of government by king, lords, and commons, if it could be restored to its true spirit and efficiency, might be made to yield all the liberty, and all the happiness, of which a great and good people are capable in this world."[14]

The advocates of self-government among the colonists found themselves in the same situation as the True Whigs in England. They claimed their point of view was inherent in the system and denied

12. Joseph Priestley, *An Essay on the First Principles of Government, and on the Nature of Political, Civil, and Religious Liberty* (London, 1768), 128. Priestley, *Remarks on Some Paragraphs in the Fourth Volume of Dr. Blackstone's Commentaries on the Laws of England*, included in Blackstone, *Commentaries*, V, appendix, 21. An initial survey portraying the personalities and the intellectual history of the radical Whig tradition has been provided by Caroline Robbins, *The Eighteenth-Century Commonwealthman: Studies in the Transmission, Development and Circumstance of English Liberal Thought from the Restoration of Charles II until the War with the Thirteen Colonies* (Cambridge, Mass., 1961). On the significance of this tradition for the colonists, see Bernard Bailyn, *The Ideological Origins of the American Revolution* (Cambridge, Mass., 1967).
13. John Cartwright, *The Legislative Rights of the Commonalty Vindicated; or, Take your choice . . .* , 2d ed. (London, 1777), 20–21.
14. James Burgh, *Political Disquisitions; or An Enquiry into public errors, defects, and abuses* (Philadelphia, 1775), I, 9, and III, 299.

that they wanted to leave the consensus of 1688 behind. John Adams, then a lawyer and an aspiring politician in Massachusetts, repeated Montesquieu and Blackstone almost verbatim in the *Boston Gazette* in January 1766 when the Stamp Act crisis was at its peak. All governments (in the broadest sense of the word), Adams wrote, claimed to serve the *salus populi*. But the English constitution was unique in viewing freedom as part of the *salus populi*. It was the only constitution expressly designed to guarantee freedom: "Liberty is its end, its use, its designation, drift, and scope, as much as grinding corn is the use of a mill, the transportation of burdens the end of a ship."[15] A number of similar declarations appeared in newspapers and broadsides published in the period between the Stamp Act crisis and the Declaration of Independence.[16] Since the arguments of the colonists were based on their rights as Englishmen, even in the months immediately preceding the Declaration of Independence, when Americans appealed more and more to natural law, it was only logical that they would repeatedly assert their fundamental agreement with the English constitution. They emphasized in particular one principle that had been held sacred since the beginnings of English parliamentarianism—that an Englishman is not obliged to pay any taxes or obey any laws except those passed by his elected representatives. Constitutional theory was clear on this point, no matter how corrupt parliamentary elections were in the eighteenth century or how inequitable the distribution of seats. For this reason, "No taxation without representation" instead of "Vive la république," became the colonists' major battle cry.

15. "The Earl of Clarendon to William Pym, No. III," *Boston Gazette*, Jan. 27, 1766, in Charles Francis Adams, ed., *The Works of John Adams* (Boston, 1850–1856), III, 479. Very similar words were used by Montesquieu, *Spirit of the Laws*, trans. Nugent, I, 151, and by Blackstone in *Commentaries*, I, 6, who explicitly refers to Montesquieu.

16. References to the period 1734 to 1763 are in Clinton Rossiter, *Seedtime of the Republic: The Origin of the American Tradition of Political Liberty* (New York, 1953), 143–144. For examples from the years 1763 to 1776, see Bernard Bailyn, ed., *Pamphlets of the American Revolution, 1750–1776* (Cambridge, Mass., 1965), I, 44–45. June E. Uphouse, "The Attitude of the Colonists toward the King and Royal Family during the Decade of Controversy" (M.A. thesis, Indiana University, 1960), 1, emphasizes the unequivocal homage paid to the crown at the coronation of George III in 1760.

The Colonists' Theory of Empire

The colonists' counterideology consisted of no more than a full affirmation of the home country's political order and the spelling out of a great contradiction in it. Absolute rule over the colonies was incompatible with the concept of the social contract. The English Whigs had used the theory of social contract to justify their struggle against the autocratic claims of the Stuarts. The Americans recognized this Whig ideological commitment as the best basis for justifying their own resistance against imperial autocracy. They needed only to show that the logic of the social contract should also apply to the political relationship between the mother country and the colonies. The English Whigs could not refute this argument, but they questioned its relevance to the colonial situation and stressed instead another element of the great compromise of 1688: the principle of parliamentary sovereignty.

The parliamentary majority, which adhered to a stricter colonial policy from 1763 on, regarded the colonies by definition as subordinate entities not comparable to the English counties or to the kingdoms of Scotland and Ireland. Colonial self-government was not a right but a privilege. Since the peace treaties of 1763 had just created a firm basis for the first empire, the parliamentary majority was loathe to relinquish its view of monolithic sovereignty and to try out, for the sake of pleasing the colonists, a new division of power within a commercial world empire of a size never seen before. British constitutionalism was trapped in orthodoxy, especially as far as shaping the empire was concerned. In 1765 Blackstone observed, with the disarming openness of a disinterested jurist, that the colonists might well attempt to conduct their local business through legislative assemblies and courts but that they had no appropriate legal basis to do so. "The king in council" remained the highest court of appeal for the colonial courts, and colonial laws and constitutions were subject to change by Parliament at any time. Without an act of Parliament, not even common law could be in force in the colonies.[17] A year later, in March 1766 when the Stamp Act was repealed, Parliament affirmed its uncompromising view of parliamentary sovereignty over the colonies in a statute appropriately entitled the Declaratory Act. Without explanation, the king and Parliament succinctly "declared" that they had the right "to bind the colonies and people of *America*, subjects of

17. Blackstone, *Commentaries*, I, 107–109.

the crown of *Great Britain*, in all cases whatsoever."[18] During the debate on this act in the lower house, William Pitt had tried without success to prevent its passage.[19] In the upper house, Lord Lyttelton had presented the majority position, rejecting the colonists' claim to equal rights in the empire as an attempt to undermine the constitution: "We have a constitution which, with all its faults, is a good one, but the doctrine of equality may be carried to the destruction of this monarchy." There should be no "*imperium in imperio.*"[20] At the end of the Stamp Act crisis crown and Parliament on the one hand, and the leadership of the colonies on the other, had clearly articulated their positions on the division of power and on decision-making processes and found those positions incompatible. The clarification of these basic issues has rightly been called the most important result of the Stamp Act crisis.[21]

In 1774 and 1775, during the last phase of public debate before the outbreak of war, the colonial pamphleteers, basing their argument on the theory of social contract, once again proposed their idea of a number of equal parliaments under one crown as an alternative to the British parliament's claim of exclusive sovereignty.[22] James Wilson, an attorney who had emigrated from Scotland in 1765, while writing in Philadelphia during this period, proposed to modify Parliament's claim to sovereignty by subordinating that sovereignty to a higher purpose. His argument was based on the theory of social contract: The purpose of all government is to increase the happiness of the governed, and only for the sake of happiness do men enter into a contract to create political authority. "All men are, by nature, equal and free: no one has a right to any authority over another without his

18. For text of the Declaratory Act, see Henry Steele Commager, ed., *Documents of American History*, 7th ed. (New York, 1963), I, 61.
19. Pitt's speech of Jan. 14, 1766, in John Wright, ed., *The Parliamentary History of England, from the Earliest Period to the Year 1803*, XVI (London, 1813), column 99.
20. Lyttelton's speech of Feb. 10, 1766, *ibid.*, columns 167–168.
21. Edmund S. Morgan and Helen M. Morgan, *The Stamp Act Crisis: Prologue to Revolution*, 2d ed. rev. (New York, 1962), 352.
22. Debate concerning the British Commonwealth in the context of the 20th century prompted Randolph G. Adams, in 1919, to survey the ideas of the Englishmen in America on the organization of the first empire. See Adams, *Political Ideas of the American Revolution: Britannic-American Contributions to the Problem of Imperial Organization, 1765 to 1775*, 3d ed. (New York, 1958), with commentary by Merrill Jensen.

consent: all lawful government is founded on the consent of those who are subject to it: such consent was given with a view to ensure and to increase the happiness of the governed, above what they could enjoy in an independent and unconnected state of nature. The consequence is, that the happiness of the society is the *first* law of every government." The application of this principle to the immediate political situation led Wilson to the following conclusion: "The commons of Great Britain have no dominion over their equals and fellow subjects in America: they can confer no right to their delegates to bind those equals and fellow subjects by laws."[23] When the Continental Congress summarized the rights and grievances of the colonists on October 1, 1774, it based its case on the theory of social contract and argued that the colonists themselves had to approve any law they were asked to obey.[24]

In the spring of 1775 John Adams began publishing in the *Massachusetts Gazette* a series of articles that continued to appear until war began. In this series he once again outlined a concept of the empire that most of the members of the First Continental Congress would probably have subscribed to. Adams granted to Parliament only the regulation of trade for the benefit of the entire commercial empire. "America has all along consented, still consents, and ever will consent, that parliament, being the most powerful legislature in the dominions, should regulate the trade of the dominions. This is founding the authority of parliament to regulate our trade, upon *compact* and *consent* of the colonies, not upon any principle of common or statute law; not upon any original principle of the English constitution; not upon the principle that parliament is the supreme and sovereign legislature over them in all cases whatsoever."[25] The response of the

23. [James Wilson], *Considerations On The Nature And The Extent Of The Legislative Authority Of The British Parliament* (Philadelphia, 1774), cited here from Robert Green McCloskey, ed., *The Works of James Wilson* (Cambridge, Mass., 1967), II, 723–724, 741.

24. "Declaration of Rights and Grievances," Worthington Chauncey Ford *et al.*, eds., *Journals of the Continental Congress, 1774–1789* (Washington, D.C., 1904–1937), I, 63–73.

25. "Novanglus VII," in Adams, ed., *Works of John Adams*, IV, 99–100. Thomas Jefferson had offered a similar argument a year earlier in *A Summary View of the Rights of British America* (Williamsburg, Va., 1774). Alexander Hamilton followed the same line of thinking in Feb. 1775 in *The Farmer Refuted: or, A more impartial and comprehensive View of the Dispute between Great-Britain and the Colonies . . .* (New York, 1775), also in Harold C. Syrett and Jacob E. Cooke,

parliamentary majority and of the crown was a decisive "No!" They emphatically rejected any attempt to break up the total sovereignty they had appropriated to themselves. When the organization of a local administration for the Province of Quebec came up for debate in May 1774, the attorney general, later Lord Thurlow, spoke in favor of the restrictive solution the Quebec Act offered and put the following rhetorical question to his opponents who advocated colonial self-government: "Do you mean to vest the sovereignty of the province . . . in any other place than in the House of Lords and Commons of Great Britain?" Extensive self-government in the colonies, he argued, would produce a "federal union" that would depend on the coopera-tiveness of its members and breed a particularism like that of the German states.[26] Since the concept of monolithic sovereignty under-lay all British attempts to negotiate peace during the Revolutionary War, diplomatic compromise was bound to fail.[27]

Part of the significance of the American Revolution for world history is that it eventuated in the first successful secession of colonies from the empire of a major European power. But the Revolution did not produce any explicit denunciations of colonialism as such. In-stead, the colonists justified their resistance by appeals to the British constitution. Those who were seeking liberation were Europeans themselves, who above all wanted equality within a world-wide commercial empire. That British citizens in America refused to accept

---

eds., *The Papers of Alexander Hamilton* (New York, 1961–), I, 81–165. In mak-ing his case Hamilton audaciously turned around the argument that there could be no *imperium in imperio* (and hence no substantial self-government of the colonists): "A supreme authority, in the Parliament, to make any special laws for this province, consistent with the internal legislature here claimed is impossible; and cannot be supposed, without falling into that solecism, in politics, of *imperium in imperio*." *Ibid.*, 164.

26. Debate of May 26, 1774, quoted in George Bennett, ed., *The Concept of Empire: Burke to Attlee, 1774–1947*, 2d ed. (London, 1962), 34, 35.

27. In his 14-volume study of the English commercial empire before the American Revolution, Lawrence Henry Gipson came to the following conclu-sion: "The war begun in 1775 was not waged . . . to secure the withdrawal of the Thirteen Colonies from the British Empire; rather it had as its original purpose to give these colonies an autonomous position within the Empire—a status to which their leaders felt they had a right both by the common law and the law of nature. But there was really no place under the eighteenth-century British constitution for autonomous local governments." Gipson, *The British Empire before the American Revolution*, XIII (New York, 1967), 213.

an inferior colonial status for themselves and finally rejected even the expression "mother country" is no proof that Americans rejected colonialism in principle.[28]

The American Concept of a Constitution

The central role played by British constitutionalism in justifying colonial resistance was carried over into American thinking about constitutions when the colonies began writing their own in 1776. The basic premise of the colonists' argument was that the political order created in 1688, though formulated only in statutes, could not be changed even by a majority decision in Parliament approved by the crown. This English constitution, the colonists argued, was a permanent code to which the stewards of governmental power—the king and Parliament—were subject and that they had no authority to alter. Decades before the colonists created their own constitutions, they emphasized, almost more than the Whigs in the home country had done, the inviolability of the rulings of 1688 and 1689.

The colonists saw all constitutions as analogous to the constitutional documents with which they were most familiar—their charters. Colonial assemblies had to function within the limits imposed on them by their charters.[29] Parliament, too, the colonists maintained,

---

28. "The Americans had never lived under colonialism in its more recent sense." Palmer, *Age of the Democratic Revolution*, II, 518–519. On the rejection of thinking in terms of the "mother-country" and "infant colonies," see Edwin G. Burrows and Michael Wallace, "The American Revolution: The Ideology and Psychology of National Liberation," *Perspectives in American History*, VI (1972), 167–306.

29. The constitution of a colony was made up of (1) the letters patent of the crown, on which the charters of colonies like Massachusetts Bay, Rhode Island, Connecticut, Pennsylvania, and Maryland were based; (2) the governor's instructions and letter of appointment, in the case of a crown colony; (3) laws affecting colonial administration that had been passed by the colonial assembly and approved by the Privy Council; (4) laws of Parliament affecting colonial affairs. In contrast to Portuguese, Spanish, and French colonies in the Western Hemisphere, the English colonies were subject not only to the crown but also to the combination of the upper house, lower house, and crown working together in the High Court of Parliament. From 1688 on, the king was unable to make any major decisions affecting the colonies without the approval of the majority in the lower house. In 1696 Parliament deter-

was operating under a "charter." In a statement of October 1765 opposing the Stamp Act, the Massachusetts house of representatives compared the English constitution to its own charter of 1691: "The *charter* of the province invests the General Assembly with the power of making laws for its internal government and taxation. . . . The Parliament has a right to make all laws within the limits of *their own constitution*. . . . There are certain original inherent rights belonging to the people, which the Parliament itself cannot divest them of, consistent with *their own constitution*."[30] This constitutional concept was perhaps most clearly formulated in a circular letter published by the Massachusetts house of representatives in February 1768. The letter openly called upon the assemblies of the other colonies to join in common resistance to the Townshend Acts, passed by Parliament the year before. The Massachusetts legislators conceded that the king and Parliament exercised the highest legislative authority in the empire. However: "In all free states the constitution is fixed; and as the supreme legislative derives its power and authority from the constitu-

---

mined that a law passed by a colonial assembly would be void if it conflicted with a law of Parliament. A series of acts of Parliament established the trade goods and trade partners of the colonies as well as provided for the regulation of details of domestic policy, such as the sale of land and other matters of internal economics. A list compiled in 1753 contained 84 "Acts of Parliament relative to Plantation Trade" that had been passed since 1660. From 1688 to 1750 the colonists had not questioned Parliament's legislative competence in these matters. Gipson, *British Empire*, III, 273–275, 289. For surveys of colonial governments, see Alfred H. Kelly and Winfred A. Harbison, *The American Constitution: Its Origins and Development*, 3d ed. (New York, 1963), chaps. 1 and 2. A much earlier study is Oliver Morton Dickerson, *American Colonial Government, 1696–1765: A Study of the British Board of Trade in Its Relation to the American Colonies, Political, Industrial, Administrative* (New York, 1962 [orig. publ. Cleveland, Ohio, 1912]).

30. Resolution of Oct. 23, 1765, in Alden Bradford, ed., *Speeches of the governors of Massachusetts, from 1765 to 1775 . . .* (Boston, 1818), 45. Italics mine. The evening before he and two other lawyers were to argue before the governor and council of Massachusetts why the courts should be opened again but not use any stamped paper, John Adams wrote in his diary, "Shall we contend that the Stamp-Act is void? That the Parliament have no legal Authority to impose Internal Taxes upon Us?—Because We are not represented in it? And therefore that the Stamp Act ought to be waived by the Judges, as against natural Equity and the Constitution?" Dec. 19, 1765, L. H. Butterfield *et al.*, eds., *Diary and Autobiography of John Adams* (Cambridge, Mass., 1961), I, 266.

tion, it cannot overleap the bounds of it, without destroying its own foundation: that the constitution ascertains and limits both sovereignity and allegiance, and therefore his Majesty's American subjects, who acknowledge themselves bound by the ties of allegiance have an equitable claim, to the full enjoyment of the fundamental rules of the British constitution."[31] It was not uncommon, therefore, in political rhetoric between 1763 and 1776, for the colonists to brand certain parliamentary decisions and crown decrees as "unconstitutional" and hence not binding.

In his plea for independence in January 1776, Thomas Paine used the now famous image of the coronation of an American constitution rather than of a king. It is notable that for the word "constitution" he used simply "the charter": "Let a day be solemnly set apart for proclaiming the charter; let it be brought forth placed on the divine law, the Word of God; let a crown be placed thereon, by which the world may know, that so far as we approve of monarchy, that in America the law is king. For as in absolute governments the king is law, so in free countries the law ought to be king; and there ought to be no other. But lest any ill use should afterwards arise, let the crown at the conclusion of the ceremony be demolished, and scattered

31. This circular was distributed in England in a small anthology compiled by Thomas Hollis, entitled *The True Sentiments of America* . . . (London, 1768), 50–51. In a letter of Jan. 22, 1768, to the marquis of Rockingham, the house of representatives had expressed the relationship between "government" and "constitution" in similar terms. "All his Majesty's happy subjects, in every part of his wide extended dominions have a just and equitable claim to the rights of that constitution, upon which government itself is formed." Bradford, ed., *Speeches of the governors*, 143. The town meeting of New London, Connecticut, introduced its unanimous rejection of the Stamp Act with the following two principles: "1st. That every form of government rightfully founded, originates from the consent of the people. 2d. That the boundaries set by the people in all constitutions are the only limits within which any officer can lawfully exercise authority." Resolution of Dec. 10, 1765, in Merrill Jensen, ed., *American Colonial Documents to 1776*, in David C. Douglas, ed., *English Historical Documents*, IX (New York, 1955), 670. In 1774, when an assembly of freeholders in Albemarle County in Virginia denied to Parliament any legislative competence over Virginia, it based its case for the authority of the Virginia House of Burgesses on "the common rights of mankind, confirmed by the political constitutions they have respectively assumed, and also by several charters of compact from the crown." Resolution of July 26, 1774, in Julian P. Boyd *et al.*, eds., *The Papers of Thomas Jefferson* (Princeton, N.J., 1950–), I, 117–118.

among the people whose right it is."[32] Paine's vision of a constitutional cult, when seen against the background of Anglo-American constitutional developments since 1688, seems almost within the realm of possibility. A new act of founding had become necessary. In the American context monarchical government had lost its power to evoke a sufficiently strong sense of legitimacy. A new sense of legitimacy had to be created by satisfying the principle of popular sovereignty as well as the basic demand of constitutionalism: the limitation of the power of those in public office by a set of rules unalterable by the rulers.

Linguistic usage varied in the discussion that accompanied the writing of constitutions between 1776 and 1780. In this period, Americans inconsistently used the term "constitution" in the current sense. They also used "form of government," not in the abstract sense of a mode of government, but in the concrete sense of a detailed plan for governing. The constitution of New Hampshire speaks only of the need for "A Form Of Government." South Carolina also avoided the term "constitution" and proposed "some mode . . . for regulating the internal polity of this colony." The Virginia constitution, which went into effect just before the Declaration of Independence was written, is entitled "The Constitution or Form of Government." New Jersey combined the two terms. After long deliberation about the implications, the assembly agreed on the phrase "form of a Constitution." The last article in this constitution, which left the way open to reconciliation with England, referred to the entire document as "this charter." Delaware chose the variation, "The Constitution, or System of Government." The Pennsylvania constitution was the first to use "constitution" as a generic term that subsumed both a "declaration of rights" and a "frame of government." Maryland and North Carolina made no distinction between "constitution" and "form of government." Georgia and New York used only "constitution." And finally in 1780 Massachusetts adopted Pennsylvania's usage and used "constitution" as a generic term. The text of the constitution stated: "We . . . do agree upon, ordain and establish, the following Declaration of Rights, and Frame of Government, as the Constitution Of The Commonwealth."[33]

---

32. *Common Sense*, in Philip S. Foner, ed., *The Complete Writings of Thomas Paine* (New York, 1945), I, 29.
33. The quotations given here are taken either from the preambles or the conclusions of the constitutional documents in Francis Newton Thorpe, comp.

By 1776 the idea of a constitution no longer required any discussion and had almost achieved the status of a self-evident truth.[34] That these new constitutions were formulated in writing evoked neither resistance nor amazement at such a novelty. Because the provincial congresses enacted the first constitutions like laws, it was clear that the constitutions, like any other decisions of these assemblies, would be in written form. However, this assimilation of legislation with constitution making also provoked a major clarification and distinction that set American constitutionalism apart from English constitutionalism of the eighteenth century. Most provincial congresses had ratified their constitutions while acting in their capacity as a legislative assembly with an executive committee. Others had followed the procedures normally used for passing bills. In Massachusetts the signal step was taken of formally separating legislative activity and the task of creating a constitution.

The Founding Spirit

Hannah Arendt has suggested that the term revolution should not be used indiscriminately for almost any act of politically motivated organized violence, but "only where change occurs in the sense of a new beginning, where violence is used to constitute an altogether different form of government, to bring about the formation of a new body politic, where the liberation from oppression aims at least at the constitution of freedom."[35] In terms of this definition, the events in America between 1764 and 1789—or between 1775 and 1781 if we focus only on the years of extensive military activity—represent a clear case of a revolution and the founding of a nation. The movement for independence and the establishment of the new order occurred

---

and ed., *The Federal and State Constitutions, Colonial Charters, and Other Organic Laws of the States, Territories, and Colonies Now or Heretofore Forming the United States of America* (Washington, D.C., 1909), hereafter cited as Thorpe, ed., *Constitutions*.

34. On the early history of American constitutionalism, see Benjamin Fletcher Wright, Jr., *American Interpretations of Natural Law: A Study in the History of Political Thought* (Cambridge, Mass., 1931); Wright, "The Early History of Written Constitutions in America," in *Essays in History and Political Theory in Honor of Charles Howard McIlwain* (Cambridge, Mass., 1936); Andrew C. McLaughlin, *The Foundations of American Constitutionalism* (New York, 1932).

35. Arendt, *On Revolution*, 28.

simultaneously and interacted constantly with each other. There was no logical sequence of events in which a declaration of independence came first, followed by a war to force its recognition, and finally, by the writing of constitutions. The First Continental Congress, for example, agreed as early as September and October 1774 on the distribution of votes among the colonies represented and on other questions of procedure. The solutions to constitutional questions the Congress found at this early date were later incorporated into the Articles of Confederation. When hostilities began on April 19, 1775, no one was aware that an actual war for independence had begun. And from the summer of 1775 on, constitutional issues were part of political discussions—both in the Continental Congress and among the people—that resulted a year later in the Declaration of Independence.

Political leaders gradually became aware that they were involved in founding a new nation, and they invoked the founding to encourage each other and to influence both their colleagues and the public. In January 1776 Thomas Paine appealed to the pride of the colonists, urging them not to shrink back from the uncertainties of a completely new order but to rejoice in this unique opportunity:

The present time, likewise, is that peculiar time which never happens to a nation but once, viz. the time of forming itself into a government. Most nations have let slip the opportunity, and by that means have been compelled to receive laws from their conquerors, instead of making laws for themselves. First, they had a king, and then a form of government; . . . but from the errors of other nations let us learn wisdom, and lay hold of the present opportunity. . . . We have every opportunity and every encouragement before us, to form the noblest, purest constitution on the face of the earth. We have it in our power to begin the world over again.[36]

A few weeks later, when the Continental Congress was on the verge of recommending that the colonies write their own constitutions, John Adams, Paine's opponent in issues of domestic politics, wrote to a fellow revolutionary in Virginia: "You and I, my dear friend, have been sent into life at a time when the greatest lawgivers of antiquity would have wished to live. How few of the human race have ever enjoyed an opportunity of making an election of government, more than of air, soil, or climate, for themselves or their children! When, before the present epocha, had three millions of people full power and a fair opportunity to form and establish the wisest and happiest

36. *Common Sense*, in Foner, ed., *Writings of Paine*, I, 36–37, 45.

government that human wisdom can contrive?"[37] On August 15, 1776, the *Maryland Gazette* editorialized enthusiastically about the great opportunity the colonies had to learn from the mistakes of the past. Other nations had originated in a state of ignorance and carried the seeds of their own destruction in them. This same mood is reflected in a number of public appeals and private letters written in 1776.[38]

One element in the American idea of nation founding was the Enlightenment belief in progress. This belief, which was not peculiar to Americans alone, represented a step away from the classical concept of the rise and inevitable fall of all forms of government. At least some of the founding fathers of 1776, after surveying two thousand years of experimentation with political organization, conceived of themselves as free to borrow and put to rational use the sum of this experience.[39] Utopias may be built on the distant experience of others, but not enduring governments. The references to ancient and modern European history that occur in the oral and written debates of the founding generation were essentially no more than rhetorical devices used to defend conclusions that had long since been reached on the basis of the much more immediate Anglo-American constitutional tradition. This tradition was the decisive element in founding the new nation.

37. *Thoughts on Government*, in Adams, ed., *Works of John Adams*, IV, 200. In a letter of June 9, 1776, to William Cushing, Adams invoked "the lives and liberties of millions yet unborn." *Ibid.*, IX, 391.
38. See, for instance, "Serious Questions proposed . . . ," *Pennsylvania Journal; and the Weekly Advertiser* (Philadelphia), May 22, 1776, hereafter cited as *Pa. Jour.*; "The Address of the Deputies from the Committees of Pennsylvania, assembled in Provincial Conference," June 22, 1776, *Journals of the House of Representatives of the Commonwealth of Pennsylvania* (Philadelphia, 1782), I, 42; William Shippen, member of one of the most prominent families of Philadelphia, to his brother Edward Shippen, July 27, 1776, Shippen Family Papers, XII, fol. 41, Historical Society of Pennsylvania, Philadelphia; *Maryland Gazette* (Annapolis), Aug. 15, 1776, hereafter cited as *Md. Gaz.*
39. On the relationship between belief in progress and the doctrine of the inevitable decline of all governments, see Stow Persons, "The Cyclical Theory of History in Eighteenth Century America," *American Quarterly*, VI (1954), 147–163. See, too, Rutherford E. Delmage, "The American Idea of Progress, 1750–1800," American Philosophical Society, *Proceedings*, XCI (1947), 307–314, and W. Warren Wagar's survey, "Modern Views of the Origins of the Idea of Progress," *Journal of the History of Ideas*, XXVIII (1967), 55–70.

Americans both hoped to escape the cycle of forms of government and prepared for the worst. A skeptical view of human nature, which gives the lie to clichés about Enlightenment optimism and which influenced the thinking of many American political leaders, balanced off the pervasive belief in inevitable progress.[40] The possibility of failure and the hope for a permanent solution could appear together in a single argument. In his *Notes on the State of Virginia,* written in 1780 and 1781, Jefferson pleaded for an immediate legal guarantee of religious freedom in Virginia, on the grounds that freedom had to be secured during this initial phase of nationhood. With a clarity unusual even in the political literature of the Revolutionary period, Jefferson realized that the idealism of this early period would be dissipated once the War of Independence was over. At the present time, he said, the popular mood supported religious tolerance in Virginia, and the people would not allow anyone to be executed for heresy:

But is the spirit of the people an infallible, a permanent reliance? Is it government? Is this the kind of protection we receive in return for the rights we give up? Besides, the spirit of the times may alter, will alter. Our rulers will become corrupt, our people careless. A single zealot may commence persecutor, and better men be his victims. It can never be too often repeated, that the time for fixing every essential right on a legal basis is while our rulers are honest, and ourselves united. From the conclusion of this war we shall be going down hill. It will not then be necessary to resort every moment to the people for support. They will be forgotten, therefore, and their rights disregarded. They will forget themselves, but in the sole faculty of making money, and will never think of uniting to effect a due respect for their rights. The shackles, therefore, which shall not be knocked off at the conclusion of this war, will remain on us long, will be made heavier and heavier, till our rights shall revive or expire in a convulsion.[41]

Jefferson saw in the founding period a transitional and ephemeral political constellation in which lasting reforms could be institutionalized with the general approval of all concerned. The pessimism implicit in this view was probably shared by many members of the political elite of the founding generation, and it is one of the reasons

40. See Gerald Stourzh, *Alexander Hamilton and the Idea of Republican Government* (Stanford, Calif., 1970), chap. 3.
41. Thomas Jefferson, *Notes on the State of Virginia*, ed. William Peden (Chapel Hill, N.C., 1955), 161.

why Jean Jacques Rousseau's trust in a sovereign popular will that can be mobilized at any time found so few adherents in America.[42] The founding situation of American political culture was not conducive to such simple-minded theory or to the establishment of neatly coordinated institutions. The American situation demanded that conflicting principles and overlapping institutions be accomodated in the new system of government. It was a new form of "mixed government," made up of sometimes conflicting republican, constitutional, and federal components. Just as several contradictory values had been incorporated into the credo of 1688, so a number of potentially conflicting values became part of the system developed in 1776. A compromise had to be reached immediately between the principle of popular sovereignty and the need to protect both the private property and the basic rights of the individual, even against decisions of the majority. The principles of rotation in office and the accountability of elected officials, for instance, had to be reconciled with an independent judiciary consisting of judges who held office practically for life. A doctrinaire understanding of popular sovereignty would have left no room for this. Also, for the sake of continental union, basic norms of the new system had to be violated: the issue of slavery had to be postponed for elementary reasons of political survival. Similarly, the colonists had to find a concept of sovereignty that would unify the thirteen states on a federal level and at the same time would allow highly developed regional and state interests to function as vehicles of the political process. A monolithic concept of sovereignty could not have met these conditions.

The new order had to be republican in nature. That much was clear. The new order had to rest on the idea of popular sovereignty. But it was unclear to what degree this principle could be put into practice. "It is certain, in theory," John Adams wrote in May 1776, "that the only moral foundation of government is, the consent of the people. But to what an extent shall we carry this principle?"[43] The great majority of the colonists in the summer of 1776 were against rule by a monarch and an aristocracy, but some were more republican than others.

42. Paul M. Spurlin, "Rousseau in America," *French-American Review*, I (1948), 8–16.
43. John Adams to James Sullivan, May 26, 1776, in Adams, ed., *Works of John Adams*, IX, 375.

CHAPTER I

Government by Congresses and Committees, 1773–1776

All commissions under the former authority being annulled, the courts of justice were shut, and the sword of magistracy was sheathed. The Provincial Convention directed the general affairs of the war; and town committees had a discretionary but undefined power to preserve domestic peace. Habits of decency, family government, and the good examples of influential persons, contributed more to maintain order than any other authority. The value of these secret bonds of society was now more than ever conspicuous.

Jeremy Belknap, *History of New-Hampshire* (1791).

The Assumption of Power

What seems in European eyes to be the almost unrevolutionary character of the American Revolution can be explained in part by the colonists' adherence to the social structure that Jeremy Belknap called the "secret bonds of society." Despite widespread fear of a decline in public morality, these bonds remained basically intact and made possible a transitional period—one dominated by local committees and provincial congresses—that was remarkably peaceful in comparison with other political upheavals of this magnitude.[1] The colonial administration had suffered a steady loss of authority following the Tea Act of May 10, 1773. Once news had spread of the skirmishes at Lexington and Concord and of the siege of Boston in April 1775, government in all thirteen colonies devolved upon the committees

1. We still do not have a study that goes beyond Belknap here and provides a comprehensive analysis of this aspect of the Revolution, taking into account the relationship between social structure and political process. Jeremy Belknap, *The History of New-Hampshire* (Philadelphia, 1784; Boston, 1791–1792).

and congresses that had developed independently of the British constitutional system. These groups existed at all levels, ranging from town meetings on up to the Continental Congress. The preparedness for personal sacrifice during this phase of the Revolution and the readiness to participate in the political process are the essence of the "spirit of 1776" that would often be invoked later in admonition or celebration.

The actual assumption of power had taken place in most instances well before the ratification of the new constitutions beginning in January 1776 and before the first republican senators, representatives, governors, and judges swore their oaths of office. It had taken place quietly by European standards, without the storming of prisons or governors' residences, and without the execution of any of the crown's governors or other high officials. A plot to hang the governor of Virginia remained no more than a rumor.[2] The governors had no police force in the modern sense, but only regular troops at their disposal. The colonial militia, which formerly could be called upon for protection, was generally useless to the British side. Thus, after the outbreak of war, several governors, especially those in the crown colonies, sought protection from mob violence in forts, which were usually located in the harbor area, or on the ships of the Royal Navy that patrolled there. After a futile attempt to administer the colony from this floating residence at a safe distance from the shore, a governor could easily decide to lift anchor and make a bloodless escape. Governor Josiah Martin of North Carolina thought he would be able to defend his seat of office in Newbern with six cannons. While he was meeting with his council in April 1775, a band of local citizens, aided and abetted by the town committee, stole the cannons. The next night the governor fled to Wilmington on the coast and later sought refuge in Fort Johnston. Governor John Wentworth of New Hampshire retreated to the harbor fort in Portsmouth after a mob, threatening him with a cannon rolled up in front of his house on a cart, had forced him to hand over to them a loyalist member of the assembly.[3] New York's governor, William Tryon, after October 1775 conducted his office on board ship. The mayor of New York and the

---

2. Allan Nevins, *The American States during and after the Revolution, 1775–1789* (New York, 1924), 77. On the end of rule by the governors throughout the colonies, see *ibid.*, 75–87 and 93–95.

3. Jere R. Daniell, *Experiment in Republicanism: New Hampshire Politics and the American Revolution, 1741–1794* (Cambridge, Mass., 1970), 89–91.

city committee had assured him that they anticipated no danger "to his person or property" but refused him the guarantee of protection he had demanded. Only in August 1776, when New York became headquarters for the British troops, did the governor reassume some of his duties on land.[4] By the end of 1775, no governor, whether appointed by the king or by a proprietor, was able any longer to exercise political authority. After he refused to approve defense measures, even the governor of Rhode Island, who owed his office to annual election by that colony's freemen, was suspended in June 1775 by vote of the assembly. The only exception was Jonathan Trumbull, the elected governor of Connecticut, who retained his office beyond the end of the war because of his leading role in the movement for independence.

Lord Dunmore properly sized up the situation in 1775 when he wrote to the secretary of state in London that the extralegal convention of representatives from Virginia counties, called to meet in Richmond in March, would become the major body in a "new government" that would supersede that of His Majesty and completely undermine the constitution.[5] It is a good indication of the smoothness of the transition that Peyton Randolph, who had been speaker of the constitutionally sanctioned House of Burgesses, extended the invitations for the Richmond convention.

Units of Revolutionary Action

In the Whig theory of social contract, "the people" were the final authority to which all political power reverted in cases of flagrant abuse of delegated governmental power. But in the actual assumption of political power, no unit as vast and amorphous as "the people" could possibly act as the vehicle of the political process. It was instead the remarkably stable territorial units of towns, cities, counties, and colonies that took control. The economic, political, and, in the broadest sense, social authority established within these familiar units

4. Carl Lotus Becker, *The History of Political Parties in the Province of New York, 1760–1776* (Madison, Wis., 1960 [orig. publ. 1909]), 225, 243.
5. Mar. 14, 1775, C.O. 5/1353, Public Record Office; cited in Merrill Jensen, *The Founding of a Nation: A History of the American Revolution, 1763–1776* (New York, 1968), 543. Compare Larry Bowman, "The Virginia County Committees of Safety, 1774–1776," *Virginia Magazine of History and Biography*, LXXIX (1971), 322–337.

did not melt away in a single stroke of revolutionary integration. Indeed, the system of political representation, which was generally accepted despite cries of "Anarchy!" and "Mob rule!" was itself based on the continuing existence of this local authority.

The very form of the organized resistance of the colonists was determined by a clear sense of the independence of territorial units that had evolved during the past 150 years. The borders England had drawn between the colonies continued to be respected as political demarcation lines even during the struggle against the mother country. Perhaps even more important for building a new governmental system was the integrity of the smaller units, called counties or districts in different colonies, and of the lowest level of political organization, cities, towns, townships, and parishes. All these units remained intact during the Revolution, and only the quasi-feudal manors in the Hudson River valley disappeared as political entities.

These smaller governmental units lent the principle of representation the credibility and efficacy it needed to form and legitimize committees and congresses. The organization of the American Revolution was characterized by faith in the political importance of territorial representation combined with the awareness that specific tasks had to be delegated to ad hoc committees, elected representatives, and delegates chosen in turn by those representatives. This way of reacting to a crisis did not have to be invented by the colonists; it was part of the Anglo-American political tradition. During the English civil war, county committees had assumed governmental power in a similar fashion.[6]

Mass demonstrations, particularly in the larger harbor cities, undermined the authority of the governors, but because of a strong sense of local identity and the effectiveness of the principle of delegation, they also strengthened the new authority the people considered legitimate.[7] The Boston Tea Party of December 1773 was preceded not

6. "When the Civil War came, it led to the formation of County Committees in Kent and all over the kingdom: once the central administration was withdrawn, that is to say, the local administration took its place as a matter of course. The running, recruitment and financing of the hostilities were conducted on a county basis." Peter Laslett, *The World We Have Lost* (New York, 1965), 182.

7. There is no study of violent demonstrations in the American Revolution comparable to George Rudé, *The Crowd in History: A Study of Popular Disturbances in France and England, 1730–1848* (New York, 1964). Beginnings have been made by Jesse Lemisch, "Jack Tar in the Streets: Merchant Seamen

only by meetings of the committees of correspondence from Boston and surrounding towns but also by public meetings of more than five thousand people. On the day after the Tea Party, John Adams described the event in his journal as an undisguised "Exertion of popular Power."[8] When Isaac Sears, Alexander McDougall, and John Lamb wanted to revive the Sons of Liberty in New York, they organized a mass meeting on November 29, 1773, and had the crowd approve the previously organized association of the Sons of Liberty.[9] When the legally constituted assembly of Pennsylvania refused to appoint a committee of correspondence, the advocates of this measure called a meeting of the freeholders and freemen of the city and county of Philadelphia for June 18, 1774, and appointed on the authority of that meeting a committee of forty-three members.[10]

The third mechanism involved in the assumption of power, in addition to the use of local units of government and of mass action, was the forming of associations, temporary committees organized to handle a single project. The new governing bodies in the colonies emerged from committees whose original task had been to supervise a consumer boycott and an embargo on imports. After war began the boycott associations were joined by defense and loyalty-oath associations that hastened polarization between the supporters of the extralegal congresses and committees and those of the governors, the

in the Politics of Revolutionary America," *William and Mary Quarterly*, 3d Ser., XXV (1968), 371–407; Pauline Maier, "Popular Uprisings and Civil Authority in Eighteenth-Century America," *ibid.*, XXVII (1970), 3–35; Maier, *From Resistance to Revolution: Colonial Radicals and the Development of American Opposition to Britain, 1765–1776* (New York, 1972); James H. Hutson, "An Investigation of the Inarticulate: Philadelphia's White Oaks," *WMQ*, 3d Ser., XXVIII (1971), 3–25; and Dirk Hoerder, *Crowd Action in Revolutionary Massachusetts, 1765–1780* (New York, 1977).

8. Benjamin Woods Labaree, *The Boston Tea Party* (New York, 1964), chaps. 6 and 7. Entry of Dec. 17, 1773, Butterfield *et al.*, eds., *Diary of John Adams*, II, 86.

9. "The following association," the preamble read, "is signed by a great number of the principal gentlemen of the city, merchants, lawyers, and other inhabitants of all ranks, and it is still carried about the city, to give an opportunity to those who have not yet signed to unite with their fellow-citizens, to testify their abhorrence to the diabolical project of enslaving America." Text dated Dec. 15, 1773, in Hezekiah Niles, ed., *Principles and Acts of the Revolution in America* (Baltimore, 1822; reprinted New York, 1876), 188.

10. For text, see *ibid.*, 179–180.

crown, and Parliament. Similarly, hard pressed loyalists tried to band together for mutual protection in several localities in Massachusetts, New Hampshire, and New York. Single purpose associations for the redress of grievances had an established place in Anglo-American political culture.[11]

The successful resistance to the Stamp Act in 1765 and 1766 was a kind of general rehearsal for actively coordinating the already constituted organs of colonial self-government with mass demonstrations, mob actions, and new citizen groups created for specific purposes. The Stamp Act Congress that met in New York in October 1765 still had a legal basis in the sense that it was a meeting of delegates from the houses of representatives in nine colonies and did nothing more than compose letters to George III and to both houses of Parliament. The Sons of Liberty, however, which was established in all the colonies during the winter of 1765/1766 and which counted the most radical opponents of the Stamp Act among its members, operated "privately." It resorted to violence and terror to prevent the implementation of the law. Shortly before the Stamp Act was annulled in March 1766, the Sons of Liberty constituted the de facto government in several colonies. The governors of those colonies were forced to recognize their helplessness, and they reported to London that orderly government was no longer possible.[12]

Events followed a similar pattern once the infringements on colonial self-government implicit in the Townshend Acts of 1767 became known. The embargo and the consumer boycott that some mass meetings and the houses of representatives in most of the colonies had adopted could only be enacted with the cooperation of a great many local committees. The committees often forced merchants suspected of violating the boycott to open their books for inspection,

11. Arthur Meier Schlesinger, *The Colonial Merchants and the American Revolution, 1763–1776* (New York, 1957), 477, 484, 493. Schlesinger's book also contains the most thorough study available on the various associations. On associations and similar organizations in England, see Robbins, *Eighteenth-Century Commonwealthman*, particularly p. 364; Maier, *Resistance to Revolution*, chap. 6; and on the organization of dissenters, Carl Bridenbaugh, *Mitre and Sceptre: Transatlantic Faiths, Ideas, Personalities, and Politics, 1689–1775* (New York, 1962).
12. Morgan and Morgan, *Stamp Act Crisis*, 253. Maier, *Resistance to Revolution*, 98, found that "rather than usurp the powers of local magistrates, the Sons of Liberty often worked closely with the regular governments of their towns."

and in cases of actual violation, they imposed punishments as if they were competent authorities.[13]

A Case Study: The Assumption of Power in Massachusetts

In New England, Revolutionary politicians could resort to the town meetings whenever the governor attempted to prevent political action by cutting off a legislative period or by refusing to convene the General Court.[14] When the representatives of Massachusetts decided in 1768 to send a circular letter to their counterparts in other states, urging them to protest the Townshend Acts, the governor dissolved the legislature. When he refused to grant the petition of the Boston town meeting and convene the General Court, the town meeting took the initiative itself and asked all the towns in Massachusetts to send delegates to a convention in Boston set for September 1768. Over 100 of the 250 towns sent delegates, and this convention, composed largely of the same members as the house of representatives, accomplished what the governor had not allowed the house to do. The convention's legitimation was based on the understanding that the towns behind it were themselves sovereign political units.[15]

13. The most detailed account of resistance by means of embargoes and boycotts between 1767 and 1773 is contained in Schlesinger, *Colonial Merchants,* chaps. 3–6. See, too, Maier, *Resistance to Revolution,* chap. 5, esp. 135–138.
14. Detailed accounts are in Harry A. Cushing, *History of the Transition from Provincial to Commonwealth Government in Massachusetts* (New York, 1896). See also the exhaustive documentation in L. Kinvin Wroth *et al.*, eds., *Province in Rebellion: A Documentary History of the Founding of the Commonwealth of Massachusetts, 1774–1775* (Cambridge, Mass., 1975), with a set of documents on microfiche.
15. John C. Miller, "The Massachusetts Convention of 1768," *New England Quarterly,* VII (1934), 445–447; Richard D. Brown, "The Massachusetts Convention of Towns, 1768," *WMQ,* 3d Ser., XXVI (1969), 94–104; and Brown, *Revolutionary Politics in Massachusetts: The Boston Committee of Correspondence and the Towns, 1772–1774* (Cambridge, Mass., 1970), 29–30. Brown writes: "The towns behaved as if sovereignty was theirs. . . . Many towns assumed that their powers to meet, discuss, and send representatives to confer with others were unlimited." *Ibid.,* 30. On the significance of the town as a social and political unit in New England, see Charles S. Grant, *Democracy in the*

In November 1772 the town meeting of Boston appointed a twenty-one-man committee of correspondence at the suggestion of Samuel Adams. Completely independent of the governor and the General Court, this committee could meet as often as it deemed necessary and pursue policies it had to justify only to the town meeting. The committee published political articles in the newspapers and distributed its own broadsides and handbills. It urged all the towns of Massachusetts to form similar committees. Most of the towns did so, and the Boston committee became a central agency for information and agitation that was far more effective than any comparable agency the governor had ever had.[16]

The arrival in May 1774 of General Thomas Gage as both commander-in-chief of the British troops in North America and as governor of Massachusetts hastened the end of British civil government in Massachusetts. The colonists rejected as "Intolerable Acts" the new sanctions that Parliament had enacted in March and May of 1774 and that Gage was to enforce.[17] The announcement that the organs of self-government in Massachusetts were to be suppressed in retaliation for the Boston Tea Party, which was staged by an anonymous mob that could not be brought to court, produced a wave of solidarity

---

Connecticut Frontier Town of Kent (New York, 1961), esp. chap. 9; J. R. Pole, *Political Representation in England and the Origins of the American Republic* (London, 1966), 38–53; G. B. Warden, *Boston, 1689–1776* (Boston, 1970), 28–33; Michael Zuckerman, *Peaceable Kingdoms: New England Towns in the Eighteenth Century* (New York, 1970).

16. Edward D. Collins, "Committees of Correspondence of the American Revolution," American Historical Association, *Annual Report . . . for the Year 1901* (Washington, D.C., 1902), I, 245–249; John C. Miller, *Sam Adams: Pioneer in Propaganda* (Boston, 1936), chap. 10; Warden, *Boston*, 257–264, and chap. 13. For a comprehensive picture, see R. D. Brown, *Revolutionary Politics*, chaps. 3 and 4.

17. The Boston Port Act of Mar. 31, 1774, closed Boston harbor until £10,000 sterling was paid to the East India Company for tea destroyed in the Boston Tea Party. The Massachusetts Government Act of May 20, 1774, suspended the Charter of 1692 and gave the governor unprecedented powers. Even town meetings, except the regular ones held in the spring, could not be convened without his permission. The Administration of Justice Act of May 20, 1774, authorized the governor to transfer trials for murder of crown officials to other colonies or to England if he thought this measure necessary to ensure a "fair trial." The Quartering Act of June 2, 1774, legalized the obligatory quartering of soldiers in private homes. The texts of the Intolerable Acts are available in Jensen, ed., *American Colonial Documents*, 779–785.

that reached as far as South Carolina. The assumption of power in Massachusetts took place in the summer and fall of 1774. Committees on the county level played a decisive role. The towns of each county sent delegates to county conventions. The county conventions not only organized the consumer boycotts and formulated the justification for them but also assumed police powers. In the western counties, they used controlled mob action to interfere with trials, particularly debtors' trials, arguing that the unconstitutional Massachusetts Government Act had deprived the judges of their legitimation.[18]

The committees of correspondence from the counties of Worcester, Middlesex, and Suffolk and from the harbor cities of Boston, Salem, and Marblehead met jointly from August 26 to September 9, 1774, and called for the abolition of Governor Gage's "unconstitutional" administration. The decisions they reached became known as the Suffolk Resolves and urged disobedience to the Intolerable Acts. Committees were to replace the judges Gage had appointed by virtue of his new plenipotentiary power. The new members of the governor's council, the "mandamus councillors," also appointed by the governor, were asked to resign; and the officers of the militia he had appointed were requested to turn in their commissions and submit to election by their companies. The tax collectors were required to deliver their returns to the provincial county treasurers. All trade with Great Britain, Ireland, and the West Indian colonies was to cease, and British goods were to be boycotted, especially the tea of the East India Company. The coordination of these measures throughout the entire colony was to be entrusted to a provincial congress made up of delegates from all the towns.[19]

Much of the political significance of the Suffolk Resolves derives from their having been immediately communicated to the Continental Congress in Philadelphia and treated there as a vote of the people in the debate between the advocates of reconciliation and the uncompromising defenders of colonial self-government. On September 17, 1774, the Continental Congress endorsed the Suffolk Resolves.[20]

The first provincial congress of Massachusetts met in Salem from October 7 to October 29, 1774. In a letter to Governor Gage demanding that he cease fortifying the Boston Neck, the congress referred to

18. R. D. Brown, *Revolutionary Politics*, chap. 9.
19. Peter Force, comp., *American Archives* . . . (Washington, D.C., 1837–1853), 4th Ser., I, 776–779, hereafter cited as *American Archives*.
20. Ford *et al.*, eds., *Journals of the Continental Congress*, I, 31–37.

itself as "the Delegates from the several Towns in the Province of the *Massachusetts Bay*, having convened in general Congress." From this point on, the political initiative clearly lay with the provincial congress. It attempted to increase its authority by inviting to its next meeting the fourteen members of the governor's council who had been elected in May 1774 but whom the governor refused to recognize. The purpose of the councillors' presence at the meeting was to let the congress have "the benefit of their advice." The question of whether they would be voting members was not raised. Before the first provincial congress adjourned, it appointed an executive committee, known as the council of safety, and authorized it to call out the militia if necessary. The second provincial congress (November 23 to December 10, 1774) urged the towns to arm the militia better and to execute carefully the decisions of the Continental Congress and the provincial congresses. It scheduled the next session of the congress for February through May 1775 and asked that the towns allow only those men who met the property qualifications for electing members to the old house of representatives to vote for delegates to the congress.[21] By the end of 1774, Massachusetts had a new governmental system that had taken over the crucial tasks previously performed by the British administration.

To give an accurate picture of the local variations in the assumption of power, we would have to reconstruct thirteen revolutions. The peculiar situation of Connecticut and Rhode Island as provinces with de facto self-government has already been mentioned.[22] In New York, the long-standing rivalry of the Livingstons and the DeLanceys colored the struggle for independence. In Pennsylvania, proprietary government and the special role of the firmly established Quakers shaped the movement for independence, influencing even the decision for a unicameral legislature under the new constitution. Developments in the South were affected by the social and economic features of the plantation system, which separated these colonies from those centered around the commercial cities of Philadelphia, New York, and Boston.[23]

21. For the minutes of the provincial congress, see *American Archives*, 4th Ser., I, 829–853. The invitation to the councillors is on p. 848, the title of the congress is on p. 835. The council of safety is dealt with on p. 843, the election on pp. 1005–1007.
22. See p. 6 above, pp. 66–68 below.
23. Schlesinger, *Colonial Merchants*, 22*ff*, provides general descriptions of "commercial provinces" and "plantation provinces."

But despite regional differences, a sufficiently large segment of the political leadership throughout the colonies felt threatened by the new English policies. This leadership reacted in similar ways that could be coordinated. In the various houses of representatives those factions that advocated self-government—usually the majority groups—supported the provincial congress and the towns of Massachusetts by issuing declarations of principle and by providing concrete help until the governors of their colonies dissolved the constitutional assemblies. The representatives then either reconvened immediately as provincial congresses or returned to their towns and counties, conducted discussions and mass meetings, and held elections—usually retaining the old property qualifications for voters—for delegates to a provincial congress.

In New York, to take an example, widely differing territorial units and social groupings played a role in the election of delegates to the first provincial congress in May 1775. (1) In the city of New York, a "Committee of Sixty" had called for an election on April 28, 1775. (2) In counties with few activists, some twenty or thirty men would hold a public meeting and elect a delegate in the name of the county. (3) Already existing county committees appointed delegates without consulting the electorate. (4) In some counties, committees were specially elected for this task. (5) The committees of several townships could meet and appoint delegates for a county. (6) Individual townships could elect a delegate in a public meeting.[24] But whatever election processes the counties had used, when the New York provincial congress met on May 23, 1775, the fourteen counties stood as the units represented. If representatives of eight counties were present, the assembly had a quorum. The city and county of New York had four votes; the city and county of Albany had three. All other counties had two votes. Before adjournment, the provincial congress established for the next session a system of representation by which each county's number of delegates would be proportional to its population.[25]

---

24. Becker, *Political Parties*, 201. For the other points cited, see *ibid.*, 202–204.
25. Resolution of Oct. 18, 1775. The city and county of New York were to have 21 delegates; the city and county of Albany, 12; Dutchess and Westchester counties, 9 each; Ulster, Suffolk, and Queens, 8 each; Orange, 6; Kings, Richmond, and Tryon, 4 each; Cumberland, 3; Gloucester and Charlotte, 2 each. *American Archives*, 4th Ser., III, 1295.

The Committees of Correspondence
and the First Continental Congress

On March 12, 1773, the House of Burgesses in Virginia established a committee of correspondence, which, with the aid of similar committees from other colonial legislatures, was to gather reliable information on future measures that Parliament and the governors might take. The decision to form this committee ushered in the period of close cooperation preceding the First Continental Congress. Active politicians such as Richard Henry Lee, Edmund Pendleton, Patrick Henry, and Thomas Jefferson were elected to this committee. Its task was "to obtain the most early and authentic intelligence of all such acts and resolutions of the British Parliament, or proceedings of administration, as may relate to, or affect the British Colonies in America," and to "maintain a correspondence and communication with our sister colonies, respecting these important considerations."[26] The houses of representatives in the other colonies responded immediately. Between March 1773 and February 1774, all the houses, with the exception of the Pennsylvania legislature, established committees of correspondence.[27] As such, there was nothing illegal about these committees. The governors declared, however, that they would become unconstitutional if they remained active once the legislative period set by the governors had come to an end. In his history of Massachusetts, Governor Thomas Hutchinson noted that the movement for independence began with the creation of the committees of correspondence: "It was a most glaring attempt to alter the constitution of the colonies, by assuming to one branch of the legislature the powers of the whole. . . . It was an act which ought to have been considered as an avowal of independency, because it could be justified only upon the principle of independency."[28]

The First Continental Congress met from September 5 to October 27, 1774, in Carpenters Hall in Philadelphia. All the British provinces in North America were represented except the four most

---

26. William J. Van Schreeven, comp., and Robert L. Scribner, ed., *Revolutionary Virginia: The Road to Independence*, I (Charlottesville, Va., 1973), 91.
27. Jensen, *Founding of a Nation*, 431.
28. Thomas Hutchinson, *The History of the Province of Massachusetts Bay, from the Year 1750 until June 1774* (London, 1828 [manuscript completed 1778]), III, 397.

northerly—Quebec, Nova Scotia, St. John's Isle (now Prince Edward Island), and Newfoundland—and the three most southerly—Georgia and East and West Florida.

The Congress, which was the first meeting of representatives from a majority of the colonies since the Stamp Act Congress of 1765, was described in the instructions of the Massachusetts delegation as "a meeting of Committees from the several Colonies on this Continent" and in the instructions of the Connecticut delegates as a "congress, or convention of commissioners or committees of the several colonies."[29]

The Continental Congress's mode of operation and its claim to political authority were based on the fiction that it represented the twelve territorial units from Massachusetts to South Carolina. The electorates or constituencies of the delegates, however, were no more uniform than the constituencies that had chosen delegates for the provincial congresses. In three colonies (Rhode Island, Connecticut, and Pennsylvania), the legally constituted houses of representatives had chosen the delegates.[30] In Massachusetts, on June 17, 1774, the governor's secretary stood before the barred door of the house of representatives reading a decree that officially dissolved the house while inside the chamber the five delegates who would go to Philadelphia were being chosen.[31] In South Carolina, a general meeting of 104 representatives from almost all the counties appointed five delegates in Charleston between July 6 and July 8, 1774. Any free white adult male who entered the room was entitled to vote. The house of representatives officially sanctioned the election afterward.[32] In New York, a campaign that lasted several months and that was centered in New York City preceded the selection of delegates. Associations of merchants and mechanics took the initiative and put up a list of candidates. In the seven wards of the city, any taxpayer could vote. In rural areas, the delegates were mostly selected by county committees.[33] In the other eight colonies, extralegal conventions usually made up of country representatives appointed the delegates for the

29. Ford *et al.*, eds., *Journals of the Continental Congress*, I, 15, 17.
30. Edmund Cody Burnett, *The Continental Congress* (New York, 1941), 20–22; Schlesinger, *Colonial Merchants*, chaps. 8–10.
31. *American Archives*, 4th Ser., I, 421–422.
32. *Ibid.*, 526, 531–532, 672.
33. Becker, *Political Parties*, 122–141.

Continental Congress. The county committees of New Jersey, for example, were created for this specific purpose.[34]

The basic question in any confederation came up on the first day of the meeting: How could decisions binding for all be reached? Patrick Henry of Virginia suggested representation for each colony in proportion to its population, excluding slaves. Thomas Lynch of South Carolina urged that both population and property provide the basis for representation. Samuel Ward of Rhode Island, the smallest colony, demanded the same number of votes for every colony. He reminded Patrick Henry of the mode of representation in Virginia. Every county there, regardless of size, sent two delegates to the provincial congress. The small colonies stood firm, and the unanimity that was politically necessary for successful resistance against England could only be achieved by the willingness of the larger colonies to compromise. The delegation of every colony was given one vote.[35]

The delegates were not in agreement about the current state of the constitution. Patrick Henry assumed that the way was clear for a new start. "Government is dissolved. . . . We are in a State of Nature." John Jay of New York replied to him: "Could I suppose, that We came to frame an American Constitution, instead of indeavouring to correct the faults in an old one—I cant yet think that all Government is at an End. The Measure of arbitrary Power is not full, and I think it must run over, before We undertake to frame a new Constitution."[36]

The approval of the Suffolk Resolves on September 17, 1774, was the first step the Continental Congress took toward a new constitution. But those who sought a solution through reform of the English constitutional system had not yet given up. Joseph Galloway of Pennsylvania made a proposal based on the Albany Plan of 1754. He envisaged a "Grand Council" elected by the houses of representatives of the colonies. Laws that affected the colonies would have to be approved by the Grand Council and Parliament. Self-government within the colonies would have continued to exist in the established form. Galloway found little support among his fellow delegates and

34. Collins, "Committees of Correspondence," A.H.A., *Annual Report for 1901*, I, 255–257.
35. John Adams's entries for Sept. 5 and 6, 1774, Butterfield *et al.*, eds., *Diary of John Adams*, II, 122–126.
36. Notes on speeches in John Adams's journal entry for Sept. 6, 1774, *ibid.*, 124–126.

might have found less in England, had his plan been adopted by the Congress. After a discussion that was disproportionately brief in view of the potential importance of the plan had it been adopted, the proposal was taken off the agenda by a vote of six delegations to five.[37] The most politically significant result of the First Continental Congress soon proved to be the forming, on October 20, 1774, of a "Continental Association" for enforcing an embargo on imported goods. Articles 10 and 11 of the association assigned complete control over imports and prices to committees to be chosen in every town, city, and county by the electorates of the old houses of representatives. If any committee felt that any citizen was disregarding the boycott of British goods, the Continental Congress recommended that that person be publicly declared an enemy of "American freedom" and that he be ostracized. The committees were to confiscate goods imported after December 1, 1774.[38]

A few weeks later, a violently antimonarchical article in the *Pennsylvania Packet* praised the Continental Congress, calling it a legislative assembly authorized by the people: "The *American Congress* derives all its power, wisdom and justice not from scrolls of parchment signed by Kings, but from the *People.* . . . The Congress, like other legislative bodies, have annexed penalties to their laws."[39] Whether those members of the First Continental Congress who were still hoping for reconciliation liked it or not, a new system of government had been formed on the continental level by the time the Congress adjourned.[40]

After war began the leading role of the Continental Congress

37. Ford *et al.*, eds., *Journals of the Continental Congress*, I, 43–51; Burnett, *Continental Congress*, 47–50. David Ammerman, *In the Common Cause: American Response to the Coercive Acts of 1774* (Charlottesville, Va., 1974), 57–60, has convincingly rejected the textbook account that there was a 6:5 vote concerning the contents of Galloway's proposal.
38. Text in Jensen, ed., *American Colonial Documents*, 813–816. On the activities of the various committees, see Ammerman, *Common Cause*, chap. 8.
39. "Political Observations, Without Order; Addressed to the People of America," *Dunlap's Pennsylvania Packet, or, the General Advertiser* (Philadelphia), Nov. 14, 1774; also in *American Archives*, 4th Ser., I, 976–977.
40. Compare Carl Becker's interpretation: "One of two things had happened: either the colonies were subject to Great Britain, in which case Congress was engaged in systematic robbery, or the colonies had ceased to be subject to Great Britain, in which case Congress was something very like a *de facto* government enforcing its own law." Becker, *Political Parties*, 155.

became clearer than ever before. Judging by the example of New York, Hugh M. Flick concluded that by the time the Second Continental Congress met, a pyramid of authority had begun to emerge. In principle at least, the Continental Congress stood at the top as the "ultimate source of authority" and was accepted as such by the provincial congress of New York, by the fourteen county committees, and by the approximately 150 town, city, and district committees.[41]

The End of Government by Congresses and Committees

More and more the provincial congresses assumed the role of unicameral legislatures with executive committees. The congresses appointed committees of safety that exercised considerable power, particularly when the congresses were not in session. The New York committee of safety, formed on July 8, 1775, received almost all the powers of the provincial congress. Every county was represented in it.[42] The New Hampshire committee of safety was given extensive powers in May 1775 to see "that the public sustain no damage." The phrase was a literal translation of the formula used in Rome when a temporary dictator was empowered to administer martial law in emergency situations: *ne quid detrimenti respublica capiat*.[43]

The provincial congresses exercised increasing control over the counties. In Virginia, the provincial congress—officially known as "the Delegates of the several Counties and Corporations in the Colony of Virginia, assembled in General Convention"—instructed the counties in August 1775 to appoint twenty-one freeholders to each county committee. The committee members were to hold office for one year and, among other duties, to be responsible for implementing the decisions of the provincial congress. As the Continental Congress had directed, only the electorate for the old House of Burgesses would be allowed to vote for these committee members.[44] In New

41. Hugh M. Flick, "The Rise of the Revolutionary Committee System," in Alexander C. Flick, ed., *History of the State of New York*, III (New York, 1933), 241.

42. Becker, *Political Parties*, 211.

43. Belknap, *History of New-Hampshire*, II, 395.

44. "An Ordinance for regulating the election of Delegates . . . and . . . of Committee-Men in the several Counties . . . ," *American Archives*, 4th Ser.,

York election procedures for a third provincial congress to be held in April 1776 had already been established. The second provincial congress had determined that even citizens who had not signed the association articles could vote, and it prescribed the number of delegates from each of the fourteen counties. The county committees were in charge of the elections.[45]

Despite these efforts at stabilization, "Government by congresses and committees"—as the preamble to the New York constitution called it in retrospect—lasted only about two years at the local level. Only the Continental Congress itself—that unicameral assembly of delegations without an independent executive—survived until 1788. By then it also had lost its usefulness and was succeeded by a more powerful central government shaped along the lines of the new state governments, just as the local committees, county conventions, and provincial congresses had themselves been replaced by the new state governments. There is no doubt, however, that during the critical phase of dismantling the old regime's credibility and efficacy the numerous local committees and county conventions had served an important function by mobilizing popular support. By regulating prices and successfully encouraging the manufacture of clothing, household goods, and other finished products customarily imported from England, they demonstrated a certain degree of economic self-sufficiency in the colonies and furthered the spirit of opposition to colonial rule. In sum, government by congresses and committees helped develop a sense of patriotic frugality and willingness to suffer.[46]

Yet despite this success, the committees could never hope to become the permanent heirs to the old regime for the simple reason that the American Revolution was not a movement to introduce grassroots democracy; not only the word, but also the idea would have been an anachronism in the America of 1776. For two or three generations, the government of each colony had been proudly and pur-

III, 420–424. The ordinance also prescribed how many delegates each county could send to the next provincial congress and that these delegates were to be elected from among "the Freeholders . . . who are by law properly qualified to vote for Burgesses." See also, Ammerman, *Common Cause*, 104–105.

45. *American Archives*, 4th Ser., V, 364–365.

46. Ammerman, *Common Cause*, 109–124. In her study of the organized form resistance took from 1764 on, Pauline Maier has shown that there was a persistent effort to limit the use of force and to work toward "regular" modes of governing. Maier, *Resistance to Revolution*, 272.

posefully considered as a complete, if dependent, replication of the British model, with a fully developed set of separate branches of government. For over a century in most colonies it had been firmly established in the public mind what "real" government looked like: it consisted of a governor, a governor's council, an assembly, and a provincial judiciary. The fact that before 1775 the governors had been the instruments of monarchical government, and that the judges had been their appointees, did not suffice to discredit either these offices or the principle of the separation of powers. The political leaders of the colonists wanted effective government in their own interest, but they expected it to have a traditional structure. They wanted one of their own to move into the governor's mansion; they did not want to turn it into a museum.

What had enabled the committees to propagate effective resistance to imperial government was, at the same time, their greatest weakness as organs of the new government: they were too dependent on the constituencies directly affected by their decisions. This flaw was bound to interfere with the functioning of the government. It was a relatively easy task under the circumstances to enforce a consumer boycott or to close a court. But the committees shied away from collecting unpopular taxes and from levying troops. Loyalty to the new government was too fragile to put to such severe tests.[47] Even the influential Boston committee of correspondence lost its political effectiveness when its measures went against the general consensus. And the county conventions of Massachusetts could maintain order in the summer and fall of 1774 only because they were not called upon to resolve any serious conflicts of interest.[48]

Criticism of government by committees and congresses on the state level arose from different political situations in each colony. In Pennsylvania the old assembly still appointed public officials, disposed of public funds, and refused to sign a declaration of independence. A writer in the *Pennsylvania Packet* of April 15, 1776, protested these conditions and demanded that the coexistence of assembly and congresses come to an end. The "indirect ways" of the committees and conventions, the unknown writer argued, were less effective than the "instructions" of a legislature; the administration of justice

47. For the situation in New York, for example, see Becker, *Political Parties*, 255, and Bernard Mason, *The Road to Independence: The Revolutionary Movement in New York, 1773–1777* (Lexington, Ky., 1966), 191–197.
48. R. D. Brown, *Revolutionary Politics*, 199, 219.

by the committees was either too indecisive or too repressive, and trials by jury were practically a thing of the past; Pennsylvania was on the road to anarchy.

In Maryland, an anonymous commentator who signed himself "An American," took to task the provincial conventions of December 1775 and May 1776, as well as the committees of safety they had appointed, and called for a division of governmental powers into three branches. The eighty members of the convention had appointed fifty militia officers from their own ranks, the "American" noted. Eighteen members of the convention could pass a law even if forty-four other members voted against it, because the voting was done by counties, not by individuals. The committee of safety seemed to be coming under the permanent control of a certain group. The convention held in May had left in office those members of the committee appointed by the December convention despite the fact that an earlier convention had ruled that half of the committee be newly appointed at each convention. The administration of justice by the legislature also came under attack. The Maryland conventions had still not established any new courts. When cases of treason or other serious crimes came up for trial, this critic argued, the same men who made the law acted as judges. Legislative, executive, and judicial powers were all in the same hands. "A complete tyranny is established by such a combination of powers." Montesquieu, he reminded his readers, had warned against such concentration of power. Government by conventions is justified only temporarily and as an emergency measure. It should be immediately replaced by "a proper, effectual, and well-regulated Government."[49]

49. "To the People of Maryland," by "An American," *American Archives*, 4th Ser., VI, 1094–1096. William Moultrie, who served as a major general under Washington, describes in his memoirs the need his home state of South Carolina felt for a new constitution: "The affairs of the province became too unwieldly for the management of [the provincial] Congress, and the council of safety or general committee: Every thing was running into confusion, and although our criminal laws were still of force, yet they were virtually repealed for want of proper officers to execute them, all those under the royal authority being suspended from office, it was therefore thought absolutely necessary to frame a constitution for the purpose of forming a regular system of government, and for appointing public officers for the different departments to put the laws into execution." William Moultrie, *Memoirs of the American Revolution, So Far as It Related to the States of North and South Carolina, and Georgia* (New York, 1802), I, 125.

In Massachusetts, there were a number of reasons for dissatisfaction with continued adherence to the Charter of 1691 and with the legal fiction, maintained from the summer of 1775 through the summer of 1776, that the council of twenty-eight acted as the executive in place of the merely "absent" governor.[50] A newspaper article written early in September 1775 argued for a new "regular system" because reconciliation with England could no longer be expected and war could not be conducted successfully unless the government could act with a free hand. Other writers asked what actions besides an embargo could be taken against England. They concluded that it was time to sort through those elements of the English constitution still in effect. Both church and state were burdened with much dead wood. The colonies should no longer fear innovations such as a unicameral legislature.[51]

The first groups to urge open defiance of the authority of the house of representatives were the towns of Berkshire County in western Massachusetts. In mid-December 1775, an assembly of town delegates called on the inhabitants of the county to deny recognition to any public official appointed by the house of representatives and to elect their own judges as a first step toward a new constitution. Around Christmas 1775, the citizens of Pittsfield, who headed the resistance under the leadership of their minister, Thomas Allen, wrote a petition to the General Court in which they cited the present system of appointing officials, particularly judges, as justifying the need for a new constitution. The charter, they wrote, had established this dangerous method of having elected representatives appoint public officials, and it should therefore be annulled.[52] Demands of this kind were unsettling to the leadership of resistance in Massachusetts. Early in June 1776, John Adams, who was in Philadelphia at the time, received reports about the "spirit of innovation" rampant in his home state. "It seems as if every thing was to be altered," John Winthrop wrote to him. "Scarce a newspaper but teems with new projects."

50. *American Archives*, 4th Ser., III, 289.

51. "To the People of Massachusetts," dated Salem, Sept. 8, 1775, *ibid.*, 676–679; "Massachusettensis," *New-England Chronicle* (Boston), May 2, 1776, hereafter cited as *N.-E. Chron.*

52. Resolution of the Convention of Stockbridge, Dec. 15, 1775, in Robert J. Taylor, ed., *Massachusetts, Colony to Commonwealth: Documents on the Formation of Its Constitution, 1775–1780* (Chapel Hill, N.C., 1961), 16–17; Petition of Pittsfield, *ibid.*, 17–19. On the "Berkshire Constitutionalists," see Taylor, *Western Massachusetts in the Revolution* (Providence, R.I., 1954), 88–101.

But, he added, there was no point in trying to repair a burning house until the fire was put out.[53]

As long as they had majority support in their provincial congresses, cautious revolutionaries like James Duane, one of the New York representatives in the Continental Congress who was still hoping for reconciliation with England, remained content with the system of congresses and committees. The election for the third provincial congress of New York in April 1776 had strengthened Duane's faction, and he therefore warned against changing the present form of government.[54] But on May 31, 1776, the majority of the New York provincial congress urged its constituents to authorize their present delegates to introduce a new form of government or to elect new delegates for this purpose. In doing this, the provincial congress referred to the recommendation made by the Continental Congress on May 10 and May 15, 1776.[55] The provincial congress claimed that the present system of government was inadequate and that it had been devised only as an interim system until reconciliation with Great Britain could be achieved. But that was no longer a realistic hope. The uniting of legislative, executive, and judicial powers in one agency had proved to be disadvantageous.[56] A few weeks later a newspaper article urging the election of men able to work out a new system of government declared, however, that such a step was by no means a declaration of independence and would not interfere with reconciliation. On the contrary, a regularly constituted government

53. John Winthrop to John Adams, June 1, 1776, Massachusetts Historical Society, *Collections*, 5th Ser., IV (Boston, 1878), 308. The town of Topsfield used the same argument in its instructions of June 14, 1776, to its delegate in the house of representatives. Oscar Handlin and Mary Handlin, eds., *The Popular Sources of Political Authority: Documents on the Massachusetts Constitution of 1780* (Cambridge, Mass., 1966), 97–98.

54. James Duane to John Jay, May 18, 1776, Henry P. Johnston, ed., *The Correspondence and Public Papers of John Jay* (New York, 1890–1893), I, 61.

55. See pp. 59–62 below.

56. "The present Government of this Colony, by Congress and Committees, was instituted while the former Government, under the Crown of *Great Britain*, existed in full force, and was established for the sole purpose of opposing the usurpation of the *British* Parliament, and was intended to expire on a reconciliation with *Great Britain*, which it was then apprehended would soon take place, but is now considered as remote and uncertain." *American Archives*, 4th Ser., VI, 1351–1352. The preamble to the New York constitution of 1777 adopted this resolution word for word.

could more easily reach agreement with England than could a "lawless multitude" led by an "ambitious man, or set of men." At the moment there was no real government. No one could be legally punished, and neither the congress nor the committees were able to guarantee law and order.[57]

Just how great the dissatisfaction was with rule by committees and congresses in 1775 and 1776 and just who encouraged it and for what purposes has not been sufficiently researched to make the identification of persons or groups possible. It is clear, however, that several motives were at work. Filling the office of governor again and having more than one assembly take part in legislation meant a step toward more familiar conditions. Private property and individual freedoms seemed better protected under such a system. Moreover, the advocates of independence were no less inclined than the loyalists to describe current circumstances as lawless and anarchistic, for they correctly saw that the writing of constitutions independent of crown and Parliament would be a major step toward their goal. Paine, for instance, made effective use of this argument. In *Common Sense* he evoked a picture of impending anarchy. America was being held together, he wrote, only by a constellation of feelings that could not last. There was no law and only as much governmental power as people were inclined by "courtesy" to recognize. No one's property was safe. No action was criminal, not even treason, and the people had no clear goal in view. "The mind of the multitude is left at random, and seeing no fixed object before them, they pursue such as fancy or opinion presents."[58] The successful defense of American independence, Paine argued, required a clearer structure of authority than congresses and committees could provide.

57. "Columbus," June 12, 1776, *ibid.*, 825–826.
58. *Common Sense*, in Foner, ed., *Writings of Paine*, I, 43. On opposition to government by committees in Massachusetts, see Hoerder, *Crowd Action*, 321–330.

CHAPTER II

The Role of the Continental Congress, 1775–1776

It has ever appeared to me that the natural course and order of things was this; for every colony to institute a government; for all the colonies to confederate, and define the limits of the continental Constitution; then to declare the colonies a sovereign state, or a number of confederated sovereign states; and last of all, to form treaties with foreign powers. But I fear we cannot proceed systematically, and that we shall be obliged to declare ourselves independent States, before we confederate, and indeed before all the colonies have established their governments.

John Adams to Patrick Henry, June 3, 1776

None of the thirteen colonies adopted a state constitution without an explicit previous recommendation from the Continental Congress to do so. This fact might suggest that, as Abraham Lincoln told Congress years later when the authority of the federal government was threatened by the states as never before, "The Union is older than any of the States and, in fact, it created them as States."[1] But the relationship between the Continental Congress and the nascent states was by no means as simple as that. The Continental Congress proclaimed independence and recommended that the colonies adopt new constitutions, but it was the colonial assemblies and Revolutionary conven-

1. Special Session Message, July 4, 1861, James D. Richardson, ed., *A Compilation of the Messages and Papers of the Presidents, 1789–1897* (Washington, D.C., 1897), VI, 27. On the precedence of the Union over the individual states, see Curtis Putnam Nettels, "The Origins of the Union and of the States," Mass. Hist. Soc., *Proceedings*, LXXII (Boston, 1963), 68–83. For a different view, see Merrill Jensen, *The Articles of Confederation: An Interpretation of the Social-Constitutional History of the American Revolution, 1774–1781* (Madison, Wis., 1940), chap. 7.

tions that had formed the Congress by sending delegates and that instructed them on how to vote on crucial issues such as independence. It is clear from the way the first constitutions came into being and from their contents that not all the powers of the central colonial administration reverted to the provincial congresses, much less to the committees of the counties and towns. On the other hand, the Continental Congress also could not gather to itself a monopoly of power. When the power of the old colonial administrations crumbled, new structures of political authority developed simultaneously on both state and continental levels. Both spheres of political activity were obviously dependent on each other and influenced each other reciprocally, just as within individual colonies power had been shared during the transition period by town meetings, county committees, and provincial congresses.

In such a situation, long debates about the true locus of sovereignty (which would have had to go beyond the undisputed but vague maxim that the consent of the governed was the only source of legitimate power) were of academic interest at best. Only later, in the 1780s, did members of the Continental Congress begin to reflect on their situation and to use the term "sovereignty" more frequently in their speeches and letters. By then the question of sovereignty had become the practical issue of the distribution of power between the two levels of government. But that each level had its own legitimate existence was already at that point a generally accepted fact.

The course of events in the spring and summer of 1776 developed its own logic and did not conform to preexistent constitutional theories. John Adams, who had a clear understanding of both constitutional theory and political practice, was keenly aware of the gap opening between them. Early in June 1776 he wrote to Patrick Henry that he would have considered it "the natural course and order of things . . . for every colony to institute a government; for all the colonies to confederate, and define the limits of the continental Constitution; then to declare the colonies a sovereign state, or a number of confederated sovereign states; and last of all, to form treaties with foreign powers." But political reality, Adams added, did not permit this kind of logical procedure.[2] What proved to be crucial was not the sequence in which these steps were taken but that the decision for

2. See epigraph to this chapter, John Adams to Patrick Henry, June 3, 1776, in Edmund C. Burnett, ed., *Letters of Members of the Continental Congress* (Washington, D.C., 1921–1936), I, 47.

independence and the decision to draft new constitutions occurred simultaneously on several interlocking levels.

The actual ambiguities of the political situation are brought out further when it is recalled that members of the Congress once considered drawing up a model state constitution for all the colonies to use, but never acted on the idea. In May 1775 the provincial congress of Massachusetts entertained the possibility of adopting such a constitution drafted by the Continental Congress.[3] But even the adoption of a model constitution by one of the states would not have implied that the Continental Congress, because it had proclaimed independence, was in a position to "give" the individual states their constitutions in the same way that the crown had issued charters to the colonies or that European monarchs would "give" constitutions in the nineteenth century. The vote that the delegations from twelve colonies entered in favor of independence reflected the instructions they had received from the entities they represented. (The New York delegation, because it had received no such instruction, ended up not voting.) None of the delegations had been instructed to work toward a model constitution for all states. The Continental Congress had a difficult enough time defining its own role in constitutional terms. Indeed, it was not until 1781 that the Articles of Confederation were ratified by all thirteen states and became the constitution of the Confederation.[4]

Massachusetts Requests Advice

The Continental Congress was to meet again on May 10, 1775. When John Adams set out for this meeting as a member of the Massachusetts delegation, he had with him a plan of action involving six steps he wanted the Congress to implement: (1) The Continental Congress should urge all thirteen colonies to arrest all crown officials and hold them as hostages until Boston was freed from British military rule. (2) The Continental Congress should urge the colonies "to institute" without delay "Governments for themselves, under their own Authority." (3) The Continental Congress should declare the colonies free, sovereign, and independent states. (4) The Continental Congress should indicate to Great Britain the willingness of the colonies

3. See pp. 55–56 below.
4. See chap. 13 below.

to settle the conflict between the two countries. (5) The Congress should use the threat of an alliance with France, Spain, and other European powers to exert pressure on Great Britain. (6) The Congress should recognize the army mustered outside Boston as the "Continental Army" and assume control of it by appointing a general to command it.[5] Even if this autobiographical account is not correct in every detail, it still makes clear that "instituting government" was not to be a consequence of independence but was considered as part of the political strategy necessary to achieve independence.

The problem of "instituting government" inevitably played an important role in the interaction between the Continental Congress and the provincial congresses. It was not always a sign of helplessness or indecision when a provincial congress asked for a recommendation on how it should react to the flight of a royal governor and the imminent collapse of all political authority. A colony's delegation in Philadelphia might have written home suggesting that a certain instruction or request be sent to them in order to enable them to introduce a new "fact" into congressional debate. On the other hand, if the Continental Congress made a recommendation, whether asked for or not, it was likely to influence the political situation in that colony.

As early as October 1774, the Continental Congress had made a first attempt to reorganize government in the colonies. In its Declaration of Rights and Grievances, it demanded that those members of the governors' councils who had been appointed by the crown (instead of having been elected) no longer be allowed to participate in legislative activity. Since the period of office of such council members was arbitrarily determined by the crown, they were not as independent, the Congress claimed, as branches of a government should be.[6] A more radical recommendation was not possible at that time.

In Massachusetts the question of whether the provincial congress should reinstate the Charter of 1629 had already been considered, but other delegations in the Continental Congress were shocked by the suggestion.[7] Several rural counties in Massachusetts had been calling since the summer of 1774 for a restitution of the first charter, which had provided the basis for almost complete self-government from 1629 to 1684. Other counties felt free "to take what form of

5. Butterfield et al., eds., *Diary of John Adams*, III, 315.
6. Jensen, ed., *American Colonial Documents*, 807.
7. John Adams to Joseph Palmer, Sept. 26, 1774, Burnett, ed., *Letters of the Continental Congress*, I, 48.

government they please" because the Massachusetts Government Act, as they saw it, had nullified the contract between the king and the people.[8]

On June 2, 1775, the Continental Congress considered the request of the provincial congress of Massachusetts for advice on the exercise of the "powers of civil government." For the sake of unity among the colonies, the provincial congress had written, it would refuse to take over the "slack reins of government" in the province without the advice and consent of the Continental Congress. The present state of affairs, it claimed, was dangerous for two reasons. First, ever since the Massachusetts Government Act of May 20, 1774, the corrupt administration in London and the military government in Boston had made impossible the exercise of the powers of government as established by the charter under the principles of the English constitution. Without orderly government, the Massachusetts revolutionaries argued, a people could not be prosperous, happy, or certain of their liberty. Second, what liberty remained was threatened by the very troops mobilized to defend it. The military, the provincial congress emphasized, should be under the control of a properly constituted government; in a free state the military always had to be subordinated to civil authority. The Massachusetts congress saw only two measures possible in this situation: it could either accept a state constitution drafted by the Continental Congress for all the colonies, or it could draw up its own constitution.[9] John Adams utilized the opportunity he had helped create to make a speech on the need for setting up new governments and forming a "Confederacy of States," comparable to those the Greeks, the Dutch, and the Swiss had established. But according to Adams's diary, the majority of his colleagues in Philadelphia in June 1775 still considered these ideas "strange and terrible Doctrines."[10]

After a committee had deliberated on the Massachusetts request for a week, the Continental Congress formulated a careful reply that made great concessions to those delegations that still believed in

8. Joseph Warren to Samuel Adams, Sept. 12, 1774, Richard Frothingham, *Life and Times of Joseph Warren* (Boston, 1865), 376.
9. Ford *et al.*, eds., *Journals of the Continental Congress*, II, 76–78. On May 16, 1775, the Massachusetts provincial congress had resolved to send this request to Philadelphia. *American Archives*, 4th Ser., II, 1842.
10. Butterfield *et al.*, eds., *Diary of John Adams*, III, 351–352; Burnett, ed., *Letters of the Continental Congress*, I, 106–109.

reconciliation with Britain. In order not to be accused of moving closer to independence, the Congress took several measured steps. It declared Parliament's recent violation of the Massachusetts Charter of 1691 (through the Massachusetts Government Act) unconstitutional, and it agreed with the provincial congress that the present state of affairs in Massachusetts was intolerable. But the Congress did not go as far as the Massachusetts leaders had hoped it would. It recommended that the Charter of 1691 be respected as still in force, adding, however, that it was permissible to consider the governor and lieutenant governor absent from the colony and their offices vacant until the crown appointed a new governor who was willing to govern the colony according to the provisions of the charter. New elections should be held immediately, the existing election laws should be followed, and the new house of representatives should elect a new governor's council.[11]

The provincial congress acted on these recommendations immediately. The newly elected house of representatives met on July 19, 1775. After rephrasing the oaths of office and reformulating the language used in making appointments, it elected a council of twenty-eight members who assumed executive power without a governor. Thus, by the end of July 1775, a year ahead of most of the other colonies, Massachusetts ended the period of government by committees and congresses.[12] But Adams's six-stage plan for the whole continent had made little progress. His hope in mid-June 1775 that government —"legislative, executive, and judicial"—would soon be taken over by the colonists (unless crown and Parliament became converted to the colonists' view of their rights), was temporarily dashed.[13]

11. Recommendation of the Continental Congress, June 9, 1775, Ford *et al.*, eds., *Journals of the Continental Congress*, I, 79, 83–84. In a letter of Sept. 24, 1774, to Joseph Warren, John Adams had developed the idea of regarding the governor's office as vacant. Frothingham, *Joseph Warren*, 377.

12. Minutes of the house of representatives, *American Archives*, 4th Ser., III, 271–366. On the election of the council, see p. 275; on recognizing the council as the executive branch, p. 289.

13. John Adams to Abigail Adams, June 18, 1775, Burnett, ed., *Letters of the Continental Congress*, I, 132–133. Adams expressed his disappointment in a letter of July 24, 1775, to James Warren. Frothingham, *Joseph Warren*, 176.

A Model Constitution for All the States?

In its inquiry of May 16, 1775, the provincial congress of Massachusetts had said it was ready to accept a state constitution drafted by the
Continental Congress.[14] One argument for identical constitutions in
all the colonies was the necessity for overcoming the already existing particularism. An appeal published in May 1776 in Connecticut
pointed out that it would be unrealistic to hope for "exact uniformity"
because political institutions had differed from colony to colony for a
long time. But it was still essential for the cohesion of the colonies
that their constitutions at least be similar in major points.[15] "Would
not a uniform plan of government, prepared for America by the
Congress, and approved by the colonies, be a surer foundation of
unceasing harmony to the whole?" Richard Henry Lee asked John
Adams in May 1776. Lee thought that the differences between the
colonies should not be augmented by differing constitutions. John
Adams did not respond to this point and only replied that every
colony should have the privilege of determining its own form of
government. Furthermore, he said, he expected greater uniformity in
the new governments than would have seemed likely even a few
months ago.[16] The speaker of the Massachusetts house of representatives, James Warren, was not as clearly in favor of uniform state
constitutions as Lee was, but he was also not as decisive as Adams in
his rejection of the idea.[17] Another Virginian, Thomas Ludwell Lee,
had also favored a standard constitution.[18] But the majority of the
provincial congress of Virginia rejected the idea. When, on May 15,

14. *American Archives*, 5th Ser., II, 621.
15. "To the Freeborn Sons of America in General, and of Connecticut in
Particular," dated "New-York, March 21, 1776," *ibid.*, 4th Ser., V, 450–451.
Possibly from a New York newspaper, but Force does not identify this
publication beyond the date.
16. Richard Henry Lee to John Adams, May 18, 1776, Adams, ed., *Works of
John Adams*, IX, 374. For Adams's reply of June 4, 1776, see *ibid.*, 389.
17. James Warren to John Adams, June 2, 1776, *Warren-Adams Letters: Being
Chiefly a Correspondence among John Adams, Samuel Adams, and James Warren*
(Mass. Hist. Soc., *Colls.*, LXXII [Boston, 1917]), I, 252.
18. Thomas Ludwell Lee to Richard Henry Lee, May 18, 1776, William Wirt
Henry, *Patrick Henry: Life, Correspondence and Speeches* (New York, 1891), I,
408.

1776, it instructed its delegates to the Continental Congress to vote for independence, it added that the drafting of state constitutions should be left to the state legislatures.[19]

In the end the Continental Congress never seriously considered drafting a model state constitution, basically because there was too little agreement on what it should say. It would have been only "natural" if the Continental Congress had worked out a constitution for the individual states, John Adams said in retrospect. However, he had not supported this course of action himself, because in the summer and fall of 1775 he had feared that the advocates of a uni-cameral legislature with an executive committee instead of a governor would have found widespread support. During this period, Samuel Adams and Thomas Cushing of Massachusetts had indeed favored "the most democratical forms" and a single "Sovereign Assembly." If the Continental Congress had presented any model of a constitutional draft at all, John Adams was afraid, it would have been along these lines and therefore completely unacceptable to him.[20]

The Initiatives of New Hampshire, South Carolina, and Virginia

On October 18, 1775, the delegation from New Hampshire asked the same question that Massachusetts had put to the Continental Congress in May: how could the administration of justice and other badly neglected governmental functions best be reorganized?[21] The seemingly innocent question was pressed by those who had given up hope for reconciliation with crown and Parliament. It was a badly disguised way of forcing the Continental Congress to face the issue of independence. As long as the majority of the delegates in the Congress were not prepared to pursue independence openly, the answers that were sent back to the provincial capitals had to be reconcilable with British constitutional law; an unguarded recommendation to draft new constitutions would rightly have been considered as equivalent to declaring independence.

As early as July 8, 1775, the president of the provincial congress of New Hampshire had reported to the Continental Congress that all

19. *American Archives*, 4th Ser., VI, 1524.
20. Butterfield *et al.*, eds., *Diary of John Adams*, III, 358, 354.
21. Ford *et al.*, eds., *Journals of the Continental Congress*, III, 298.

governmental powers were in the hands of the provincial congress and the town meetings and that the situation needed clarification, which could not be brought about without "Direction" from the Continental Congress.[22] The instructions that New Hampshire's delegates, Josiah Bartlett and John Langdon, received from home shortly thereafter described the situation in dramatic terms: the Continental Congress would have to come to a decision quickly. The political scene in New Hampshire was confused, "the people not suffering things to proceed in their former manner." More specific grievances were not cited.[23]

The decision New Hampshire desired from the Continental Congress was a long time in coming. Bartlett and Langdon received several reminders from home.[24] When in October 1775 the president of the New Hampshire provincial congress, Matthew Thornton, was called before a committee of the Continental Congress, Bartlett and Langdon advised him to make use of this opportunity to speak not only about the questions of military strategy on the agenda but also to raise the issue of reorganizing governmental power. It would be useful, they told him, if he could bring to Philadelphia a "Petition for Government" from the provincial congress. The need for a new constitution, they suggested, could well be justified by the necessity for effective tax collection.[25] But no petition for government came forth, and on October 18, 1775, the two delegates acted without the additional support they had requested from home and simply put the instructions they had received earlier before the Continental Congress.[26]

Among those in favor of advising New Hampshire to establish a new form of government was John Adams, who argued that unsettled conditions and the general laxity in carrying out the functions of government endangered the "Morals of the People." Without insti-

22. Meshech Weare to the Continental Congress, Nathaniel Bouton *et al.*, eds., *The Provincial and State Papers of New Hampshire* (Concord, N.H., 1867–1943), VII, 561.

23. *Ibid.*, 560.

24. Richard Francis Upton, *Revolutionary New Hampshire: An Account of the Social and Political Forces Underlying the Transition from Royal Province to American Commonwealth* (Hanover, N.H., 1936), 67; Daniell, *Experiment in Republicanism*, 106.

25. Bouton *et al.*, eds., *N.H. State Papers*, VII, 615.

26. Report to the New Hampshire committee of safety, Oct. 26, 1775, Burnett, ed., *Letters of the Continental Congress*, I, 242.

tuting a new government, the full authority of law and government could not be turned to suppressing pro-British uprisings, nor could informants of British troops be prosecuted as spies. Not only was it absurd, Adams maintained, that oaths of allegiance were sworn every day to a king with whom the colonies were at war, but also the colonies would not be able to mobilize their military and economic capabilities unless they took all the powers of government into their own hands.[27] The majority of the Congress, however, still shied away from an unambiguous recommendation that would have made the consent of the governed the sole foundation of legitimate government. At stake in this debate, which Bartlett and Langdon proudly described as "truly Ciceronial," was the consequence that any recommendation the Congress made would set an important precedent. Unlike Massachusetts, New Hampshire did not have a charter that could be interpreted to permit continuing government in the absence of a governor. From 1680 on, the colony had been governed by virtue of the "royal commission" the king granted all governors when they took office.[28] The Continental Congress, therefore, had to find a formulation that recommended establishing governmental agencies outside the framework of the English constitution yet that did not explicitly declare independence.

Finally, on November 3, the Continental Congress recommended that New Hampshire "call a full and free representation of the People, and that the Representatives if they think it necessary, establish such a form of Government, as in their Judgment will best produce the happiness of the People." The Congress went on to stress its readiness for reconciliation by adding that this reorganization would remain in effect only for the duration of the conflict with Britain.[29] In the letter accompanying the resolution of the Congress, the New Hampshire delegates explained to their colleagues in Portsmouth that the time limit had been added only to appease the more timid members of the Congress who were still afraid of declaring independence. But the qualification was meaningless, they claimed, because governments once established could be dissolved again only after negotiations with England. They no longer believed such negotiations would ever take

27. Butterfield *et al.*, eds., *Diary of John Adams*, III, 354–355.
28. William Henry Fry, *New Hampshire as a Royal Province* (New York, 1908), 74; Burnett, ed., *Letters of the Continental Congress*, I, 246.
29. Ford *et al.*, eds., *Journals of the Continental Congress*, III, 319; see also p. 298.

place.[30] Samuel Adams thought this recommendation to New Hampshire would open the way for all the governments of the New England colonies to be established on "the same footing." And once this step had been taken, he hoped, the middle and southern colonies would also see the need for new constitutions.[31]

South Carolina was the third colony to turn to the Continental Congress for advice on adopting a new constitution. On November 4, 1775, it received the identical recommendation that New Hampshire had been given.[32] And when Governor Lord Dunmore of Virginia declared martial law, and thus in the eyes of the Continental Congress overstepped the limits of legitimate government, the Congress recommended on December 4, 1775, that Virginia, too, hold new elections and reorganize its government.[33]

The Resolution of May 10 and 15, 1776

By February 1776 the advocates of independence were working for three objectives in opposition to the more conservative Dickinson-Duane wing: the opening of colonial harbors to all countries except Great Britain, "new Governments," and a proclamation of independence.[34] The fate of an address drawn up by James Wilson of Pennsylvania suggests how the strength of the group in favor of reconciliation was waning. On February 13, 1776, Wilson presented the Continental Congress with a committee draft for a declaration addressed to all the inhabitants of the colonies. This draft claimed that the actions taken by the Congress so far were compatible with the English constitution. If the existence of the Congress was incompatible with that constitution, then so were the actions of the barons at Runnymede, the Convention Parliament that Charles II called, and the assembly that had offered the throne to William and Mary. The sole intent of the Continental Congress was to defend the rights of the colonists under the English constitution. The new forms of gov-

30. Nov. 3, 1775, Burnett, ed., *Letters of the Continental Congress*, I, 246.
31. Samuel Adams to Elbridge Gerry, Oct. 29, 1775, *ibid.*, 245.
32. Ford *et al.*, eds., *Journals of the Continental Congress*, III, 326.
33. *Ibid.*, 403–404. See also, Samuel Adams to James Warren, Dec. 5, 1775, Burnett, ed., *Letters of the Continental Congress*, I, 270.
34. Butterfield *et al.*, eds., *Diary of John Adams*, III, 367. On the conflict between the Adams-Lee and Dickinson-Duane wings, see H. James Henderson, *Party Politics in the Continental Congress* (New York, 1974).

ernment established in some colonies were mentioned in an apologetic tone as interim solutions that could be annulled at any time.[35] The majority of the delegations disapproved of the draft address because they had lost hope for a reconciliation within the British empire; the proposal did not even come up for a vote.[36] The majority required for a declaration of independence was gradually forming.

In March 1776 the Continental Congress came close to approving a general recommendation for new constitutions. In retrospect, John Adams regarded March 13 as the crucial day. After months of avoiding the issue, the decisive question was once again on the agenda. Should the Congress advise all colonies to disregard and abolish all remnants of "Royal Authority"?[37] The majority of the delegations still shied away from an unequivocal "yea." Instead, something more concrete but hardly less revolutionary was recommended to the various assemblies, provincial congresses, and committees of safety: they were to disarm all persons known to be "notoriously disaffected to the cause of America."[38]

A few days later, on March 20, 1776, when the Continental Congress instructed its emissaries to urge the French Canadians to join the United Colonies, it also recommended that they be encouraged to adopt a new constitution.[39] Even this merely rhetorical move was opposed by some. John Jay of New York, for instance, equated this recommendation, especially if it were not qualified by the time limit set in the New Hampshire recommendation, with a call for independence, and he therefore refused to support the resolution.[40]

It was not until May 10 and 15, 1776, a whole year after the Second Continental Congress had convened, that a majority was ready

35. Ford *et al.*, eds., *Journals of the Continental Congress*, IV, 134–146.
36. Richard Smith's journal entry, Burnett, ed., *Letters of the Continental Congress*, I, 348.
37. Butterfield *et al.*, eds., *Diary of John Adams*, III, 369–370.
38. Ford *et al.*, eds., *Journals of the Continental Congress*, IV, 205.
39. *Ibid.*, 215–219.
40. Richard Smith's journal, Burnett, ed., *Letters of the Continental Congress*, I, 383. This move to involve the Canadians had been in the making for a long time. As early as Oct. 11, 1775, Philip Schuyler, president of the Continental Congress, had officially requested that he be informed about the possibility of establishing a new form of government in Quebec. "The Establishment of a Civil Government in Canada," he thought, "is a Subject of great Consequence." *Ibid.*, 227. Compare Gustave Lanctot, *Canada and the American Revolution, 1774–1783* (Cambridge, Mass., 1967), 103.

to take the decisive step. On May 10 the Congress recommended to all those colonies "where no government sufficient to the exigencies of their affairs have been hitherto established to adopt such Government as shall, in the Opinion of the Representatives of the People, best conduce to the Happiness and Safety of their Constituents in particular and America in general." The preamble, added on May 15, dismissed all hope of reconciliation and declared that now it was "necessary that the exercise of every kind of authority under the said crown should be totally suppressed, and all the powers of government, exerted under the authority of the people of the colonies, for the preservation of internal peace, virtue, and good order, as well as for the defence of their lives, liberties, and properties."[41] This was a de facto declaration of independence; James Duane rightly called it "a Machine for the fabrication of Independence." John Adams, who together with Edward Rutledge of South Carolina and Richard Henry Lee of Virginia had been commissioned to write the draft, thought the preamble actually achieved independence.[42]

What form the new governments should take, the Congress did not say. It even refrained from using the term "republican" to distinguish them from the colonial institutions. In the records of the Congress's debates before July 1776, the terms "republican" and "republicanism" appeared only incidentally. When, for instance, in October 1775 John Joachim Zubly of Georgia had argued for opening colonial ports and for rapid reconciliation with England, he warned against breaking out of the British constitutional framework and declared that "a Republican Government is little better than Government of Devils. I have been acquainted with it from 6 Years Old."[43] Even these harsh words did not stir the assembly to a debate on the merits of republican government.

The resolution of May 10 and 15 merely recommended procedures to be followed: governmental power should derive from the "authority of the people" as expressed in "full and free representation." Similarly, the Declaration of Independence, passed six weeks

41. Ford *et al.*, eds., *Journals of the Continental Congress*, IV, 342, 357–358.
42. For Duane's and Adams's reactions, see Butterfield *et al.*, eds., *Diary of John Adams*, III, 386. For similar reactions by others, see Burnett, ed., *Letters of the Continental Congress*, I, 445, 449, 453–455, 464.
43. Butterfield *et al.*, eds., *Diary of John Adams*, II, 204, debate of Oct. 12, 1775. Zubly was born in St. Gall, Switzerland, in 1724, and came to South Carolina in 1744. *Dictionary of American Biography*, s.v. "Zubly, John Joachim."

later, did not relieve the states of the task of deciding for themselves what shape their governments should take. It only reasserted the principle that "just powers" derive from the consent of the governed and that "the people" may "alter or abolish" unjust governments and establish new ones whose principles and structure would best seem to safeguard their security and happiness. The Declaration of Independence went beyond the May resolution in that it added the political values that government should serve: equality and certain inalienable rights such as those to life, liberty, and the pursuit of happiness. But it was left to the politically active citizens of each state to determine what consequences followed from these guiding values for the organization of republican government.

CHAPTER III

"Choosing Deputies to Form a Government": The Making of the First State Constitutions

Q. *Who ought to form a new Constitution?*
A. *The people.*
Q. *Should the officers of the old constitution be entrusted with the power of the making of a new one when it becomes necessary?*
A. *No. Bodies of men have the same selfish attachments as individuals, and they will be claiming powers and prerogatives inconsistent with the liberties of the people.*

Pennsylvania Journal, May 22, 1776

Organizing the "Constituent Power"

When in its resolution of May 10 and 15, 1776, the Continental Congress advised the thirteen colonies to reorganize their governments solely on the basis of "the authority of the people," American political leaders found themselves faced with a task that had never before been accomplished in political entities of comparable size.[1] From decades of debate on the colonists' right to self-government, popular sovereignty had emerged as the basic principle of legitimate government. But how was this principle to be realized in practice? How could the making of constitutions be organized to satisfy the principle? There was no monarch to be forced to give or grant a constitution drawn up by his advisers. Somehow "the people" had to be the originators of the basic law of the land.

The solution to this problem developed in two stages. At first the provincial congresses drafted and ratified constitutions in the same

1. See pp. 59–61 above.

way they drafted and passed bills. They considered themselves to be the "full and free representation of the people" that the Continental Congress had recommended. Since they were already acting as legislatures, it was only natural for them to take on the new task in legislative fashion. Just as there was no referendum on a new law, so there was no plebiscite on, no popular ratification of, the first of the state constitutions.

The congresses that enacted the constitutions were not altogether unaware of the special character of these "laws," however. Most of the constitutions stressed in their preambles the representative character of the assembly that put them in force and, in several cases, noted that in the preceding election voters had known of the special task awaiting their representatives. This awareness was recorded in introductory clauses such as: "appointed by the free suffrages of the people . . . and authorized . . . to establish some form of government" (New Hampshire); "the representatives of the freemen of Pennsylvania, in general convention met, for the express purpose of framing such a government" (Pennsylvania); and "chosen and assembled in Congress, for the express purpose of framing a Constitution" (North Carolina).[2]

In justification of this procedure it could have been said (although it was not at the time) that the momentous question of independence was also decided without a plebiscite. The delegations assembled in Philadelphia voted for independence on no other basis than that of the instructions from the provincial congresses that had sent them there. It could, therefore, hardly have been considered illogical if these same bodies enacted state constitutions.

Within a few years, however, a second stage was reached when legislation and constitution making came to be considered two entirely distinct steps in the political process, each requiring a separate representative body. The specially elected "constitutional convention" became the initial embodiment of the "constituent power" of the people. In addition, the convention's proposal had to be submitted for final ratification to the adult free male citizenry. This practical and eventually much celebrated procedure was developed in Massachusetts because a minority of town meetings demanded it.[3] Rather than being the offspring of one of the founding fathers, it originated in the mistrust the towns and counties felt toward the

2. Thorpe, ed., *Constitutions*, IV, 2451, V, 3082, 2790.
3. See below, pp. 88–91.

house of representatives and the council sitting in Boston. Within only a few years, however, the nation's political leaders made apt use of a constitutional convention and more or less popular ratification for creating the constitution of the United States.[4]

The concept underlying the distinction between legislation and constitution making, that of a fundamental "constituent power," was also formulated in these years. The *Oxford English Dictionary on Historical Principles* is quite wrong when it describes "constituent power," in the sense of "having the power to frame or alter a political constitution as in *constituent assembly, power*," as a post-1789 translation of "pouvoir constituant." Americans invented not only the thing but also the name for it. The phrase seems to have been first used in the context of the struggle for Vermont statehood. Thomas Young, one of the Pennsylvania radicals urging the rebels of the New Hampshire Grants to adopt the constitution of Pennsylvania, made use of the term to support the Vermonters' right to adopt a constitution without any outside interference. He distinguished between the "supreme delegate power" of elected representatives and the "supreme constituent power" of the settlers: "They are the supreme constituent power, and of course their immediate Representatives are the supreme delegate power; and as soon as the delegate power gets too far out of the hands of the constituent power, a tyranny is in some degree established."[5] It was not wholly accidental that the concept was first so clearly defined in connection with the conflict over Vermont. Those who had an interest in justifying the attempt to carve

4. John Adams, in the version of *Thoughts on Government* that he sent to John Penn, mentioned electing a "representative assembly" as the first step toward new constitutions, but he thought this assembly could then be divided to form the upper and lower houses of the new legislature. Adams, ed., *Works of John Adams*, IV, 205. In *Common Sense*, Paine went no further than some considerations on forming the federal government. To this end, he suggested creating "some intermediate body," a specially elected "continental conference." Paine was aware of his own lack of clarity on this issue and abandoned the subject with the remark: "Could the straggling thoughts of individuals be collected, they would frequently form materials for wise and able men to improve into useful matter." Foner, ed., *Writings of Paine*, I, 28.

5. An open letter dated Apr. 11, 1777, by Thomas Young, *To the Inhabitants of Vermont, a Free and Independent State, bounding on the River Connecticut and Lake Champlain*, bound together with the broadside, *In Congress, May 15, 1776. Whereas His Britannic Majesty* . . . (Philadelphia, 1777). For more on Vermont, see below, pp. 93–94.

another state out of territory claimed by already existing states were tempted to argue that they only repeated on a smaller scale what had happened on the continental level. When the Continental Congress had declared the thirteen colonies independent states, it had asserted the constituent power of their inhabitants (even if it did not use those words). Why, then, could not the same process be repeated within the American setting, if that was what "the people" of a certain area wanted?

Connecticut and Rhode Island

Despite the gradual emergence of a uniform political philosophy, the practical transition from colonial government to republican governments under new constitutions varied considerably from colony to colony. In Connecticut and Rhode Island, the assemblies saw their mandate confirmed so consistently, even in the midst of the Revolution, that they did not think a new constitution was necessary. The transition from colony to state could therefore easily take place under the assumption that the existing government was already based on the will of the people. In the charters of 1662 and 1663, the crown had granted the representative assemblies in both colonies the right to elect their own governors. Advocates of independence needed only to argue that the charters from then on received their legitimation not from the monarch but from the consent of the voting inhabitants. A unilateral nullification of the charters by the crown was inconsequential as long as "the people" wanted to live by them.[6]

In accordance with this view, the general assembly of Connecticut, at the beginning of its session in October 1776, confirmed by means of a simple law that the charter was still in effect.[7] Between March and October 1776 only a few voices had publicly called for a

6. J. Hammond Trumbull, *Historical Notes on the Constitutions of Connecticut, 1639–1818* . . . (Hartford, Conn., 1901), 14–15. Connecticut's charter of 1662 corresponds in all major points with the Fundamental Orders that the settlers adopted without royal sanction in 1639. Richard J. Purcell, *Connecticut in Transition, 1775–1818* (Washington, D.C., 1918), 113.

7. "The form of civil government in this State shall continue to be as established by charter received from *Charles* the Second, King of *England*, so far as an adherence to the same shall be consistent with an absolute independence of this State on the Crown of *Great Britain.*" *American Archives*, 5th Ser., III, 447.

different solution. Some of the changes suggested were that the towns and counties, not the assembly, should make appointments to public offices, that delegates to the Continental Congress should be elected by the towns, not by the assembly, and that the election of council members should be reorganized.[8] But all of these changes would have been possible without giving up the charter. Only one newspaper article at the time seems to have demanded a completely new constitution for Connecticut.[9] Calls for a new constitution did not gather political backing until after 1780. In 1784 the general assembly enacted a declaration of rights in the same way it enacted laws; but in 1786 and 1787, for the first time, the assembly seriously discussed the constitutional question.[10]

Rhode Island did not even consider it necessary to prolong its charter by an explicit legislative act. In May 1776 the general assembly merely resolved, in a law that was widely regarded as a kind of declaration of independence, that the name of the king in all appointments, oaths of office, and similar documents be replaced by "The Governour and Company of the *English* Colony of *Rhode-Island and Providence Plantations.*" In July 1776 the assembly voted approval of the Declaration of Independence and made public prayers for the king illegal.[11] But this convenient official solution came under attack somewhat earlier in Rhode Island than it had in Connecticut. Two towns instructed their representatives in 1779 to work toward drafting a real constitution. They argued that in accepting the charter of 1663 the settlers had recognized the king's "power of Government." When the king violated this contract, he in effect annulled the charter, and governmental power reverted to the people. Because no new contract had established a new form of government, the current government of Rhode Island had no legal basis.[12]

It was not until 1818 and 1842 that Connecticut and Rhode Island

8. "To the Freeborn Sons of America in General, and of Connecticut in Particular," *ibid.*, 4th Ser., V, 450–452; instructions of an unnamed town to its delegates in the assembly, Sept. 1776, *ibid.*, 5th Ser., II, 113–114.

9. "A.B.," *Connecticut Journal* (New Haven), Oct. 23, 1776; compare Oscar Zeichner, *Connecticut's Years of Controversy, 1750–1776* (Chapel Hill, N.C., 1949), 219.

10. Purcell, *Connecticut in Transition*, 115–117.

11. *American Archives*, 4th Ser., V, 1215–1217; *ibid.*, 5th Ser., I, 475; compare David S. Lovejoy, *Rhode Island Politics and the American Revolution, 1760–1776* (Providence, R.I., 1958), 192–194.

12. Instructions of the town of Scituate, *Providence Gazette; and Country Journal*

respectively replaced their charters with what by then had come to be considered regular state constitutions.

The State Constitutions, 1776–1780

NEW HAMPSHIRE, JANUARY 5, 1776

On November 14, 1775, a few days after the recommendation from the Continental Congress had been received, the provincial congress of New Hampshire determined what it understood by "full and free representation." The congress that was assembled to draft the new constitution and perform certain other legislative and executive tasks would be made up of men who owned land valued at three hundred pounds sterling or more and who had been elected by voters whose land holdings were valued at twenty pounds or more.[13] We have no record of the debates in the newly elected congress, which sat from December 21, 1775, to January 5, 1776. The journal of this session only lists the members present and records the routine daily work of a government at war: accepting petitions, approving funds for military suppliers, ordering the construction of fortifications, and so forth.[14]

On December 27, 1775, a committee "to draw up a Plan for the Government of this Colony" was appointed, and the following day it was resolved to limit the new form of government to the duration of the conflict with the mother country. At the same time, it was decided that the current congress would begin to form the new two-chamber legislature by declaring itself the house of representatives under the new constitution. This body would then elect the second chamber, to be called the council. The institutional skeleton of the new constitution was thus determined.[15] On January 5, 1776, the congress voted

---

(R.I.), Apr. 24, 1779. For the reply of "The American Whig," see *ibid.*, Apr. 24, May 29, and Aug. 14, 1779.

13. Belknap, *History of New-Hampshire*, II, 398.

14. *American Archives*, 4th Ser., V, 1–35, contains the journal of this session, which lasted from Dec. 21, 1774, to Mar. 23, 1776. Compare Daniell, *Experiment in Republicanism*, 94, 108–112.

15. Bouton *et al.*, eds., *N.H. State Papers*, VII, 703–704. We know of at least two proposals for the constitution that may have been considered by the congress. New Hampshire's delegates to the Continental Congress had recommended the charter of Massachusetts as a model, with the exception of a

on the constitution in the same way it would have on any ordinary bill. The text was phrased in the form typical of a parliamentary resolution: "We, the members of the Congress of New Hampshire . . . Do Resolve. . . ." The preamble referred to the recommendation made to the colony by the Continental Congress on November 3, 1775, and to the special mandate for drafting and adopting a new constitution that the representatives had received at the last election.[16]

The next day the house of representatives chose twelve council members from its own ranks, and "then the Honble the Council and Secretary left the House." In the following days the house added supplements to the constitution in the form of ordinary laws governing such questions as the continuing validity of English laws and the establishment of an executive committee for the period when the house and the council were not in session.[17] One thing the congress was unable to do at this time: according to Meshech Weare (probably New Hampshire's most influential politician in the first decade of independence), an oath of loyalty to the new government was desired by some, but the idea met with so much resistance that it had to be dropped.[18]

At first the constitution ran into strong opposition not because specific regulations in it were objectionable but because the whole enterprise was considered a step toward independence.[19] After the

---

governor, who would not be needed at the moment. Letter of Nov. 3, 1775, *ibid.*, 642. Another proposal came from Gen. John Sullivan, encamped near Boston, who held the Connecticut charter up as a model. The general favored the election of a governor, following the Connecticut example. Letter to the committee of safety, Dec. 12, 1775, Otis G. Hammond, ed., *Letters and Papers of Major-General John Sullivan* (Concord, N.H., 1930), I, 141–148.

16. Thorpe, ed., *Constitutions*, IV, 2451–2453.

17. Bouton *et al.*, eds., *N.H. State Papers*, VIII, 6, 9, 21–22.

18. Undated draft of a letter by Meshech Weare to "Mr. King," probably written in mid-Jan. 1776, Weare Papers, Library of Congress.

19. On Dec. 18, the town meeting of Portsmouth presented the following argument against framing a constitution: "The present times are too unsettled to admit of perfecting a form, stable and permanent; . . . to attempt it now would injure us, by furnishing our enemies in Great Britain with arguments to persuade the good people there that we are aiming at independency, which we totally disavow." Bouton *et al.*, eds., *N.H. State Papers*, VII, 701–702. The printer of the *New-Hampshire Gazette* (Portsmouth) was summoned before the house of representatives for printing, on Jan. 9, 1776, an anonymous open letter against the constitution. Bouton *et al.*, eds., *N.H. State Papers*,

Declaration of Independence opposition to the new constitution grew even more determined, but on different grounds. The small inland towns, no longer willing to let the large coastal towns dominate the political scene, objected to the distribution of seats in the house of representatives.[20] It was not until 1784 that a second constitution replaced the provisional one. In 1779 a draft prepared by a convention elected expressly for the purpose of drawing up a constitution was submitted to the town meetings for approval but was rejected.[21]

SOUTH CAROLINA, MARCH 26, 1776; MARCH 19, 1778

In response to the recommendation the Continental Congress made to South Carolina on November 4, 1775, the provincial congress of the colony initially did no more than define the powers of the committee of safety, which was responsible for handling the most urgent business of government during those months when the provincial congress was not in session.[22] The provincial congress did not appoint a committee to discuss the recommendation of the Continental Congress until February 8, 1776, and it did so then without special

VIII, 24. For the text of this letter, see *ibid.*, 25–27. For other protests against the constitution as a step toward independence, see *ibid.*, 14, 17.

20. Everett S. Stackpole, *History of New Hampshire* (New York, 1916), II, 120, and Isaac W. Hammond, comp., *Town Papers. Documents Relating to Towns in New Hampshire* . . . (Concord, N.H., 1882–1884), XI, 2, 328–329, XII, 23–24, 57.

21. Neither the journal of the constitutional convention of 1779 nor the town meetings' critiques of the draft are extant. Some information on the convention and on the text of the draft is in Bouton *et al.*, eds., *N.H. State Papers*, IX, 833–834, 837–842. The draft prepared by the constitutional convention of 1781 was modeled completely on the Massachusetts constitution and was voted on by the town meetings. See Stackpole, *History of New Hampshire*, II, 232–236, and Bouton *et al.*, eds., *N.H. State Papers*, IX, 873–919.

22. William Edwin Hemphill, ed., *Extracts from the Journals of the Provincial Congresses of South Carolina, 1775–1776* (Columbia, S.C., 1960), 154–156. This edition is a complete reprint of the original of 1776, which also contains the word "Extracts" in its title. The original handwritten text is not extant in its entirety. *Ibid.*, preface, xxvi. The text is also in *American Archives*, 4th Ser., IV, 27–76, V, 561–609; *ibid.*, 5th Ser., III, 1–84. On the pre-Revolutionary period in South Carolina, see Stourzh, "William Blackstone," *Jahrbuch für Amerikastudien*, XV (1970), 184–200.

authorization or instructions from its constituents and without new elections.[23] When several members objected on February 10 that it was too early to begin discussion of a constitution, Christopher Gadsden, quoting from *Common Sense*, spoke in favor of a new constitution and American independence. His speech provoked great dispute in the assembly. Many who advocated a constitution that would be in effect only for a limited time period were not prepared to take the step Gadsden urged on them, but a majority could be found to support an interim solution.[24] A drafting committee was appointed on February 11, and on March 4, 1776, it presented its proposal. An attempt was made the next day to table the entire issue and to convene a new assembly that would truly be based on "full and free representation," but the congress voted it down.[25] During the following two weeks, the congress discussed clause after clause of the constitution while also handling the routine business of government. On the morning of March 26, a provisional constitution, which was to be valid only for the duration of the conflict with Great Britain, was passed by the provincial congress like any other law. At five o'clock that afternoon, the same assembly convened as the first general assembly under the new constitution and filled all public offices from the president of the general assembly on down to the sheriffs of the counties.[26]

After the Declaration of Independence, South Carolina was the first state to replace an explicitly provisional constitution with a permanent one. In October 1776 the general assembly appointed a committee to revise the constitution, and in the same month it discussed and passed amendments.[27] The general assembly that met in January 1777 had been elected with the understanding that it was authorized not only to pass laws but also to enact a constitution. However, the

23. Hemphill, ed., *Extracts*, 181, and Fletcher M. Green, *Constitutional Development in the South Atlantic States, 1776–1860: A Study in the Evolution of Democracy* (Chapel Hill, N.C., 1930), 61.

24. John Drayton, *Memoirs of the American Revolution* . . . (Charleston, S.C., 1821), II, 172–173, 176. John Drayton's work is based on the papers of his father, William Henry Drayton, and on notes his father made for writing a history of the American Revolution. *Ibid.*, I, viii.

25. Hemphill, ed., *Extracts*, 184–185, 223; Drayton, *Memoirs*, II, 176.

26. Hemphill, ed., *Extracts*, 263; Drayton, *Memoirs*, II, 239–243.

27. *American Archives*, 5th Ser., III, 61, 71–74; Green, *Constitutional Development*, 107–108.

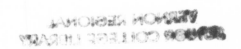

assembly decided to allow a year for public discussion.[28] Following legislative procedures used for any bill, the assembly submitted a new constitutional draft to President John Rutledge on March 5, 1778. Rutledge refused to sign it, however, arguing that the constitution of 1776 gave him an absolute veto over legislation, a power not granted to the governor in the new document. His oath of office, he correctly reminded the legislators, obliged him to uphold the constitution of 1776. Rutledge was also opposed to the proposed election of the second chamber by the general electorate in the parishes and districts.[29] But the president did not have sufficient backing in the assembly. He offered his resignation, and on March 19, 1778, a new president signed the constitutional amendments.[30] Once again a state constitution had been treated as no more than a series of laws.

VIRGINIA, JUNE 29, 1776

The provincial congress of Virginia did not appoint a committee to draft a declaration of rights and a constitution until May 15, 1776, nearly six months after the Continental Congress recommended that it take such action. The reason for this delay was probably that many of the great planters who made up the political leadership of Virginia looked upon a new constitution as the equivalent of a declaration of independence. Few of them seem to have favored an interim solution of the New Hampshire and South Carolina type. Only after the Virginia provincial congress decided to authorize its delegates in Philadelphia to vote for independence did it appoint a drafting committee for a declaration of rights and a constitution.[31] In the weeks that followed, the Virginia provincial congress probably worked harder than any legislative assembly has ever worked. Often the committees met from seven to nine in the morning, the congress from nine to five, and the committees again after dinner until nine or ten at

28. David Ramsay, *The History of the Revolution of South-Carolina, from a British Province to an Independent State* (Trenton, 1785), II, 129, 131.
29. Edward McCrady, *The History of South Carolina in the Revolution, 1775–1780* (New York, 1901), 238–239. For text of Rutledge's speech, see Ramsay, *Revolution of South-Carolina*, II, 132–138.
30. McCrady, *South Carolina in the Revolution*, 240.
31. Journal from May 6 to July 5, 1776, *American Archives*, 4th Ser., VI, 1509–1616. On the instruction of the delegates to the Continental Congress and the establishment of a drafting committee, see p. 1524.

night.[32] On May 27, a draft for the declaration of rights, written by George Mason and gone over by the drafting committee, was read twice to the congress. In the days following, it was discussed repeatedly, and on June 12, 1776, after a third reading, it was passed unanimously, following procedures used for any law.[33] The drafting committee then set to work immediately on a constitution. An amended form of Mason's draft was passed unanimously on June 29, 1776, after a third reading. On the same day, the new constitution was partially implemented when Patrick Henry was elected governor and the members of the new executive council appointed.[34]

NEW JERSEY, JULY 2, 1776

The loyalists in New Jersey considered the Continental Congress's recommendation of May 15, 1776, "a touchstone, by which we may certainly distinguish those of us who wish for absolute and perpetual independence from those who are desirous of a reconciliation."[35] When the New Jersey provincial congress convened on June 10, 1776, for its summer session, petitions streamed in from public meetings, some claiming to represent whole towns and city districts and others only "sundry Inhabitants." About a dozen of these petitions were for independence and the establishment of a new government, and a dozen were against.[36] Some of the petitions contained concrete sug-

32. Robert L. Hilldrup, "The Virginia Convention of 1776" (Ph.D. diss., University of Virginia, 1935), 150.

33. *American Archives*, 4th Ser., VI, 1537; for draft the committee presented to the convention, see pp. 1537–1538; for discussion of the draft in the committee of the whole, see pp. 1543, 1550–1557, 1560. Hilldrup, "Virginia Convention," 180–207, describes in detail the changes the text of the declaration of rights underwent, beginning with Mason's draft and progressing through the committee's drafts to the final version. Final text is in Thorpe, ed., *Constitutions*, VII, 3812–3814.

34. *American Archives*, 4th Ser., VI, 1578–1601. Hilldrup, "Virginia Convention," 254–269, follows the changes made from Mason's first draft on through the final text. The final text is in Thorpe, ed., *Constitutions*, VII, 3814–3819, and in *American Archives*, 4th Ser., VI, 1598–1601.

35. "Reflections on Publick Affairs," dated June 6, 1776, *New-York Journal: or, the General Advertiser*, June 20, 1776; also in *American Archives*, 4th Ser., VI, 724.

36. See the journal for the period June 10 to Aug. 20, 1776, *American Archives*,

gestions: elections by secret ballot should be held annually; anyone holding public office should come up for election every year and be paid modestly; no individual should be allowed to hold both a paid public office and a seat in the legislature.[37]

We have no documentation on the framing of the New Jersey constitution beyond the journal of the provincial congress.[38] On June 21, 1776, the congress voted 54 to 3 to follow the Continental Congress's recommendation of May 15, 1776, and to draft a new constitution. From June 27 to July 2, the plenum discussed a committee draft and then passed it by a vote of 26 to 9. The constitution, like a law, became effective immediately.[39]

DELAWARE, SEPTEMBER 21, 1776

The assembly of Delaware, which by the spring of 1776 still had not been replaced by a Revolutionary provincial congress, created in fact a republican transition government on June 15, 1776, when it requested all public officials to continue to exercise their power from that date on "in the name of the Government of the Counties of *Newcastle, Kent,* and *Sussex,* upon *Delaware,*" and no longer "in the name of the King." But loyalist sentiment continued strong. A petition addressed to the Continental Congress rejecting the idea of a new

4th Ser., VI, 1615–1665. For petitions urging "that the Government of the Province of *New-Jersey* may not be changed," see *ibid.,* 1621, 1625, 1627. For petitions urging "that a new mode of Government may be established," see *ibid.,* 1622, 1623, 1625, 1627, 1629, 1632.

37. *Ibid.,* 1623, 1626, 1640.

38. Leonard Lundin, *Cockpit of the Revolution: The War for Independence in New Jersey* (Princeton, N.J., 1940), 257. Charles R. Erdman, Jr., *The New Jersey Constitution of 1776* (Princeton, N.J., 1929), viii, reported that he was unable to find detailed sources on the debates in the provincial congress. Compare Donald L. Kemmerer, *Path to Freedom: The Struggle for Self-Government in Colonial New Jersey, 1703–1776* (Princeton, N.J., 1940) and David Alan Bernstein, "New Jersey in the American Revolution: The Establishment of a Government amid Civil and Military Disorder, 1770–1781" (Ph.D. diss., Rutgers University, 1970).

39. *American Archives,* 4th Ser., VI, 1623, 1628–1629, 1631–1637. The text of the constitution is in Thorpe, ed., *Constitutions,* V, 2594–2598, and in *American Archives,* 4th Ser., VI, 1635–1638.

constitution allegedly had five thousand signatures on it.[40] When the assembly decided on July 27 to hold elections for a convention "to order and declare the future form of Government," they restricted the right to vote to those qualified men who swore an oath "to . . . support and maintain the independence of this Government."[41]

The idea of calling a special convention for the express purpose of enacting the constitution (in neighboring Pennsylvania the same decision had been reached weeks before) and thus separating the fundamental law from ordinary legislation, was a great step forward in the practical development of modern constitutionalism, as we have noted. The idea was sufficiently radical to have provoked the opposition of some of the whig leaders, particularly those who wanted a smooth and unthreatening transition from colonial government to independence.[42]

On September 2, 1776, the Delaware constitutional convention formed a committee to draft a declaration of rights and, a few days later, one to work out the text of a constitution. By September 11 the committee's draft for a declaration of rights was presented, amended, and passed.[43] The committee was able to work with unusual speed

40. The petition was intercepted by force and destroyed before it reached the Congress. Harold Hancock, "Thomas Robinson: Delaware's Most Prominent Loyalist," *Delaware History*, IV (1950–1951), 3; H. Clay Reed, "The Delaware Constitution of 1776," *Delaware Notes*, VI (1930), 9; *American Archives*, 4th Ser., VI, 884.

41. Reed, "Delaware Constitution," *Del. Notes*, VI (1930), 16; *American Archives*, 5th Ser., I, 618; Harold Hancock, "The Kent County Loyalists," *Del. Hist.*, VI (1954–1955), 16.

42. In May, Caesar Rodney, writing from Philadelphia, called the formation of an illegal convention in Pennsylvania a bad example and emphasized that he regarded the Continental Congress's recommendation of May 15, 1776, as an address to the regular colonial assemblies. "The Recommendation of Congress was certainly meant to go to the Assemblies, where there were such who had authority. . . . The people of this province [Pennsylvania] having taken the matter up upon other Grounds have occasioned very great disturbance, such as I would not wish to see in our Government." Undated letter to Thomas Rodney, probably written in the second half of May 1776, quoted in Reed, "Delaware Constitution," *Del. Notes*, VI (1930), 10.

43. *Proceedings of the Convention of the Delaware State, Held at New-Castle On Tuesday the Twenty-seventh of August, 1776* (Wilmington, Del., 1927 [orig. publ. 1776]), 17–20. The text of the declaration of rights is reprinted there and in

because it adopted most of the clauses in its declaration from Pennsylvania's declaration of rights, which had been published on August 21, and from an unpublished first draft of Maryland's declaration.[44] On September 20 the plenum accepted the committee's amended draft of a constitution.[45]

Unlike those congresses in New Hampshire, South Carolina, New Jersey, and Virginia that enacted state constitutions, the constitutional convention of Delaware concerned itself only minimally with normal legislation. It was also the first such convention to dissolve itself after its work was done, rather than to immediately declare itself the legislative body under the new constitution. Thomas McKean, a member of the constitutional convention and one of the most passionate advocates of independence, expressed unequivocally the new awareness of the difference between constitution making and legislation when he stated: "We are not vested with the legislative power."[46]

PENNSYLVANIA, SEPTEMBER 28, 1776

Pennsylvania, like Delaware, still had a legal assembly in the spring of 1776. But the Pennsylvania assembly differed from Delaware's in

---

American Archives, 5th Ser., II, 286–287; it has been omitted from Thorpe, ed., *Constitutions*.

44. Max Farrand, "The Delaware Bill of Rights of 1776," *American Historical Review*, III (1897–1898), 641–650, has been superseded by Reed, "Delaware Constitution," *Del. Notes*, VI (1930), but Farrand's work continues to be useful because of its detailed comparison of the Delaware, Maryland, and Pennsylvania declarations of rights.

45. On Sept. 17, 1776, three days before deliberations ended, the president of the convention reported to Caesar Rodney in Philadelphia that Rodney would not have benefited much from knowing what the first draft had contained because so much had been changed in it. The president added that a "great appearance of harmony" had ruled in the convention up to that point. Reed, "Delaware Constitution," *Del. Notes*, VI (1930), 41–42.

46. The Delaware constitutional convention was compelled to decide a few pressing issues of military finance, because no other representative assembly existed. *Convention of the Delaware State*, 43. Thomas McKean to Caesar Rodney, Sept. 19, 1776, Reed, "Delaware Constitution," *Del. Notes*, VI (1930), 35. Compare G. S. Rowe, "Thomas McKean and the Coming of the Revolution," *Pennsylvania Magazine of History and Biography*, XCVI (1972), 3–47.

that it lacked a moderate group capable of holding the opponents and advocates of independence together in one representative body. When the election of May 1, 1776, did not give the advocates of independence a majority in the assembly, they demanded that a special convention be called to draft a new constitution.[47] The Continental Congress's recommendation of May 15, 1776, spurred on the supporters of independence more than it had in any other colony. As early as May 20, over four thousand Philadelphians gathered in a public meeting that, according to the opening speaker, was taking place at the request of a large number of "respectable citizens."[48] Daniel Roberdeau, who had become wealthy in the West Indies trade, presided. The recommendation of the Continental Congress was read aloud, and the meeting expressed its approval in three rousing cheers. In November 1775, the assembly had instructed Pennsylvania's delegates to the Continental Congress to vote against independence and any change in form of government. The May 20 meeting countermanded those instructions and resolved that the regular assembly had not been elected with a mandate to frame a new constitution and was consequently not authorized to follow the Continental Congress's recommendation. The reorganization of government was, however, urgently needed, and a "Provincial Convention" should therefore be called. The committees of inspection in Philadelphia and in the counties were to organize the election for this convention. The existing assembly would remain in power until the new government was fully established.[49]

The supporters of the assembly responded promptly. On May 22, 1776, a number of Philadelphia citizens published a petition to the assembly in the *Pennsylvania Gazette*. They pointed out that the May 15 message of the Continental Congress was not an order to introduce a new constitution in every colony. It was instead no more than a recommendation valid only for those colonies that no longer had a duly established government. The assembly, they claimed, was still governing Pennsylvania satisfactorily. The courts were functioning,

47. Theodore Thayer, *Pennsylvania Politics and the Growth of Democracy, 1740–1776* (Harrisburg, Pa., 1953), 179. See also, J. Paul Selsam, *The Pennsylvania Constitution of 1776: A Study in Revolutionary Democracy* (Philadelphia, 1936) and David Hawke, *In the Midst of a Revolution* (Philadelphia, 1961).
48. *American Archives*, 4th Ser., VI, 517; Selsam, *Pennsylvania Constitution*, 117.
49. *American Archives*, 4th Ser., VI, 518–520.

and public finances were in order. Governmental experiments, however, could easily threaten this fiscal stability. The examples of Connecticut and Rhode Island were cited. There, the petitioners claimed, the old assemblies were still governing on authority "derived by Charter" and not "under the authority of the people." In conclusion, they urged that if governmental reorganization should become absolutely necessary, the example of South Carolina be followed and the new constitution be valid only until reconciliation with England was achieved.[50]

Responding to the initiative of the Philadelphia committee of inspection, 108 delegates of the county committees of inspection met in June 1776, for a week-long "Provincial Conference of Committees of the Province of Pennsylvania." Their main task was to make arrangements for the election of a "Provincial Convention" that would frame a constitution.[51] Suffrage for this election was the main question the conference had to settle. The conference decided that in addition to those who already had the vote, adult militia members were to be given the franchise and the right to be candidates for the convention.[52] In a concluding statement, which Benjamin Rush, who would soon violently oppose the new constitution, helped draft, the people of Pennsylvania were urged to take advantage on July 8, 1776, of an opportunity Providence had granted to very few men, the opportunity of "choosing Deputies to form a Government." Unconsciously adhering to the view of the English Puritans in 1649, the conference felt that only those citizens of Pennsylvania who recognized the new regime should have a hand in forming the new government. Thus, only those citizens who rejected the authority of the English crown and wanted a constitution at this time would be allowed to elect representatives to the convention.[53]

In the meantime, the absence of the radical proponents of inde-

50. *Ibid.*, 522–523.

51. *Ibid.*, 521, 951, and Thayer, *Pennsylvania Politics*, 184. James E. Gibson made a detailed study of this conference to find further support for the view that the course this conference took made a declaration of independence on July 4 possible. Gibson, "The Pennsylvania Provincial Congress of [June 18 to 25] 1776," *PMHB*, LVIII (1934), 312–314.

52. *American Archives*, 4th Ser., VI, 553. Every county was to be allowed eight delegates. This decision put an end to the dominance of the East Coast and assured a majority of 64 to 24 in favor of the western counties. Thayer, *Pennsylvania Politics*, 183–184.

53. *American Archives*, 4th Ser., VI, 962.

pendence had deprived the assembly of a quorum. The conference therefore took over some legislative and executive functions, such as the levying of troops. But it felt obliged to offer an apologetic explanation for temporarily assuming this authority.[54]

On July 15, 1776, the ninety-six members of the newly elected constitutional convention began their deliberations. Voters had been required to take an oath that contained a clear renunciation of allegiance to England. Not surprisingly, this prescreened electorate gave the advocates of independence the majority in the convention.[55] The first draft of a declaration of rights was presented to the plenum on July 25, 1776. More than a month passed before this declaration, which drew heavily on Virginia's in many points, found a majority.[56] The draft of the constitution was presented on August 19 and came under discussion almost daily for the next four weeks. The decision for a unicameral legislature—a decision that would soon be violently criticized—was reached on August 2. On September 27, 1776, the convention agreed on the final texts of both the declaration of rights and the constitution, and on the next day both were voted on and became effective immediately.[57] The practice of "choosing Deputies to form a Government" was widely accepted as a solution to the

54. The conference of committees declared that its purpose was "to put an end to our own power in the Province, by fixing upon a plan for calling a Convention to form a Government under the authority of the people; but the sudden and unexpected separation of the late Assembly has compelled us to undertake the execution of a resolve of [the Continental] Congress for calling forth four thousand five hundred of the Militia of the Province. . . . We presume only to recommend the plan we have formed to you, trusting that, in a case of so much consequence, your love of virtue and zeal for liberty will supply the want of authority delegated to us expressly for that purpose." *Ibid.*, 965–966.

55. See journal, *ibid.*, 5th Ser., II, 1–62, also in *Journals of the House of Representatives of Pennsylvania*, I, 49–96, and in *The Proceedings relative to calling the Conventions of 1776 and 1790* (Harrisburg, Pa., 1825). Selsam, *Pennsylvania Constitution*, 146–165, gives a detailed account of the convention's proceedings.

56. *American Archives*, 5th Ser., II, 5, 9–12, 22. The printed handbill, "An Essay of a Declaration of Rights, Brought in by the Committee appointed for that Purpose, and now under the Consideration of the Convention of the State of Pennsylvania," Historical Society of Pennsylvania, Philadelphia, is probably a copy of the version that went to print on July 29, 1776. It contains a limitation on the inviolability of property that the convention later struck from the text; see below, p. 194.

57. *American Archives*, 5th Ser., II, 51–59.

problem of framing a republican constitution, but popular ratification of the constitution was not yet demanded in Pennsylvania.

M A R Y L A N D ,   N O V E M B E R   8 ,   1 7 7 6

Maryland's provincial congress did not react to the Continental Congress's recommendation of May 15 until July 3, 1776. Then the provincial congress decided that a new congress should be elected "for the express purpose of forming a new Government by the authority of the People only, and enacting and ordering all things for the preservation, safety, and general weal of this Colony." This assembly was expected not only to frame a new constitution but also to attend to the tasks that constantly presented themselves to the government of a colony at war. The old suffrage law with the usual property qualifications was to remain in effect for the election of the convention members.[58] This decision by the provincial congress failed to meet the demands of the western counties for more adequate representation, but despite the strength of this dissent, which in the spring had led to disturbances, progress toward a new constitution was not impeded.[59]

The fifty-three members of the convention authorized to work out a new constitution met on August 14, 1776, and they needed the relatively long period until November 8 before they could agree on a declaration of rights and a constitution. The declaration of rights came under debate almost every day from October 10 to November 3. The convention resolved on October 14 not to deal with any but the most pressing legislative and executive business until a declaration of rights and a constitution were ratified. On November 3 the plenum passed the declaration of rights.[60] From November 3 to 8 suggestions

58. *Ibid.*, 4th Ser., VI, 1496. Public calls for a new constitution are in "To the People of Maryland," by "An American," *Md. Gaz.*, June 27, 1776, also in *American Archives*, 4th Ser., VI, 1094–1096. For demands made by the militia of Arundel County, see pp. 1092–1094; of Talbot County, pp. 1019–1021; of Charles County, pp. 1018–1019.

59. "An American," *Md. Gaz.*, July 18, 1776; Chilton Williamson, *American Suffrage: From Property to Democracy, 1760–1860* (Princeton, N.J., 1960), 108–109; Elisha P. Douglass, *Rebels and Democrats: The Struggle for Equal Political Rights and Majority Rule during the American Revolution* (Chapel Hill, N.C., 1955), 49–50.

60. Journal in *American Archives*, 5th Ser., III, 83–182. Nov. 11 is often cited

for changes in the constitutional draft were made every day. Some of the suggestions that were not adopted were to lower the property qualification for common voters from thirty to five pounds, to extend the term of office for the house of representatives to two or three years, and to leave the appointment of all sheriffs to the governor.[61] On November 8, the "Convention of the Delegates of the freemen of Maryland" enacted and put into force the constitution without providing for its consideration by the voters of Maryland.

NORTH CAROLINA, DECEMBER 18, 1776

The advocates of a declaration of independence soon won a dominant position in the provincial congress of North Carolina. As early as April 12, 1776, the congress authorized North Carolina's delegates to the Continental Congress to vote for independence. In its instructions, the provincial congress laid claim to the exclusive right to adopt the constitution and laws of the colony. The next day a committee was charged with drafting a constitution that was explicitly intended to be "temporary," and on May 11 the provincial congress passed "sundry Resolutions" that made up a "temporary Civil Constitution." North Carolina thus chose an even more obvious interim solution than those arrived at in New Hampshire, South Carolina, and New Jersey. Its constitution consisted basically of the establishment of a council of safety for the entire colony. This council would exercise the powers of government without supervision from the legislature until the provincial congress convened again, provided the council did not violate decisions passed by previous congresses.[62]

A radical faction in the provincial congress was dissatisfied with this interim solution, but the resistance of the undecided members had been too great for them to overcome. Samuel Johnston, a power-

---

incorrectly as the day of ratification. All that was passed on Nov. 11 was the resolution to have the constitution printed. *Ibid.*, 165, 182.

61. See the text of the draft presented to the committee of the whole on Nov. 3, *ibid.*, 147–159. Compare Philip A. Crowl, *Maryland during and after the Revolution: A Political and Economic Study* (Baltimore, 1943) and Ronald Hoffman, *A Spirit of Dissension: Economics, Politics, and the Revolution in Maryland* (Baltimore, 1973), chap. 8.

62. Journal of the fourth provincial congress from Apr. 4 to May 14, 1776, in *American Archives*, 4th Ser., V, 1315–1368; quotation is on p. 1361.

ful proponent of independence but an enemy to egalitarian trends, stated with great relief on May 2, 1776: "Affairs have taken a turn within a few days past. All ideas of forming a permanent Constitution are, at this time, laid aside."[63] In the decisive months between mid-May and mid-November 1776, when congresses were meeting in the other colonies, reaching momentous decisions, and enacting constitutions, North Carolina was in the unique position of being governed by a council of safety with only thirteen members. In August 1776, the council announced elections for October 15 and urged the voters to exercise their responsibility with particular seriousness because the elected representatives would not only pass laws but would also draft a constitution.[64]

The new congress met on November 12, 1776. Within a month a committee had ready a draft of a constitution and a declaration of rights. For the most part, the North Carolinians did not work out original formulations, particularly in the declaration of rights. Most of the clauses in their declaration were taken over from Virginia, Pennsylvania, and Maryland. The congress debated the constitution for only three days and, after a third reading, passed it like a law on December 14. The declaration of rights followed in the same manner on December 17.[65]

GEORGIA, FEBRUARY 5, 1777

Georgia, like North Carolina, first settled on a transitional arrangement. Eight "Rules and Regulations" that were adopted by the provincial congress on April 15, 1776, formed the legal basis for selecting a president, an executive council, and a chief justice and for establishing several courts of law. The provincial congress was to remain as

63. Samuel Johnston to James Iredell, in Griffith J. McRee, *Life and Correspondence of James Iredell . . .* (New York, 1857–1858), I, 279. Douglass, *Rebels and Democrats*, 121, sees this interim solution as a defeat for a "democratic faction." Allan Nevins, *The American States during and after the Revolution, 1775–1789* (New York, 1924), 130–131, thinks the main motivation for it was fear of a "schism in the patriot party."
64. Aug. 9, 1776, *American Archives*, 5th Ser., I, 1373.
65. *The Journal of the Proceedings of the Provincial Congress of North-Carolina, held at Halifax the 12th day of November, 1776* (Newbern, N.C., 1777), 13–51. Compare Robert L. Ganyard, "North Carolina during the American Revolution: The First Phase, 1774–1777" (Ph.D. diss., Duke University, 1963).

the legislative body.[66] After news of the Declaration of Independence reached Savannah on August 8, the council of safety scheduled elections for a congress that in addition to its task as a legislature was to draft and put into effect a new permanent constitution. The council explicitly referred to the recommendation of the Continental Congress of May 15, 1776.[67] The new congress met in Savannah at the beginning of October 1776, but we have practically no documentation on its work. On January 24, 1777, it appointed a committee to rework an existing constitutional draft. The congress decided against a declaration of rights. On February 4, after a third reading, the new constitution became law, and five hundred copies of it were published.[68] Its characteristic feature was the one-chamber legislature on the Pennsylvania model. This choice was probably also one of the reasons why the new constitution ran into opposition. One discrediting report claimed that it had been "framed and agreed upon at a nightly meeting in a tavern."[69] In 1789 the opponents of the constitution succeeded in replacing it with a new instrument that provided for a two-chamber legislature.

NEW YORK, APRIL 20, 1777

In New York, the introduction of a new constitution had been debated and specific suggestions on what should be in it had been published months before the Continental Congress's recommendation of May 15, 1776. But the new constitution was not passed until April 20, 1777.[70] At the meeting of the provincial congress on May 24, 1776,

66. Text of the "Rules and Regulations" in *American Archives*, 4th Ser., V, 1107–1109, and in Allen D. Candler, comp., *The Colonial Records of the State of Georgia* (Atlanta, Ga., 1904–1916), I, 276–277. Compare Albert Berry Saye, *A Constitutional History of Georgia, 1732–1945* (Athens, Ga., 1948), 93–95.
67. Saye, *Constitutional History of Georgia*, 96–97.
68. Text in Thorpe, ed., *Constitutions*, II, 777–785. Compare Ethel K. Ware, *A Constitutional History of Georgia* (New York, 1947), 32; Douglass, *Rebels and Democrats*, 340–347; and Kenneth Coleman, *The American Revolution in Georgia, 1763–1789* (Athens, Ga., 1958).
69. John Wereat to Henry Laurens, Aug. 30, 1777, Frank Moore, ed., *Materials for History Printed from Original Manuscripts* (New York, 1861), 39.
70. Mason, *Road to Independence*, chap. 7, has traced the development of New York's first constitution in detail. Compare Charles Z. Lincoln, *The Constitutional History of New York . . .* (Rochester, N.Y., 1906), I, 498–557; Becker,

twenty-four-year-old Gouverneur Morris urged that the state act on
the recommendation of May 15 and proposed that notices be posted
for elections "for the choosing of persons to frame a Government."[71]
He met resistance from two opposing quarters. One side argued that
in spite of the recommendation of the Continental Congress the time
was not ripe for this step. James Duane, one of New York's delegates
in Philadelphia, had warned only a few days earlier that the returns
from New York's last elections had clearly shown the extremists to be
lacking in popular support. It was wise to follow the people, he
argued, rather than to push them into making decisions of such
consequence.[72] But the ardent supporters of independence also rejected Morris's proposal. Their leader, John Morin Scott, claimed that
new elections were not necessary because the provincial congress
already had the "power to form a Government." He granted, however, that opinions could well differ on this point, and he suggested
that a committee be appointed to clarify it. The congress voted 28 to 4
to establish such a committee, and on May 27, 1776, the committee
presented a report that called for new elections: "The right of framing,
creating, or remodelling Civil Government is and ought to be in the
People. . . . As the present form of Government by Congress and
Committees in this Colony originated from, so it depends on, the free
and uncontrolled choice of the inhabitants thereof." Through new
elections, a new provincial congress was to receive the authority to
frame a new constitution, provided a majority of the voters thought
this step necessary.[73]

The only objections to this plan came from the organized artisans
and "mechanics" of the city and county of New York. They disputed
the right of a provincial congress to pass into law a constitution it had

Political Parties; Alfred F. Young, *The Democratic Republicans of New York: The
Origins, 1763–1797* (Chapel Hill, N.C., 1967), 17–22; Richard B. Morris *et al.*,
eds., *John Jay: The Making of a Revolutionary* (New York, 1975–), I.

71. Journal in *American Archives*, 4th Ser., VI, 1332. The authenticity of frag-
ments of this speech that Jared Sparks presents in *The Life of Gouverneur
Morris* . . . (Boston, 1832), I, 91, 94–107, has not been established. Compare
Willi Paul Adams, "'The Spirit of Commerce Requires That Property Be
Sacred': Gouverneur Morris and the American Revolution," *Amerikastudien /
American Studies*, XXI (1976), 309–334.

72. James Duane to John Jay, May 18, 1776, Johnston, ed., *Jay Papers*, I, 61.

73. *American Archives*, 4th Ser., VI, 1332, 1338, 1352. Published version of the
committee's report is on pp. 1351–1352.

itself framed. This power belonged exclusively to "the inhabitants at large" and was not a privilege but a right, "the right which *God* has given them, in common with all men, to judge whether it be consistent with their interest to accept or reject a Constitution framed for that State of which they are members." Up to this point, the crown and Parliament had prevented the colonists from exercising this right; and if the colonists now forfeited it themselves, they would once again be under the sway of despicable "oligarchic principles" and of a "corrupt oligarchy." This early call for popular ratification of a constitution was thus publicly issued by urban artisans at the same time and with the same reasoning as that of the town meeting of rural Pittsfield in Massachusetts.[74]

The newly elected congress met on July 9, 1776, in White Plains, outside New York City, which was no longer safe from the Royal Navy. Its first act was to subscribe to the Declaration of Independence, but it postponed discussion of the Continental Congress's recommendation of May 15.[75] On August 1 a committee was charged with immediately preparing drafts for a constitution and for a bill of rights. Yet despite repeated reminders to the committee, no draft was presented until March of the following year.[76] One reason for the delay was the threatening military situation. From August 1776 on, British troops occupied five counties and parts of two others. New York City was in British hands from November 1776 until 1783. Two members of the congress suggested drily that it might have been better "first to

---

74. The resolution passed on June 14, 1776. "To the Honourable the Delegates elected by the several Counties and Districts . . . in Colonial Congress convened," was published in the *New-York Gazette: and the Weekly Mercury*, June 17, 1776, cited according to *American Archives*, 4th Ser., VI, 895. Compare Staughton Lynd, "The Mechanics in New York Politics, 1774–1788," *Labor History*, V (1964), 225–246. For Pittsfield, see p. 88 below.
75. *American Archives*, 5th Ser., I, 1391, 1394, 1410. On July 10, 1776, the assembly changed its title from "The Provincial Congress of the Colony of New-York" to "The Convention of the Representatives of the State of New York." *Ibid.*, 1393.
76. *Ibid.*, 4th Ser., VI, 1465–1466; *ibid.*, 5th Ser., III, 202, 307, 331, 371. The journal for the period Dec. 14, 1776, to Mar. 5, 1777, has not been preserved. *Ibid.*, I, 374, and *Journals of the Provincial Congress, Provincial Convention, Committee of Safety and Council of Safety . . . of New-York. 1775–1776–1777 . . .* (Albany, N.Y., 1842), I, 751. For mention of the committee, see *ibid.*, 820, 821, 823, 833.

endeavour to secure a State to govern, before we established a form to govern it by."[77] But the provincial congress never relinquished its claim to represent the occupied territory. Politicians like John Jay, James Duane, and John Morin Scott, who had left the city, retained their mandates or had the congress elect them to other offices. The congress paid several delegates from the occupied territories who obviously could not be paid by their constituents.[78]

After the constitutional draft of March 12, 1777, was submitted, the congress discussed it almost daily for a month and revised the text heavily. On April 20 the draft was accepted with only one opposing vote and, like the constitutions enacted by the other states, it went into effect without the approval of the voters.[79]

MASSACHUSETTS, JUNE 16, 1780

At the end of January 1776, the General Court of Massachusetts had distributed and made public throughout the colony a proclamation against demands for a new constitution. The proclamation defended the interim government, which was based on the Charter of 1691, as one that met all the conditions of the Continental Congress's recommendations. The new government, "in all its branches, under the influence and control of the people," was more "popular" than any other in the history of Massachusetts.[80] Nevertheless, on May 1, 1776, the General Court gave up the charter as its basis of legitimation and struck from its letters of appointment all references to the crown.[81]

77. Flick, ed., *History of New York*, III, 269, IV, 43. Christopher Tappen and Gilbert Livingston to the convention, Aug. 24, 1776, *American Archives*, 5th Ser., I, 1542.
78. Lincoln, *Constitutional History of New York*, I, 46; Becker, *Political Parties*, 275–276.
79. *Journals of the Provincial Congress of New York*, I, 898. Three thousand copies of the constitution were distributed. On the contribution of individual politicians to the drafting of the text, see Frank Monaghan, *John Jay* . . . (New York, 1935), 94; Morris *et al.*, eds., *John Jay*, I, 389–417; George Dangerfield, *Chancellor Robert R. Livingston of New York, 1746–1813* (New York, 1960).
80. Jan. 23, 1776, Taylor, ed., *Massachusetts*, 20–22.
81. "An Act for Establishing the Style of Commissions," *American Archives*, 4th Ser., V, 1301.

In the next month the house of representatives appointed a committee to draft a constitution, made up of one delegate from each county. Since the committee was to meet only when other "more pressing matters" permitted, by mid-September it still had no draft to submit.[82] At the same time, the house of representatives decided to seek a special mandate from the town meetings. Its circular of September 17, 1776, requested the towns to give their approval to the suggested plan: the house and council would draft a constitution, publish it "for the Inspection and Perusal of the Inhabitants," and only then take the final vote on it.[83] Similarly, a few months earlier the house of representatives had refused to decide the issue of independence of its own authority and had sent the town meetings a request for their opinions.[84] By October it was evident that a clear majority of the towns wanted to leave to the General Court the task of framing and passing the constitution. Like Georgia and New York, Massachusetts could have had a new constitution in the summer of 1777. But twenty-three out of the ninety-seven replies received from the towns expressed objections to the plan, and this dissent proved to be large enough to deflect quick action.[85]

Some of these towns rejected the General Court as being un-

82. *A Journal Of The Honorable House of Representatives, Of The Colony Of The Massachusetts-Bay, in New-England* [May 29 to June 27, 1776] (Boston, 1776), 25, 42.

83. Taylor, ed., *Massachusetts*, 41. The abruptness with which this step was taken is obvious in the sources Oscar and Mary Handlin have gathered in *Popular Sources*. No petitions or instructions from the summer of 1776 questioned the General Court's competence to frame a constitution. Even the Berkshire Constitutionalists demanded only that the town meetings ratify the draft. Handlin and Handlin, eds., *Popular Sources*, 88–89. Charles Evans's *American Bibliography* lists as no. 14877, *A Journal of the Honorable House of Representatives . . .* [29 May to 9 October 1776] (Boston, 1776), but only portions of this document, which may well have contained relevant petitions or instructions, have been preserved.

84. For the replies of the towns to this question, sent out on May 10, 1776, see the manuscripts in the Massachusetts Archives, CLVI, fol. 98–118, State House, Boston, hereafter cited as Mass. Archives.

85. Fred E. Haynes, "Struggle for the Constitution in Massachusetts" (M.A. thesis, Harvard University, 1891), 85, cited in Samuel Eliot Morison, "The Vote of Massachusetts on Summoning a Constitutional Convention, 1776–1916," Mass. Hist. Soc., *Procs.*, 3d Ser., L (Boston, 1917), 242.

representative and demanded a redistribution of seats and broader suffrage before a constitution could be drafted.[86] A more fundamental objection concerned the authority of the legislature to draft and enact a constitution under any circumstances. As early as May 1776, the town meeting of Pittsfield, in repeating its demand for a new constitution, had also asked for ratification by a vote of the town meetings. When George III had broken his contract, Pittsfield argued, the colonies had reverted to the state of nature without any constitution:

The first step to be taken by a people in such a state for the Enjoyment or Restoration of Civil Government amongst them, is the formation of a fundamental Constitution as the Basis and ground work of Legislation.

That the Approbation of the Majority of the people of this fundamental Constitution is absolutely necessary to give Life and being to it. That then and not 'till then is the foundation laid for Legislation. . . .

That a Representative Body may form, but cannot impose said fundamental Constitution upon a people. They being but servants of the people cannot be greater than their Masters, and must be responsible to them. If this fundamental Constitution is above the whole Legislature, the Legislature cannot certainly make it, it must be the Approbation of the Majority which gives Life and being to it.[87]

Similarly, Lexington in October 1776 refused to grant the General Court the approval it desired because there had been no mention of a constitution at the last election and because the mere public discussion of the draft was not of much value to the towns: "It does not appear from thence, that there is any just Provision made for the Inhabitants, as Towns, or Societies, to express their approbation, or the Contrary."[88] The town meeting of Norton made still another suggestion. In addition to a newly elected "State Convention," it proposed there be assemblies on the county level that would gather ideas for the constitution.[89]

The town meeting of Concord has been credited by proud local historians with inventing the constitutional convention in October 1776.[90] The arguments that Concord used in denying approval to the

86. The returns from Sept. to Nov. 1776 are available in Handlin and Handlin, eds., *Popular Sources*, 101–166.
87. Taylor, ed., *Massachusetts*, 27–28.
88. Handlin and Handlin, eds., *Popular Sources*, 150.
89. *Ibid.*, 124–125; resolution of Oct. 22, 1776.
90. R. S. Hoar, "When Concord Invented the Constitutional Convention," *Boston Transcript*, July 3, 1917. Andrew C. McLaughlin, *A Constitutional History*

General Court's plan derived logically from the function of a constitution and a declaration of rights. The constitution, Concord argued, had the purpose of protecting the individual from arbitrary actions of "the Governing Part." The same body that creates a constitution naturally has the power to change it. A constitution that can be changed by the legislature therefore offers no protection against the legislature. For this reason, the people of Concord wanted a special convention, "a Convention, or Congress . . . to form and establish a Constitution."[91] Concord did not at the same time ask for ratification by the town meetings, as Pittsfield and Lexington had demanded. But in any case Concord's October town meeting of 1776 did not develop the crucial combination of constitutional convention and popular ratification; and, as we have seen, the clear distinction between legislative assembly and constitution-making convention had been made in other states before.

Although only a minority of the towns had joined Concord's call for a constitutional convention, the committee that evaluated the towns' replies recommended to the General Court at the end of January 1777 that elections for a special constitutional convention be held.[92] Politicians disagreed on whether the committee's advice should be followed.[93] In April 1777, the *Independent Chronicle* wrote in an editorial that the issue of a new constitution was occupying the public more than any other topic. The paper feared that such a large

---

of the United States (New York, 1936), 111, n. 11, commenting on Hoar's article, doubted the usefulness of further debating "exactly when and where the idea of the character of the full-fledged constitutional convention came to light." John Alexander Jameson did not deal with the town meeting returns in his otherwise exhaustive monograph, *The Constitutional Convention: Its History, Power and Modes of Proceeding*, 3d ed. (Chicago, 1873), 141–144.

91. Town meeting resolves of Oct. 21, 1776, Taylor, ed., *Massachusetts*, 45–46.

92. *Ibid.*, 48; for other town meeting requests for a special constitutional convention, see *ibid.*, 44, 47, and Handlin and Handlin, eds., *Popular Sources*, 105, 125, 169.

93. On Feb. 22, 1777, James Warren reported to John Adams in Philadelphia: "When we shall form our Constitution, or in what manner we shall do it, I am unable to say. Our own delays have embarrassed us, and I am persuaded the longer we delay this business the greater will be the difficulty in executing it. I am therefore constantly urging the necessity of going about it. Various are the opinions both as to the manner of doing it, and as to the thing itself. Many are for having it done by a Convention, and many are for one Branch only." *Warren-Adams Letters*, I, 296.

number of opinions would make it impossible for any suggestion to win a majority.[94]

By May, the house of representatives and the council had agreed on the next step. They recommended that the towns, in the next general election, give to the new members of the house of representatives full authority to draft a constitution, along with the "ordinary Powers of Representation." The house would then join with the council to work out a proposal, which would be made public by printing it in the Boston newspapers and by distributing handbills to all towns. Special town meetings would then be called to vote on the text, and reports sent back to Boston indicating not merely whether the majority had accepted or rejected it, but also the numbers of those present and those voting for and against. This procedure was intended to make it possible for the General Court to determine whether two-thirds of those voting had accepted the constitution. Thus the individual voter, not the corporate entities of the towns, was considered the basic unit in this fundamental decision-making process. Yet another procedural decision showed that the General Court believed a particularly wide political base was needed for the ratification of the constitution. The town meetings called to vote on it were to be open to all males "free and twenty-one Years of Age, belonging to this State." The regular property qualifications for voters were to be waived in this case.[95]

The newly elected house of representatives, equipped with its special authorization, gathered in June 1777.[96] On June 17, house and council in joint session appointed a drafting committee that agreed in a few days to adopt the "main points in the Connecticut Form." Determining the number of representatives each town was to have under the new constitution presented the only issue. By December a draft

94. *Independent Chronicle. And the Universal Advertiser* (Boston), Apr. 17, 1777.
95. Resolution of May 5, 1777, Handlin and Handlin, eds., *Popular Sources*, 174–175.
96. On each of the 31 days on which the court and council discussed the constitutional draft, they declared themselves a "convention" and kept a separate journal, reprinted *ibid.*, 177–189. The instructions the towns issued in response to the General Court's recommendation of May 5, 1777, have not been preserved. A committee commissioned with examining these instructions reported to the house of representatives on June 12, 1777, that the resolution of May 5, 1777, could be considered accepted by the towns. Taylor, ed., *Massachusetts*, 48.

was ready, and in February 1778 the convention agreed on a final version. It had not considered drawing up a declaration of rights.[97]

In March 1778, for the first time in American history, a constitution was voted upon in an election open to all adult male citizens. About 180 returns from the towns, some of them very detailed, have come down to us. Among them is the Essex Result, an essay in political theory and constitutional practice comparable to *The Federalist* in the sophistication of its argument (and in its political outlook).[98] According to the count made at the time, there were 2,083 votes for the proposed constitution and 9,972 against.[99] The very situation that the opponents of popular ratification had feared had come about. There were so many differing opinions on the thirty-six articles of the constitution that a majority for a combination of all of them was not very likely. Arguments frequently brought against the draft were: the disqualification of Negroes, Indians, and mulattoes as voters was not justifiable; property qualifications were too high; it was dangerous to allow the governor and council to make appointments to public office; a constitution should be accompanied by a declaration of rights; and—the most frequent objection—the distribution of seats in the house of representatives was unfair.[100]

The General Court hesitated an unusually long time before deciding on the next step, and it is easy to see how the suspicion arose that those in power were less than eager for government reorganization because it would mean a loss of power for them.[101] The General Court waited almost a year before it stated formally that the constitutional draft of 1777/1778 had failed to win a majority. The house of representatives then decided to start all over again and asked the

97. James Warren, a member of the drafting committee, reported these details to John Adams in Philadelphia as early as June 22, 1777. *Warren-Adams Letters*, I, 334–335. Journal in Handlin and Handlin, eds., *Popular Sources*, 179, 188, 189; the proposed constitution is on pp. 190–201.

98. Handlin and Handlin, eds., *Popular Sources*, 202–365. On the writing of the Essex Result, see Cushing, *History of Government in Massachusetts*, 221–223.

99. *Continental Journal, and Weekly Advertiser* (Boston), Oct. 8, 1778, hereafter cited as *Cont. Jour.*

100. Taylor, ed., *Massachusetts*, 49, and Taylor, *Western Massachusetts*, 89–90.

101. William Gordon thought the constitutional draft of 1778 had been purposely written in such a way that it was sure to be rejected. Handlin and Handlin, eds., *Popular Sources*, 21.

towns whether they indeed wanted a new constitution and whether they wanted to authorize their representatives in the next house of representatives to call "a State Convention, for the sole Purpose of forming a new Constitution." The town meetings that were to answer these questions were no longer to be open to the adult male inhabitants but only to those "duly qualified to vote for Representatives."[102] At the town meetings in April 1779 the affirmative votes outnumbered those in the negative 6,612 to 2,659.[103] Now the house and the council reacted more promptly, and on June 21, 1779, announced elections for a constitutional convention that was to meet in September.[104]

The first true constitutional convention in Western history, a body of representatives elected for the exclusive purpose of framing a constitution, met in Cambridge on September 1, 1779. It appointed an unusually large drafting committee of thirty-one, which in turn selected three of its most prominent members, James Bowdoin, Samuel Adams, and John Adams, as a subcommittee. The subcommittee in its turn left all of the work to John Adams. His drafts of a declaration of rights and of a constitution were accepted with only minor changes. The only significant clause the convention did not accept was Adams's proposal that the executive have absolute veto power over legislation.[105] Debate on the draft lasted four months on and off, beginning October 28, 1779. Finally, on March 2, 1780, the convention agreed on a text, which was then printed in eighteen hundred copies and presented to the towns for their judgment.[106] In a letter accompanying the draft, the convention sought support by explaining its

102. Taylor, ed., *Massachusetts*, 116.
103. Cushing, *History of Government in Massachusetts*, 245–246. For table and selection of replies, see Handlin and Handlin, eds., *Popular Sources*, 385–401.
104. Taylor, ed., *Massachusetts*, 116–117. Some towns gave their delegates detailed instructions. A selection of these is available in Handlin and Handlin, eds., *Popular Sources*, 404–431.
105. *Journal of the Convention for framing a Constitution of Government for the State of Massachusetts Bay, from . . . September 1, 1779, to . . . June 16, 1780* (Boston, 1832), 28–30. For a detailed report on the work of the convention, see William V. Wells, *The Life and Public Services of Samuel Adams . . .* (Boston, 1865), III, 80–90. See Adams, ed., *Works of John Adams*, IV, 219–267, for the text of the draft and the points in which it differed from the version finally adopted.
106. *Journal of the Convention of Massachusetts Bay*, 168–169. Samuel Eliot Morison, "The Struggle over the Adoption of the Constitution of Massachusetts, 1780," Mass. Hist. Soc., 3d Ser., *Procs.*, L (Boston, 1917), 356–359.

intentions and countering anticipated objections to some clauses, such as the property qualifications for voters.[107] Throughout the spring the town meetings considered the draft. In accordance with the convention's recommendation, the towns did not vote on the constitution as a whole but discussed and voted on each article separately. If the majority rejected an article, the town meeting often replaced it with a proposal of its own.[108]

When the constitutional convention reconvened on June 7, 1780, to evaluate the towns' responses, it faced an impossible task. How could the formless and extremely disparate returns and suggestions for changes be subjected to a statistically meaningful evaluation? After two weeks of frantically tallying votes, the convention decided to cut through the maze with a trick of logic. Instead of counting votes it simply declared that the draft had been accepted by more than two-thirds of the voters. On October 25, 1780, the new constitution went into effect.[109]

Constituent Power on the Frontier

The settlers in the territory that is now Vermont reacted in a unique fashion to the Continental Congress's recommendation of May 15, 1776. Led by the Allen family, the inhabitants of this area, which both New Hampshire and New York claimed, refused to be incorporated into either state. On January 15, 1777, an assembly of settlers, acting explicitly on the authority of the Declaration of Independence and on the recommendation of the Continental Congress, proclaimed the state of "New Connecticut."[110] The assembly rejected as presumptuous the New York constitution of 1777, which had granted this territory nine seats in the house of representatives of New York and three in the senate of that state. Citizens of "Vermont"—they had chosen

107. Handlin and Handlin, eds., *Popular Sources*, 432–440. The drafts of the declaration of rights and the constitution are on pp. 441–472.
108. Of the town meeting returns, 181 have been preserved; they represent the major portion of Handlin and Handlin, eds., *Popular Sources*, 473–930.
109. *Journal of the Convention of Massachusetts Bay*, 186. Morison, "Adoption of the Constitution," Mass. Hist. Soc., 3d Ser., *Procs.*, L, 363–412, offers the most detailed account of the evaluation of the town meeting returns. For the logical trick applied, see below, pp. 96–97.
110. Chilton Williamson, *Vermont in Quandary: 1763–1825* (Montpelier, Vt., 1949), 60–61, and Belknap, *History of New-Hampshire*, II, 336–351.

this new name in June 1777—held a one-week convention in July 1777 and adopted a constitution and a declaration of rights, both of which they had taken almost word for word from Pennsylvania.[111] This same convention optimistically elected delegates to represent the self-proclaimed state in the Continental Congress. But not until 1791 was Vermont to be accepted as the fourteenth state.

Unlike the thirteen original colonies, Vermont had acted against the will of the Continental Congress. The Congress, which was much more interested in peace between New York and New Hampshire than in the desire of a relatively small number of settlers for recognition as a fourteenth state, was now confronted with its own recommendation of May 1776. For the first time on the domestic scene, a situation arose that up until then had only occurred in the context of the Anglo-American conflict: the inhabitants of a newly settled territory adopted a constitution as a means of substantiating their claim to recognition as an independent political entity.

This same process took place repeatedly west of the Appalachians. In the Monongahela River valley, a territory claimed by both Pennsylvania and Virginia, the settlers had formed a committee of correspondence in May 1775 and petitioned the Continental Congress in the summer of 1776 to be recognized as the state of "Westsylvania." "No Country or People," they wrote, "can be Either rich, flourishing, happy or free . . . whilst annexed to or dependent on any Province, whose Seat of Government is . . . four or five hundred Miles distant, and separated by a vast, extensive and almost impassible Tract of Mountains." The Continental Congress ignored this petition, and the territory later became part of west Augusta County in Virginia.[112]

111. Williamson, *Vermont in Quandary*, 61–63. Thomas Young, an advocate of Pennsylvania's constitution, had suggested the name "Vermont" to the Vermont delegates who were working in Philadelphia for the recognition of the disputed area as an independent territory, and he also gave them a copy of the Pennsylvania constitution. *DAB*, s.v. "Young, Thomas." See also, Nathaniel Hendricks, "A New Look at the Ratification of the Vermont Constitution of 1777," *Vermont History*, XXXIV (1966), 136–140. Compare Matt Bushnell Jones, *Vermont in the Making, 1750–1777* (Cambridge, Mass., 1939), 386–393.
112. On the claims to self-government of the territories west of the Appalachians, see Frederick Jackson Turner, *The Significance of Sections in American History*, with an introduction by Max Farrand (New York, 1950), 86–138; George Henry Alden, *New Governments West of the Alleghanies before 1780: Introduction to a Study of the Organization and Admission of New States* (Madison, Wis., 1897); Thomas Perkins Abernethy, *Western Lands and the American Revo-*

In part of what would later be Kentucky, a group of speculators, the Transylvania Company, tried in 1775 to make their land more attractive to settlers by offering them an agreement resembling a constitution by which the settlers would have legislative powers. Following the model of the proprietary colonies, the company tried to secure executive authority and veto power for itself. The settlers decided for their part that they had the right as a "political body" to determine the rules for governing their "little society." But neither the company nor the settlers could maintain their claims against Virginia and North Carolina's opposition, and in December 1776 the area became part of Virginia as Kentucky County.[113]

Of all the trans-Appalachian efforts to form new states, those of the settlers in the Holston and Watauga river valleys in what is now Tennessee progressed further than any others. An assembly of settlers met in 1784 and drafted for their proposed state of "Franklin" a declaration of independence, a declaration of rights, and a constitution, which was essentially identical with North Carolina's. The Continental Congress did not want to act against the express will of North Carolina, which claimed the territory, and therefore did not accept the new state.[114]

These unsuccessful attempts to found new states showed that even frontier settlers understood the political effectiveness of the constituent power of free citizens, although they rarely used the term. When the Continental Congress undertook to regulate the constitutional side of the development of the western territories from frontier areas to member states of the Union, it had to recognize this readiness for self-determination.[115]

lution (New York, 1937); John D. Barnhart, *Valley of Democracy: The Frontier versus the Plantation in the Ohio Valley, 1775–1818* (Bloomington, Ind., 1953). On Westsylvania, see Alden, *New Governments*, 64–68, quotation on p. 66; Barnhart, *Valley of Democracy*, 48–52.

113. *American Archives*, 4th Ser., IV, 552; William S. Lester, *The Transylvania Colony* (Spencer, Ind., 1935); Patricia Watlington, *The Partisan Spirit: Kentucky Politics, 1779–1792* (New York, 1972).

114. Samuel Cole Williams, *History of the Lost State of Franklin*, rev. ed. (New York, 1933), and Walter Faw Cannon, "Four Interpretations of the History of the State of Franklin," East Tennessee Historical Society, *Publications*, No. 22 (1950), 3–18.

115. Compare Robert F. Berkhofer, Jr., "Jefferson, the Ordinance of 1784, and the Origins of the American Territorial System," *WMQ*, 3d Ser., XXIX (1972), 231–262.

Practical Limits of the Constituent Power

What had happened in Massachusetts and Vermont made vividly clear the limits and the problems that would present themselves to the former colonies in the course of realizing the constituent power of the people. The petitions of frontier inhabitants and land speculators to form states called attention to a conflict between different constitutionally justifiable claims, a conflict that could only grow more acute in the future. In the territory north of the Ohio River, the Continental Congress took over England's claim to sovereignty, while in the territory south of the river, several states did the same. The Continental Congress and the legislatures of the states concerned could therefore determine how these territories would be settled and what degree of self-government the settlers would enjoy. This claim to sovereignty came into conflict with the claim of settlers and land speculators to self-government. Thomas Paine was aware of this conflict and of the need for compromise when in 1780 he urged the individual states to relinquish their claims in the West. But even if the states did transfer their claims to the Confederation, a conflict still remained between the Confederation and the settlers. "The vacant territory is their [the confederated states'] property collectively, but the persons by whom it may hereafter be peopled will also have an equal right with ourselves."[116] Without an interim solution that gave the Continental Congress priority, it would have been nearly impossible to found new states in the West. Even Paine thought it essential that the Congress at first *give* a new territory a temporary constitution that would be valid until the population reached a certain number. Only then could the settlers frame their own constitution. In the frontier setting the vague and sometimes mythical concept of a "people" with a legitimate claim to constituent power was reduced to a simple question of numbers; five thousand adult free men on a certain territory, the Continental Congress decreed in its Northwest Ordinance of 1787, had a valid claim to elect a legislature, and only with sixty thousand inhabitants could a territory apply for membership in the Union and enact its own state constitution.

Another problem that could be solved only by compromising principles presented itself in Massachusetts in the evaluation of the town meetings' responses to the constitutional draft. As has already

116. Thomas Paine, *Public Good* (Philadelphia, 1780), in Foner, ed., *Writings of Paine*, II, 332.

been mentioned, the last task the convention had to perform was to ratify the constitution "if upon a fair Examination it shall appear that it is approved of by at least two thirds of those who are free and twenty one years of age, belonging to this State, and present in the several Meetings."[117] The convention had 174 town meeting returns in hand, and new ones kept arriving every day.[118] Many articles were only approved on the condition that they be amended in certain ways. But these alterations could, of course, have moved other towns to reject articles they had previously accepted. The committee finally gave up distinguishing between votes of "yes" and "yes, if amended." This procedure made it much more likely that a two-thirds majority would be found for every article in its original form.[119] Meanwhile, the convention was becoming impatient with the committee and pressed for a concluding report. On June 15, 1780, a rescue operation was designed that strongly reminds one of the German story of the baron von Münchhausen lifting himself out of a bog by a mighty pull at his pigtail. As article by article of the constitution was read to the convention, the chairman asked, "Is it your opinion that the people have accepted this article?" The result was "a very great majority" for every article. After a final vote on the entire document the convention declared "that the people . . . have accepted the Constitution as it stands."[120]

Of all the constitutions put into effect by 1780, only that of Massachusetts had in any sense obtained the consent of the people. But it became clear in the process that the people, however powerful

117. Resolution of the house of representatives on June 15, 1779, Taylor, ed., *Massachusetts*, 117.
118. *Journal of the Convention of Massachusetts Bay*, 175.
119. Douglass, *Rebels and Democrats*, 209–210, cites the case of Middleboro, a town that rejected the proposed constitution with a vote of 220 to 0. After making a number of substantial changes, the town voted 173 to 3 for their own draft. By recording Middleboro's votes in the "pro-if" column, the evaluation committee registered 220 votes for the original text. When Samuel Eliot Morison published his detailed study of the ratification of the Massachusetts constitution, he said he was fully conscious of how grave a matter it was to accuse this venerable assembly of wrongdoing. Yet, he wrote, "it is difficult to avoid the conclusion that there was not a two-thirds majority for at least two articles of the constitution, and that the Convention deliberately juggled the returns in order to make it appear that there was." Morison, "Adoption of the Constitution," Mass. Hist. Soc., 3d Ser., *Procs.*, L, 400.
120. *Journal of the Convention of Massachusetts Bay*, 180.

they were in theory, could exercise their constituent power only with certain limitations. It was certainly a sign of the political maturity of the American founding generation that in the face of such difficulties two obvious dangers were avoided: the theoretically inclined were not allowed to become doctrinaires fighting mainly for the purity of their principles, and those with a taste and talent for the mere exercises of power were not enabled to throw all principles overboard simply because they made the politician's life more difficult. It was this tempered combination of adherence to ideals and pragmatism in concrete situations that made possible the comparatively quick, smooth, and successful founding of the American constitutional system. The attempts at similarly incisive constitutional innovation soon to be launched in France were to be of a quite different nature.

CHAPTER IV

"Republic" and "Democracy" in Political Rhetoric

By a democracy *is meant, that form of government where the highest power of making laws is lodged in the common people, or persons chosen out from them. This is what by some is called a republic, a commonwealth, or free state, and seems to be most agreeable to* natural right and liberty.

Providence Gazette, August 9, 1777

What ideas about government and society guided the members of the provincial congresses and constitutional conventions when they drafted their constitutions? Historians who have explored this question recently have focused on republicanism as the concept that best synthesizes and explains the thinking of the founders.[1] But this approach is useful only up to a point. If the term "republican" is applied to everything the founders thought and did, it soon ceases to explain anything. Besides, the adjective and the all-inclusive "-ism" that goes with it tend to create an impression of purposefulness and consensus when, in fact, uncertainty, the need to experiment, and conflicts of both interest and opinion actually determined the course of action taken. The men who drafted and discussed the first constitutions had no detailed concept of what constituted "republican" government, no blueprint that could be simply set down on paper in so many paragraphs. On the day of the Declaration of Independence, there was no specifically "republican" model of government that Americans could automatically adopt the moment British monarchical government ceased. Nor was there in the colonies a monolithic movement

1. Robert E. Shalhope, "Toward a Republican Synthesis: The Emergence of an Understanding of Republicanism in American Historiography," *WMQ*, 3d Ser., XXIX (1972), 49–80.

determined to establish a new political order called "republican" or anything else.

It is true that in the public discussions accompanying the decision for independence and the adoption of the first constitutions, the terms "republic," "republican," and "republicanism" played an important role as slogans. But in no way did these words contain a clear prescription for the form of government that would soon be identified with them. The Continental Congress shied away from using the words when on May 15, 1776, it recommended that the new state constitutions be based on "the authority of the people." And again it refrained from employing the terms in the Declaration of Independence. Clearly, well-defined republicanism had not motivated the rebelling colonists after 1764 any more than the goal of proclaiming a republic had guided the revolutionary movements of 1581 in the Netherlands, of 1641 in England, or of 1789 in France. Looking back toward the British constitution and their own charters for guidance, and demanding the full rights of British subjects, the colonists moved, crablike, toward republicanism.

"Republican" as a Smear Word

In the political rhetoric employed during the conflict between the colonists and the mother country, which drew on historical experiences going back long before 1776, both "democracy" and "republic" had basically negative connotations. Ever since the inglorious end of the Puritan Commonwealth in 1660 and the glorification of the revolution of 1688, the terms republic, republican, and republicanism, along with commonwealth and democracy, had been used in English political rhetoric to stigmatize opponents of government. The ruling Whigs discredited critical writers like Robert Molesworth, Joseph Priestley, John Cartwright, and James Burgh as confessed or secret republicans and branded them with the name of "Commonwealth-men." The Tories, still hoping for a restoration, thought even John Locke had gone too far and tried to pillory him as a republican, although Locke had never supported republican government and had even proposed in the constitution of the Carolina colony that a provincial aristocracy be established. It was common to accuse unruly colonists in America of republicanism. Crown officials in the colonies thought they could win sympathy from their superiors in England if they blamed their difficulties with the uncooperative assemblies on the alleged republicanism of the colonists.[2]

Colonists who opposed independence also made use of the derogatory value attached to the term republican. When the assembly of Pennsylvania, prodded by extralegal revolutionary committees and mass meetings, was about to decide whether to send delegates to an extralegal continental congress, a piece from the Philadelphia press was passed around by members of the legislature. The anonymous author warned them against accepting instructions from committees bare of any legal authority: "Setting up a power to control you, is setting up anarchy above order—It Is The Beginning Of Republicanism."[3] It was republican, in other words, to disregard the procedural rules of the English constitution and to give the demands of mass meetings priority over the decisions of a regularly elected representative assembly.

After the successful conclusion of the First Continental Congress in October 1774, which had shown that political leaders of twelve out of thirteen colonies were ready and able to form a united front, warnings against republicanism and praise of the English constitution became more frequent in colonial newspapers and pamphlets. Englishmen, both in the home country and in the colonies, were so accustomed to thinking of the English constitution as unsurpassable that many shrank from the idea of giving up the much lauded triad of king, lords, and commons in favor of some untried form of "popular" government. How could a multitude of voters, they asked, make the decisions that up to then had seemed to require the education and political acumen of an experienced political elite? And how could a state of any extent survive without a monarch as an impartial judge to resolve the conflicts between opposing interest groups? And how could a league of thirteen separate republics endure if it were based on no higher authority than the sovereignty of the people?

2. Robbins, *Eighteenth-Century Commonwealthman*. Examples are cited in W. Paul Adams, "Republicanism in Political Rhetoric before 1776," *Political Science Quarterly*, LXXXV (1970), 397–421. The article deals more fully with this question than the present chapter does.

3. *American Archives*, 4th Ser., I, 607–608. Force does not give the source of the item datelined "Philadelphia, July 23, 1774."

Criticism of Monarchical Government

Independence and republican government were inseparable in 1776. The political leaders and the pamphleteers of resistance could not deny that connection; they therefore avoided advocating either goal as long as they could.

During the Stamp Act crisis, newspapers in Virginia and in New England published anonymous articles that criticized not only the individual decisions and person of the monarch but also the crown as an institution.[4] The colonists attacked in particular the notion that the monarch could not be held responsible for the actions of his ministers, a principle in British constitutionalism that was expressed in the phrase "the king can do no wrong." This principle provided as useful a target for colonial journalists as had Parliament's claim in 1766 to legislative authority over the colonists "in all cases whatsoever." But this open criticism did not call for deposing George III or for abolishing the monarchy. It was meant as an appeal to the king to fulfill the obligations of his contract as a ruler and to restrain his ministers from violating the rights of his subjects. Only when the king failed to uphold the law to the satisfaction of the political leadership in the colonies did the crown lose its usefulness as a last resort in the colonial assemblies' struggle with Parliament. The crown from then on could no longer be considered an impartial arbiter between competing interests, and it could not even be relied upon for competent, uniform, and just colonial administration.

Rule by the grace of God had been dead as a constitutional principle at least since 1688, but in the minds of the people there still lingered traces of faith in the monarch's special, transcendentally justified claim to political power, to sovereignty. In the winter of 1775/1776, an anonymous writer published in New York newspapers a series of articles favoring independence. One of these articles attacked any form of emotional attachment to the monarch. The writer thought it necessary to remind his countrymen that kings were merely human, and he urged his fellow citizens to rid themselves of monarchical superstition, just as they had rid themselves of religious superstition.[5]

---

4. Stella F. Duff, "The Case against the King: The *Virginia Gazettes* Indict George III," *WMQ*, 3d Ser., VI (1949), 383–397; Louise Burnham Dunbar, *A Study of "Monarchical" Tendencies in the United States from 1776 to 1801* (Urbana, Ill., 1923), 16–17.
5. No. XII of the "Monitor" series, *N.-Y. Jour.*, Jan. 25, 1776.

But many colonists seem to have felt themselves bound to the crown by their oath of loyalty. An "Amicus Constitutionis" in New York tried to weaken that feeling by arguing that "allegiance" meant no more than fulfillment of a contract. He referred to the theory of social contract and the trusteeship of rulers and explained that even a king was only a contractual partner of the people. A breach of contract on his part released the people from their obligations to him. In such a case, he said, a king "unkings himself."[6]

Avowal of Republicanism

In the public debate preceding Independence, no future republican presented either a coherent theoretical argument against the British variant of monarchy or a comprehensive justification of republican government. The American Revolution produced no single classic of political theory as the Whig revolution of the 1680s had produced Locke's *Treatises of Government*. Even the Declaration of Independence can hardly be read as a republican manifesto. After listing its twenty-seven grievances against king and Parliament, the Continental Congress merely stated: "A Prince, whose character is thus marked by every act which may define a Tyrant, is unfit to be the ruler of a free people." According to this statement, a monarch would be acceptable as long as he did not assume tyrannical powers.

The turn toward republicanism was first evident in anonymous newspaper articles that attacked those who used republican as a smear word. Advocates of independence in 1775 began to ridicule the bleak visions conjured up by loyalists who kept repeating clichés about republican factionalism and anarchy. In November 1775 the governor of New Jersey, after deploring those influential men who had publicly declared themselves for independence, sternly disap-

6. "Allegiance to crowned Heads upon the British Throne," *ibid.*, Oct. 19, 1775. In Jan. 1776, the *Va. Gaz.* published one of those halfhearted criticisms of monarchy typical of the time. In an article entitled "Of the Nature and Use of Riches and Power," the anonymous author rejected all supernaturally founded claims to rule, including the *jus divinum*. He did not object to monarchy on principle but only when it ran counter to "the good of the community." Experience has shown, he added, that kings tend to be men of either extremely weak or extremely strong character. The weak ones are overtaxed by their duties; ambition and restlessness make the strong ones dangerous. Dixon and Hunter's *Va. Gaz.*, Jan. 20, 1776.

proved also of newspapers that were publishing articles making light of the evil consequences of independence in an attempt to lessen the people's justified "Aversion to Republican Government."[7] The same development was taking place in other colonies. The *Virginia Gazette* attacked the warnings of the loyalists as hypocritical: since they had realized they could not impose their "scheme of despotism" on the colonies, they were trying to exploit the colonists' respect for the English constitution in order to create mistrust toward the Continental Congress and instill fear of an "unsettled and imperfect republick."[8] A newspaper article in Pennsylvania tried to unmask the tories' tactics: "Intestine confusions, continual wars with each other, Republicks, and Presbyterian Governments, compose the bugbear of the day, and the very name of them frightens people more than the whole force of *Great Britain*. My present design is to remove this dreadful chimera from your imaginations." Pointing to the Dutch republic, this author tried to quell the myth, which had hung on from the time of the Puritan Commonwealth, that republican government was synonymous with religious tyranny. In Holland, state and church were strictly separated. Furthermore, ambitious monarchs started wars more often and more readily than the elected representatives of a free people. A "Republick well regulated," he claimed, was better than other forms of government at preventing the enrichment of some at the cost of all.[9]

A first step toward the open affirmation of republican government was thus made. But it was not until the publication of Paine's *Common Sense* in January 1776 that republicanism was represented as a positive good. This pamphlet comes as close to being a justification of American republicanism as any document we have. That an outsider, who had immigrated only thirteen months before, was needed to set the journalistic campaign for republicanism in motion suggests how cautious and restrained colonial leaders had been in their public statements before 1776. John Adams later remarked with some envy that Paine had done no more than write down ideas already in the air.[10] But the fact was that native political leaders ranging from

7. Speech of Nov. 16, 1775, reported in the *N.-H. Gaz.*, Dec. 5, 1775.
8. Purdie's *Va. Gaz.*, Mar. 8, 1776.
9. "To the People of Pennsylvania," Mar. 1776, signed "Salus Populi," *American Archives*, 4th Ser., V, 96, 98.
10. Butterfield *et al.*, eds., *Diary of John Adams*, III, 330. Paine had at least discussed his manuscript with influential native-born Americans like Benjamin Rush and David Rittenhouse. Foner, ed., *Writings of Paine*, I, xiii.

Thomas Jefferson and Patrick Henry in Virginia to Samuel and John Adams in Massachusetts continued to keep their silence even after the newcomer broke the taboo by demanding not just that the rights of British subjects in the colonies be respected, but by calling for unconditional independence and republican government.

Paine's radical rejection of monarchy and indeed of the whole English constitution was unparalleled in the journalistic writings of the colonists.[11] In the first two sections of *Common Sense*, entitled "On the Origin and Design of Government in General, With Concise Remarks on the English Constitution" and "Of Monarchy and Hereditary Succession," Paine rejected monarchy in any form, even with constitutional limits imposed on it.[12] In the typical fashion of political theorists in the eighteenth century, he began the theoretical part of his essay by inquiring into the origins of legitimate government. In his opinion, the legitimation, strength, and success of a government depended on a sense of common destiny and a united effort to achieve the common good. The idyllic picture he painted of the first parliament, held in the shade of a large tree and affording both a seat and a vote to everyone, was not meant to be historically accurate. It was intended as an image to bolster the colonists' sense of their accomplishment in self-government. The principle of representation, Paine added immediately, does not conflict with everyone's basic right to have a voice in government. But to single out one family from the community and to invest it with a hereditary claim to rule is incompatible with legitimate government. Republican and monarchical principles are mutually exclusive, because in a community of equals there is no place for a monarch. Paine appealed to his readers to deny "the unmeaning name of king" its authority, to be guided by reason and "the simple voice of nature," and not to let themselves be duped by pomp. He granted that the British constitution had once served a useful purpose. But now it was obsolete, and the time had come to break free of old attachments. The checks and balances for which the British form of limited monarchy was famous were no longer functioning. Furthermore, the fact that the English Whigs' constitutional theory provided for control over the king by the House of Commons proved that the king's power could hardly rest on

11. It was only in the course of the year 1775 that Paine himself seems to have become an uncompromising republican. Compare his articles published in Jan., Sept., and Oct. 1775, Foner, ed., *Writings of Paine*, II, 20, 47–49, 1092.
12. For text, see *ibid.*, I, 4–46.

divine sanction. Paine's theory of legitimate government, in sum, projected the principle of equality into the immemorial past, and he condemned as an arbitrary human invention the division of mankind into kings and subjects.

Paine represented republican government not only as the natural government of the long distant past, but also as the form of government of the future, something modern that Americans could realize as soon as they turned their backs on the bankrupt monarchical systems of Europe. He therefore explicitly denied to the British constitution the appellation of "republic" that had sometimes been applied to it by writers who celebrated British limited monarchy as a system based on the rule of law in contrast to French absolutism. Paine wanted to see the term "republic" reserved only for communities that governed themselves and provided for the control of government by the governed. He granted that at some point in the past, the House of Commons had guaranteed the famous English liberties and had therefore once justly been called "the republican part of the constitution." But now these "republican virtues" were lost, and the government of Britain was just as monarchical as that of Spain or France.

Common Sense sparked a public debate that marked the breakthrough of open republicanism in America. The roots of American republicanism may be traced back to the Jamestown and Plymouth settlements; but not until 1776 did it become a publicly recognized body of political principles and institutions. It seems clear that the decision for independence and the avowal of republicanism were integral parts of the same process. As long as there was no serious prospect of gaining independence, public praise of republican government would have worked against American ambitions of attaining extensive self-government within the empire.

"Republic" and "Democracy" as Synonyms

In May 1776 Patrick Henry called himself "a Democrat on the plan of our admired friend, J. Adams." A few weeks later, Richard Henry Lee approvingly described the constitution that was taking shape in Virginia as "very much of the democratic kind." In July 1776 Samuel Adams agreed with a correspondent that "the Soul or Spirit of Democracy" was *"Virtue."* "Spartanus," who developed his view of the new order in the *New York Journal* in June 1776, took for granted that New York would now have to become "a proper Democracy." In August 1776 the *Maryland Gazette* called for the introduction of that most just of all governmental forms, a "well regulated democracy." The county convention of Mecklenburg in North Carolina demanded in November 1776 that the new constitution should be "a simple Democracy or as near it as possible." In May 1777 Alexander Hamilton spoke positively of the New York constitution as "a representative democracy."[13] Other examples could be given of the use of the terms "democrat," "democratic," or "democracy," in 1776 and 1777, but at the same time an equal number of instances could be cited when "republic," "republican," and "republicanism" were used. The *Providence Gazette* published an essay in August 1777 on different forms of government, and by its definition of democracy it acknowledged the interchangeability of "democracy" and "republican government" in current American usage: "By a *democracy* is meant, that form of government where the highest power of making laws is lodged in the common people, or persons chosen out from them. This is what by some is called a republic, a commonwealth, or free state, and seems so the most agreeable to *natural right and liberty*."[14]

The interchangeable use of "republican government" and "de-

13. Patrick Henry to R. H. Lee, May 20, 1776, cited according to H. J. Eckenrode, *The Revolution in Virginia* (Boston, 1916), 162; R. H. Lee to Charles Lee, June 29, 1776, in James Curtis Ballagh, ed., *The Letters of Richard Henry Lee*, I (New York, 1911), 203; Samuel Adams to Benjamin Kent, in Harry Alonzo Cushing, ed., *The Writings of Samuel Adams* (New York, 1904–), III, 305; "Spartanus," using the title "The Interest of America—Letter III," *N.-Y. Jour.*, June 20, 1776, in *American Archives*, 4th Ser., VI, 994; *Md. Gaz.*, Aug. 15, 1776; instructions to the provincial congress at Halifax in Nov. 1776, Nov. 1, 1776, William L. Saunders, ed., *The Colonial Records of North Carolina . . .* (Raleigh, N.C., 1886–1890), X, 870a; Alexander Hamilton to Gouverneur Morris, May 19, 1777, Syrett and Cooke, eds., *Hamilton Papers*, I, 255.

14. *Providence Gaz.*, Aug. 9, 1777. Robert W. Shoemaker, " 'Democracy' and 'Republic' as Understood in Late Eighteenth-Century America," *American Speech*, XLI (1966), 83–96, deplores the "confusion" he found in the usage of both terms. R. R. Palmer, "Notes on the Use of the Word 'Democracy,' 1789–1799," *Pol. Sci. Qtly.*, LXVIII (1953), 203–226, concentrates on European usage. Roy N. Lokken, "The Concept of Democracy in Colonial Political Thought," *WMQ*, 3d Ser., XVI (1959), 568–580, does not deal with usage of these terms in the public discussion leading up to Independence and the first state constitutions.

mocracy" is first noticeable in the colonies in the rhetoric of the opponents of independence, who had an interest in magnifying the negative associations of both concepts by merging them into one vision of mob rule and anarchy. But the advocates of independence, after they openly admitted to republicanism from January 1776 on, also avoided making a sharp distinction between republic and democracy for the contrary reason that they did not want to be accused of not fully accepting the principle of popular sovereignty. In short, no one contributing to public discussion from 1774 to 1780 seems to have insisted on making a clear division between the two.

Even an examination of the rather technical debates over the classification of the various forms of government reveals no clear distinctions. Pamphlets published by leading American whigs before the appearance of *Common Sense* rarely attempted to make comparisons of governmental forms, because the colonists had been fully committed to the English constitution. A pamphlet reprinted anonymously in Philadelphia in 1775 shows with what caution forms of government other than British limited monarchy were publicly discussed before the publication of *Common Sense*. In this pamphlet, entitled *An Essay upon Government, Adopted by the Americans . . .* , the unknown author rejected any form of absolute monarchy as beneath discussion but also maintained that it was difficult to determine what the best form of government is for any given country because that decision will always depend on the circumstances and needs of the particular people involved. However, due homage was paid to the British constitution. In his classification of governments, the author resorted to a variation of the well-known Aristotelian triad. The three basic forms—monarchy, aristocracy, and democracy—could each appear in "absolute" or "mixt" and in "dependent" or "independent" forms. Republic, as a category, did not seem to exist for this writer.[15]

15. *An Essay upon Government, Adopted by the Americans . . .* (Philadelphia, 1775), 119, 32. Aristotle used the term "democracy" to describe a degenerate form of a "politeia." Democracy was a form of government aimed at serving only the needs of "the poor." *Politics* 3.7. Similarly, Montesquieu's classification scheme was not accepted by colonial writers, despite the popularity that other parts of his political theory enjoyed. He listed despotism, monarchy, and republicanism as the basic forms of government and differentiated between aristocratic and democratic republics. He defined a republic as a state "où le peuple en corps, ou seulement une partie du peuple a la souveraine puissance." Montesquieu, *De l'Esprit des lois*, ed. Gonzague Truc (Paris, 1961), I, 11–12. In the discussion of the new constitutions, no American made use of

Thomas Paine, on the other hand, avoided any use of the terms democracy or democratic in *Common Sense*. He also refused to distinguish between limited and absolute monarchies and condemned all forms of monarchical government. Nor did he stop in his celebration of republican government to distinguish between aristocratic and democratic republics, as Montesquieu had done. Does that mean that Paine advocated republican but not democratic government? Is it not more plausible to suppose that he knew both words were used interchangeably in America and that he strove to achieve a stonger rhetorical effect by limiting himself to the clear opposition of republican and monarchical government?[16]

John Adams, in his pamphlet of early 1776, *Thoughts on Government*, similarly avoided using the terms democracy and democratic and offered no explication of the traditional terminology concerning forms of government. But it is not at all evident that he had in mind at that early date a rigorous distinction between a republic and a democracy. Not until a decade later, when the Federal Constitution was being discussed, did he first vigorously argue against equating republican and democratic governments.[17]

The newspaper articles and pamphlets opposing independence that *Common Sense* provoked also used republic and democracy interchangeably, but with a negative connotation. Paine's major journalistic opponent, William Smith, refuted the idea that the Bible favored "democratical" government over "monarchical."[18] Smith repeatedly used "democratical" even though Paine had avoided the term, and he employed the phrase "a pure Republick" in much the same sense that other writers spoke of simple or pure democracy. By contrasting republican government with "mixed forms," he tried to create the impression that it was impossible for republican government to in-

---

Montesquieu's distinction to argue that he wanted a republic but not a democratic one. See Paul Merrill Spurlin, *Montesquieu in America, 1760–1801* (Baton Rouge, La., 1940), and F.T.H. Fletcher, *Montesquieu and English Politics (1750–1800)* (London, 1939).

16. Paine did not deal with the distinction between "republic" and "democracy" until 1792 in the second part of the *Rights of Man*, chap. 3, "On the Old and New Systems of Government," in Foner, ed., *Writings of Paine*, I, 363–375.

17. John Adams, *Thoughts on Government*, in Adams, ed., *Works of John Adams*, IV. On his definition of "republic" in 1775 see below, p. 123.

18. "To the People of Pennsylvania—Letter VI," signed "Cato," *American Archives*, 4th Ser., V, 840, 843.

corporate the principles of representation and a system of separation of powers. He accused Paine of propagating a Greek marketplace kind of democracy and took obvious pleasure in citing Algernon Sidney, the English politician beheaded in 1683 for his alleged republicanism. Even Sidney, the reader was asked to conclude, had rejected what Paine was recommending to the colonists, because Sidney had known that democracy was impractical in modern times:

As to popular Governments in the strict sense, (that is, pure Democracy) where the People in themselves, and by themselves, perform all that belongs to Government, I know of no such thing; and if it be in the world, I have nothing to say for it. . . . Being no way concerned in the defence of Democracy, I may leave our Knight, [Robert] (*Filmer,*) like *Don Quixotte*, fighting against the phantasm of his own brain, and to say what he pleases against such Governments as never were, unless in such a place as *San Marino*, near *Senegaglia*, in *Italy*, where a hundred men govern a barbarous rock, that no man invades. . . . I believe it can suit only with the convenience of a small town, accompanied with such circumstances as are seldom to be found.

Smith concluded that the thirteen colonies were already "too unwieldy for such a Government."[19] But of course Paine had not proposed such a government, and in reality Smith was a Don Quixote fighting an imaginary opponent. Equally misleading was Smith's attempt to create the impression that republics, by definition, had unicameral legislatures.[20] Eager as he was to exploit all the negative associations that the terms republic and democracy could have, he constantly used both words synonymously. Another loyalist responding to *Common Sense* did the same thing when he accused Paine of being "a violent stickler for Democracy or Republicanism."[21]

Supporters as well as opponents of independence saw occasion to denigrate alleged republican or democratic principles in 1776. Vir-

19. "To the People of Pennsylvania—Letter VIII," signed "Cato," *ibid.*, 1050–1051. The first part of the Sidney quotation is from chap. 2, section 19, of the *Discourses Concerning Government* (Philadelphia, 1805 [orig. publ. London, 1698]), II, 179. The reference is to Robert Filmer, *Patriarcha, or the Natural Power of Kings* (London, 1680).
20. "To the People of Pennsylvania—Letter VII," *American Archives*, 4th Ser., V, 852–853. This letter appeared in the *Pa. Packet*, Apr. 15, 1776.
21. [Charles Inglis], *The True Interest of America Impartially Stated, in Certain st[r]ictures on a Pamphlet Intitled Common Sense* (Philadelphia, 1776), 70; see also, pp. 52–53.

ginia's Carter Braxton, for instance, tried to convince the convention that was preparing the new constitution of Virginia that it would be a mistake for that body to depart from the basic principles of the English constitution. He deplored the daily attacks by the advocates of "popular Governments" on the time-tested principles of the British constitution and predicted that the constitutional drafts submitted so far would expose Virginia to all the dangers of a "simple Democracy." The often quoted saying, "Virtue is the principle of a Republick," in Braxton's opinion only illustrated that "the principle of democratical Governments" places dangerously high expectations on the people.[22]

In May 1776, an article appeared in the *Virginia Gazette* defending republican government that may have been intended as a reply to Braxton's address. The English constitution, the anonymous writer claimed, had proved to be unsuitable for America. He admitted that Holland, Switzerland, Venice, Genoa, and Lucca were imperfect republics, but in America he expected to see the "best republicks, upon the best terms that ever came to the lot of any people."[23]

In the northern states, writers were no more precise in distinguishing republican from democratic government. New Hampshire's *Freeman's Journal* explained in June 1776 that "Proper Democracy" was that form of government "where the people have all the power in themselves, who choose whom they please for their head for a time, and dismiss him when they please; make their own laws, choose all their own officers, and replace them at pleasure."[24] Strikingly unorthodox was the terminology of an article in the *Providence Gazette* in August 1777. There were three species of forms of government, the author of this piece said, "the republican, the monarchical, and the despotic." To these three forms, he claimed without further explanation, political writers had given the names of democracy, aristocracy, and monarchy. In an attempt at clarification the writer added: "By a *democracy* is meant, that form of government where the highest power of making laws is lodged in the common people, or persons chosen out from them. This is what by some is called a republic." If this nomenclature was confusing for a student of Aristotle and Montesquieu,

22. *American Archives*, 4th Ser., VI, 751–752. Following Montesquieu, Braxton defined "democracy" or "popular Government" as a form of government in which sovereignty rests with "the body of the people." *Ibid.*, 749.
23. Purdie's *Va. Gaz.*, May 17, 1776.
24. "The Interest of America," *Freeman's Journal, or New-Hampshire Gazette* (Portsmouth), June 15, 1776, cited in Cushing, *History of Government in Massachusetts*, 252.

the writer nevertheless made it very clear, with the help of a time-honored metaphor in English radical politics, what the spirit of the new form of government, whatever it might be called, was to be. It was to be built on the truth that "it cannot reasonably be imagined that the *Almighty* intended, that the greater part of mankind should come into the world with saddles on their backs, and bridles in their mouths, and a *few* ready booted and spurred, to ride the rest to death."[25]

Only among the cautious whig leaders of Essex County in Massachusetts, and then only in 1778, does one find a public statement distinguishing democracy from republican government, at least by implication. Their well-reasoned extensive comments on the unsatisfactory 1778 draft of the Massachusetts constitution, probably written by lawyer Theophilus Parsons, listed as possible forms of government "despotic government," "monarchy," and "a republican form," obviously following Montesquieu. Anyone in Massachusetts who seriously proposed a despotic government, the town delegates of Essex declared, insulted the people; and anyone who considered monarchy would be hissed off the stage. Only republican government was compatible with the desires of Americans. In its ideal form it should incorporate both aristocratic and democratic elements: "Among gentlemen of education, fortune and leisure, we shall find the largest number of men, possessed of wisdom, learning, and a firmness and consistency of character. . . . Among the bulk of the people, we shall find the greatest share of political honesty, probity, and a regard to the interest of the whole. . . . The former are called the excellencies that result from an aristocracy; the latter, those that result from a democracy."[26] This usage tried to subordinate democracy to the more encompassing term republican government by limiting its meaning to the plebiscitarian element. Such an interpretation foreshadowed the later attempt by Federalist writers to endow democracy with this particular connotation.

---

25. *Providence Gaz.*, Aug. 9, 1777. On the history of this egalitarian metaphor, see "Rumbold's Dying Speech, 1685, and Jefferson's Last Words on Democracy, 1826," in Douglass Adair, *Fame and the Founding Fathers*, ed. Trevor Colbourn (New York, 1974), 192–202.
26. Handlin and Handlin, eds., *Popular Sources*, 330, 334–335.

The Federalists' Usage in 1787

It was not until the debate over the Federal Constitution was in progress, and the advocates of a new distribution of power between the states and the Union found it advantageous to dismiss the state constitutions of the 1770s as immature experiments, that for the first time political leaders in America introduced a sharp distinction between republican government and democracy.[27] When Edmund Randolph presented the Virginia Plan to the constitutional convention in Philadelphia, he claimed that the immature element in the state constitutions had been the undue influence of "the democracy." His proposal, he explained, was based on "republican principles" that were meant to counter the dangers implicit in "the democratic parts of our constitutions." Randolph thought the main flaw in the state constitutions had been the lack of "sufficient checks against the democracy." When Randolph used the phrase "the democratic parts of our constitutions," he was following, by analogy, English usage of the previous 150 years and meant the lower houses of the state legislatures as distinguished from the governors' councils and senates. In later discussions of the duties of the United States Senate and of procedures for its election, democracy continued to be used in this sense. The Senate was intended to act as a check on the House of Representatives and to guard against "the follies of democracy" and "the fury of democracy."[28]

Elbridge Gerry, a delegate from Massachusetts, also warned the convention against giving the electorate a direct voice in the federal government. He did not question the good will of the voters, but he doubted their ability to govern. In his speech, as recorded by James Madison, his use of the terms "republican," "democratic," "popular," and "levilling spirit" suggests a developing distinction. In Massachu-

27. Benjamin Rush stated in 1787 that in 1776 no one had had clear ideas of how a republican government should be organized: "We had just emerged from a corrupted monarchy. Although we understood perfectly the principles of liberty, yet most of us were ignorant of the forms and combinations of power in republics. . . . Remember, we assumed these forms of government in a hurry, before we were prepared for them." Alden T. Vaughan, ed., *Chronicles of the American Revolution* (New York, 1965), 334, 337.
28. Max Farrand, ed., *The Records of the Federal Convention of 1787*, rev. ed. (New Haven, Conn., 1937), I, 26–27, 51, 58; see also, pp. 29, 27.

setts, Gerry argued, it had become clear how easily the people could be influenced by misinformation. Most people in his home state, for example, refused to recognize that government and administrative officials had to be decently paid: "It would seem to be a maxim of democracy to starve the public servants. He mentioned [Madison reports] the popular clamour in Massts. for the reduction of salaries and the attack made on that of the Govr. though secured by the spirit of the Constitution itself. He had he said been too republican heretofore: he was still however republican, but had been taught by experience the danger of the levilling spirit."[29] Gerry meant to make a distinction between republican and democratic. He identified democracy with "popular clamour" and suggested that the "levilling spirit" gave too much power to the uninformed masses. Republican government meant government in the interest of the people but without "popular clamour." Gerry's statement that he had been "too republican heretofore" but would remain "republican" no doubt reflected the mood of many delegates but also muddled the distinction he was trying to make. Gerry could have said that he had held opinions before that he now rejected as "democratic" or "popular." But when he described his earlier position as too republican and then felt obliged to add that he was still a republican (and therefore not in favor of monarchical or aristocratic government), he indicated that democratic and republican still meant the same thing for him after all.

The choice of words of the next speaker, George Mason, confirms this suspicion. Mason disagreed with Gerry. He favored the election of the House of Representatives by the voters of the individual states, but he was in accord with Gerry on one point: "We had been too democratic." He was clearly using Gerry's phrase except that he substituted "too democratic" for "too republican." That republican and democratic meant the same thing seems to be confirmed by Mason's warning against going to the opposite extreme. What Mason meant by democratic becomes clear in his remark, intended for Gerry, that the constitutional convention was obliged "to attend to the rights of every class of the people. He had often wondered [Madison reports] at the indifference of the superior classes of society to this dictate of humanity and policy, considering that however affluent their circumstances, or elevated their situations, might be, the course

---

29. *Ibid.*, 48. Since Madison, who recorded this speech of Gerry's, made a sharp distinction between "democracy" and "republic" himself, it is likely that his notes reflect Gerry's precise usage.

of a few years, not only might but certainly would, distribute their posterity throughout the lowest classes of Society."[30] For Mason, democracy was synonymous with the political influence of the "lowest classes of Society." The convention never arrived at a clarification of the terms republican and democratic, even in the debate over the clause in Article IV, section 4, which empowers the federal government to guarantee to every state in the Union "a republican form of government." Leading Federalists like James Wilson still used both words synonymously in the ratification debate of 1787/1788. To monarchy and aristocracy Wilson offered only one alternative: "a republic or democracy, where the people at large *retain* the supreme power, and act either collectively or by representation."[31]

During the ratification period Federalist spokesmen attempted to introduce a distinction between the meanings of republic and democracy in public debate, notably John Adams in the *Defence of the Constitutions of Government* and the authors of *The Federalist*. In the tenth and fourteenth numbers of *The Federalist*, James Madison took up the question at length and based his argument in the two essays on a rigorous distinction between the two terms. Madison knew that the proposed constitution was vulnerable to the argument that republics could guarantee freedom only within small, easily surveyable territories. Large territories needed monarchs. Therefore, it was argued, the new Federal Constitution should leave the states as independent as possible and the central government as weak as possible. Because Madison felt he could not easily counter this widely held view, he conceded the point, but only for democracies, not for republics. He agreed that only a small area could be governed democratically because in "a pure democracy . . . a small number of citizens . . . assemble and adminster the government in person." In a republic, however, government is in the hands of elected representatives. A republic therefore can extend over a large area without infringing either on the efficacy of government or on the freedom of its citizens.[32]

John Adams, too, tried to prevent the identification of republic

---

30. *Ibid*., 49. We have to assume that Madison's notes accurately reflect the terms the speakers used.

31. Jonathan Elliot, ed., *The Debates in the Several State Conventions on the Adoption of the Federal Constitution, as Recommended by the General Convention at Philadelphia, in 1787* (Washington, D.C., 1836–1845), II, 433. Speech given at the ratifying convention of Pennsylvania. Further examples are in Shoemaker, " 'Democracy' and 'Republic,' " *Am. Speech*, XLI (1966), 83, 85, 89.

32. Clinton Rossiter, ed., *The Federalist Papers* (New York, 1961), 81–82.

with democracy. Instead of distinguishing sharply between the two, as Madison did, Adams made the term republic so all-inclusive that it became meaningless. He spoke of democratic republics, aristocratic republics, and monarchical or regal republics, and showed that each of the categories contained elements of the other two. The only examples of true "simple democracies" we have, Adams claimed, came from the history of antiquity. Even San Marino, which was always cited as an example of a modern democracy, was not a perfect democracy at all, Adams claimed, but a mixture of monarchy, aristocracy, and democracy. Sparta and Rome represented similar mixed forms in the past, and Massachusetts, New York, and Maryland did in the present.[33] Adams was equally disinclined to see Bern, Lucerne, Geneva, Venice, and Genoa as purely aristocratic republics, and Poland and England as purely monarchical ones. He claimed to be able to find all three elements in any existing state.[34]

In these writings, neither Madison nor Adams was concerned with creating unambiguous scholarly terminology. In the course of pleading a specific case, they used these terms to serve their argument. Whoever adopted their usage afterwards assumed with them a part of their political intention: to warn against the dangers inherent in unmodified majority rule.

In her history of the American Revolution, published after the turn of the century, Mercy Otis Warren provided a possible key to understanding the confusion that later arose around the terms democracy and republic. She probably had John Adams in mind when she wrote: "In 1783 interested and ambitious men endeavored to confound ideas and darken opinion, by asserting that republicanism was an indefinite term." John Adams indignantly denied this assertion.[35] He had certainly never consciously set out to obscure the meaning of a key concept of the Revolutionary period. But the fact remains that in 1776 he had seen no need to distinguish two concepts that he clearly, and for obvious purposes, distinguished in 1787.

Whatever or whomever the advocates of the Federal Constitution thought they were invoking when they differentiated between repub-

---

33. John Adams, *A Defence of the Constitutions of Government of the United States of America*, in Adams, ed., *Works of John Adams*, IV, 303, 308.
34. Correa Moylan Walsh, *The Political Science of John Adams: A Study in the Theory of Mixed Government and the Bicameral System* (New York, 1915), 20–36.
35. John Adams to Mercy Warren, Aug. 8, 1807, Mass. Hist. Soc., *Colls.*, 5th Ser., IV, 431–432.

lican government and democracy, they were not invoking the usage of 1776. The new constitutional order soon developed its own momentum after 1789, and one of the results was that the terminology of a few articulate Federalists gained acceptance in the course of the nineteenth century. Even today one still encounters the pseudo-learned argument that the founding fathers intended the United States to be a republic but not a democracy.[36]

36. In 1951, Henry Steele Commager noted that "some students, especially in our own day, have . . . attempted to distinguish between 'republicanism' and 'democracy.'" He rightly added that this distinction is "artificial and misleading." Commager, ed., *Living Ideas in America* (New York, 1951), 204.

CHAPTER V

Forms versus Principles of Government: Harnessing Enlightenment Ideas to Anglo-American Institutions

Forms in government are not like forms in religion. They are essential to the very existence of freedom in a government. There cannot be a greater mistake therefore than Mr. Pope's position, that that "form of government is best which is best administered."

"Maxims for Republics,"
by "Sidney," *United States Magazine*, I (1779)

Forms versus Principles

The abundance of patriotic rhetoric and the many declarations of political principle that accompanied the movement toward independence and the making of the first state constitutions should not lead us to forget the basically undoctrinaire character of the American Revolution. It was undoctrinaire in the sense that even guiding principles remained subject to the test of practicability. Where the test revealed irreconcilability with existing interests and institutions, where no compromise could be reached between the ideal and the practical, the ideal was—at least temporarily—abandoned. This pattern was not only true with regard to slavery, but is also apparent in the case of other issues, such as the right to vote, the right to stand for public office, and the question of equal treatment for all religious groups. These and other controversial issues were not resolved in one stroke by the disinterested application of the political norms professed in the founding situation. The discrepancy between principles and practice was permitted to stand until compromise or change became possible with majority support.

The pragmatic attitude of submitting principle to practicability was expressed by such diverse political temperaments as John Adams and Patrick Henry. Shortly before Independence, in a letter to a general of the Continental army, Adams raised a question that in another revolution might have brought him to the guillotine. "It is certain, in theory," Adams admitted, "that the only moral foundation of government is, the consent of the people. But to what an extent shall we carry this principle?"[1] Popular sovereignty, in other words, although the first axiom in the new political catechism, could not be the overriding organizing principle; it had to be modified by other considerations. Similarly, the ardent Patrick Henry was no visionary when it came to positing the fundamentals of the new political order. In 1775 he declared: "I have but one lamp by which my feet are guided, and that is the lamp of experience. I know of no way of judging the future but by the past."[2] The American leaders found support for this attitude in the revered model of the Glorious Revolution. In 1688, too, new political principles had been accommodated within traditional governmental forms.

In the writings of the founders we discover many instances of a pragmatic attitude, but very few reflections on the attitude itself. When they discussed it, the few theoretically minded among them did so in the context of defending the existence of "the science of political government." That branch of knowledge, they insisted, demanded a clear distinction between the "forms" and the "principles" of government.[3] When, for example, the physician and politician Benjamin Rush wrote a pamphlet in 1777 opposing Pennsylvania's new constitution, he invoked "science." In his opinion, the authors of the constitution, by providing for a unicameral legislature, had proved themselves incompetent state builders. He reproached them particularly with failing to distinguish clearly between principles and forms and with allowing the voting majority too much direct influence on the exercise of government. He granted that they were true

1. John Adams to James Sullivan, May 26, 1776, Adams, ed., *Works of John Adams*, IX, 375.
2. H. Trevor Colbourn, *The Lamp of Experience: Whig History and the Intellectual Origins of the American Revolution* (Chapel Hill, N.C., 1965), epigraph.
3. During the election campaign for the third provincial congress of New York in Apr. 1776, the group favoring independence but opposing "popular" leaders distributed a broadside reading: "Trust not men who are only remarkable for their noise and bustle; but seek for men of sound judgment . . . who really know the science of political government." Becker, *Political Parties*, 257.

whigs and had followed the right principles. But the writing of a lasting constitution required more than that: "It is one thing to understand the *principles*, and another to understand the *forms* of government. The former are simple; the latter are difficult and complicated. There is the same difference between principles and forms in all other sciences. Who understood the principles of mechanics and optics better than Sir Isaac Newton? and yet Sir Isaac could not for his life have made a watch or a microscope. Mr. Locke is an oracle as to the *principles*, Harrington and Montesquieu are oracles as to the *forms* of government."[4]

Rush's political intention became even more evident in an article opposing Pennsylvania's constitution published in 1779. Writing under the pseudonym of "Sidney," he openly asserted that the mass of the voters was incapable of deciding upon the best governmental organization: "There is a material difference between the principles and form of government. We judge of the principles of a government by our *feelings*—of its form by our *reason*. The bulk of mankind are judges of the *principles* of a government, whether it be free and happy. Men of education and reflection only are judges of the *form* of a government, whether it be calculated to promote the happiness of society by restraining arbitrary power and licentiousness—by excluding corruption—and by giving the utmost possible *duration* to the enjoyment of liberty, or otherwise."[5] The argument that both erudition and the lessons of experience were needed for the science of government was also to be turned against learned but inexperienced Europeans. John Adams, for instance, in his defense of the American constitutions of 1787 conceded that Turgot's love of liberty was genuine, but he thought Turgot, like most continental Europeans, had an inadequate understanding of "the science" of republican legislation.[6]

The significance of the science of government was obvious in an

4. Benjamin Rush, *Observations Upon the Present Government of Pennsylvania* . . . (Philadelphia, 1777), 20. Compare Montesquieu's distinction between "la nature du gouvernement" (or "sa structure particulière") and "ce que le fait agir" (or "les passions humaines qui le font mouvoir"). Montesquieu, *De l'Esprit des lois*, ed. Truc, I, 23.

5. "Maxims for Republics," *United States Magazine*, I (1779), 18–19. Stylistic parallels suggest that Rush was the author of these maxims. Stourzh, *Hamilton and Republican Government*, 3–6, and chap. 1, discusses the intellectual background for this distinction between principles and forms and indicates the importance this distinction had for the founding generation.

6. Adams, ed., *Works of John Adams*, IV, 558.

age that concerned itself with discovering laws not only in physics, biology, and other natural sciences but also in all areas of human activity. The great reputation won by Montesquieu reflected a widespread desire to understand the function and organization of social processes.[7] Americans were the first to have the opportunity to draw up a whole new political system. (And they were also the only ones who could make a radically new beginning without having to introduce great changes.) European Enlightenment thinkers, therefore, looked at the American experiment with some envy and some real pleasure at seeing their ideas realized.[8]

Unlike the French experiment soon to follow, the American effort was characterized by a great compromise: the new political order was determined only in part by the moral and political values of 1776. The direct experience with self-government within the British system, on which the dominant middle classes could look back, was the other determining influence. Revolutionary republicanism had to adjust itself to Anglo-American constitutionalism. Enlightenment ideas were harnessed to Anglo-American experience and institutions whenever a conflict between the two arose.

Thomas Paine and John Adams

In the spring of 1776, Thomas Paine emphasized political principles in his writing, while John Adams emphasized organizational forms. Paine did not provide a detailed plan for a constitution in *Common Sense*. The goals he wanted to achieve in January 1776 were independence from England and basic acceptance of republican government by the colonists. He outlined his ideas for a constitution in only a few sentences, remarking that all he hoped to do at that stage was to allay any fears of the unknown that might frighten the colonists away from the idea of independence. He was offering only "hints, not plans," he

7. Compare Carl L. Becker, *The Heavenly City of the Eighteenth-Century Philosophers* (New Haven, Conn., 1932), chap. 2; Becker, *The Declaration of Independence: A Study in the History of Political Ideas* (New York, 1942). Sheldon S. Wolin, *Politics and Vision: Continuity and Innovation in Western Political Thought* (Boston, 1960), chap. 10, esp. section 8, offers an interpretation of the further development, through the 19th and into the 20th century, of the belief in "organization."

8. Peter Gay entitled the concluding chapter of *The Enlightenment*, II, on the American Revolution and the Enlightenment, "The Program in Practice."

said. Paine obviously did not intend to provide the conventions and congresses with a blueprint of republican government but wanted simply to demonstrate that the framing of new constitutions after a declaration of independence would not be difficult. For the state constitutions he recommended unicameral legislatures with a president. These legislatures were to be subordinate to a continental congress, which would also be headed by a president. Paine did not think an independent executive branch was necessary at either the state or federal level.[9]

John Adams's reaction to *Common Sense* was typical of that of most of the whig leaders. They approved of and admired Paine's convincing plea for independence, but they rejected his suggestions for political organization. Being identified as the probable author of *Common Sense* somewhat flattered Adams but also annoyed him. He recalled in his autobiography that he immediately rejected two of the three sections in the pamphlet. The arguments against monarchy based on the Old Testament were ridiculous, Adams thought. Furthermore, Paine's ideas concerning a constitution displayed outright ignorance and only served the ends of the "democratic Party" in Philadelphia.[10] At the end of March or early in April 1776, Adams himself decided to publish a pamphlet that he hoped would counter any trend toward unicameral legislatures initiated by Paine's popular work.[11] A comparison of Adams's *Thoughts on Government* and Paine's *Common Sense* (both published anonymously) will make clear the schools of thought these two men represented.

Both pamphlets advocated republican government. Both authors rejected as flippant and irresponsible Pope's sarcastic couplet: "For forms of government let fools contest, That which is best administered is best."[12] Both writers used the same criterion for determining the best form of government: the security and happiness of the largest number of citizens.[13]

The differences begin with the very intention the publications were meant to serve. Paine wrote as an agitator in order to rouse a militant republican spirit. Adams's purpose was to give reassurance

9. *Common Sense*, in Foner, ed., *Writings of Paine*, I, 27, 28, 37.
10. Butterfield *et al.*, eds., *Diary of John Adams*, III, 330–331.
11. On Adams's decision to write this pamphlet, see *ibid.*, 331n.
12. Cited in Adams, *Thoughts on Government*, Adams, ed., *Works of John Adams*, IV, 193.
13. *Common Sense*, in Foner, ed., *Writings of Paine*, I, 5; Adams, ed., *Works of John Adams*, IV, 193.

and to build trust in the coming new order that he and other educated and principled men would lead. Adams feared that fiery appeals calling for innovation and experimentation and emphasizing the novelty of the new order would only lead to dangerous unrest. His text was meant to show how easily the transition from colony to republic could be made. Moved by these considerations, in November 1775 Adams sent Richard Henry Lee a set of proposals for use in the debate then beginning about Virginia's new form of government. In these proposals, which formed the basis of his *Thoughts on Government* published a few months later, Adams did not take as his starting point the question of what would have to be changed in Virginia's political organization if republican government were introduced. He asked instead: "What form of government is most readily and easily adopted"? He encouraged the introduction of new constitutions that would bring about a radical break in foreign policy but at the same time would make as few changes as possible on the domestic scene. While Paine rejected the English constitution totally, pitting the idea of unified government and the common interest of the people against the English premise that government should be tripartite and a mediator between conflicting interests, Adams tried to rescue for the republican order as much of the English constitution as possible. To this end he adopted the old broad definition of a republic, which covered both British limited monarchy and a self-governing American state. "The very definition of a republic," he claimed, "is 'an empire of laws, and not of men.' "[14]

Adams's suggestions for a republican constitution included the maxim that the voters should delegate the exercise of governmental power to a few of the most wise and good. Possession of property seemed to him to be the most obvious criterion for eligibility to vote. Under no circumstances did he want to see all the representatives gathered in one legislative assembly. There must be two chambers, he insisted, that could act as checks on each other. The new executive branch would, of course, be stripped of all the prerogatives the royal governors had enjoyed. But the head of the executive branch should be allowed considerable independence and, most important of all, be

14. John Adams to Richard Henry Lee, Nov. 15, 1775, Adams, ed., *Works of John Adams*, IV, 185–187. On Adams's conservative attitudes based on the New England tradition, see Timothy H. Breen, "John Adams' Fight against Innovation in the New England Constitution: 1776," *NEQ*, XL (1967), 510–520. Adams, ed., *Works of John Adams*, IV, 194.

"an integral part of the legislature." By this Adams meant that the governor should have the power to veto bills already passed by the two legislative chambers. The governor, aided by his executive council, would appoint all judges and all military and administrative officers. In short, Adams wanted to replace the "king in parliament" with a "governor in assembly."

In their pamphlets, both Paine and Adams proceeded logically to the conclusion that a republic is the best of all governmental forms. Paine came to this conclusion by way of the theory of social contract. Natural necessity, a necessity arising from human weakness, obliged human beings to form societies. Government was needed to compensate for a lack of moral virtue and represented nothing more than the fig leaf of lost innocence. But still, everyone had the right to participate in government, and the happiness of the governed remained the criterion for making decisions.

Adams, on the contrary, made no mention of a social contract or of natural necessity. He cited the generally accepted view at the time, derived from Montesquieu's political theory, that virtue is the peculiar attribute of the citizens of a republic. The primary obligation of government is to promote human happiness; happiness follows from virtue; and virtue, as everyone knew, is the principle on which republican government rests. But where Montesquieu was specific about the relationship between political virtue and republican government, Adams was vague. He did not clarify what he meant by virtue, nor did he say whether he considered it a premise or a result of a functioning republic.[15]

It is an additional indicator of the undoctrinaire character of the American Revolution that in the public debate surrounding the making of the first state constitutions, the principle-oriented attitude represented by Paine soon was dominated by the experience-oriented and more compromising attitude represented by Adams.

15. Adams, ed., *Works of John Adams*, IV, 196. Compare Gerald Stourzh, "Die tugendhafte Republik: Montesquieus Begriff der 'vertu' und die Anfänge der Vereinigten Staaten von Amerika," in H. Fichtenau und H. Peichl, eds., *Österreich und Europa: Festgabe für Hugo Hantsch zum 70. Geburtstag* (Graz, 1965, 247–267.

Ten Principles of Republican Government

How many colonists in 1776 had a fairly clear grasp of the political principles professed by their leaders, we will never know. What we do know is that political ideas were widely debated in newspapers and pamphlets, and that many local groups, such as town meetings, were quite capable of buttressing their demands with extensive theoretical considerations. It is the multitude of such local documents that convincingly demonstrates the remarkable maturity of political culture in the colonies and justifies the epithet, "founding" generation.

One example, admittedly of a degree of sophistication above the average, is the instructions that the town meeting of Stoughton, a small town southwest of Boston, gave its delegate to the Massachusetts constitutional convention of 1779. After reaffirming that "a republican form of Government is the most agreeable to the Genius of the people," the town of Stoughton listed ten propositions it considered "essential leading principles of a free Government." The first two principles summarized the theory of social contract and presented the argument for limiting all governmental power:

1t   That man in a State of Nature, unconected with society Cannot Justly be Controuled by any Earthly power whatever but when united to Society he is under the Controul of the Supreme power thereof in a Certain limited degree.

The social contract provides a basis for the claims of the citizens on their government:

2d   That the Design of man in entering into society and Submitting himself to Controul of the Supreme Power of the State is to obtain greater benefitts and advantages than he Could possiblely enjoy by being out of it that is he . . . is justly entitled to the Protection and Security of his person and property together with the enjoyment of all those natural Rights . . . that he has not explicitly given up to the Controul of the Supreme power in the Social Contract.

The common good is the sole reason for accepting the authority of government:

3d   That in the Social Contract every individual is bound with each other to the Supreme Power to Submit to its Controul where the good of the whole Requirest it.

The highest authority lies with the majority of the state's "Members":

4th   That the Supreme Power of the State is Composed of the power of individuals united Together and Exercised by the Consent of the Majority of the Members of the State for the good of the whole.

But even the highest authority is not empowered to infringe upon basic civil rights:

5th   That the Supreme power is limited and cannot Controul the unalienable Rights of mankind.

The exercise of governmental power should be organized according to the principle of checks and balances:

6th   That the Supreme power Should be So ajusted and balanced as to exert the Greatest possible energy wisdom and Goodness;
7th   That the Supreme power is divisible into Several Deparments, viz the legislative Judicial and executive; and that the powers particular to each may and ought to be delegated to Certain Disstinct and seperate Bodies of men in Such Manner that the power belonging to all or either two of the branches may not be exercised by any one of them.

Recognition of the need to delegate power to public officials is linked with the demand for strict control by the people:

8th   That the Majority of the people wherein the Supreme power is vested has a Controul over all the delegated Powers of the State. . . . All persons entrusted with any of the Delegated powers of the State are Servants of the people and as Such are elected by them and accountable to them and removable for breach of Trust.

The control of government by the governed seemed so essential to the people of Stoughton that they repeated this demand in metaphorical form:

9th   That all the Delegated Powers of the State are to be Considered as so many Streams issuing out or flowing from the Grand fountain of Supreme power and that the people ought with care, jealouscy and circumspection to prevent these Streams from flowing too copious and rapid least in time the Grand fountain be exhausted and their Liberties Deluged in a flood of Tyranny.

The final principle declared that "republican Liberty" consisted primarily in having a voice in legislation, particularly in any legislation affecting taxes:

10th   Where Political and republican Liberty fully Subsists no law can be enacted or tax imposed that Shall be binding on any person whether property holder or not with out his consent.[16]

These ten principles obviously are not as irreducible and logically rigorous as the axioms of a mathematical system. They are not *the* ten republican principles. But they impressively document how political theory had reached the common town meeting participant's level.

The dynamic element in this political theory was the call for greater participation in political decisions by those concerned, and it was especially this element that, from 1776 on, came to be considered the essential characteristic of republican government. But in addition, a whole series of classic political concepts, as the instructions of the Stoughton town meeting demonstrate, played a role in the justification and development of the forms as well as the principles of the new system of government. Popular sovereignty, liberty, property, equality, representation, the common good, the separation of powers, and federalism were the major ones, and they have been chosen for closer analysis in the following chapters. This list, again, is not a pyramid of syllogisms; it is not even exhaustive. Other concepts, particularly the ideas of "natural law" and "social contract," could have been singled out for separate discussion.[17] But since both of these ideas form an integral part of the founding generation's political thinking they will be dealt with whenever they become relevant in connection with any one of the other major concepts.

European commentators tended to see the realization of republican constitutions primarily as an adoption of the principle of popular sovereignty. It seems reasonable, therefore, to take "the great repub-

---

16. Taylor, ed., *Massachusetts*, 120–123.

17. For good introductions focusing on these two concepts, see Thad W. Tate, "The Social Contract in America, 1774–1787: Revolutionary Theory as a Conservative Instrument," *WMQ*, 3d Ser., XXII (1965), 375–391, and Dieter Grimm, "Europäisches Naturrecht und amerikanische Revolution: Die Verwandlung politischer Philosophie in politische Techne," *Ius Commune*, III (1970), 120–151, and Paul K. Conkin, *Self-Evident Truths* (Bloomington, Ind., 1974).

lican principle of popular 'supremacy" as the starting point for an analysis of the political ideas of the American Revolution as they were articulated in the public debate accompanying the decision for independence and the making of the first state constitutions and the Articles of Confederation.[18]

18. Quotation from G. Usher, *Republican Letters; or, An Essay, shewing the Evil Tendency of the Popular Principle* . . . (London, 1778), p. ii. For further identification of this pamphlet, see chap. 6, n. 1.

CHAPTER VI

Popular Sovereignty

It has been said often, and I wish the saying was engraven over the doors of every State-House on the continent, that "all power is derived from the people," but it has never yet been said, that all power is seated in the people. Government supposes and requires a delegation of power: It cannot exist without it.

"Ludlow," *Pennsylvania Journal*, June 4, 1777

We think a Convention ought to be made certain in the Year 1795 in order that mistakes and Errors which the wisest Bodies of Men are liable to, may be then rectifyed and corrected; and if it should be then necessary that the people might recurr to first principles in a Regular Way, without hazarding a Revolution in the Government.

Town meeting of Roxbury, Massachusetts, May 29, 1780

A European Perspective

From the perspective of European monarchists as well as Enlightenment thinkers, the proclamation of the principle of popular sovereignty in the American founding documents was a momentous innovation. It was received with a mixture of apprehension, renewed faith in the progress of mankind, and skepticism about the durability of the experiment.

One of the most violent public rejections of the idea of popular sovereignty appeared in London in 1778 when the otherwise unknown author G. Usher's *Republican Letters* was published. This pamphlet of over 160 pages attempted to rally the inhabitants of the British Isles around their king and pleaded with the colonists to reconsider their course; if they insisted on remaining a separate political entity, they should at least invite a European of royal blood to serve as a proper head of the new state. The booklet's subtitle revealed its thesis: *An Essay, shewing the Evil Tendency of the Popular Principle; Proving that a Republic is more dangerous to the Liberties of the People than a Monarchy; and that it is our interest to support our present free Constitution.* "The great republican principle," Usher declared, is that of "popular supremacy" or "popular authority"; it was not only utterly incompatible with the time-tested British constitution but a threat to any orderly government. "If the constitution be only a delegation of the people, liable to their control and censure, and that the people are born with an inherent, inalienable supremacy, all governments that pretend to be absolute and uncontrollable are tyrannous, unjust encroachments on the natural rights of mankind, and may justly be extirpated off the face of the earth when the sons of sedition think proper to set out on the meritorious cruisade."[1]

Usher had a number of other objections to republican government: (1) If the people control governmental power, those who govern are only representatives. Rather than governing, they are themselves obliged to obey; (2) The people are not capable of making decisions for the common good. They are an unreliable mass no less guided by passions than are absolute monarchs and their ministers; (3) The people are subject to the machinations of demagogues whose selfish ambitions can only be checked by a monarch; (4) The rule of demagogues leads to "an eternal succession of revolutions in power and property," with complete cycles from the anarchy of the state of nature, to tyranny, to just and civilized monarchical government. In the course of his argument Usher did not reject the theory of social contract completely; he simply assumed that the contract contained different terms. Like Thomas Hobbes, he believed that when men leave the state of nature behind them they must also relinquish forever certain claims to control over government: "Mankind at the institution of society must be supposed for the sake of peace to have resigned for ever a part of their original, natural liberties and all claim to them."[2]

We know as yet too little about European reactions to the American Revolution to say with confidence how representative Usher's

1. Only the copy in the Library of Congress gives Usher's name on the title page; the copy in the Beinecke Library of Yale University does not. The reference departments of the Library of Congress, the British Library, and the National Library of Ireland were unable to locate any further information on G. Usher. The quotations and paraphrases are from pp. ii, 39, 40, 156.
2. Usher, *Republican Letters*, 18–24, 27.

pamphlet was.[3] It seems fairly clear, however, that there was hardly an argument against republican government and the idea of popular sovereignty that any European monarchist could have thought of that was not contained in its pages.

European historians in the mid-nineteenth century confirmed the contemporary estimate of the signal effect of the idea of popular sovereignty. When Leopold von Ranke, speaking in 1854 from a Central European point of view, interpreted the consequences of the establishment of the American republic, he saw manifested in it primarily the principles of popular sovereignty and representation in a world otherwise dominated by the monarchical principle. He explained in a private lecture to the king of Bavaria:

By abandoning English constitutionalism and creating a new republic based on the rights of the individual, the North Americans introduced a new force into the world. For ideas spread most rapidly when they have found adequate concrete expression. Thus, republicanism entered our Romanic-Germanic world. . . . Up to this point, the conviction had prevailed in Europe that monarchy best served the interests of the nation. Now the idea spread that the nation should govern itself. But only after a state had actually been formed on the basis of the theory of representation did the full significance of this idea become clear. All later revolutionary movements would now have this same goal. . . . This was a revolution of principle. Up to this point, a king who ruled by the grace of God had been the center around which everything turned. Now the idea emerged that power should come from

3. The major synthesis of European reactions to the American Revolution has not yet been written. Good monographs are: Bernard Fay, *L'Esprit révolutionnaire en France et aux États-Unis à la fin du XVIIIe siècle* (Paris, 1925), translated as, *The Revolutionary Spirit in France and America: A Study of Moral and Intellectual Relations between France and the United States at the End of the Eighteenth Century* (New York, 1927); Durand Echeverria, *Mirage in the West: A History of the French Image of American Society to 1815* (Princeton, N.J., 1957); Palmer, *Age of the Democratic Revolution*; Elisha P. Douglass, "German Intellectuals and the American Revolution," *WMQ*, 3d Ser., XVII (1960), 200–218; Gerald John Ghelfi, "European Opinions of American Republicanism during the 'Critical Period,' 1781–1789" (Ph.D. diss., Claremont Graduate School and University Center, 1968); Horst Dippel, *Germany and the American Revolution, 1770–1800: A Sociohistorical Investigation of Late Eighteenth-Century Political Thinking*, trans. Bernhard A. Uhlendorf (Chapel Hill, N.C., 1977); and the exhaustive bibliography by Horst Dippel, *Americana Germanica 1770–1800. Bibliographie deutscher Amerikaliteratur* (Stuttgart, 1976).

below. . . . These two principles are like two opposite poles, and it is the conflict between them that determines the course of the modern world. In Europe the conflict between them had not yet taken on concrete form; with the French Revolution it did.[4]

Ranke did not feel it necessary to discuss earlier examples of republican government that had emerged in Europe, possibly because these had failed or, being limited to the scope of the Swiss cantons, had never been perceived as a challenge to monarchical government. Only the events in America and in France succeeded in giving popular sovereignty "adequate concrete expression" and in stimulating political thought in Europe. For contemporary Englishmen in the colonies and in the mother country, the new principle had, of course, come as much less of a surprise. England had not had a monarch who claimed to rule solely by the grace of God since 1688, and the idea that "power should come from below," as Ranke put it, had been discussed in England and its colonies for over a century and partially realized.

European observers had a tendency to forget, however, that "sovereignty" in the new American state took on a less monolithic, less doctrinaire, and less threatening shape than it did in Europe. This point has been forcefully made by Hannah Arendt in her comparative study of revolutions. The new American system of government rejected any claim to sovereignty by those exercising the powers of government, Arendt noted, for "in the realm of human affairs sovereignty and tyranny are the same."[5] The contrasting European example that Arendt had in mind was of course the French Revolution. The political conditions and political thought of the ancien regime caused the revolutionaries there to announce in the Declaration of the Rights of Man and of the Citizen of 1791, "The nation is essentially the source of all sovereignty; nor shall any individual exercise authority which is not expressly derived from it."[6] No similarly abstract and sweeping statement about the seat of sovereignty

4. Leopold von Ranke, *Über die Epochen der neueren Geschichte*, ed. Theodor Schieder and Helmut Berding (Munich, 1971), 415–417, my translation.
5. Arendt, *On Revolution*, 152.
6. *France Amérique, 1776–1789–1917: Déclaration d'Indépendance, Déclaration des droits de l'homme et du citoyen* . . . , trans. P.-H. Loyson and J. H. Woods (Paris, 1918), Article III, 77–79. "Le principe de toute souveraineté réside essentiellement dans la Nation. Nul corps, nul individu ne peut excercer d'autorité qui n'en émane expressément."

ever issued from the chambers of the Continental Congress. It did not have an absolutist regime to battle and saw no need to replace "l'état c'est moi" with "la nation c'est nous"; the third estate reigned supreme over the new continent and did not feel the need to solemnly declare the obvious.

Sovereignty Modified by Federalism

The American problem with sovereignty was of a different sort. The thirteen political units whose legislatures had for some time felt themselves to be the equals of the British parliament were not easily persuaded to part with power and money in favor of a newly constructed seat of "sovereignty."

In America, a monolithic concept of sovereignty had already been undermined in the course of the colonists' struggle for increased self-government within the empire. In justification of their demands they had introduced a distinction between the authority to legislate and the crown's more abstract and less effective "sovereignty" over the whole empire. When the defenders of the privileges of the crown and of the authority of Parliament answered that sovereignty was indivisible and that according to one of the tenets of classical political science there could not be *imperium in imperio*, the colonists accepted the principle but twisted its application to their advantage. In 1775, for example, Alexander Hamilton declared in an argument with a supporter of Parliament: "In every civil society there must be a supreme power, to which all the members of that society are subject; for, otherwise, there could be no supremacy, or subordination, that is no government at all." But, he added, this meant that Parliament must stay out of intracolonial legislation.[7] The necessity to evade a clearcut stand on the issue of sovereignty before independence led naturally to the Revolutionaries' less than fervent belief in it afterwards.

Yet another factor in the American founding situation worked in the same direction. Whig social contract theory specified that sover-

7. Hamilton, *Farmer Refuted*, cited according to Syrett and Cooke, eds., *Hamilton Papers*, I, 98. On the relationship of Hamilton's position to Hobbes's and Blackstone's theories, see Stourzh, *Hamilton and Republican Government*, 16–17, 22. John V. Jezierski, "Parliament or People: James Wilson and Blackstone on the Nature and Location of Sovereignty," *Jour. Hist. Ideas*, XXXII (1971), 95–106, shows how English and American views of sovereignty followed separate developments. Compare Conkin, *Self-Evident Truths*.

eignty resided in the will of the majority of the participants in the contract, limited only by the individual member's right to life, liberty, and property. Applied to the colonies, the question was, who were the legitimate participants in the new polity based on contract, a majority of whom were to decide the momentous question of independence? Was there an American "people," or maybe thirteen "peoples," the largest number of whom could claim the sovereignty to decide? The opponents of independence rightly argued that the two and a half million inhabitants of the mainland colonies did not make up a majority of English citizens.[8] Since the colonists could not deny this fact, they had to muddle the issue. From the time of the Stamp Act crisis on, in order to ward off the idea that their grievances might be settled by proportional representation at Westminster, they cited the practical difficulties of colonial representation in Parliament.[9] Finally, the First Continental Congress began to speak of "the English colonists" as a collective entity that possessed the right to self-government within the empire.[10] In July 1775, when the Second Continental Congress justified the colonies' right to defend themselves by military force, it used as the subject of crucial sentences a broadly defined "we" that sometimes represented the population of the colonies and sometimes the Congress itself. The Congress spoke here of the rights and achievements of "our forefathers," designated "the Americans" as "one people," and referred to America as "our native land," just as the inhabitants of the mother country used that phrase to refer to England.[11]

A year later, the Continental Congress presupposed the existence of an American "people" when it began the Declaration of Indepen-

8. For example, see Daniel Leonard in his seventeenth "Massachusettensis" article, Apr. 3, 1775, John Adams and Daniel Leonard, *Novanglus, and Massachusettensis; or, Political Essays . . . on the Principal Points of Controversy between Great Britain and her Colonies* (Boston, 1819), 11. "A Dispassionate Englishman" expressed similar views in the *Massachusetts Gazette; and the Boston Weekly News-Letter*, Feb. 22, 1776.

9. See below, pp. 232–233.

10. "As the English colonists are not represented, and from their local and other circumstances, cannot properly be represented in the British parliament, they are entitled to a free and exclusive power of legislation in their several provincial legislatures." "Declaration and Resolves of the First Continental Congress," Oct. 14, 1774, Commager, ed., *Documents*, I, 83.

11. "Declaration of the Causes and Necessity of Taking up Arms," July 6, 1775, *ibid.*, 93–95.

dence with the statement that it might become necessary "for one people to dissolve the political bands which have connected them with another." When Thomas Hutchinson, the former governor of Massachusetts, read this sentence in London, he commented: "They begin . . . with a false hypothesis, that the Colonies are one *distinct people*, and the kingdom another, connected by political bands. The Colonies, *politically* considered, never were a *distinct* people from the kingdom."[12] Because of the delicacy of the issue, the Declaration of Independence was vague about the new seat of sovereignty. The authors introduced themselves as "We, . . . , the Representatives of the united States of America, in General Congress, Assembled." They spoke "in the Name, and by Authority of the good People of these Colonies" and declared that "these United Colonies are, and of Right ought to be Free and Independent States." A clear statement about the degree of sovereignty of the individual colony/state was elegantly avoided by the sentence: "As Free and Independent States, they have full Power to levy War, conclude Peace, contract Alliances, establish Commerce, and to do all other Acts and Things which Independent States may of right do."[13] It was merely one possible reading of these words that only collectively would the thirteen ex-colonies exercise the rights of a sovereign state.

The summer of 1776 was obviously not the time to debate this question, and thus the term sovereignty was for good reason avoided in the proclamations of the Continental Congress. The issue only arose indirectly in the guise of the more practical questions of how power was to be divided between the states and the Congress, and how their difference in size and economic importance was to be acknowledged in the composition of that assembly.[14]

The Sovereignty Clauses in the State Constitutions

In addition to the Declaration of Independence, the constitutions of several states asserted that the people were the sole source of legitimate power and insisted on the accountability of elected representa-

---

12. Thomas Hutchinson, *Strictures upon the Declaration of the Congress at Philadelphia*, ed. Malcolm Freiberg, Old South Leaflets, no. 227 (Boston, 1958 [orig. publ. London, 1776]), 10.
13. Commager, ed., *Documents*, I, 100–102.
14. See chap. 13 below.

tives to their constituents. The American version of the republican theory of sovereignty was stated in constitutionally binding form for the first time in the Virginia bill of rights of June 1776: "All power is vested in, and consequently derived from, the people; . . . magistrates are their trustees and servants, and at all times amenable to them."[15] The New Jersey constitution, also adopted before independence, was more limited in its claims because it still left open the possibility of reconciliation with Great Britain. The central issue in its preamble, therefore, was not the relationship of the people of New Jersey to their state government, but the justification of their resistance against the king, which was formulated in terms of the Whig theory of limited monarchy.[16]

Delaware's constitution, the first to be adopted after independence had been declared, was particularly concise: "All Government of Right originates from the people, is founded in Compact only, and instituted solely for the Good of the Whole." Therefore, "Persons intrusted with the legislative and executive Powers are the Trustees and Servants of the Public, and as such accountable for their Conduct." Delaware also introduced the concept of "internal police" to deal with the incipient problem of federal distribution of power. Without defining the term, the Delaware declaration of rights stipulated "that the people of this State have the sole exclusive and inherent Right of governing and regulating the internal Police of the same."[17] Pennsylvania, after making minor editorial changes, adopted Virginia's definition of sovereignty and Delaware's reference to internal police.[18] Maryland followed Delaware word for word.[19] North Carolina, similarly, declared all political power to be "vested in and derived from the people only" and subjected "the internal government and police" to the control of the people of North Carolina.[20] Georgia

15. Thorpe, ed., *Constitutions*, VII, 3813.

16. "All the constitutional authority ever possessed by the kings of Great Britain over these colonies, or their other dominions, was, by compact, derived from the people, and held of them, for the common interest of the whole society; allegiance and protection are, in the nature of things reciprocal ties." *Ibid.*, V, 2594.

17. *Convention of the Delaware State*, 17–18. On federalism and "internal police," see p. 288 below.

18. Thorpe, ed., *Constitutions*, V, 3082–3083.

19. *Ibid.*, III, 1686–1687.

20. *Ibid.*, V, 2787.

also followed this concise formulation.[21] New York included the complete Declaration of Independence in its constitution and repeated in its own words that "no authority shall, on any pretence whatever, be exercised over the people or members of this State but such as shall be derived from and granted by them."[22]

The Massachusetts bill of rights of 1780, drafted by John Adams, contained the most comprehensive and mature explanation of state sovereignty. In its definition of state rights it was the first to speak of "expresly delegated" powers: "The people of this Commonwealth have the sole and exclusive right of governing themselves as a free, sovereign, and independent state; and do, and forever hereafter shall, exercise and enjoy every power, jurisdiction, and right, which is not, or may not hereafter, be by them expresly delegated to the United States of America, in Congress assembled."[23]

These statements of principle expressed the very heart of the consensus among the victors of 1776. After decades of debate between the colonies and England, no revolutionary act was needed to assure the principle of popular sovereignty its place in the newly established governments. But in order not to test it prematurely, the first constitutions avoided spelling out all its ramifications and practical consequences for the state governments as well as for the Confederation. The full implications of the principle of popular sovereignty were left to be developed through future political action.

The Right to Resist Government

Having proclaimed the sovereignty of the people and the accountability of their representatives in public office, several of the state constitutions went on to affirm in principle the existence of a continuing right to oppose government and to make constitutional changes. It was, of course, in order to justify resistance to British rule that the Continental Congress insisted on "the Right of the People to alter or to abolish it [the form of government], and to institute new Government, laying its foundation on such principles and organizing its powers in such form, as to them shall seem most likely to effect their

21. *Ibid.*, II, 788.
22. *Ibid.*, V, 2628.
23. Taylor, ed., *Massachusetts*, 129.

Safety and Happiness."[24] Virginia's bill of rights, the first constitutional document to apply the idea to new American state government, went one step toward more precision by adding that only "a majority of the community" had the right to reform, alter, or abolish government. Pennsylvania granted the same power to "the people . . . by common consent," or "the community." Delaware's clause went back to the vaguer phrase "the People," and so did that of Massachusetts.[25] It is notable, however, that the right of the people to resist or alter government was not made explicit in the Articles of Confederation or in the Constitution of 1787 and its amendments.

The conditions under which the people or the majority of the community were thought to be entitled to make use of this right were left unspecified in most constitutions. The only explanations given consist of references to previously defined human rights and purposes of government. The Declaration of Independence says, "Whenever any Form of Government becomes destructive of these ends . . ."; the Virginia bill of rights stipulates, "When any government shall be found inadequate or contrary to these purposes . . ."; the Delaware bill of rights chose the unique formulation, "Whenever the Ends of Government are perverted, and public Liberty manifestly endangered by the Legislative singly, or a treacherous Combination of both . . ."; and the Massachusetts bill of rights made the people's right to institute or alter government contingent upon a situation "when their protection, safety, prosperity and happiness require it."[26]

Missing in the existing clauses was any reference to the right of an individual to resist governmental authority on grounds of conscience. In this respect, Americans did not go beyond an assertion of the collective right to resist on which the Whigs had rested their justification of the Glorious Revolution. The Maryland constitution expressly referred to the English when it vehemently rejected the Tories' central argument against the legitimacy of the new regime of 1689 and declared, "The doctrine of non-resistance, against arbitrary power and oppression, is absurd, slavish, and destructive of the good and happiness of mankind."[27] The Marylanders were thus only re-

24. Commager, ed., *Documents*, I, 100.
25. Thorpe, ed., *Constitutions*, VII, 3813, V, 3081; *Convention of the Delaware State*, 18; Taylor, ed., *Massachusetts*, 129.
26. Commager, ed., *Documents*, I, 100; Thorpe, ed., *Constitutions*, VII, 3813; *Convention of the Delaware State*, 18; Taylor, ed., *Massachusetts*, 129.
27. Thorpe, ed., *Constitutions*, III, 1686–1687.

peating the basic Whig tenet that no earthly authority could claim to rule by divine right or could declare resistance sinful on the basis of Paul's well-known injunction in Romans 13: "The powers that be are ordained of God. Whosoever therefore resisteth the power, resisteth the ordinance of God."

The Right to Change a Constitution

In another respect, however, the Americans went an important step beyond the English Whigs when they institutionalized the right to change a constitution. The defenders of the Glorious Revolution only had to justify Parliament's resistance against the crown, not popular resistance against Parliament. It is true that, according to Locke, Parliament's power was solely "fiduciary," and he asserted that there remained "still in the people a supreme power to remove or alter the legislative, when they find the legislative act contrary to the trust reposed in them." But he added the crucial qualification that the community is not the supreme power "under any form of government, because this power of the people can never take place till the government be dissolved."[28] In other words, those entrusted with the powers of government must first disqualify themselves by endangering the happiness of the community to such a degree that civil society can be said to have reverted to a state of nature. Only then, Locke argued, were the people entitled "to put the rule into such hands which may secure to them the ends for which government was at first erected."[29] Two generations later, the influential Whig jurist Blackstone also failed to give practical guidance for any likely situation in which the people might resume governmental powers.[30]

The Americans went beyond Locke and Blackstone in 1776 by giving the people a practical role to play before civil society had relapsed into a more or less anarchical state of nature. They did so by institutionalizing peaceful means of making and amending constitutions. The development of the constitutional convention and popular

28. John Locke, *The Second Treatise of Government*, ed. Thomas P. Peardon (Indianapolis, Ind., 1952), 84–85, section 149; similarly section 134.
29. *Ibid.*, section 225; see also sections 226 and 89.
30. Blackstone's ideas on natural law and revolution are analyzed in Stourzh, *Hamilton and Republican Government*, chap. 1, and by the same author in "William Blackstone," *Jahrbuch für Amerikastudien*, XV (1970), 184–200.

ratification has already been discussed.[31] The amending procedure was of equal importance and developed in a similarly haphazard way.

The possibility of constitutional amendment was first touched upon implicitly in the constitutions of New Jersey and Delaware, which introduced a special category of clauses that the legislature was expressly forbidden to change, such as the right to trial by jury, the division of the legislature into two chambers, the mode of election, and the bill of rights. Whether and how these somewhat more fundamental constitutional provisions could ever be altered was left unmentioned.[32] Pennsylvania's constitution was the first to institutionalize the amending process. Every seven years each county and city would elect two representatives, twenty-four all together, to form a council of censors. If sixteen of the censors agreed that an amendment was needed, a constitutional convention had to be called within two years. The legislature had no power to alter the constitution in any way. The council of censors had venerable predecessors in Greek and Roman history, but only Vermont's constitution followed the Pennsylvania model.[33]

Maryland pioneered an ideologically less pure method. The legislature itself was permitted, by a two-thirds vote in both houses, to draft amendments to the constitution. They would take effect only after the next election and another two-thirds vote by the newly elected senators and representatives.[34] The election obviously was meant to function as a referendum on amendments. Georgia adopted still another, very practical method. If a majority of voters in the majority of the counties petitioned the legislature, a constitutional convention would have to be called.[35] South Carolina, however, even in its revised constitution of 1778, allowed a simple majority in both houses of the legislature to change the constitution.[36] Yet another way was provided in the Massachusetts constitution. It enjoined the legislature to poll the town meetings in 1795 about their desire to

31. See pp. 75, 78–80, 85, 88, above.
32. Thorpe, ed., *Constitutions*, V, 2998, I, 568. Compare Walter Fairleigh Dodd, *The Revision and Amendment of State Constitutions* (Baltimore, 1910). North Carolina also denied the legislature the right to change any clause in the bill of rights. Thorpe, ed., *Constitutions*, V, 2794.
33. Thorpe, ed., *Constitutions*, V, 3085, 3091–3092, VI, 3748. Compare Lewis H. Meader, "The Council of Censors," *PMHB*, XXII (1898), 265–300.
34. Thorpe, ed., *Constitutions*, III, 1701.
35. *Ibid.*, II, 785.
36. *Ibid.*, VI, 3257.

amend the constitution. If two-thirds of those voting throughout the state demanded it, a constitutional convention had to be called.[37] By 1780, fewer than half of the states had a constitutionally fixed amending procedure, but the principle that the fundamental law could be peacefully altered by popular will was firmly established.

The idea itself could hardly have caused surprise after a decade of confrontation with a British constitutional order that had proved inflexible and had left the colonists no avenues for change but war. The need for means of nonviolent change was repeatedly mentioned in public debate. The townspeople of Lexington, for instance, rejected the 1778 draft of the Massachusetts constitution because it did not provide for amendment by the majority of voters. Only that method, Lexington argued, "might give Satisfaction to the People; and be an happy Means, under Providence, of preventing popular Commotions, Mobs, Bloodshed and Civil War."[38] An anonymous article in the *Providence Gazette* protested against the power of the legislature of Rhode Island to change the constitution because, if the legislature had that power, "we should have no remedy left us, but downright rebellion against that power we have vested them with."[39] The town meeting of Roxbury, Massachusetts, in its resolutions on the constitution of 1780, demanded (successfully, as we have seen) a new constitutional convention to be scheduled for 1795 in order that "the people might recurr to first principles in a Regular Way, without hazarding a Revolution in the Government."[40] And in the same context the town delegates of Essex County, Massachusetts, had registered the opinion in 1778 that "the constitution should make provision, that recourse should constantly be had to those principles within a very small period of years, to rectify the errors that will creep in through lapse of time, or alteration of situations. The want of fixed principles of government, and a stated regular recourse to them, have produced the dissolution of all states, whose constitutions have been transmitted to us by history." The redistribution of seats in the legislature would be one regulation that needed periodic adjustment.[41]

The words chosen by the town of Roxbury and by Essex County to justify their demands for an amending procedure provide one more

37. *Ibid.*, III, 1911.
38. Taylor, ed., *Massachusetts*, 67–68.
39. *Providence Gaz.*, Nov. 23, 1776.
40. Handlin and Handlin, eds., *Popular Sources*, 793.
41. *Ibid.*, 343.

expression of the hope that the revolution of 1776 would make future revolutions in America superfluous. They also remind us of the significance to the founders of a political concept that seems to have been all but totally ignored by historians of political thought in America, the concept of "recurrence to fundamental principles."[42] Virginia's declaration of rights included the phrase, and although the context may be such that the modern reader sees in it little more than a moralistic rhetorical appeal, there can be no doubt the point was taken seriously. "No free government, or the blessings of liberty, can be preserved to any people," the Virginia declaration read, "but by a firm adherence to justice, moderation, temperance, frugality, and virtue, and by frequent recurrence to fundamental principles."[43] Two months later the Pennsylvania declaration of rights announced, "A frequent recurrence to fundamental principles, and a firm adherence to justice, moderation, temperance, industry, and frugality are absolutely necessary to preserve the blessing of liberty, and keep a government free." Pennsylvania drew from these sentiments the practical conclusion that "the people ought therefore to pay particular attention to these points in the choice of officers and representatives and have a right to exact a due and constant regard to them from their legislators and magistrates, in the making and executing such laws as are necessary for the good government of the state."[44] The same train of thought was suggested by the North Carolina declaration of rights, which prescribed in one clause that elections ought to be held often and added in the next that "a frequent recurrence to fundamental principles is absolutely necessary to preserve the blessings of liberty."[45] Massachusetts, finally, followed Pennsylvania's words with only slight stylistic changes.[46]

The point at issue clearly was the relationship between the sovereign people and their elected rulers. Having shifted the source of legitimate government from the grace of God to the sovereignty of the people was not enough to avoid a cycle of oppression and revolution. The people had to insist on a permanent role and be ready to

42. My teacher Gerald Stourzh seems to have been the first scholar to have pointed out and analyzed its significance. See his *Hamilton and Republican Government*, chap. 1.
43. Thorpe, ed., *Constitutions*, VII, 3814, section 15.
44. *Ibid.*, V, 3083–3084.
45. *Ibid.*, 2788.
46. *Ibid.*, III, 1892.

intervene in the political process before it came to a violent halt. This could be achieved by frequent elections and timely reforms of the constitutional system.

The colonists had encountered the demand for recurrence to fundamental principles in English radical Whig writings that called for reform of the corrupt system of parliamentary representation. Reformers like Charles Davenant and James Burgh had insisted that they were not agitating for republican government but for purification of the existing British constitution by reaffirming its original principles. In contrast to the human body, the body politic could escape the cycle of growth and decline, "by wisdom and conduct that is to be made long lived, if not immortal; . . . a mixed government grows young and healthy again, whenever it returns to the principles upon which it was first founded."[47] To enhance their credibility the opposition Whigs referred to the authority of Machiavelli, who in his *Discourses* had advised that "to render a commonwealth long lived, it is necessary to correct it often, and reduce it towards its first principles, which is to be done by punishments and examples."[48]

In the decade before Independence, colonial pamphleteers argued much like the radical Whigs in England, calling for measures to stop the ongoing corruption of the British constitution. In a mixed government of the British kind, and especially in the colonies, John Dickinson wrote in his "Farmer" letters, Machiavelli's advice ought to be heeded that "a state, to be long lived, must be frequently corrected, and reduced to its first principles."[49] During the debate over the question of reconciliation versus independence, both sides made use of Machiavelli's principle, the loyalists saying that the British constitution was not beyond repair and could be brought back to its first principles, and the proponents of independence and new constitutions claiming, "We have it now in our hands . . . to obtain

47. Burgh, *Political Disquisitions*, III, 288–290. On Charles Devanant, whom Burgh quoted here, see Robbins, *Eighteenth-Century Commonwealthman*, 367.
48. Burgh, *Political Disquisitions*, 298. Davenant, whom Burgh was again quoting here, did not give the source of his paraphrase. Machiavelli deals with the question in his *Discorsi*, book 3, chap. 1, under the heading, "To insure a long existence to religious sects or republics, it is necessary frequently to bring them back to their original principles." Niccolò Machiavelli, *The Prince and the Discourses*, ed. Max Lerner (New York, 1940), 397–402. Compare Stourzh, *Hamilton and Republican Government*, 34–36.
49. Letter no. 11, *The Political Writings of John Dickinson* . . . (Wilmington, Del., 1801), I, 256.

substantial justice for the people . . . by carrying back the Constitutions of the several Colonies to their original principles."[50] The colonists could even argue that they were not innovators but defenders of the true old order, of "the ancient Saxon, or English Constitution," and that the time had come to return to it because "all human Constitutions are subject to corruption, and must perish, unless they are *timely renewed* by reducing them to their first principles."[51]

The basic idea had changed little since Machiavelli: a state or political system endures only as long as it does not stray too far from the conditions that had prevailed at its founding. To prevent such departures from the virtues of the founders, Machiavelli had counseled periodic reinforcement of the subjects' fear of their rulers. Above all, the willingness of the citizens to sacrifice, i.e., the exercise of political "virtue," was essential for avoiding corruption and decay. The first American constitutions continued to call for civic virtue and republican frugality. But instead of placing faith in the chance that a great lawgiver or ruler would arise to halt the decay of the system, they institutionalized the process of "reverting to first principles" through the amending procedure and through frequent elections.[52] Neither resistance on the grounds of individual dissent, nor collective violence, was to be the last resort of the sovereign people, but rather constitutional change by the ballot.

Sovereignty Limited by Civil Rights

The "people" in America did not become a collective tyrant because this new sovereign accepted a basic limitation of its powers in the form of bills of rights. That is why Jean Jacques Rousseau, who endowed the majority with unlimited power, provided the majority was acting for the common good—or said it was—went almost unmentioned in the public deliberations on the first American constitu-

50. "Cato," *Pa. Packet*, Apr. 15, 1776; "To The People of Massachusetts," dated Salem, Massachusetts, Sept. 8, 1775, quoted from *American Archives*, 4th Ser., III, 677.

51. Advertisement in *Pa. Packet*, July 15, 1776, for the pamphlet by "Demophilus," *The Genuine Principles of the ancient Saxon, or English Constitution* (Philadelphia, 1776).

52. "To the Electors of Massachusetts," *Thomas's Massachusetts Spy Or, American Oracle of Liberty* (Worcester), May 18, 1776, quoted from Taylor, ed., *Massachusetts*, 35.

tions.[53] The use of a bill of rights to curtail the power of the sovereign majority was a new step in the development of Western constitutionalism. From their origin, bills of rights had imposed limits on rulers. The development of civil rights in England ever since Magna Charta had been carried forward by the struggle of subjects who wanted to place restrictions on the monarch, or, later, on Parliament, and until 1776 the colonists were in a similar situation of opposition to the ruling authority.[54] But with independence the enemy disappeared, and the question arose whether there still was any need for this kind of safeguard against arbitrary power. The dangerous turn that the history of civil rights in America might have taken from then on was spelled out by Alexander Hamilton a decade later when he justified the absence of a bill of rights in the draft of the Federal Constitution with the historically accurate observation, "Bills of rights are, in their origin, stipulations between kings and their subjects, abridgments of prerogative in favor of privilege, reservations of rights not surrendered to the prince. . . . They have no application to constitutions, professedly founded upon the power of the people and executed by their immediate representatives and servants."[55] This conclusion happily was not shared by many. Since 1776, bills of rights had acquired a new function, one that was no less essential in the republican system than it had been under the monarchical. They now not only obliged those in public office to adhere to specific modes of procedure but also delimited certain areas of individual behavior over which the sovereign majority relinquished control.

The state bills of rights were based on the conviction that in cases of conflicting interest, the life, liberty, and property of the individual should have precedence over the will of the majority. The need to keep the sphere of the individual inviolable against governmental power and the will of the majority found concrete expression in catalogs of "inalienable" personal rights. Both the natural law tradition and the theory of social contract provided the intellectual basis for these catalogs.

53. "Un acte de souveraineté . . . ne peut avoir d'autre objet que le bien général"; and "Le pouvoir souverain . . . ne peut pas passer les bornes des conventions générales." Jean Jacques Rousseau, *Du Contrat social; ou, principes du droit politique* . . . (Paris, 1960), 255; also book 2, chap. 4.
54. Zechariah Chafee, Jr., comp. and ed., *Documents on Fundamental Human Rights: The Anglo-American Tradition* (Cambridge, Mass., 1951–1952).
55. Rossiter, ed., *Federalist Papers*, no. 84, 512–513.

The town delegates from Essex County in Massachusetts, in their demand for a state bill of rights, offered an elaborate argument for such a bill. Drawing on the theory of natural law, the Essex spokesmen noted that everyone has in relation to his fellow man two kinds of rights: "alienable rights" and "inalienable rights." Inalienable rights are those that cannot be given up under any circumstances. Among these inalienable rights were "the rights of conscience," i.e., primarily the right to free exercise of religious worship. When an individual enters society, he relinquishes only his alienable rights in the process of creating a "supreme power." In return he is granted security of person and property. The contract becomes void, however, if the people become "slaves," that is, if they cannot maintain control over the supreme power or if the supreme power is not directed toward the common good. The bill of rights was to list all the conditions of the contract in unambiguous language. Through it, the fictitious social contract would take on concrete form.[56]

The practical value of the American bills of rights lay in the fact that they were not merely vague phrases in need of interpretation; rather, they listed casuistically, as in the Ten Commandments, precisely what government and the majority of the voters were not permitted to do. Creating such a list of prohibitions must have been a particularly fascinating project for eighteenth-century rationalists. The knowledge that one lived in a community that had agreed on such a code undoubtedly provided a special feeling of security. The individual could learn from the Ten Commandments what the deity expected of him. From the bill of rights, he could learn what secular authorities could demand of him and what they could not. "The Bill of Rights should contain the great principles of *natural* and *civil liberty*," wrote an anonymous praiser of the Pennsylvania bill of rights. "It should be to a community, what the eternal laws and obligations of morality are to the conscience. It should be unalterable by any human power."[57]

The first constitutions represented only the initial phase in the development of civil rights in the United States. As late as 1780, by which time all of the former colonies had already adopted republican constitutions, not even half of them had also adopted a bill of rights, and in the states that had done so, court decisions based on them—

56. Essex Result, in Handlin and Handlin, eds., *Popular Sources*, 330–332.
57. "Ludlow," *Pa. Jour.*, May 21, 1777.

for instance in slavery cases—were slow in coming.[58] The codification and application of civil rights were part of a political process that had a promising beginning under the favorable conditions of the founding, but a long time would elapse before the value of bills of rights fully emerged in practice.

Popular Sovereignty as the Criterion of Political Radicalism

The development of republican government in the New World was accompanied by conflicts over the claim that political power comes "from below." In the process of working out the first constitutions, a minority was not satisfied with the mere recognition of popular sovereignty as a principle. They demanded that the principle be put into practice more and more extensively by increasing the number of those who would control governmental power.

In the historiographical controversy over the "revolutionary" character of the American Revolution, writers have often warned against a "dichotomous analysis" and have rejected as an oversimplification any sharp division of the various positions "into two clearly defined groups, radical and conservative, more or less constant in composition."[59] Although this point may be granted, there is no doubt that there were certain situations that gave rise to meaningful radical/conservative splits. Because radical and conservative are relative terms, they take their meaning from specific situations in which they describe concrete political options. The task of framing new constitutions created such situations. In the previous phase of the Revolution, resistance to king and Parliament had been the criterion

58. Virginia, Delaware, Pennsylvania, Maryland, North Carolina, and Massachusetts each had a "declaration of rights," which was the formal title for bills of rights. In 1777, the territory of Vermont adopted Pennsylvania's declaration. On the first trials (1781–1783) in Massachusetts in which slavery was allegedly declared incompatible with the declaration of rights, see Arthur Zilversmit, "Quok Walker, Mumbet, and the Abolition of Slavery in Massachusetts," *WMQ*, 3d Ser., XXV (1968), 614–624.

59. Cecelia M. Kenyon, "Republicanism and Radicalism in the American Revolution: An Old-Fashioned Interpretation," *ibid.*, XIX (1962), 155. Oscar and Mary F. Handlin expressed a similar view in "Radicals and Conservatives in Massachusetts after Independence," *NEQ*, XVII (1944), 343–355.

for political radicalism. In the constitution-making phase, willingness to realize popular sovereignty fully, or at least to a greater degree than it had been realized in the past, became the criterion for political radicalism.

The political confessions of a "True Patriot" from New Jersey provide an example of the conservative position that sought to realize the principle of popular sovereignty only to a limited and previously established degree:

There are two extremes in republican governments, which it behoves us carefully to avoid. The one is, that *noble birth, or wealth and riches*, should be considered as an hereditary title to the government of the republic. . . . The other extreme is, that the government be managed by the *promiscuous multitude of the community*, as in some of the States of ancient Greece. . . . The happy medium is, where the people at large have the sole power of annually electing such officers of state as are to be entrusted with the *most invaluable rights, liberties and properties* of the people.[60]

An element of this same conservatism can be found in the position of "Ludlow," quoted in the epigraph to this chapter. This writer insisted on a clear distinction between the *source* of legitimate power, which is rightly the people, and the actual *seat* of that power, which is held by those who govern.

The radicals, on the other hand, feared that new, unrestrained interest groups would undermine the exercise of government for the good the majority. This attitude was strikingly expressed by the warning in the *New-York Journal* a few weeks before Independence. "There are always a number of men in every State who seek to rise above their fellow-creatures, and would be so much above them as to have them and their estates at their disposal, and use them as their footstool to mount to what height they please."[61] Or as the town of Pittsfield, Massachusetts, put it: "As all men are equal by nature, so, when they enter into a state of civil government, they are entitled precisely to the same rights and privileges, or to an equal degree of political happiness."[62] The fact that the radical position was adopted only by a minority does not justify its neglect. The radical minority

60. "A True Patriot," *New-Jersey Gazette* (Trenton), May 12, 1779.
61. "The Interest of America—Letter III," signed "Spartanus," *N.-Y. Jour.*, June 20, 1776, quoted according to *American Archives*, 4th Ser., VI, 995.
62. Pittsfield's instructions to its representative at the constitutional convention, summer 1779, Taylor, ed., *Massachusetts*, 118.

carried enough weight in the framing of the first constitutions to affect the dominant opinion, if only by forcing public discussion of previously unquestioned convictions.

The differences in attitude toward the exact application of the ideal of popular sovereignty we also find expressed in the debate over related concepts and issues, particularly the ideals of liberty and equality, the protection of private property from the arbitrary action of the majority, equal representation, the distribution of powers among the different organs of government, and the establishment of a federal government. To these questions the following chapters will be devoted.

CHAPTER VII

Liberty

The idea of liberty has been held up in so dazzling colours, that some of us may not be willing to submit to that subordination necessary in the freest States.

Essex Result, 1778

There are many very noisy about liberty, but are aiming at nothing more than personal grandeur and power. . . . The people are now contending for freedom; and would to God they might not only obtain, but likewise keep it in their own hands.

The People the Best Governors, 1776

An Asylum for Which Liberty?

In the new political order the Americans developed, popular sovereignty was the principle of legitimation that subsumed all others under it, but freedom or liberty was the preeminent goal of political action. The colonists were told they were fighting for more than political independence; they were defending the ideal of liberty itself. "We do not fight for a few acres of land," the New York house of representatives proclaimed in 1776, "but for freedom—for the freedom and happiness of millions yet unborn."[1] Freedom or liberty, used interchangeably, was the battle cry as well as the unrivaled central concept in the founding fathers' vision of the future.

With each new measure that England had taken to tighten her hold over her American possessions, the conviction had grown for many colonists that freedom in the English sense had been destroyed everywhere else in the world and that its last bastion was now under siege. In his classic statement on this theme, Thomas Paine captured

1. Dec. 23, 1776, "Address of the Convention of the Representatives of the State of New York to Their Constituents," Johnston, ed., *Jay Papers,* I, 103, 113.

both the colonists' sense of foreboding and their confidence that they were destined to meet the threat: "Every spot of the old world is over-run with oppression. Freedom hath been hunted round the globe. Asia and Africa have long expelled her. Europe regards her like a stranger, and England hath given her warning to depart. O! receive the fugitive, and prepare in time an asylum for mankind."[2]

The idea of an asylum for liberty was not new, either in the colonies or in Europe. We find words similar to Paine's even in sermons, such as the one delivered by Pastor Samuel Williams of Massachusetts many months before *Common Sense* appeared. Most of mankind was subservient to a tiny minority of absolute monarchs, the idea of liberty was unknown in Asia and Africa, and its flame was now being extinguished in Europe, too, Williams had preached. Sweden and Poland, he observed, had lost their liberty within a year of each other, and the free German cities would not enjoy their free-dom a day longer than it pleased their powerful neighbors. Holland still subscribed to the forms of freedom, but its spirit was no longer alive there. Switzerland was the only country that still enjoyed a full measure of liberty.[3] Presbyterian pastor John Joachim Zubly, who was Swiss born and a delegate from Georgia to the Continental Congress, held the same view. In a sermon published in 1775 in both English and German he noted that Asia, Africa, and the South Ameri-can continent were not free and cautioned that efforts were under way to abolish this birthright of man on the North American conti-nent also.[4] The image of America as the land of the free did not originate with Paine, Williams, and Zubly, however. They all drew on a figure of speech that had been in currency since at least the first half of their century.[5]

But what practical shape would liberty take in the land of the free? To many it was obvious that the new system of government should be that of a "free republic." The house of representatives of Massachusetts had asked in May 1776 whether the towns of the

2. Paine, *Common Sense*, in Foner, ed., *Writings of Paine*, I, 30, 31.
3. Samuel Williams, *A Discourse on the Love of Our Country* . . . (Salem, Mass., 1775), quoted in Bailyn, ed., *Pamphlets of the American Revolution*, I, 82.
4. John Joachim Zubly, *Eine Kurzgefasste Historische Nachricht von Den Kämpfen Der Schweitzer für Die Freyheit* (Philadelphia, 1775), 1. Translated as *The Law of Liberty: A Sermon on American Affairs* (Philadelphia, 1775). See also, "Caracta-cus," *Pa. Packet*, Oct. 31, 1774.
5. Bailyn, *Ideological Origins*, 138–141, esp. n. 42.

colony would support a declaration of independence issued by the Continental Congress. Several replies of town meetings explicitly called for "a Free and Independent Republic" and for "independence and a free republic."[6] Constitutional drafts published anonymously in newspapers also combined the two concepts of liberty and republican government. The *Boston Gazette* of July 12, 1779, began its suggestions for a constitution by announcing that it would first list "the principles of a free Republican form of Government." The *New-York Journal* wrote in June 1776: "It is proposed that we should form into a free popular Government."[7] The delegates of Mecklenburg County in North Carolina were instructed by their electorate to "endeavor to establish a free government under the authority of the people."[8] The Massachusetts constitutional convention of 1779 resolved unanimously that "the government to be framed by this convention shall be a Free Republic."[9]

The close combination of liberty and republican government was prompted by the fear that popular government threatened to degenerate either into "mobocracy" or "aristocracy." The half-literate anonymous pamphlet with the programmatic title *The People the Best Governors* expressed fears of a republican aristocracy: "There are many very noisy about liberty, but are aiming at nothing more than personal grandeur and power. . . . The people are now contending for freedom; and would to God they might not only obtain, but likewise keep it in their own hands." To this unknown author, extending the right to vote and establishing unicameral legislatures were necessary precautions to safeguard liberty.[10] On the other hand, fear of dis-

6. House resolve of May 10, 1776; reply of the town of Acton, June 14, 1776, Mass. Archives, CLVI, fol. 108; reply from Pittsfield quoted according to Richard Frothingham, *The Rise of the Republic of the United States* (Boston, 1872), 507–508.

7. *Boston-Gazette, and Country Journal*, July 12, 1779; "The Interest of America —Letter III," *N.-Y. Jour.*, June 20, 1776, also in *American Archives*, 4th Ser., VI, 994.

8. Nov. 1, 1776, "Instructions to the Delegates from Mecklenburg to the Provincial Congress at Halifax in November, 1776," Saunders, ed., *N.C. Col. Recs.*, X, 870a.

9. Adams, ed., *Works of John Adams*, IV, 215.

10. *The People The Best Governors: Or A Plan Of Government Founded On The Just Principles Of Natural Freedom* (n.p., 1776), in Frederick Chase, *A History of Dartmouth College and the Town of Hanover, New Hampshire*, ed. John K. Lord, I (Cambridge, Mass., 1891), 654, 662.

orderly and arbitrary government by the mob was expressed by the delegates of Essex County, Massachusetts. They reminded the authors of the rejected draft of the state constitution that "all republics are not Free."[11]

The great challenge the colonial leaders faced was to demonstrate that republican government could protect freedom of speech, religious toleration, and other civil rights at least as effectively as limited monarchy had done in Britain. Loyalists and European skeptics doubted that republican government would be as tolerant as the balanced British system had been.

English Liberties and the Debate on Colonial Government and Independence

Ever since the revolution of 1688, not only English patriots but also many political commentators in Europe looked upon the English constitution as the freest in the world, and well into the year 1776 numerous articles and pamphlets in the colonies continued to praise the English constitution because it protected freedom better than any other.[12] The opponents of independence exploited this assumption for their own use and argued that freedom would be lost under an independent American regime. The removal of the constraints imposed by the British constitutional tradition would result in domination by the capricious will of the people. The main reply to Paine's critique of the British constitution, therefore, was the assertion that for all its defects this constitution effectively guaranteed the liberty of a British subject. Moreover, it was pointed out, the republican experiment in England in the seventeenth century had utterly failed. One "Cato," for example, writing in the *Pennsylvania Packet* in 1776, cited Montesquieu's definition of political liberty—"that tranquillity or peace of mind arising from the opinion each person has of his safety"—and doubted that a government without a king could guarantee this kind of security. Paine himself, Cato reminded his readers, had called the House of Commons "the new Republican materials" of the English system, yet the colonists complained bitterly of its policies. This fact, Cato concluded, ought to teach the colonists that unbalanced republican government could easily become a source of

11. Essex Result, in Handlin and Handlin, eds., *Popular Sources*, 330.
12. See Introduction, pp. 11–13.

tyranny rather than the guardian of liberty.[13] Another loyalist asserted that limited monarchy was still most conducive to liberty, even if an occasional "crackbrained zealot for democracy" failed to understand that truth. Still another, using Holland as an example, claimed that the citizens of a republic could lose their freedom more quickly than the subjects of a constitutionally limited monarch; for despite the blood shed in the struggle for freedom there, the people of Holland now no longer enjoyed liberty. This same view of the English constitution was reflected in appeals to the colonists to support the king's troops because the Redcoats were fighting for "British Liberties."[14]

But the debates among the colonists incorporated more than the traditional Whig argument that the separation of powers and the interdependence of crown, lords, and commons guaranteed freedom. The colonists also drew on the English radical Whigs' denunciation of the growing discrepancy between constitutional theory and political practice. From the radicals' point of view the concentration of power in the hands of the king and his ministers and the increasing corruption of the members of Parliament had already resulted in the erosion of liberty in England. Trenchard and Gordon's *Cato's Letters*, that most powerful expression of radical Whig thinking in the 1720s, parts of which were repeatedly reprinted in colonial newspapers, argued that those in power always strive to increase that power and that a people must remain constantly vigilant to preserve its freedom against this incessant political greed. The English system, Trenchard and Gordon conceded, was a free government because there were "Checks and Restraints appointed and expressed in the Constitution itself."[15] But they demanded more than constitutional limitation of

13. "To the People of Pennsylvania—Letter VII," signed "Cato," *Pa. Packet*, Apr. 11, 1776, also in *American Archives*, 4th Ser., V, 851–852. Similar warnings were expressed in [James Chalmers], *Plain Truth; Addressed To The Inhabitants of America* . . . (Philadelphia, 1776), 1, and the *Pennsylvania Ledger: or the Virginia, Maryland, Pennsylvania, and New-Jersey Weekly Advertiser* (Philadelphia), Apr. 6, 1776.

14. Inglis, *True Interest of America*, 52–53; "Rationalis," *Pennsylvania Gazette* (Philadelphia), Feb. 28, 1776; also in *American Archives*, 4th Ser., IV, 1527–1529; "Z." in *Rivington's New York Loyal Gazette*, Nov. 8, 1777.

15. John Trenchard and Thomas Gordon, *Cato's Letters; or, Essays on Liberty, Civil and Religious, And other important Subjects*, 3d ed. (London, 1733), II, 214, letter no. 59 of Dec. 30, 1721. The importance of these four volumes of radical Whig writing for political debate in the colonies was first pointed out by

governmental powers. They claimed a "natural right" of the individual to liberty; liberty defined comprehensively as "the Power which every Man has over his own Actions, and his Right to enjoy the Fruits of his Labour, Art, and Industry, as far as by it he hurts not the Society, or any Members of it, by taking from any Member, or by hindering him from enjoying what he himself enjoys." Trenchard and Gordon's broad understanding of liberty included "the Right of every Man to pursue the natural, reasonable, and religious Dictates of his own Mind; to think what he will, and act as he thinks, provided he acts not to the Prejudice of another."[16]

A generation later, writers like Joseph Priestley and Richard Price, who were heirs to the radical tradition of Trenchard and Gordon, expanded the concept of liberty by adding to the conventional idea of "civil liberty" that of "political liberty." Priestley defined the former as "that power over their own actions, which the members of the state reserve to themselves and which their officers must not infringe," and as "the right [a man] has to be exempt from the control of the society, or its agents; that is, the power he has of providing for his own advantage and happiness." Every individual, Priestley claimed, was entitled to a certain area of privacy where he was safe from the interference not only of the government but of his fellow subjects. But in addition, there was the more active kind of freedom, political liberty, which he defined as the possibility "of arriving at public offices; or at least, of having votes in the nomination of those who fill them." Political liberty, Priestley said, could therefore also be called "the right of magistracy," and it included the chance for any member of the state "to have his private opinion or judgment become that of the public, and thereby control the actions of others." Men who are by their birth or fortune excluded from public offices, or from voting for persons to fill them, may enjoy civil liberty, but no political liberty because they have "no share in the government."[17]

After the outbreak of the War of Independence, Priestley's politi-

---

Clinton Rossiter, *Seedtime of the Republic*, 141. See also the modern selection by David L. Jacobson, ed., *The English Libertarian Heritage: From the Writings of John Trenchard and Thomas Gordon in* The Independent Whig *and* Cato's Letters (Indianapolis, Ind., 1965), and Stourzh, *Hamilton and Republican Government*, 229, n. 99.

16. Trenchard and Gordon, *Cato's Letters*, II, 244, 248, letter no. 62 of Jan. 20, 1721.

17. Priestley, *First Principles of Government*, 12–14.

cal ally Richard Price, in a pamphlet that went through at least ten printings in London in 1776 and was immediately reprinted in Philadelphia, New York, and Boston, also emphasized the active element in the four types of liberty that he distinguished. In physical as well as in moral, religious, and civil liberty, "there is one general idea, that runs through them all," he wrote, "the idea of *Self-direction* or *Self-government*."[18]

These English critics of the ruling Whig factions were often more articulate and daring than their colonial counterparts, and we have to take their political language into account when we try to comprehend the thinking of the authors of the American constitutional documents of 1776. It seems quite probable that their usage at least contributed to the colonists' abandonment of the language of feudal constitutional law, which spoke of "Liberties, Privileges, Franchises, and Immunities," and their subsequent adoption of the more modern concept of political liberty as the right to self-direction.[19]

Liberty and Liberties in the State Constitutions

The Declaration of Independence and several of the American bills of rights proclaimed liberty to be a "right" of every man. "All men are by nature equally free and independent," read the classic statement in the first of them, the Virginia bill of rights. They "have certain inherent rights, of which, . . . they cannot, by any compact, deprive or divest their posterity; namely, the enjoyment of life and liberty, with the means of acquiring and possessing property, and pursuing

18. Richard Price, *Observations on the Nature of Civil Liberty, the Principles of Government, and the Justice and Policy of the War with America* (London, 1776), 2–3. John Adams accepted Price's definitions as his own. Adams, ed., *Works of John Adams*, IV, 401. The *Connecticut Courant, and Hartford Weekly Intelligencer* printed Price's pamphlet in serial form from July 29 to Sept. 16, 1776. In an advertisement, the printer said he had chosen the serial form in hopes of achieving wider distribution for the pamphlet, even though he would have made more money if he had published it in its entirety as a reprint. Excerpts appeared in the *Md. Gaz.* on Aug. 22 and Dec. 19, 1776, as well as in other newspapers.

19. Resolution of the Virginia House of Burgesses against the Stamp Act, May 30, 1765, in Edmund S. Morgan, ed., *Prologue to Revolution: Sources and Documents on the Stamp Act Crisis, 1764–1766* (Chapel Hill, N.C., 1959), 47.

and obtaining happiness and safety."[20] In contrast to the Declaration of Independence, this formulation did not invoke a divine source of this right but rested its claim on secular natural law and social contract thinking. Pennsylvania adopted Virginia's draft after making a few editorial changes.[21] Delaware's declaration of rights did not speak of all men but only of "every Member of Society" who has a right to be protected in the enjoyment of "Life, Liberty and Property." In the article guaranteeing trial by jury as "one of the greatest Securities of the Lives, Liberties and Estates of the People," the same document used the plural version of the concept, which was more familiar to lawyers trained in English medieval constitutional law.[22] The medieval form clearly had changed its content and had come to be used interchangeably with the more abstract singular modern version of individual liberty. This fact is also illustrated by the Massachusetts bill of rights, drafted by as thorough a scholar of English constitutional law as John Adams. Without invoking divine authority, he declared as one of the "natural, essential, and unalienable rights" of all men "the right of enjoying and defending their lives and liberties." But in the clause that guaranteed an independent judiciary Adams used the classical Lockean triad in the singular version of "life, liberty, property."[23]

The active component of the modern concept of liberty as political self-determination found clear expression in the Maryland bill of rights and in that of Delaware, which declared that "the Right in the People to participate in the Legislature, is the Foundation of Liberty and of all free Government."[24]

The practical potential of these statements of principle was not lost on their authors and other contemporaries. We know of opposi-

20. Thorpe, ed., *Constitutions*, VII, 3813.

21. *Ibid.*, VI, 3082.

22. *Convention of the Delaware State*, 18–19. On the plural and singular forms of the concept, Harold Laski observed, "Until the end of the fifteenth century, roughly, the defense of particular liberties against the invasion by external authority was the work of a functional group, such as the barons of Runnymede or the merchants of London. In this period liberty may be said to have resolved itself into a system of liberties or customary negative rights which were bought and sold between the parties for hard cash." *Encyclopedia of the Social Sciences*, IX, 442.

23. Thorpe, ed., *Constitutions*, III, 1889, 1893.

24. *Convention of the Delaware State*, 18, and Thorpe, ed., *Constitutions*, III, 1687.

tion to the liberty clause in the convention that drafted the Virginia bill of rights.[25] And exgovernor Hutchinson of Massachusetts, suffering an exile's fate in London, pounced on the liberty clause of the Declaration of Independence in order to show up the inconsistencies of the revolutionaries. In a pamphlet published in London he asked the representatives of the slave states in the Continental Congress how they reconciled this confession of political belief with the continuation of slaveholding.[26] In America itself opponents of slavery also made full use of the liberty clauses in their rhetoric, but only the Vermont constitution drew the practical conclusion from these express principles and went ahead to outlaw slavery.[27]

Other specific liberties protected by the first constitutions, in addition to the previously mentioned trial by jury and the right to elect representatives, were freedom of the press and freedom of religion.[28] It would be wrong, however, to count the separation of state and church as one of the achievements of 1776. An important step was taken in that after 1776 the freedom to exercise one's religion in private was constitutionally guaranteed. But it was not until later decades that this tolerance was transformed into such concrete measures as the abolition of universal taxes for the support of state churches and the permission for non-Protestant religious groups to worship in public, and that a number of other detailed enactments were passed truly disestablishing state churches and finally achieving a genuine separation of civil and religious authority. The prohibition of religious tests in the Federal Constitution of 1787 referred only to federal offices. In most states, oaths of office for public officials continued well into the nineteenth century to include various religious clauses that automatically prevented non-Protestants from holding public office.[29]

25. Thomas Ludwell Lee to Richard Henry Lee, June 1, 1776, in Kate Mason Rowland, *The Life of George Mason, 1725–1792* (New York, 1892), I, 240. See also p. 175 below.
26. Hutchinson, *Declaration of the Congress*, ed. Freiberg, 11.
27. Philip F. Detweiler, "Congressional Debate on Slavery and the Declaration of Independence, 1819–1821," *AHR*, LXIII (1957–1958), 598–616; Thorpe, ed., *Constitutions*, VI, 3739–3740.
28. See Leonard William Levy, *Legacy of Suppression: Freedom of Speech and Press in Early American History* (Cambridge, Mass., 1960), and Levy, ed., *Freedom of the Press from Zenger to Jefferson: Early American Libertarian Theories* (Indianapolis, Ind., 1966).
29. Anson Phelps Stokes and Leo Pfeffer, *Church and State in the United States,*

Liberty and Law

The founding generation's understanding of liberty was by no means dominated by the potential of the concept to compel change and to inspire reforms such as an expansion of popular participation in the political process. The innovative impulse was balanced by a concern for order and stability. When the new leaders began curbing the plebiscitarian element, they found themselves in a situation similar to that of most leaders of political revolutions, that is, attempting to call a halt to the process of rapid change and violence without at the same time betraying the origins of the movement that put them in power. The American leaders justified this cessation by pointing out that under the new republican governments the laws were clearly of the people's own making and therefore only by obeying them could the people find true liberty. They were "free not from the law, but by the law."[30] Or, in the words of the constitutional convention of Massachusetts, "It is of the essence of a free republic, that the people be governed by Fixed Laws Of Their Own Making."[31]

The interdependence of liberty and law was a strong element in Anglo-American constitutionalism that the colonial leaders saw no reason to give up. For several generations liberty had been contrasted with licentiousness in English political debate. In addition, defenders of republican government had frequently defined its essential characteristic as "the rule of law" or *imperium legum non hominum*, rather than as the mere absence of a king.[32] In Europe, the phrase had come to be used as a major argument against the arbitrariness of absolutist government; in America it soon was in use as a standard argument

---

rev. ed. (New York, 1964); William G. McLoughlin, *New England Dissent, 1630–1833: The Baptists and the Separation of Church and State* (Cambridge, Mass., 1971); Bailyn, *Ideological Origins*, 246–272; Sydney E. Ahlstrom, *A Religious History of the American People* (New Haven, Conn., 1972), 379–380.

30. *The Freeholder's Political Catechism. Very necessary to be studied by every Freeman in America* (London and New York, 1769), 2–3. On the authorship of the *Catechism* and on excerpts from it that appeared in the *Virginia Gazettes* in 1770 and 1775, see Duff, "Case against the King," *WMQ*, 3d Ser., VI (1949), 392.

31. Adams, ed., *Works of John Adams*, IV, 215.

32. For example, Trenchard and Gordon, *Cato's Letters*, II, 25–26, letter no. 36 of July 8, 1721; John Adams in *Thoughts on Government*, in Adams, ed., *Works of John Adams*, IV, 194; see also, pp. 204, 230, 401–402. Compare Stourzh, *Hamilton and Republican Government*, 56–63.

against the arbitrariness of the new ruler, the majority of voters. The Massachusetts bill of rights perfectly expressed the new function of the ancient formula when it equated "government of laws" with the separation of powers and thereby with the rejection of an all-powerful one-chamber legislature.[33]

The rule of law, and with it the great powers of an independent judiciary, thus became from the very beginning a countervailing power to the plebiscitarian component in the American system of republican government. Its effectiveness in this role was strikingly illustrated in February 1776 when popular demands for relief measures to help the indebted farmers in western Massachusetts and the Connecticut River valley were parodied in the *Connecticut Journal*. To discredit calls for the postponement of court trials and for the suspension of imprisonment of farmers for debt, the newspaper published a mock resolution that proclaimed in stilted language that in future debts would be paid "by inclination" only and that from now on liberty meant "liberty without law."[34]

Liberty and Property

The linking of liberty and property, long taken for granted, began to break down during the American Revolution. Before the Declaration of Independence, political rhetoric had combined the two catchwords in a single appeal: England threatened the colonists' liberty and property to the same degree. One could not exist without the other. If property were not secure, freedom could not exist. But debate on the new constitutions brought into the open the inherent conflict between these two values. Locke's triad of life, liberty, and property seemed increasingly problematic, and even the modified version of it in the Declaration of Independence—life, liberty, and the pursuit of happiness—could not disguise this conflict.

The increasing awareness of the tensions between the ideal of

33. Article XXX, Thorpe, ed., *Constitutions*, III, 1893. R. A. Humphreys, "The Rule of Law and the American Revolution," *Law Quarterly Review*, LIII (1937), 80–98, equates the rule of law with appeals to "natural law." I find the evidence for such an interpretation unpersuasive.
34. *Conn. Jour.*, Feb. 28, 1776. The parody was prefaced with a quotation from Mark 5:9: "And the Devil answered, saying my name is Legion, for we are many."

political liberty and the ideal of fully protected private property can easily be recognized in the rhetoric of the Revolutionary period. Gouverneur Morris, the outspoken representative of New York's social and political elite, provides a remarkable example in his speech on government before the provincial congress of his state in 1776 or early 1777. He exposed as unrealistic and naive the belief that "political liberty" was compatible with the social conditions necessary for the development of commerce. Morris rejected Rousseauistic dreams of "natural liberty." Members of civilized society could demand no more than "political liberty," i.e., the right to approve or disapprove by voting on governmental measures. And even perfect political liberty was impossible because that could exist only where all laws were agreed to by everybody who would be affected by them. History showed how unrealistic this view was. The *liberum veto* of the Polish aristocracy, for example, had not created a free state, and, in any case, nine-tenths of the Polish population was not included. Morris did not think the English constitution guaranteed political freedom either anymore, because it had become a matter of chance whether king, lords, and commons paid any attention to the approval or disapproval of those affected by their laws. Morris therefore regarded political liberty in the strict sense as impracticable in any advanced society. Perhaps the Mohawk and Oneida tribes could still sit down together around their campfires, but the Confederation of the Six Nations had to submit to the decisions reached by the majority of the sachems.

Perfect political liberty also conflicted directly with the necessities of commerce, Morris argued:

Where political Liberty is in Excess Property must be insecure and where Property is not secured Society cannot advance. . . . The most rapid advances in the State of Society are produced by Commerce. . . . Commerce once begun is from its own Nature progressive. It may be crippled or destroyed not fixed. It requires not only the perfect Security of Property but perfect good faith. . . . If the public be in Debt to an Individual political Liberty enables a Majority to cancel the Obligation, but the Spirit of Commerce exacts punctual Payment. In a Despotism everything must bend to the Prince. He can seize the Property of his Subject but the spirit of Commerce requires that Property be sacred. It requires also that every Citizen have the Right freely to use his Property.

Developing this latter assumption, Morris concluded that political liberty should exist only to the extent that it did not infringe upon civil liberty, i.e., the "civil or social Right" of each citizen to dispose of his property. Political liberty could serve to protect civil liberty, but it should only be a means to that end. If the freedom to dispose of one's property is cramped by the principle of political liberty, then the end has been sacrificed to the means. Devices such as the separation of powers and the system of mutual checks and balances of organs of government, Morris argued, are necessary to prevent political liberty from destroying itself. Morris shared with Adam Smith the belief that unimpeded commerce is the spring of civilization and progress; going beyond Smith, he perceived a new variant of government interference in America, that of an all-powerful popular government.[35]

Morris was better known for bluntness than for originality as a political thinker, and it is likely that he articulated a fear that was widely felt among the commerce-oriented merchants, farmers, and land speculators whom the politics of the Revolution and the war itself had made acutely aware of their dependence on the behavior of the general population. To these groups, freedom of commerce and property rights were not subordinate to the revolutionary ideal of political liberty but were of equal, and in case of conflict probably of greater, value.

The tension between property rights and political liberty also became apparent in the controversies over equal representation, i.e., in the struggle of newly settled areas to gain seats in the state legislatures. Basing the distribution of seats on the amount of property taxes collected in a town or county was rejected by the poorer regions with the argument: "Taxation only respects property, without regard to the liberties of a person; and if representation should be wholly limited by that, the man who owns six times as much as another would consequently have six times the power, though their natural right to freedom is the same."[36] This issue was sometimes moderated by the compromise of having one legislative chamber represent property and another represent people. But in this way the conflict between the ideals of liberty and property rights was not resolved, only institutionalized.

It would be quite wrong, however, to overemphasize the divisive function of the ideal of liberty after the Revolution. Under the banner

35. The text of the speech was first published as an appendix to W. P. Adams, "'Spirit of Commerce,'" *Amerikastudien/American Studies*, XXI (1976), 309–334, quotations from pp. 329–331.
36. *People the Best Governors*, in Chase, *History of Dartmouth College*, I, 657–658.

of "liberty" Americans of all classes united to conquer the continent. Liberty to them was above all the freedom to take possession of the American continent in their own way and to their own—not to a European power's—advantage, and liberty soon evolved into an incantation of future prosperity and expansion.

CHAPTER VIII

Equality

---

*Superior degrees of industry and capacity, and above all, com-
merce, have introduced inequality of property among us, and
these have introduced natural distinctions of rank in Pennsylvania, as certain and general as the artificial distinctions of men
in Europe.*

"Ludlow," *Pennsylvania Journal*, May 28, 1777

The Revolutionary convention that adopted Virginia's bill of rights on
June 12, 1776, declared: "All men are by nature equally free and independent." And on July 4, 1776, when the Continental Congress in
Philadelphia announced the end of colonial status for thirteen English
colonies, it proclaimed: "All men are created equal." Nonetheless,
eleven years later George Mason, who wrote the sentence just cited
from the Virginia bill of rights, was the owner of 118 slaves. Thomas
Jefferson, author of the Declaration of Independence, owned 149.
George Washington, already glorified as the victorious commander-
in-chief in the War of Independence and, like Mason and Jefferson, a
citizen of Virginia, owned 390 slaves.[1] Moreover, the new state constitutions codified suffrage laws that made the right to vote dependent on wealth, and they denied the vote to large numbers of white
males because of church affiliation.

The contrast between rhetoric and reality prompts us to ask what
moved the leadership of 1776, to which Mason, Jefferson, and Washington belonged, to espouse the postulate of equality so deliberately
and vigorously. Even if we wanted to depict the leading American
whigs as rapacious, power hungry, hypocritical bourgeois, we would
still have to explain why they chose these words rather than some
other political rhetoric to disguise their true motives and interests.
Why did they choose to emphasize the postulate of equality in the
new nation's canon of values and thus provide their political oppo-

---

1. Jackson T. Main, "The One Hundred," *WMQ*, 3d Ser., XI (1954), 354–384.

nents with an argument that would soon be turned against them? To say that the founding fathers' espousal of equality did not amount to an advocacy of "social leveling" although it expressed their conflicting feelings toward this "beautiful but ambiguous ideal" describes the conflict between word and deed, but hardly offers an explanation for it.[2] How did the postulate of equality acquire its status as one of the most significant articles of belief formulated in 1776?

Equality in the Empire

Between 1763 and 1776 the political leadership in the colonies adopted the postulate of equality as part of its active vocabulary because it provided a most effective argument for justifying resistance to colonial rule. They could make good use of the postulate because in 1688 the English Whigs had adopted the concepts of a social contract and of a contract between ruler and subjects, and as part of it the principle of equality had become part of English constitutional theory. Social contract thinking implicitly repudiated the existence of second-class citizens under the name of colonists. If all citizens voluntarily joined society with the same need for protection, then it was unjust that some citizens claimed more rights than others once the contract was closed. Even though Locke did not explicitly call for the full realization of equality—he did not demand, for example, any more than the Levellers did, that everyone have the right to vote—the postulate of equality was inherent in the logic of social contract thinking. As one of its basic elements, it could not be ignored for long.[3]

As early as 1762, in the last year of the war that France and England fought over colonial territories in North America, James Otis, a prominent lawyer and a member of the Massachusetts legislature, was already publicly arguing along the same lines as the Continental Congress would be twelve years later. The insignificance of the incident that prompted Otis's statements indicates how strained

2. Gordon S. Wood, *The Creation of the American Republic, 1776–1787* (Chapel Hill, N.C., 1969), 70, 71, 73, 75. See also, Richard B. Morris, *The Emerging Nations and the American Revolution* (New York, 1970), 20–25.
3. What Heinz Kläy has said of Rousseau is equally true of Locke; his ahistorical concept of a "social contract" provided the theoretical basis for sharing political rights equally among all members of society, because everyone enters into the contract as an equal partner. *Zensuswahlrecht und Gleichheitsprinzip* (Bern, 1956), 21.

relations had become between the inhabitants and the colonial administration: the governor of Massachusetts had decided to increase the crew of a warship from six men to twenty-four. Arguing that the governor had frequently acted without consulting the assembly and had thereby incurred additional expenses, the legislature refused to give retroactive approval to the decision. According to the town delegates, the governor was disregarding the fiscal prerogatives of the provincial parliament and had gone a long way toward despotism. The governor in return demanded that the assembly reverse its stand, on the grounds that it contained an insult to the king. The assembly responded that if George III collected taxes or funds resembling taxes without the approval of the parliament, he would be a tyrant like Louis XV. Otis's pamphlet justified the assembly's position by fully articulating the premises on which it had built its case:

1. God made all men naturally equal.
2. The ideas of earthly superiority, preheminence and grandeur are educational, at least acquired, not innate.
3. Kings were (and plantation Governor's should be) made for the good of the people, and not the people for them.
4. No government has a right to make hobby horses, asses and slaves of the subject, nature having made sufficient of the two former, for all the lawful purposes of man, from the harmless peasant in the field, to the most refined politician in the cabinet; but none of the last, which infallibly proves they are unnecessary.
5. Tho' most governments are *de facto* arbitrary, and consequently the curse and scandal of human nature; yet none are *de jure* arbitrary.[4]

Otis buttressed his argument with long quotations from Locke's *Second Treatise of Government* and concluded that legitimate government can originate only with the consent of a free people. He also anticipated objections from the governor's followers: "It is possible there are a few, and I desire to thank God there is no reason to think there are many among us, that can't bear the name of Liberty and Property, much less that the things signified by those terms, should be enjoyed by the vulgar. These may be inclined to brand some of the principles advanced in the vindication of the house, with the odious epithets *seditious* and *levelling*."[5] Otis's words revealed with unusual clarity the

4. James Otis, *A Vindication of the Conduct of the House of Representatives of the Province of the Massachusetts-Bay* (Boston, 1762), 15, 17–20.
5. *Ibid.*, 17–20.

linking of "sedition," or resistance against colonial rule, with differences of opinion among the colonists about the share that the lower classes should have in political freedom and in property. Colonial whig leaders like Otis did not call for more social equality. But they observed with some complacency the degree to which property had come to be distributed in North America, and they pointed out that in the colonies the claim of the common man to freedom and property was more widely recognized than in Britain.

Otis's explanation of the assembly's political beliefs clearly indicates the fundamental position the colonists gave the postulate of equality. It comes first on his list for the same reason that it would be listed first in the Declaration of Independence. Its function is the same in both cases: the inhabitants of the colonies insisted on equality with the inhabitants of the home country and, indeed, all Europeans. "The colonists, being men, have a right to be considered as equally entitled to all the rights of nature with the Europeans," Otis declared during the Stamp Act crisis. At the same time, however, Otis cautioned against applying the principle of equality in domestic politics. He thought "equality and the power of the whole," taken as principles for the organization of government, were as dangerous as oligarchy or monarchy. In his view, only a very small society could base its form of government on one of these "simple" principles. A larger society would have to introduce some mixed form containing elements of all three.[6]

The anticolonial function of the postulate of equality was still more evident in a pamphlet Richard Bland published in 1766 opposing the Stamp Act. Bland, a long-standing member of the Virginia House of Burgesses, emphasized that the English colonies in North America were not conquered territories whose inhabitants could be dominated by the victor according to the rules of war and forced to pay tribute. English citizens had settled the colonies in full possession of their civil rights.[7] Bland therefore rejected restrictive commercial

6. James Otis, *The Rights of the British Colonies Asserted and proved* (Boston, 1764), 30, 14. On the colonists' awareness of the advantages of the English constitution as a mixed form of government, see chap. 12 below.
7. Pamphleteers on the colonists' side made use of their knowledge of the classics by pointing out that North America was not a conquered territory with a native population but consisted of colonies in the Greek sense. Defenders of parliamentary sovereignty rejected the parallels with the ancient world as anachronistic. Furthermore, they objected, the Roman "coloniae"

and shipping laws because they discriminated against merchants in the colonies and thus "constituted an unnatural Difference between Men under the same Allegiance, born equally free, and entitled to the same civil Rights." Bland turned to his own purpose an argument that British Secretary of the Treasury Thomas Whately had recently used in defense of the Stamp Act. If it were true, as Whately had said, that the colonists were not a separate people, then there could be no discriminatory laws for them: "If 'the *British* Empire in *Europe* and in *America* is the same *Power,*' if the 'Subjects in both are the same People, and all equally participate in the Adversity and Prosperity of the Whole,' what Distinctions can the Difference of their Situations make, and why is this Distinction made between them?"[8] Also writing in support of resistance to the Stamp Act was John Adams, a young lawyer and fledgling politician, who said in the *Boston Gazette* that the English constitution was the freest in the world. It was based, he claimed, on the principle that not the king nor the aristocracy nor the wealthy had inherited the world or had the right to exploit the rest. According to the inviolable laws of God and of nature, the lowliest people have the same right to air, nourishment, and clothing that any other people have: "All men are born equal; and the drift of the British constitution is to preserve as much of this equality as is compatible with the people's security against foreign invasions and domestic usurpation."[9] Adams's view was shared by physician Joseph Warren, who attributed the violent rejection of the Stamp Act to the broad distribution of property in America, "in consequence of which . . . influence and authority must be nearly equal, and every man will think himself deeply interested in the support of public liberty." American society, Warren thought, was quite different from feudal Europe:

In many old countries . . . in a long course of years, some particular families have been able to acquire a very large share of property, from which must arise a kind of aristocracy: that is, the power and authority of some persons

---

did not enjoy all the rights of Roman citizens; they obeyed Roman laws and served in the legions but were not entitled to vote. [Martin Howard], *A Letter From A Gentlemen at Halifax . . .* (Newport, R.I., 1765), 14–15.

8. Richard Bland, *An Inquiry into the Rights of the British Colonies . . .* (Williamsburg, Va., 1766), 13–14, 18, 23, 25. See also, David S. Lovejoy, "Rights Imply Equality: The Case against Admiralty Jurisdiction in America, 1764–1776," *WMQ*, 3d Ser., XVI (1959), 459–484.

9. Adams, ed., *Works of John Adams*, III, 480.

or families is exercised in proportion to the decrease of the independence and property of the people in general. Had America been prepared in this manner for the Stamp Act, it might perhaps have met with a more favorable reception; but it is absurd to attempt to impose so cruel a yoke on a people who are so near to the state of original equality.[10]

Warren thus countered the European idea of an inferior colonial status with the colonists' pride in a society still close to the state of nature, a society of the free and relatively equal.

Ten years before the Declaration of Independence the colonists were effectively using the postulate of equality in their defense of self-government within the empire. Soon, their claim to have been born free and equal and to be entitled to the same civil rights as inhabitants of the home country logically led them to demand that the colonial assemblies be recognized as equals of the parliament in Westminster, subordinate only to the king as head of state.[11] In a pamphlet published in 1774 and obviously intended to influence the deliberations of the Continental Congress, the logical deduction from the principle of equality to colonial self-government was once more convincingly spelled out. The sovereignty of Parliament, James Wilson argued, was only a means to an end. Since "all men are, by nature, equal and free," all lawful government is founded on the consent of those who are subject to it. And since the consent is usually given in expectation of increased happiness the consequence is that the happiness of the society is the first law of every government. Applied to the current political situation, this could lead Wilson to only one conclusion: "The commons of Great Britain have no dominion over their equals and fellow subjects in America: they can confer no right to their delegates to bind those equals and fellow subjects by laws."[12]

Supporters of Parliament rejected this claim as an expression of rebel arrogance. The anonymous pamphlet *Americans against Liberty*, published in London probably after the outbreak of hostilities in 1775, responded to the colonists' ideas of many parliaments within one empire by asserting that in an orderly state there could not be two or

10. Joseph Warren to Edmund Dana, Mar. 19, 1766, in Frothingham, *Joseph Warren*, 20–21.

11. Compare Introduction, pp. 14–18.

12. [James Wilson], *Considerations On The Nature And The Extent Of The Legislative Authority Of The British Parliament* (Philadelphia, 1774), cited here from Robert Green McCloskey, ed., *The Works of James Wilson* (Cambridge, Mass., 1967), II, 723–724, 741.

more legislatures, all with equal competence. In the English constitution, the pamphlet continued, the king and the upper and lower houses of Parliament were the undisputed authorities for the whole empire. "Every Member of our Empire is born under this Controul, must live subject to it while he is a Member, and is protected by it as such; whether he reside in Europe, Asia, Africa, or America." It was therefore impossible to grant the colonists their demand for "a Parity of Power with the Parent-State." By definition, "Colonies never enjoyed and cannot, as Colonies, enjoy any such Privilege or Emancipation."[13] Colonial advocates of Parliament's point of view occasionally accused the American whig leaders of using the postulate of equality to stir up the people. In December 1774, for instance, Massachusetts lawyer and supporter of the crown Daniel Leonard condemned the First Continental Congress for inciting to rebellion because they had tried to convince the people "that all men by nature are equal," that kings are servants of the people, and that the people can reclaim delegated power if they feel oppressed by it.[14] John Adams responded to Leonard, contending that the colonists' views did not constitute any new revolutionary doctrine but were merely a reiteration of the "revolution principles" of 1688. Adams insisted that such principles had been propounded by Aristotle, Plato, Livy, Cicero, Harrington, Sidney, and Locke and were based on nature and reason.[15] He glossed over the fact, of course, that parliamentary sovereignty had also been one of the principles of 1688.

More radical and consistent than most loyalists was Anglican minister Jonathan Boucher of Annapolis. In a sermon delivered in the summer of 1775, he rejected the theory of social contract and, along with it, the principle of equality. The claim that legitimate government derived solely from the consent of the governed, Boucher asserted, was based on the view, as popular as it was false, "that the whole human race is born equal; and that no man is naturally inferior, or, in any respect, subjected to another; and that he can be made subject to another only by his own consent." The obvious inequality of men

---

13. [Ambrose Serle], *Americans against Liberty: Or, An Essay on the Nature and Principles of True Freedom, Shewing that the Designs and Conduct of the Americans tend only to Tyranny and Slavery* (London, 1775), 26–27, 48–49.

14. Daniel Leonard, "Massachusettensis," letter of Dec. 26, 1774, quoted from Merrill Jensen, comp., *Tracts of the American Revolution, 1763–1776* (Indianapolis, Ind., 1967), 287.

15. First "Novanglus" letter, Jan. 23, 1775, *ibid.*, 301.

justified government without the consent of the governed. Boucher's basic premise was God's command that men should live in society. It was inconceivable that sinful men could live in harmony without government, and government was impossible without subordination. The theory of social contract in no way resolved the inherent conflict between the principle of equality and the necessities of government. The contract between ruler and subjects inevitably results in inequality. How could the principle of equality be applied, Boucher asked, in deciding who should give up some of his rights and who should acquire new rights in the form of governmental power? Establishing government necessarily meant institutionalizing inequality. Temporary delegation of governmental power among equals, Boucher thought, was too frail a foundation for stable government; it was bound to lead to permanent revolution and chaos.

Boucher, who was not only a loyalist but an archtory as well, offered in place of the social contract a theory of the "patriarchical origin of government" and explicitly embraced Robert Filmer's principles: just government followed from the principles of family life, and the obligation to honor and obey the king and all those who acted in his name was implicit in the Fifth Commandment. According to Christian doctrine, Boucher argued, the sinfulness and weakness of man had made the authority of one man over another necessary and had put a permanent end to the paradisiacal state of equality.[16]

All the advocates of colonial rule, whether they were loyal whigs or extreme tories like Boucher and whether they appealed to the principle of parliamentary sovereignty or to rule by the grace of God, were united by their rejection of the colonists' claim to equality with the inhabitants of Britain.

Equality in the Declaration of Independence

From 1774 to 1776 numerous writers reiterated the colonists' demand for equality, and the Continental Congress did so in several public proclamations. All of them limited the application of the principle of

16. "On Civil Liberty, Passive Obedience, and Non-Resistance" (1775), in Jonathan Boucher, *A View of the Causes and Consequences of the American Revolution* (New York, 1967 [orig. publ. London, 1797]), 514–516, 520, 525, 528–533. Robert Filmer's *Patriarcha* appeared posthumously in London in 1680.

equality to justifying the rejection of parliamentary supremacy over the colonies. Even Thomas Paine, who came closest to being an Anglo-American Rousseau, did not apply the postulate of equality to social conditions and political rights within the colonies.

Paine's plea for independence had such great force because he broke with the conventional wisdom that the colonists could enjoy life, liberty, and property best under the British constitution and within the empire. Equality was the basic premise of his rejection of the English constitution and his critique of monarchy. In accordance with the theory of social contract, Paine argued that men are originally equal, but he was aiming specifically at the institution of monarchy. The only distinctions in nature are "male" and "female," he said, and "good" and "evil" are theological distinctions. The difference between "rich" and "poor" can be explained. But the division of human beings into "Kings" and "Subjects" is without any natural or religious justification. Only this kind of inequality was the focus of Paine's agitation in January 1776.[17]

The similar purposes of the declarations issued by the Continental Congress imposed a similarity of form and argumentation on them. Two important milestones on the way to the Declaration of Independence were the resolves of the First Continental Congress, dated October 14, 1774, and the next Congress's "Declaration of the Causes and Necessity of Taking Up Arms," dated July 6, 1775. A comparison of the initial paragraphs of these documents, along with the first article of the Virginia Declaration of Rights, will show how the proposition "all men are created equal" came to be incorporated into the Declaration of Independence. Speculating about this statement outside of this context inevitably leads to false praise or unfounded accusations.[18]

Declaration and Resolves of the First Continental Congress,
October 14, 1774

[1] Whereas, since the close of the last war, the British parliament, claiming a power of right to bind the people of America by statute in all cases whatsoever, hath, in some acts expressly imposed taxes on them . . . [we] declare,
[2] That the inhabitants of the English Colonies in North America, by the

17. Foner, ed., *Writings of Paine*, I, 9–10.
18. Commager, ed., *Documents*, I, 82, 92, 103, 100.

immutable laws of nature, the principles of the English constitution, and the several charters or compacts, have the following Rights:
1. That they are entitled to life, liberty, and property, and they have never ceded to any sovereign power whatever, a right to dispose of either without their consent. 2. That our ancestors, who first settled these colonies, were at the time of their emigration from the mother country, entitled to all the rights, liberties, and immunities of free and natural-born subjects within the realm of England. 3. That by such emigration they by no means forfeited, surrendered, or lost any of those rights. . . . . 4. That the foundation of English liberty, and of all free government, is a right in the people to participate in their legislative council.

Declaration of the Causes and Necessity of Taking Up Arms, July 6, 1775

[1] If it was possible for men, who exercise their reason to believe, that the divine Author of our existence intended a part of the human race to hold an absolute property in, and an unbounded power over others, marked out by his infinite goodness and wisdom, as the objects of a legal domination never rightfully resistible, however severe and oppressive, the inhabitants of these colonies might at least require from the parliament of Great-Britain some evidence, that this dreadful authority over them, has been granted to that body. [2] But a reverence for our great Creator, principles of humanity, and the dictates of common sense, must convince all those who reflect upon the subject, that government was instituted to promote the welfare of mankind, and ought to be administered for the attainment of that end.

Virginia Bill of Rights, June 12, 1776

[1] *A declaration of rights made by the representatives of the good people of Virginia, assembled in full and free convention; which rights do pertain to them and their posterity, as the basis and foundation of government.*
[2] 1. That all men are by nature equally free and independent, and have certain inherent rights, of which, when they enter into a state of society, they cannot by any compact deprive or divest their posterity; namely, the enjoyment of life and liberty, with the means of acquiring and possessing property, and pursuing and obtaining happiness and safety. 2. That all power is vested in, and consequently derived from, the people.

Declaration of Independence, July 4, 1776

[1] When in the Course of human events, it becomes necessary for one people to dissolve the political bands which have connected them with another, and to assume among the Powers of the earth, the separate and equal station to

which the Laws of Nature and of Nature's God entitle them, a decent respect to the opinions of mankind requires that they should declare the causes which impel them to the separation.

[2] We hold these truths to be self-evident, that all men are created equal, that they are endowed by their Creator with certain unalienable Rights, that among these are Life, Liberty and the pursuit of Happiness. That to secure these rights, Governments are instituted among Men, deriving their just powers from the consent of the governed.

The progression of thought from the first to the second paragraph in all four declarations is the same. In the first paragraph, the colonists' right to self-government or the presumptuousness of Parliament's claim to dominance over the colonies is ascertained. In the second, the theory of contract is used to justify the colonists' position. In the Declaration of Independence, the postulate of equality appears between these two sections in the position that the logic of the social contract naturally provides for it. The Declaration was, above all else, the formal announcement of the whig leadership's determination to combat, with all available means, England's claim to supremacy over the colonies. Basing their reasoning on the premises of social contract thinking, they asserted that colonists had the same rights as all others, since all men were created equal.[19]

Equality Clauses in the Bills of Rights

The principle of equality was included in three of the early bills of rights because it had become so essential to the legitimacy of any government that in the end it could not be kept out of the discussions of domestic political organization.

When George Mason, who owned a plantation of five thousand acres and enough slaves to work it, wrote the draft of the Virginia bill of rights that the convention adopted with only minor changes on June 12, 1776, he certainly did not intend to call for the abolition of slavery or to initiate a movement for social reform. Public debate on

19. Erich Angermann, "Ständische Rechtstraditionen in der amerikanischen Unabhängigkeitserklärung," *Historische Zeitschrift*, CC (1965), 61–91, shows that the Declaration of Independence shared several characteristics with the legal instruments used to renounce certain feudal relationships. Stourzh, "William Blackstone," *Jahrbuch für Amerikastudien*, XV (1970), 184–200, emphasizes the role of the Glorious Revolution as a precedent.

the bill and debate within the convention are only sparsely docu-
mented, but what records we have show clearly that some members
of the convention recognized and rejected the domestic implications
of an explicit acknowledgment of the principle of equality.[20] After
four days of debate, the first article had still not been agreed upon.
One member of the convention singled out the reason for this delay:
"A certain set of aristocrats, for we have such monsters here, finding
that their execrable system cannot be reared on such foundations,
have to this time kept us at bay on the first line, which declares all
men to be born equally free and independent. A number of absurd or
unmeaning alterations have been proposed. The words as they stand
are approved by a very great majority, yet by a thousand masterly
fetches and stratagems the business has been so delayed that the first
clause stands yet unassented to by the Convention."[21] The majority
that finally passed the Virginia bill of rights was not made up of
American levelers but of members of a socially and politically dominant class that felt secure enough to be able to afford the open avowal
of the revolutionary principle.

Of the six states that passed bills of rights between 1776 and 1780,
only two others (and the territory of Vermont) followed Virginia's
example. Pennsylvania's article on equality used almost the same
words as Virginia's. When Massachusetts formulated its clause in
1780, it drew on the models provided by Virginia, Pennsylvania, and
the Declaration of Independence. John Adams, who wrote the draft
of the bill, suggested that the key phrase read "equally free and
independent." But the constitutional convention decided to follow
the wording of the Declaration of Independence more closely and
declared, "All men are born free and equal." No one seemed to feel
that there was any significant difference between "equally free and
independent" and "free and equal." One could argue, of course, that
all inmates of a prison are "equally free and independent" and that
the formulation Massachusetts chose is less ambiguous. But in the
discussions at the time these differences in wording do not seem to
have aroused any attention.[22] The little town of Hardwick, Massachu-

---

20. Rowland, *George Mason*, I, 228–250; Hilldrup, "Virginia Convention,"
169–219; and Robert Allen Rutland, *The Birth of the Bill of Rights, 1776–1791*
(Chapel Hill, N.C., 1955), 30–40.
21. Thomas Ludwell Lee to Richard Henry Lee, June 1, 1776, Rowland,
George Mason, I, 240.
22. Texts of the articles containing clauses on freedom and equality are given

setts, did, however, propose so controversial a clarification that it never seriously entered into the debate. By a vote of 68 to 10, Hardwick requested the constitutional convention to declare: "All men, whites and blacks, are born free and equal."[23]

It remains a matter of speculation why the majority of the states did not formally acknowledge the principle of equality in their first constitutional documents in the years following Independence. The clause on equality in the Declaration of Independence could hardly have been considered sufficient for all states because it did not establish a litigable right.[24] It seems likely that the political leaders in the states became increasingly aware of the potential consequences for domestic politics that such a declaration of principle would have. The majority of them were no doubt reluctant to hasten such an unsettling development.

Education and Property as Factors of Inequality

After the Declaration of Independence, equality appears to have received less emphasis in the political rhetoric of the whig leaders, but a minority soon began to protest against its violation in the first state constitutions and in legislation. The reform demands of this minority signaled the end of traditional respect for social superiors and the beginning of what would become majority opinion after 1820, at least in the area of suffrage. Three weeks after the Declaration of

above on pp. 156–158. John Adams's draft is in Adams, ed., *Works of John Adams*, IV, 220. In his inaugural address as governor of Massachusetts, Samuel Adams cited the following three sentences one after another as identical statements: "all men are born free and equal" (from the Massachusetts declaration of rights); "all men are created equal" (from the Declaration of Independence); and "all men are born free and equal in rights" (from the French Déclaration des droits de l'homme et du citoyen). "Address delivered to the House of Representatives and the Senate of Massachusetts," Jan. 20, 1794, in Cushing, ed., *Writings of Samuel Adams*, IV, 356–358.

23. Resolution of the town meeting on May 25, 1780, in Handlin and Handlin, eds., *Popular Sources*, 830.

24. Edward S. Corwin and Jack W. Peltason, *Understanding the Constitution*, 3d ed. (New York, 1964), 1. Court rulings in Massachusetts and Virginia show how uncertain the litigable status of the guarantees in the declaration of rights was. See pp. 183–186 below.

Independence, an anonymous writer in the *Pennsylvania Evening Post* pointed out:

Although it is granted on all hands, that all power originates from the people, yet it is plain that in those colonies where the government has from the beginning, been in the hands of a very few rich men, the ideas of government both in the minds of those rich men, and of the common people, are rather aristocratical than popular. The rich having been used to govern, seem to think it is their right; and the poorer commonalty, having hitherto had little or no hand in government, seem to think it does not belong to them to have any.[25]

The debates over the first constitutional drafts reveal an initial drift away from this attitude that was characteristic of a "deferential society."[26] In these debates a minority, challenged by the discrepancy between the facts of American life and the postulate of equality that had just been solemnly proclaimed, demanded reforms.

The superior education of local elites accounted for the deference granted them, and when education came under attack as a factor in inequality, this deference began to be eroded. Whig leaders like George Mason, John Adams, and Thomas Jefferson were convinced that the educated elite should have a decisive influence in public affairs. They warned against unqualified acceptance of the maxim *vox populi vox dei*. Anyone who took this maxim literally, an assembly of whigs from Essex County, Massachusetts, declared, was foolish and arrogant. They granted in principle that the common people were capable of pursuing their own happiness. But in order to do so in fact, they would have to be sufficiently well informed. It was regrettable but true, particularly for such public acts as framing a constitution, that the majority of the people had neither the time nor the means to obtain the necessary information. Only among "gentlemen of education, fortune and leisure," were the necessary knowledge, intelligence, and character to be found.[27] The leading role this elite assumed

25. *Pennsylvania Evening Post* (Philadelphia), July 30, 1776.
26. J. R. Pole, "Historians and the Problem of Early American Democracy," *AHR*, LXVII (1961–1962), 629.
27. Essex Result, in Handlin and Handlin, eds., *Popular Sources*, 333–335. In an election-time sermon preached before the Massachusetts General Court on May 29, 1779, Samuel Stillman presented a similar view: "The rulers of the people . . . should be men of leisure and abilities, whether they are called

was thereby justified, and radical implications of the postulate of equality for political participation were rejected. The assumption that men of property, leisure, and education should hold more political power than the rest of the population had long been an established element in the ideology of majority Whigs in England, and it continued to strike many American patriots as logical and natural even after 1776.

In the course of the conflict with England, those who favored granting a political voice to broader segments of the population countered the elitist view with increasing conviction. They affirmed that common sense was sufficient qualification for the exercise of political power. The political consciousness of the mechanics and small merchants of Philadelphia, for example, seems to have grown considerably following the successful American resistance to the Townshend Acts.[28] In September 1770, a group of mechanics, protesting against the traditional dominance of a few merchant families in Philadelphia, announced that they were no longer willing to leave it to "a certain company of leading men to nominate persons and *settle the ticket* for assemblymen, commissioners, assessors, etc., without even permitting the affirmative or negative voice of a mechanic to interfere." "Have we not an equal right of electing or being elected?" the mechanics asked. "Are there no ingenious, cool, sensible men well acquainted with the Constitution and lovers of their country among the Tradesmen and Mechanics?"[29] The same argument was held up to opponents of independence in the spring of 1776. An author who had doubted that the majority of the colonists were capable of self-government and who had warned against giving up the moderate English constitution in favor of a republic was asked in the *Pennsylvania Packet*: "Do not mechanicks and farmers constitute ninety-nine out of a hundred of the people of America? If these, by their occupations, are to be excluded from having any share in the choice of their rulers, or forms of government, would it not be best to acknowledge the jurisdiction of the British Parliament, which is composed entirely of Gentlemen? . . . Is not one half of the property in the city of Philadel-

---

to act in a legislative or executive department." Frank Moore, ed., *The Patriot Preachers of the American Revolution* (New York, 1862), 271–272.

28. Pole, *Political Representation*, 267.

29. "A Brother Chip," *Pa. Gaz.*, Sept. 27, 1770, also in Charles H. Lincoln, *The Revolutionary Movement in Pennsylvania, 1760–1776* (Philadelphia, 1901), 80–81n. In Aug., artisans and small businessmen had formed a patriotic society. *Ibid.*, 89–91.

phia owned by men who wear Leathern Aprons? . . . Does not the other half belong to men whose fathers or grandfathers wore Leathern Aprons?"[30] This same newly acquired self-confidence led the Committee of Mechanics of New York to call for a referendum on New York's constitution. The mechanics admitted that not every citizen could draft a constitution, but they were convinced that every citizen could judge one. "That share of common sense," they claimed, "which the Almighty has bountifully distributed amongst mankind in general, is sufficient to quicken every one's feeling, and enable him to judge rightly, what advantages he is likely to enjoy or be deprived of, under any Constitution proposed to him."[31]

One direct consequence of increased self-confidence among the "middle class of men" was the decision against a bicameral legislature in Pennsylvania. The group of reformers that overthrew the colonial legislature of Pennsylvania in the summer of 1776 broke with the principle of checks and balances in the English constitution and, in September, adopted a constitution with a unicameral legislature and an executive committee. They defended this experiment by citing the equality already prevailing among all citizens. They claimed that the balance of power between king, upper house, and lower house, much praised for the stability it provided, could only exist in a society made up of clearly distinguishable classes; and they reminded the "gentry" who were displeased with their unicameral legislature that Montesquieu had said that equality is the soul of a republic.[32] A senatorial chamber, they maintained, would only encourage the formation of an aristocracy; it would become a gathering place for the ambitious, an assembly of the "better sort."[33]

The opponents of Pennsylvania's constitutional experiment answered that the unicameral legislature, the lack of an independent executive, suffrage for all taxpayers, and the election of justices of the peace by the voters of their districts presupposed a social condition that did not exist: "perfect equality, and an equal distribution of property, wisdom and virtue, among the inhabitants." Benjamin Rush,

30. *Pa. Packet*, Mar. 18, 1776.

31. Lincoln, *Constitutional History of New York*, I, 46; Becker, *Political Parties*, 275–276.

32. "Remarks on the Resolves Published against the Plan of Government," *Pa. Evening Post*, Nov. 9, 1776. The reference is to Montesquieu, *Spirit of the Laws*, trans. Nugent, book 5, chap. 5.

33. "One of the People," *Pa. Evening Post*, Nov. 23, 1776.

the Philadelphia doctor and political ally of John Adams who voiced this opinion in 1777, denied that there was only one social class in America. To be sure, no artificial distinction was made between "noblemen" and "commoners," but there were distinctions resulting from differences in diligence and capability. Commerce had produced an unequal distribution of property, and in Pennsylvania there were marks of class that were as obvious and generally recognized as the artificial distinctions upheld by Europeans. From experience he knew that "the rich have always been an over-match for the poor in all contests for power." There would always be poor people who would sell their votes and rich people who would buy them. Rush therefore thought it only sensible for "men of middling fortunes" to combine their forces in one chamber to defend their interests against the rich. If the second chamber should begin to yearn for honors and hereditary titles, the first chamber would be there to restrain it. For as long as present social conditions prevailed and the mass of voters lacked education and political virtue, Rush was convinced, the educated would have to provide responsible leadership.[34]

Within a decade Rush's party gained control in Pennsylvania, and the constitution of 1790 established the kind of tripartite state government with a bicameral legislature that by then had come to be accepted as standard and has since proven to be a permanent feature of American state government.[35] But this political victory did not, of course, mean that the political ideas of the victors were also to prevail for centuries to come.

Race as a Factor of Inequality

The limitations of the postulate of equality in matters of political and social reform are nowhere more apparent than in the slavery issue. The founding generation was fully aware that racial discrimination and slavery were incompatible with the principles of freedom and equality. But economic and political interests outweighed ideological considerations. The immediate personal interests of the slaveholders were deeply involved in this question, and the politicians in the

34. Rush, *Observations Upon the Present Government*, 4, 9.
35. Robert L. Brunhouse, *The Counter-Revolution in Pennsylvania, 1776–1790* (Harrisburg, Pa., 1942), describes the victory of the traditionalists over the reformers.

northern and middle Atlantic colonies were unwilling to weaken colonial resistance against Great Britain or, later, to endanger the Union by pursuing the divisive issue. The cohesion of the newly formed nation clearly had priority over the realization of the postulate of equality.[36]

Neither the political theory nor the social practice of whites toward blacks changed in any basic way in the years 1764 to 1783. The outbreak of the Seven Years' War had prompted an upsurge of pacifism and abolitionism among the Quakers.[37] And as early as 1764, James Otis had unequivocally stated, in one of the first great justifications for colonial resistance, that enslavement was incompatible with the natural rights of human beings. "The colonists are by the law of nature freeborn, as indeed, [are] all men, white or black."[38] But nineteen years later the Quaker David Cooper recalled the principles of equality and freedom in the Declaration of Independence and asked whether the men who had proclaimed those great truths meant them to apply only to white men, rather than to all men.[39]

Only minor measures had been taken in the intervening years. The attempt of the Continental Congress to stop the importation of slaves as of December 1, 1774, was ineffective, as was a similar resolution passed on April 6, 1776.[40] Jefferson had urged that the Declaration of Independence cite the toleration of the slave trade as one of the king's violations of his duties as a ruler, but the delegates of South Carolina and Georgia, whose states, in contrast to Virginia, had a great economic interest in continuing the importation of slaves, protested, and the Continental Congress deleted the disputed sen-

36. Compare the two comprehensive studies, Jordan, *White over Black*, 269–311, and David Brion Davis, *The Problem of Slavery in the Age of Revolution, 1770–1823* (Ithaca, N.Y., 1975), esp. chap. 6.

37. Jordan, *White over Black*, 271. Bailyn, *Ideological Origins*, 232–242, cites condemnations of slavery in this period that make use of the ambiguity of the term and turn on American slaveholders the same arguments the colonists, who felt themselves to be "slaves," used against Parliament.

38. Otis, *Rights of the British Colonies*, 29.

39. [David Cooper], *A serious address to the rulers of America, on the inconsistency of their conduct respecting slavery* . . . (Trenton, N.J., 1783), 12–13, cited in Jordan, *White over Black*, 290.

40. Ford *et al.*, eds., *Journals of the Continental Congress*, I, 77, and IV, 258. For the position of the Continental Congress on this issue in the years 1774 to 1789, see Peter M. Bergman and Jean McCarroll, comps., *The Negro in the Continental Congress* (New York, 1969).

tences.[41] Delaware, in 1776, was the only state to prohibit the importation of slaves in its constitution.[42] In 1778, when the Virginia legislature forbade the importation of slaves to that state, the decision was not based on the equality clause in the Virginia bill of rights but on the desire to have better control over the slave market. This law was not intended as a first step toward the abolition of slavery.[43] By 1786, eleven states had, for different reasons, either outlawed the importation of slaves or levied a high tax on it, yet none of the state constitutions ratified between 1776 and 1783 contained prohibitions against slavery. Only the 1777 constitution of the territory of Vermont prohibited slavery.[44]

The Pennsylvania legislature was first to abolish slavery by law. But even there, where the Quaker influence was strong and where the majority faction of the unicameral legislature was under attack for its democratic innovations, it was impossible to put an immediate and total end to slavery. The 1780 statute gave freedom only to slave children born after the law went into effect, and then only after they turned twenty-eight. The preamble to this law, written by Thomas Paine, made no reference to the equality clause in Pennsylvania's bill of rights.[45] Other northern and middle Atlantic states followed Pennsylvania's example and drew up similar laws that gradually abolished slavery in the region.[46]

Events in Massachusetts demonstrate the secondary role of the postulate of equality in the gradual process of emancipation. By the 1830s, leading Massachusetts lawyers agreed that slavery had

41. The omitted paragraph is cited in Becker, *Declaration of Independence*, 180–181; for Jefferson's notes about the striking of the passage, see pp. 171–172.

42. "No person hereafter imported into this State from Africa ought to be held in slavery under any pretence whatever; and no negro, Indian, or mulatto slave ought to be brought into this State, for sale, from any part of the world." Thorpe, ed., *Constitutions*, I, 567.

43. Robert McColley, *Slavery and Jeffersonian Virginia* (Urbana, Ill., 1964), 164–166.

44. Richard B. Morris, *The American Revolution Reconsidered* (New York, 1967), 72–76; Thorpe, ed., *Constitutions*, VI, 3739–3740.

45. Benjamin Quarles, *The Negro in the American Revolution* (Chapel Hill, N.C., 1961), 49–50; Foner, ed., *Writings of Paine*, II, 21–22.

46. Rhode Island and Connecticut in 1784; New York in 1799; New Jersey in 1804. Compare Arthur Zilversmit, *The First Emancipation: The Abolition of Slavery in the North* (Chicago, 1967).

been abolished in their state sometime before the Constitution of the United States went into effect. But Chief Justice Lemuel Shaw was unable to say in 1836 exactly which legal act had put an end to slavery. It had been, he thought, the recognition of an English court decision of 1772 as part of the common law, or the Declaration of Independence, or the Massachusetts constitution of 1780.[47] Some textbooks claim that the bill of rights of 1780 was crucial to the abolition of slavery in Massachusetts, and they cite decisions reached by the supreme court of Massachusetts between 1781 and 1783 as evidence. In fact, however, these decisions make no reference to the bill of rights, and contemporary reactions to them ascribe no particular importance to them as precedents illustrating the incompatibility of slavery with the postulate of equality.[48]

An attempt by the Massachusetts house of representatives in 1777 to abolish slavery by law was soon dropped out of regard for the feelings of the southern partners in the war. The representatives did not want to act without assurance from the Continental Congress that such a law would not be regarded as an unfriendly gesture toward other states in the Confederation. Even John Adams spoke against the law because he feared the political consequences of offending the southern states.[49]

The town meetings of Massachusetts, on the other hand, openly discussed the incompatibility of racial discrimination and the principle of equality. Without regard for other states, they called attention to the fact in letters to the legislature, in instructions to their representatives, and, later, in instructions to their delegates to the state consti-

47. In 1772, English Chief Justice Sir William Murray Mansfield ruled that a slave who set foot on English soil was free. Emory Washburn, "Somerset's Case, and the Extinction of Villenage and Slavery in England," Mass. Hist. Soc., *Procs.*, 1st Ser., VII (Boston, 1864), 319–321. The provincial parliament and courts in the colonies seem to have ignored this ruling. Quarles, *Negro in the American Revolution*, 37. Shaw's opinion is available in Helen Tunnicliff Catterall, ed., *Judicial Cases concerning American Slavery and the Negro* (Washington, D.C., 1926–1936), IV, 507.
48. William O'Brien, "Did the Jennison Case Outlaw Slavery in Massachusetts?" *WMQ*, 3d Ser., XVII (1960), 219–241; John D. Cushing, "The Cushing Court and the Abolition of Slavery in Massachusetts: More Notes on the 'Quock Walker Case,'" *American Journal of Legal History*, V (1961), 118–144; Zilversmit, "Quok Walker," *WMQ*, 3d Ser., XXV (1968), 614–624.
49. John Adams to James Warren, June 22, 1777, *Warren-Adams Letters*, I, 335, 339.

tutional convention. The draft of the state constitution presented to the towns in the spring of 1778 contained no bill of rights and withheld the vote from Indians, mulattoes, and blacks. Many towns thereupon demanded a bill of rights and criticized the discriminatory article of the draft. In their arguments they referred less often to equality than to natural law, religious convictions, and the right of a taxpayer to a voice in public affairs.[50]

The town meeting of Hardwick, for instance, reported that a number of blacks had unsuccessfully petitioned the house of representatives for their freedom. Refusal to grant it violated the law of God and the principle of freedom the state of Massachusetts espoused. A year later, as we have already noted, the same community demanded that the first article in the Declaration of Rights be amended to read: "All men, whites and blacks, are born free and equal."[51] The townspeople of Sutton argued that continued racial discrimination would bring down the wrath of God on Massachusetts and also cited the maxim "No taxation without representation." Sutton thought it intolerable that blacks, Indians, and mulattoes should be denied the right to vote even though they might well hold property and pay taxes on it. In order to prevent misunderstandings, the town emphasized that no one should be able to vote if he were a public charge or if he owned little or no property. As a compromise Sutton suggested that all adult males who did not fall into this latter category but who had been denied the vote by the old suffrage law be granted half a vote, regardless of race.[52] The town of Boothbay could find no justification either in nature or in the Bible for the disgraceful and unchristian treatment of the Africans or for the denial to them of a privilege to which all men were entitled. Boothbay thought it equally intolerable that the Indians, the original masters and owners of the land, were excluded from civil rights.[53] The town meeting of Blandford demanded that all slaves be freed, that no new ones be imported, and that all taxpaying citizens, regardless of their color, be able to elect representatives.[54]

50. Handlin and Handlin, eds., *Popular Sources*, 192, 257, 269, 291, 295, 302, 309, 312, 317, 324, 332, 350, 410.
51. *Ibid.*, 216, 830.
52. *Ibid.*, 231–232.
53. *Ibid.*, 248–249.
54. *Ibid.*, 282. The towns of Spencer and Upton also based their rejection of racial discrimination on the principle that taxation and representation were inseparable. *Ibid.*, 302, 263.

A convention of Essex County, however, defended the denial of the vote to blacks, mulattoes, and Indians in the 1778 draft of the constitution. The county convention probably expressed the uneasy feeling and resignation of a majority in the New England states when they said: "Would to God, the situation of America and the tempers of it's inhabitants were such, that the slave-holder could not be found in the land."[55]

The spirited rejection of the discriminatory article by a number of town meetings prompted the authors of the next draft to drop it. Of the extant town meeting resolves on the draft of 1779, only three pursued the issue of slavery.[56]

The discussion in Massachusetts was surely not typical of the rest of the country. The judges and legislators in the states where most of the blacks lived rejected both in theory and practice any application of the postulate of equality to blacks and Indians in general and to slaves in particular. They refused to discuss the implications of the theory of social contract, with the explanation that slaves were "a species of property, personal estate."[57] They made up part of the property of a member of society but were not themselves members.

Court decisions in Virginia reflected this point of view. When several Indian slaves sued for their freedom in 1787, the supreme court of Virginia granted it not on the basis of the declaration of rights, but in accordance with a law of 1705 by which all Indians were permitted to trade freely anywhere in Virginia. According to this law, the court concluded, no Indian who had come to Virginia after 1705 could be a slave.[58] When in 1806 Indians who were still kept in slavery went to court, Judge George Wythe of the Court of Chancery in Richmond declared them free on the basis of the principle that "freedom is the birth-right of every human being, which sentiment is strongly inculcated by the first article of our 'political catechism,' the bill of rights." Before the trial was formally closed, Wythe died. His successor on the bench, St. George Tucker, confirmed Wythe's decision but rejected the reasoning behind it. In Tucker's opinion, the Indians were free because of the law of 1705. The first article of the Bill of Rights did not apply here. The authors of this article, Tucker

55. *Ibid.*, 340–341, 354.
56. *Ibid.*, 769, 860.
57. Samuel Chase before the Continental Congress on July 30, 1776, as recorded by John Adams, Adams, ed., *Works of John Adams*, II, 496.
58. Catterall, ed., *Judicial Cases*, I, 94–95.

stated, had clearly given much reflection to its significance and conceived of it as limited to "free citizens, or aliens." They had carefully excluded the possibility of infringing on property rights and of giving freedom to those "whom we have been compelled from imperious circumstances to retain, generally, in the same state of bondage that they were in at the revolution, in which they had no concern, agency or interest."[59]

The "logic of color" as justification for racial discrimination and slavery was called into question during the Revolutionary period, but the arguments invoked against it—the "logic of English liberties" and the postulate of equality derived from natural law—were in no way able to overcome its pernicious effect.[60] The circumstances of the struggle for independence had forced the white part of the founding generation to subscribe to the postulate of equality. The most significant effect of this commitment on the later struggle for the emancipation of the slaves was the institutionalization of a sense of guilt.

Members Only

Shared experiences in the fight for colonial rights and the economic opportunities that white Americans enjoyed created a sense of relative equality among them and made it imperative that equality become one of the guiding values of the new system of government. But American society in 1776 was, of course, neither a society of equals nor one of doctrinaire egalitarians. The implications of the ideal, as we have seen, were modified by other values such as the sanctity of property, education as a precondition for holding public office, and economic gain from the exploitation of a black lower class. Yet even within social contract thinking it was quite possible to counter the egalitarian component of the republican ideal by limiting political rights to "constituent members" of society, those free and equal men who could claim a certain autonomy by virtue of their property.

In the debate on the first article of the Virginia bill of rights in June 1776, as Edmund Randolph reported it, an opponent of the clauses on freedom and equality was pacified by this explanation: "Slaves, not being constituent members of our society, could never

59. *Ibid.*, 112; compare McColley, *Slavery and Jeffersonian Virginia*, 136–137.
60. Jordan, *White over Black*, 279.

pretend to any benefit from such a maxim."[61] That the concept of "constituent member" was crucial in the thinking of southern plantation owners is suggested by George Mason's revealing use of the term as early as June 1775. On the occasion of electing officers for a militia company, he explained how he interpreted the principle of equality in the context of Virginia society. "We came equals into this world," he said, "and equals shall we go out of it. All men are by nature born equally free and independent." After outlining the social contract idea he declared that there was a particularly suitable means of preventing the abuse of governmental power—"frequently appealing to the body of the people, to those constituent members from whom authority originated, for their approbation or dissent."[62] The difference between this statement of Mason's and his draft for the bill of rights a year later was that in 1776 he no longer explicitly limited civil and political rights to constituent members. There can be little doubt, however, that he tacitly assumed the same limitation.

A European traveler in the 1780s perceptively observed the restricted understanding of who counted among the members of society, especially in the South. The marquis de Chastellux made a point of explaining to those "half philosophers" among his countrymen "who have invariably mistaken the word *people,* for mankind in general," that a planter or farmer in Virginia had nothing in common with a European peasant, because he is "always a freeman, participates in the government, and has the command of a few negroes." He is both "citizen and master," and as such "perfectly resembles the bulk of individuals who formed what were called *the people* in the ancient republics; a people very different from that of our days."[63]

Those who opposed such a restrictive concept of civil and political rights and started what came to be a specifically American reform tradition, based their arguments on a naive and, in effect, radical reading of the contract theory.[64] If the highest purpose of the social contract was to provide the individual with a better chance to find

61. Edmund Randolph, *History of Virginia,* ed. Arthur H. Shaffer (Charlottesville, Va., 1970), 253. On the tradition of the concept of the constituent member in English political theory, see C. B. Macpherson, *The Political Theory of Possessive Individualism: Hobbes to Locke* (Oxford, 1962), 151, 181, 248–250.
62. Rowland, *George Mason,* I, 430–433.
63. Marquis de Chastellux, *Travels in North-America, in the Years 1780, 1781, and 1782* (London, 1787), II, 56–57.
64. Compare Staughton Lynd, *Intellectual Origins of American Radicalism* (New York, 1968), chap. 2.

happiness than the presocial state of nature permitted, it seemed only logical that everybody should have an equal share in the beneficent consequences of the contract. The amount of property he owned should neither increase nor decrease his share. This radical conclusion was indeed spelled out by the town meeting of Pittsfield, Massachusetts, when it instructed its delegates to the state constitutional convention in 1780. "As all men are equal by nature," the townspeople of Pittsfield asserted, "so, when they enter into a state of civil government, they are entitled precisely to the same rights and privileges, or to an equal degree of political happiness." Similarly, the town meeting of Stoughton derived from the idea of social contract the duty of every government to insure the stability of the community "and to enable individuals Equally to Enjoy all the Blessings and benfits resulting there from."[65]

The dynamics inherent in this uncompromising view of the postulate of equality consisted in the fact that it demanded not only that everyone enjoy equality before the law or have an equal voice in government but also that everyone have an equal share in the fruits of the common enterprise. On a few rare occasions we thus find the basic tenet that underlies any justification of the modern welfare state clearly expressed at a time when voting was still based on property qualifications and educational opportunities were anything but equal.

Against the intentions of its authors, the statement "all men are created equal," which had been used to justify the movement for independence, soon became an invaluable theoretical and rhetorical point of reference for the proponents of social and political reforms. The difficulties they would encounter were foreshadowed when in 1789 James Madison, during preparation of a federal bill of rights, reviewed the existing eight state bills of rights and found that "in some instances they do no more than state the perfect equality of mankind; this to be sure is an absolute truth, yet it is not absolutely necessary to be inserted at the head of a constitution."[66] At this moment it became clear that the founding fathers would refuse the principle of equality a place in the Constitution of the United States, a fateful decision not to be reversed until the Fourteenth Amendment of 1868.

65. Handlin and Handlin, eds., *Popular Sources*, 411, 423.
66. July 8, 1789, *The Congressional Register; Or, History Of The Proceedings And Debates Of The first House of Representatives of the United States of America . . .* (New York, 1789–1790), I, 429. Compare throughout, Jack P. Greene, *All Men Are Created Equal* (Oxford, 1976).

CHAPTER IX

Property

Harrington has shown that power always follows property. This I believe to be as infallible a maxim in politics, as that action and reaction are equal, is in mechanics. Nay, I believe we may advance one step farther, and affirm that the balance of power in a society, accompanies the balance of property in land.

John Adams, 1776

Rich men enjoy too great a share of power at all times, even without the addition of governmental powers. . . . Government is, or ought to be, instituted to prevent and punish oppression, and therefore ought not to confer power on rich men as such. Putting the rich and the poor on equal footing is giving the wealthy an amazing advantage.

"Whitlock," *Pennsylvania Evening Post*, May 22, 1777

The Colonists and the "natural right of property"

The idea that property is a natural right, it is usually said, triumphed with the Glorious, the American, and the French bourgeois revolutions.[1] Equally significant for an understanding of the American case is the fact that the seemingly natural connection between a person's property and a person's liberty lost its self-evident and unquestioned character in the course of the Revolution. Gouverneur Morris's warning about the incompatibility of an expanding economy and extensive "political liberty" in the sense of pure majority rule is only one example of the growing awareness of the possible tensions between

1. Richard Schlatter, *Private Property: The History of an Idea* (New Brunswick, N.J., 1951), 151. See also William B. Scott, *In Pursuit of Happiness: American Conceptions of Property from the Seventeenth to the Twentieth Century* (Bloomington, Ind., 1977).

property and liberty.[2] Morris and others of his class had become revolutionaries because, from 1764 on, they saw their idea of unrestricted control over property in the colonies increasingly threatened by the central authorities of the empire. A common interest in creating a world that would be open to unlimited material ambition firmly united them with the middle class, from whose ranks they had risen over the past few generations. The twin theme of threatened liberty and property therefore recurred in hundreds of public statements made between 1764 and 1776. When the New York assembly condemned England's new colonial policy in 1764, it did not bother to distinguish between "internal" and "external" taxation but repudiated all taxes except those levied by the colonial assemblies themselves. For, they argued, any tax reduces the value of the taxed property, and the entire wealth of a country could be reduced in this way.[3] Similarly, the Boston town meeting reasoned that whoever taxed trade goods could also tax land, what the land produced, and, finally, any and every kind of property. These Bostonians already regarded their town as a settlement of "Tributary Slaves."[4] Ten years later, when the extralegal provincial congress of New York began collecting taxes itself, the congress suggested one among dozens of compromise proposals that would let colonists continue to benefit from the English colonial empire: Parliament and the crown's ministers could continue to regulate trade, but the tariffs they collected were to be transferred to the provincial legislature; thus "the natural right of property" would be respected.[5]

American political leaders did not develop new ideas about private property. They merely demanded that the concept of property long since canonized by the English Whigs also apply in the colonies. Locke was invaluable to the colonists not only for his codification of general constitutional principles but also for his comprehensive analysis of property. Locke realized that the development of a money economy and the improved standard of living that accompanied it

2. See W. P. Adams, " 'Spirit of Commerce,' " *Amerikastudien / American Studies*, XXI (1976), 309–334.
3. Edmund S. Morgan, ed., *The New York Declaration of 1764*, Old South Leaflets, no. 224 (Boston, 1948).
4. Instructions to Boston's representatives in the general assembly, May 24, 1764, quoted in Morgan and Morgan, *Stamp Act Crisis*, 52.
5. Resolution of June 24, 1775, in Alexander C. Flick, ed., *The American Revolution in New York: Its Political, Social and Economic Significance* (Albany, N. Y., 1926), 318.

negated the factors that had originally put limits on the natural and legitimate striving for property. Among those factors were the rules that perishable goods cannot be accumulated and that all people should have the opportunity to acquire goods of comparable value.[6] Locke's moral justification of a practically unlimited striving for property suited the interests of the majority of the colonists. The acquisition and cultivation or exploitation of land was the very raison d'être for the colonies. They were a "possessive market society," in which property was the central institution and the one that society was most concerned to protect.[7] The relative ease with which land and other property could be acquired did not make the colonists more tolerant of European interference; on the contrary, it made them even less tolerant. They regarded the comparatively wide distribution of property in the colonies as a special achievement that distinguished them from Europeans.

During the debate preceding Independence, references to the distribution of property in America were used to bolster the self-confidence of the colonists. In February 1776, a "Demophilus" wrote in the *Pennsylvania Packet* that the inability of other nations to govern themselves should not discourage Americans. For nowhere else were circumstances as advantageous as in these *"pantaplebean* colonies," where—to mention but one point—most people could read. "The most just and solid foundation of social happiness was laid in the first settlement of the Continent, *the cultivation of the earth for the subsistance of its proprietor.* Here was no feudal tenure from some military Lord; every cultivator being the lord of his own soil, and content with its produce, had no thoughts of encroaching upon and subjecting his neighbour to his absolute dominion."[8] Proponents of independence used this historical construction to attack the feudal law tradition by which land in the colonies could be granted only by the English king. In 1774 Jefferson explicitly rejected the "fictitious principle" that all land originally belonged to the crown. "America," he added, "was not

6. Macpherson, *Possessive Individualism*, 197–220, 238*ff*; J. E. Parsons, Jr., "Locke's Doctrine of Property," *Social Research*, XXXVI (1969), 389–411, supports Macpherson's interpretation. Hans Medick, *Naturzustand und Naturgeschichte der bürgerlichen Gesellschaft: die Ursprünge der bürgerlichen Sozialtheorie als Geschichtsphilosophie und Sozialwissenschaft bei Samuel Pufendorf, John Locke und Adam Smith* (Göttingen, 1973), 75–97, discusses Locke's concept of property, as does Schlatter, *Private Property*, chap. 7.
7. Macpherson, *Possessive Individualism*, 53–61.
8. *Pa. Packet*, Feb. 12, 1776.

conquered by William the Norman, nor it's lands surrendered to him or any of his successors."[9] A few years later this view of a new society of landowners proved useful in patriotic rhetoric. In celebrating the second anniversary of Independence, David Ramsay, a physician who later turned historian, stated in Charleston:

Our Independence will naturally tend to fill our country with inhabitants. Where life, liberty, and property are well secured, and where land is easily and cheaply obtained, the natural increase of people will much exceed all European calculations. Add to this, the inhabitants of the Old World becoming acquainted with our excellent forms of government, will emigrate by thousands. In their native lands, the hard-earned fruits of uninterrupted labour, are scarcely equal to a scanty supply of their natural wants; and this pittance is held on a very precarious tenure: While our soil may be cheaply purchased, and will abundantly repay the toil of the husbandman, whose property no rapacious landlord dare invade. Happy America! Whose extent of territory westward, is sufficient to accomodate with land, thousands and millions of the virtuous peasants, who now groan beneath tyranny and oppression in three quarters of the globe.[10]

Just how wide the distribution of property was and in what way the Revolution influenced it are questions still under debate today. Recent monographs have modified Jackson Turner Main's thesis that the Revolution halted or even reversed the process of stratification in the colonies. The general rise in the standard of living was usually accompanied by an increasingly uneven distribution of property. Possibilities for speculation, provided by a war economy and by land acquisition in the West, account for the rapid growth of some individual fortunes. On the other hand, property was obviously divided more equally than it was in Europe. The strongest motive of the middle class, and of the upper and lower classes that shared its guiding values, was the pursuit of property in free competition, property as a guarantee of security and status.[11] This fact explains

9. Jefferson, *A Summary View*, 20.
10. David Ramsay, *An Oration on the Advantages of American Independence* (Charleston, S.C., 1778), in Robert L. Brunhouse, ed., *David Ramsay, 1749–1815: Selections from His Writings*, American Philosophical Society, *Transactions*, N.S., LV, pt. iv (1965), 187, compare p. 191.
11. See the synthesis by Richard Hofstadter, *America at 1750: A Social Portrait* (New York, 1971), chap. 5. Recent case studies on property distribution are discussed in Hermann Wellenreuther, "A View of the Socio-Economic Structures of England and the British Colonies on the Eve of the American

why even the religiously motivated, in other respects radically democratic, and at least partially egalitarian tradition of the English Dissenters remained politically insignificant, at least in the years before
and immediately after 1776.[12] In the struggle against the new colonial
policy after 1763, property was the one great unifying value; the
colonial assemblies appointed themselves as its guardians; and it was
only logical that the right to property was included in the canon of the
highest social values when the new political order was established.

Property Clauses in the State Constitutions

Much has been made of the fact that in the Declaration of Independence Jefferson used "pursuit of happiness" in a place where according to accepted Lockean language he ought to have said "property."
Vernon Louis Parrington, in his attempt to establish Jefferson as the
father of American idealism, interpreted this choice of words as "a
complete break with the Whiggish doctrine of property rights that
Locke had bequeathed to the English middle class."[13] New Left
historians in search of an American tradition of radicalism were
disappointed in their search for confirmation of Parrington's view.
They found that during the French Revolution Jefferson had struck
out "property" in Lafayette's draft of a bill of rights for France and
had replaced it by the phrase "the power to dispose of his person and
the fruits of his industry, and of all his faculties."[14] But on the whole,
Parrington's claim proved to be exaggerated.

One of the reasons was that the acquisition of property and the
pursuit of happiness were so closely connected with each other in the
minds of the founding generation that naming only one of the two
sufficed to evoke both. The property clauses in the state bills of rights

Revolution," in Erich Angermann *et al.*, eds., *New Wine in Old Skins: A
Comparative View of Socio-Political Structures and Values Affecting the American
Revolution* (Stuttgart, 1976), 14–40, and by Dirk Hoerder, "Socio-Political
Structures and Popular Ideology, 1750s–1780s," *ibid.*, 41–65.
12. Lynd, *Intellectual Origins*, 86, concluded that religious dissenters in England and in America "did not transcend private property in theory, any
more than in practice."
13. Vernon Louis Parrington, *Main Currents in American Thought: An Interpretation of American Literature from the Beginnings to 1920* (New York, 1927),
I, 344.
14. Lynd, *Intellectual Origins*, 84.

provide evidence for the close association of both values. Virginia, Pennsylvania, and Massachusetts listed the acquisition of property among the inalienable rights and included happiness and safety in the same sentence. In the words of the Virginia declaration: "All men . . . have certain inherent rights, . . . namely, the enjoyment of life and liberty, with the means of acquiring and possessing property, and pursuing and obtaining happiness and safety."[15]

The representatives responsible for drawing up constitutions were aware of the potential conflict between private property and public interest. In case of expropriation all states guaranteed just compensation. Pennsylvania's drafting committee was the only one to propose a radical statement of principle concerning maximum property holding: "An enormous Proportion of Property rested in a few Individuals is dangerous to the Rights, and destructive of the Common Happiness of Mankind; and therefore every free State hath a Right by its Laws to discourage the Possession of such Property."[16] The plenum of the provincial congress struck out every last word of this challenge to the unlimited desire for property. The Vermont constitution at least stated explicitly the potential conflict between private property and the public interest. It asserted the individual's right to acquire property and the state's duty to protect it but also declared, "Private property ought to be subservient to public uses, when necessity requires it."[17]

The first state constitutions thus clearly emphasized the individual's claim to legal protection of his property. The self-imposed limits on sovereign power that the constitutions articulated derived from a desire to guarantee not only freedom of expression and of religious exercise but also the freedom to acquire property.

Primogeniture and Entail

The two traditional legal arrangements used to refute the claim of all potential heirs to an equal share in an inheritance were primogeniture

15. Thorpe, ed., *Constitutions*, VII, 3813; similarly, V, 3082 (Pennsylvania) and III, 1889 (Massachusetts). On "happiness," see below, pp. 225–226.
16. Broadside, "An Essay of a Declaration of Rights," Historical Society of Pennsylvania, Philadelphia.
17. Thorpe, ed., *Constitutions*, VI, 3740.

—passing on the whole estate to the eldest son or the first-born child —and entail—passing on land inalienably to one heir and his descendants. In New York and in the southern colonies these arrangements had a large enough impact to evoke public objections in the 1770s. They were regarded as remnants of a feudal and aristocratic order. "In a republic," a "Gentleman" wrote in the *Pennsylvania Evening Post* of November 1776, "there should be no entails. They belong to monarchies. Estate should be divided among the children. This is *essential*."[18] Even the small town of Lenox in western Massachusetts, in rejecting the constitutional draft of 1778, demanded that an article be included in the new constitution prohibiting entail, for this arrangement was "a distructive thing in a free State and like swelled Legs and an emaciated Body Symtoms of a Disolution."[19]

In Pennsylvania and Georgia, entail was forbidden by the new constitutions, in New York by laws passed in 1782 and 1786.[20] In Virginia, Jefferson proposed abolishing entail in his constitutional draft of 1776. He reached his goal later in the same year when the new legislature passed a law, drafted by him, to prohibit entail and primogeniture. He considered this measure an essential one in a republic. For him, it represented the end of "the aristocracy of wealth" and an opening for "the aristocracy of virtue and talent."[21] The change did not go unopposed among Virginia planters. Landon Carter, a major landholder, objected violently to Jefferson's view and saw the change as ushering in "agrarian law," i.e., general restrictions on

18. "Remarks . . . by a Gentleman of Neither Party," *Pa. Evening Post*, Nov. 5, 1776; Evelyn Cecil, *Primogeniture: A Short History of Its Development in Various Countries and Its Practical Effects* (London, 1895); Richard B. Morris, *Studies in the History of American Law, with Special Reference to the Seventeenth and Eighteenth Centuries*, 2d ed. (New York, 1963), 73–103. Lynd, *Intellectual Origins*, 79–83, calls attention to a dilemma that the English opponents of hereditary monarchy faced after Locke. They wanted to put an end to hereditary political offices without endangering the hereditary character of property. For a view of this issue written at the time, see Adam Smith, *The Wealth of Nations* (London and New York, 1954 [orig. publ. 1776]), I, book 3, chap. 4, 370–371.
19. Taylor, ed., *Massachusetts*, 62.
20. Thorpe, ed., *Constitutions*, I, 74, V, 3090; Flick, ed., *History of New York*, IV, 177–178.
21. Boyd *et al.*, eds., *Jefferson Papers*, I, 363, 560; Adrienne Koch and William Peden, eds., *The Life and Selected Writings of Thomas Jefferson* (New York, 1944), 38–39.

the extent of land a person may legally own. For, Carter concluded, if the public considered it dangerous to will a large estate to a single heir, then ownership in fee simple must be equally dangerous.[22]

In point of fact, more land in Virginia was held in fee simple than in entail; and in response to petition the House of Burgesses had routinely annulled entails.[23] But here again the statistics do not reflect the importance the issue assumed for those involved. No less significant than the actuality that relatively few estates were held in entail was the perception or the feeling, shared by plantation owners in Virginia and small farmers in the Berkshires, that restrictions on the disposal of property had no place in their social order.

Property Qualifications for Voting

For the majority of those involved in framing constitutions, the right to hold property was closely linked to the issue of suffrage. Property qualifications in their strictest form called for ownership of land in fee simple. Less rigorous interpretations required ownership of other kinds of property, or, simply, the payment of a tax. The constitution adopted by the territory of Vermont was the only one to give the vote to every adult male.[24] In other states, property qualifications for voting were taken for granted. The only question under debate was what kind of property qualification was suitable, whether, for instance, tax paying was sufficient.

Just as there had been variations in election laws during the colonial period, so there were variations in the property qualifications that the new state constitutions imposed. These qualifications were an extension of an unbroken tradition of English election laws dating back to 1429. The right to vote for county representatives to Parliament as knights of the shires was first limited to landholders under

22. Jack P. Greene, ed., *The Diary of Colonel Landon Carter of Sabine Hall, 1752–1778* (Charlottesville, Va., 1965), II, 1068, "Undated Entries 1776."
23. Robert Eldon Brown, *Reinterpretation of the Formation of the American Constitution* (Boston, 1963), 8–9, and Robert E. Brown and B. Katherine Brown, *Virginia, 1705–1786: Democracy or Aristocracy?* (East Lansing, Mich., 1964), 83–92. C. Ray Keim, "Primogeniture and Entail in Colonial Virginia," *WMQ*, 3d Ser., XXV (1968), 545–586, follows the Browns' interpretation.
24. Section 7 of the Vermont constitution does not mention the payment of taxes or any other form of property qualification for voting. Thorpe, ed., *Constitutions*, VI, 3742.

Henry VI.[25] For over three hundred years, the figure of forty shillings as the minimum annual rent recurs like a mystic number in English and American suffrage laws.

In America during the Revolutionary period the medieval origins of property qualifications were not unknown. It was even argued that the law of 1429 was part of that corruption of the English constitution that had begun in 1066 and that had been steadily eroding the free constitution of the Angles and the Saxons ever since. Virginian Arthur Lee, who represented the interests of his fellow colonists in London in 1774, publicly questioned Parliament's powers to restrict the vote to persons having a freehold of forty shillings annual value.[26] There had been no significant opposition to property qualifications in the colonies before 1776. If they were not imposed in the form of instructions to the governors, the colonial assemblies had adopted them of their own accord.[27]

The table on pp. 293–307 provides a survey of property qualifications as they were formulated in the first constitutions and the last preceding election laws. Property qualifications fell into four classes. First, there were articles that required "property" without further definition. Second, there were articles that called for "freehold property" and that either did or did not set minimum limits on the size of such property. Where a minimum limit was imposed, it took the form of either a yearly rent or a given acreage. A size limit defined in acres was customary in all the colonies south of New York. Third, there were articles that permitted a combination of land and other property. The conjunctions "and" or "or" determined whether personal property could be substituted wholly or only in part for land. Finally, there were articles that recognized the payment of taxes as sufficient proof of property. Definitions in acres were the least controversial in the long run. Size or value defined in terms of annual rent makes comparison more difficult because of the different curren-

25. "The Knights of the Shires . . . shall be chosen in every County of the Realm of England by People dwelling and resident in the same Counties, whereof every one of them shall have free Land or Tenement to the Value of Forty Shillings by the Year at the least above all Charges." Quoted in Albert Edward McKinley, *The Suffrage Franchise in the Thirteen English Colonies in America* (Philadelphia, 1905), 5.

26. Arthur Lee, *An Appeal To The Justice And Interests Of The People Of Great Britain, In The Present Dispute With America*, 4th ed. (New York, 1775), 6–7.

27. McKinley, *Suffrage Franchise*, 1–4, 484–487; Williamson, *American Suffrage*, 3.

cies named and their changing value. To account for inflation, only the constitution of Massachusetts empowered the legislature to adjust the property requirements for holders of public office in accordance with the real value of currency.[28] Also, the terms freeman and freeholder were not always used in their strict legal sense in eighteenth-century America. In the present context, however, freeholder always means a landholder. (In the Latin original of the charter of Maryland of 1732, the terms *liberi homines* and *liberi tenentes* are also used synonymously, just as "Free-Men" and "Freeholders" are used in the official translation.)[29]

The Restrictive Effect of Property Qualifications

How many new voters were enfranchised in New Hampshire when the voting qualification of land in the value of fifty pounds sterling was replaced by the payment of taxes? How many more candidates could run for the Massachusetts house of representatives when the property qualification was changed to allow the substitution of any property amounting to two hundred pounds for land evaluated at one hundred pounds? How many members of the Massachusetts senate could meet the requirement of three hundred pounds in land but could not be candidates for governor because they fell short of the one thousand pounds needed to run for that office?

These questions remain unanswered. In particular, we still have no adequate information on the extent to which the significantly higher property qualifications for candidates for public office limited

28. Chap. 6, Art. 3, of the constitution of 1780. The difficulty of comparing evaluations in different currencies becomes clear from Morison's attempt to compare the property clauses in the Massachusetts constitutional draft of 1778 with the standards set in the constitution of 1780. Morison equated six shillings "lawful currency" with one silver dollar and ten silver dollars with three pounds sterling. Morison, "Adoption of the Constitution," Mass. Hist. Soc., *Procs.*, 3d Ser., L, 390. See the painstaking effort to compare the Massachusetts "ratable estate" of twenty pounds sterling with the property qualification of forty pounds sterling, in Robert E. Brown, *Middle-Class Democracy and the Revolution in Massachusetts, 1691–1780* (Ithaca, N.Y., 1955), 80–88.

29. Thorpe, ed., *Constitutions*, III, 1671–1672, 1679–1680; compare Cortlandt F. Bishop, *History of Elections in the American Colonies* (New York, 1893), 48–51; McKinley, *Suffrage Franchise*, 102.

the number of contestants.[30] Most of the studies made to date deal only with the restrictive effect property qualifications had on the number of voters. They seem to indicate that by and large the property clauses prohibited at least a quarter—and in some states possibly as many as half—of the white male adults from voting for representatives to their state legislatures. If we look for more precise figures and for details on laws and circumstances, we find them varying widely from state to state.

New Hampshire. It is impossible to say how many New Hampshire residents owned a freehold evaluated at fifty or two hundred pounds. All we know from the tax rolls is that, in the individual towns, between 50 and 90 percent of the males over twenty-one were landowners. In 1770 a law requiring much lower property qualifications for voting in town meetings was passed; but there was resistance even to this law, which called for payment of a poll tax and of property taxes amounting to at least thirty shillings. The objection to this ruling was that it excluded "many Persons" from voting. The subsequent reduction of the tax qualification to eighteen shillings in 1773 probably made any owner of a few cows or horses eligible to vote.[31] In August 1775, the provincial congress considered revising the suffrage law. A committee draft dated August 31, 1775, proposed granting the right to vote to every landowner, regardless of the size of his freehold. Candidates for the legislature would have to own land that was valued at two hundred pounds. But this draft was rejected and a more restrictive law passed. On November 4, 1775, the provincial congress established twenty pounds as the minimum property qualification for voters and three hundred pounds (the amount still in effect from 1727) as the minimum for candidates for office. But this law remained effective for only a few days. On November 14, the congress passed the suffrage law that acquired permanence and was in effect for the election of the provincial congress that enacted the 1776 constitution. This law made it possible for every "Legal Inhabitant Paying Taxes" to vote and for anyone owning land valued at two hundred pounds to run for office.[32] The range of figures proposed in

30. New York is the only exception here. Williamson, *American Suffrage*, 111. The only other study of property qualifications for candidates that I am aware of is Miller, "Legal Qualifications," A.H.A., *Annual Report for 1899*, I, 95–98. Miller says nothing about the effects of the property clauses.
31. Williamson, *American Suffrage*, 25, 36–37.
32. Bouton *et al.*, eds., *N.H. State Papers*, VII, 606, 644, 657–660.

the deliberations preceding this law seems to indicate that critics as well as defenders of high property qualifications were represented in the provincial congress in New Hampshire. In the end, the old clause requiring a freehold of fifty pounds for voters was dropped permanently, but at the same time candidates for the house of representatives and the senate still had to have freeholds valued at fifty and two hundred pounds respectively.

Massachusetts. In its preamble to the constitutional draft of 1780, the constitutional convention of Massachusetts gave some thought to the effects of property qualifications for voting. The convention suggested to the towns that a freehold "of the small annual income of Three Pounds or Sixty Pounds in any Estate" was a qualification that, in the long run, only irresponsible citizens would be unable to meet. "Your Delegates considered that Persons who are Twenty one Years of age, and have no Property, are either those who live upon a part of a Paternal estate, expecting the Fee thereof, who are but just entering into business, or those whose Idleness of Life and profligacy of manners will forever bar them from acquiring and possessing Property."[33] The mere existence of this statement suggests that there was no longer a consensus on property qualifications in Massachusetts. A number of contemporary opinions expressed the fear that property qualifications for voting, leaving aside those for candidacy, would have undesirable effects. The town meeting of Mansfield, in its response to the statement of the constitutional convention, recognized that there would always be irresponsible people who would abuse the property rights of others:

But on the other hand, how many young men Neither Profligates Nor idle persons, for some years must be debared that priviledge? how many sensable, honest, and Naturly Industerouss men, by Numberless Misfortins Never Acquire and possess propperty of the value of sixty pounds? and how many Thousands of good honest men, and Good members of Society who are at this day possessed of a comfortable Interest, which before the publick debts of the Commonwelth are discharged, will not be possessed of a soficiency to quallify them to vote for Representatives if this article takes place as it now stands; We readily allow as we said before that there are and ever will be some who pay little regard to the rights of Propperty: But shall it from thence be argued, that thousands of honest Good members of society shall be

33. "An Address of the Constitutional Convention, to Their Constituents, 1780," Taylor, ed., *Massachusetts*, 125.

subjected to laws framed by Legislators, the Eliction of whom, they could have no voice in?[34]

The town of Northampton also thought "many Persons" would be adversely affected by the proposed qualification and demanded that the payment of any tax be recognized as sufficient qualification to vote for a representative.[35] The town of Marlborough denied the General Court that met in October 1776 the right to frame a constitution because, in Marlborough's opinion, the suffrage law that was passed in the summer of 1776 and that gave the vote to any taxpayer, made new elections necessary. "A great Part of the People, who are now Impowered to Vote, are not Represented, by the present House; haveing had no Voice in the Election."[36] The earlier qualification of property in the value of forty pounds of land with an annual rent or income of forty shillings had clearly excluded a large number of men from voting. The town of Dorchester in 1780 demanded the vote for every adult man without regard to estate or income. The town meeting believed that the number of adult men who could not meet a property qualification of a freehold worth three pounds or an estate of the value of sixty pounds "is daily increasing and possibly may increase in such proportion, that one half the People of this Commonwealth will have no Choice in any Branch of the General Court."[37]

Public opinion in Massachusetts in the summer of 1776 was, if James Warren did not completely misinterpret it, clearly against any qualification for voting other than the paying of taxes. Warren revealed his own position in June 1776, when he reported to his friend John Adams how deliberations on the new election law were going. He expected the proposed law to give the vote to all adult resident freemen if they paid taxes. Warren did not approve of this measure but did not believe that any additional qualification would find a majority among the delegates.[38] Obviously, by June 1776, property qualifications were no longer accepted unquestioningly as part of the

34. *Ibid.*, 154.
35. Mass. Archives, CCLXXVI, fol. 58.
36. Town meeting return of Oct. 21, 1776, in response to the assembly's inquiry of Sept. 17, 1776, *ibid.*, CLVI, fol. 181; also in Handlin and Handlin, eds., *Popular Sources*, 152.
37. Handlin and Handlin, eds., *Popular Sources*, 778.
38. James Warren to John Adams, June 22, 1776, *Warren-Adams Letters*, I, 334–335.

Anglo-American political heritage. The element of the population that would have felt discriminated against by a minimum property law and that opposed such a measure was sufficiently large that its desires had to be taken into account.

The most comprehensive study that has been done on the effects of property qualifications in colonial Massachusetts came to the conclusion that between 53 and 97 percent of the adult male population in the individual towns could vote for representatives. The average throughout Massachusetts was at least 80 percent.[39] But does this make Massachusetts society in the 1760s and 1770s a "middle-class democracy"? Compared to the political culture of most European societies, the British colonists in North America had achieved something remarkably close to popular participation in government. But compared to the twentieth-century ideal type of democracy characterized by adult suffrage, the secret ballot, and none but age qualifications for public office, there were several phases of development yet

39. Robert E. Brown, "Democracy in Colonial Massachusetts," *NEQ*, XXV (1952), particularly p. 297 and the table on pp. 300–301. Compare John Cary, "Statistical Method and the Brown Thesis on Colonial Democracy," *WMQ*, 3d Ser., XX (1963), 251–276. John M. Murrin, "The Myths of Colonial Democracy and Royal Decline in Eighteenth-Century America: A Review Essay," *Cithara*, V (1965), 53–69, analyzes the conceptual framework of Brown's thesis. See also, J. R. Pole, "Suffrage and Representation in Massachusetts: A Statistical Note," *WMQ*, 3d Ser., XIV (1957), 560–592. The debate over property qualifications is viewed in connection with European 19th-century concepts of liberalism and democracy by Hans-Christoph Schröder, "Das Eigentumsproblem in den Auseinandersetzungen um die Verfassung von Massachusetts, 1775–1787," in Rudolf Vierhaus, ed., *Eigentum und Verfassung: zur Eigentumsdiskussion im ausgehenden 18. Jahrhundert* (Göttingen, 1972), 11–67; and Dirk Hoerder, "Vom korporativen zum liberalen Eigentumsbegriff: Ein Element der Amerikanischen Revolution," in Hans-Ulrich Wehler, ed., *200 Jahre amerikanische Revolution und moderne Revolutionsforschung* (Göttingen, 1976), 76–100. Michael Zuckerman, in "The Social Context of Democracy in Massachusetts," *WMQ*, 3d Ser., XXV (1968), 523–544, and in *Peaceable Kingdoms*, contrasts the "communal consensus" with the idea of middle-class democracy. David Grayson Allen is highly critical of Zuckerman in his essay, "The Zuckerman Thesis and the Process of Legal Rationalization in Provincial Massachusetts," *WMQ*, 3d Ser., XXIX (1972), 443–460, published with "Michael Zuckerman's Reply," *ibid.*, 461–468. In a review essay in *History and Theory*, XI (1972), 226–275, John M. Murrin presents a detailed discussion of the local, chronological, and conceptual limitations of Zuckerman's thesis.

to be gone through, and the going did not take place without conflict between defenders and critics of property qualifications.

Connecticut. A recent study of property qualifications in a frontier town in Connecticut established that only half of the male adults in that town had acquired the status of freemen and, as such, the right to vote, although 60 to 75 percent of the adult male population could have met the necessary property qualifications. Many of the nonfreemen were freeholders who were simply politically indifferent. Others were young men who in a few years would be earning enough to qualify as voters. Generally speaking, there was hardly any citizen whose lack of property kept him from voting.[40] In 1740, 79 percent of the adult males in East Guilford, now Madison, could meet the forty shilling requirement. About 56 percent of the adult males in New Haven owned enough land or other property to vote. The fear expressed by the citizens of Dorchester, Massachusetts, that the number of those excluded from voting by minimum property clauses would increase, was realized in at least two Connecticut towns. In 1740, 21 percent of East Guilford men were excluded from freemanship by property clauses. By 1800 this percentage had risen to 35. In Kent, the percentage rose from 21 to 37.[41] Freemanship and the right to vote for representatives to the legislature were not synonymous, but the property qualifications for both were nearly the same.[42]

However insignificant the number of Connecticut citizens excluded from voting may have been, there were still voices calling for the reduction or abolishment of property qualifications. Without considering the number of those actually affected, critics argued: "The Want of *Fifty Shillings* never ought to be the Criterion which distinguisheth a Bondman from a Son of Liberty."[43] In June 1779, the assembly of Connecticut debated a bill that would have granted the vote to all taxpayers, but it was not put to a vote.[44] One might ask why reducing the property qualification to the payment of taxes met

40. Grant, *Democracy in Kent*, 170–171.
41. Williamson, *American Suffrage*, 27, 123, 166.
42. Zeichner, *Connecticut's Years of Controversy*, 6–7.
43. Handbill addressed "To the Honorable General Assembly of the Colony of Connecticut to Be Holden at Hartford in May 1776," and entitled *The Memorial and Petition of a Numerous Body of the Inhabitants of Said Colony, Known by the Name of the United Company*, 1776, Beinecke Library, Yale University, New Haven, Conn., 3.
44. Williamson, *American Suffrage*, 113.

with such opposition if the higher qualifications in force barred only an insignificant segment of the population from the vote.

Rhode Island. Studies of several towns in Rhode Island for the years after 1751 have shown that, on the average, 79 percent of the adult males had enough property to qualify for freemanship and to vote in provincial elections.[45] There are also cases in which the minimum property clauses were ignored, a circumvention of the law not uncommon in other colonies either.[46] This practice, which is often cited to demonstrate that just about anyone could vote, also indicates that there were men in the towns, apart from the qualified voters, whose votes on controversial issues were sought by contending parties.

New York. The earliest study of the effects of property qualifications in New York concluded that at best only half the adult male population could attain the vote.[47] But this conclusion has been corrected by more recent research showing that in 1790, in New York City at least, just about every white adult male could vote.[48] In rural areas, the number of those unable to vote seems to have been much higher, amounting to about 35 percent of the adult male population.[49] In the two Hudson Valley counties of Dutchess and Westchester, where the manors of the quasi-aristocratic Livingstons, Van Cortlandts, and Van Rensselaers determined the social structure, the number of those who could not vote seems to have been considerably higher than elsewhere in the state. However, in these counties leaseholders as well as freeholders could vote for representatives.[50]

---

45. Lovejoy, *Rhode Island Politics*, 16.

46. Williamson, *American Suffrage*, 58. On falsification of election results, see *ibid.*, 50–51. There do not seem to have been any calls to reduce or annul property qualifications in Rhode Island until after the Revolution. Lovejoy, *Rhode Island Politics*, 14–16.

47. Becker, *Political Parties*, 11.

48. Milton M. Klein, "Democracy and Politics in Colonial New York," *New York History*, XL (1959), 233. Compare Patricia U. Bonomi, *A Factious People: Politics and Society in Colonial New York* (New York, 1971).

49. Klein, "Democracy and Politics," *N.Y. Hist.*, XL (1959), 236–237. Williamson, *American Suffrage*, 27, arrives at a figure of over 50% of male adults.

50. Klein, "Democracy and Politics," *N.Y. Hist.*, XL (1959), 233–234. Staughton Lynd has shown that in towns in the southern part of Dutchess County 90% of the taxpayers were assessed at four pounds or less. Lynd, "Who Should Rule at Home? Dutchess County, New York, in the American Revolution," *WMQ*, 3d Ser., XVIII (1961), 335.

Organized opposition to property qualifications existed as early as 1774 in New York.[51] In the course of public discussion on the constitutional draft, extension of suffrage was demanded; and in the constitution as passed in 1777, the freehold qualifications for voting in the election of representatives were cut in half.

For New York we have figures on how many voters met the requirements for electing senators and the governor. In 1790, 33 percent of all qualified voters could participate in these elections, i.e., if an average of 60 percent of the male adults could vote for representatives, then those voting for senators and governors represented only 20 percent of the entire adult male population.[52]

New Jersey. The suffrage law of February 1776 established property qualifications for New Jersey that were incorporated into the state constitution in July of that year.[53] This law, which eliminated land ownership as a requirement and recognized other property in the value of fifty pounds proclamation money as sufficient voting qualification, was the first major change to take place in New Jersey's suffrage law.[54] Assessments of the effects of this change vary from "no drastic alteration" to "popularized suffrage slightly" to "great increase in the number of eligible voters."[55] Some towns feared that minimum property qualifications would have adverse effects and favored the payment of taxes as sufficient qualification to vote for representatives.[56]

---

51. Williamson, *American Suffrage*, 84.
52. *Ibid.*, 111; see also Flick, ed., *History of New York*, IV, 175–176.
53. Thorpe, ed., *Constitutions*, V, 2595.
54. Richard P. McCormick, *The History of Voting in New Jersey: A Study of the Development of Election Machinery, 1664–1911* (New Brunswick, N.J., 1953), 68.
55. Lundin, *Cockpit of the Revolution*, 258; Edward A. Fuhlbruegge, "New Jersey Finances during the American Revolution," New Jersey Historical Society, *Proceedings*, LV (1937), 175; Richard P. McCormick, *Experiment in Independence: New Jersey in the Critical Period, 1781–1789* (New Brunswick, N.J., 1950), 80–81; J. R. Pole, "Suffrage Reform and the American Revolution in New Jersey," N.J. Hist. Soc., *Procs.*, LXXIV (1956), 192, sees "a number of people" excluded from the vote, primarily seasonal workers, the unemployed, apprentices, and young men who were earning their own livings but were still residing at home and so had not yet acquired any property. Williamson, *American Suffrage*, 29, arrives at a figure of 50 to 75% qualified voters among the male adults in some towns.
56. McCormick, *Voting in New Jersey*, 67–68; Williamson, *American Suffrage*, 85.

Pennsylvania. The effects of property qualifications in Pennsylvania have hardly been studied to date. About 60 percent of the adult males seem to have met the fifty-acre freehold qualification before the Revolution.[57] The number of those enfranchised by the constitution of 1776 has not been determined. The resistance against any qualification higher than the payment of taxes was more determined here than in any other state.[58]

Delaware. The effects of the property qualifications established in Delaware in 1734 and remaining in force after 1776 have not yet been studied.[59]

Maryland. Shortly after 1780, between 36 and 55 percent of the white male adults seem to have been landowners, most of whom had more than the required fifty acres. Nonetheless, demands for extending the right to vote were made in the summer of 1776. A company of militiamen marched to a polling place in Annapolis and demanded to vote, even though the entire company taken together owned less than forty pounds.[60] A writer in the *Maryland Gazette* who was pleased that a congress had been called to draft a constitution nevertheless complained that it had been elected only by those qualified under the old law, thus excluding "near half of the members of this state." This fact had evoked "strong sensations of disgust, and more than murmurs of resentment." The provincial congress, this critical article concluded, had therefore not followed the Continental Congress's recommendation that the constitution be based on the authority of the people.[61]

Virginia. In Virginia only a small percentage of white male adults could not vote for representatives.[62] The question then remains, why did the legislature in the election laws of 1762 and 1769 (both disallowed by the crown) bother to reduce the property qualification by half to fifty acres of unsettled freehold, and what prompted Jefferson and George Wythe, who were probably the authors of the bill, to

57. Williamson, *American Suffrage*, 33–34; Pole, *Political Representation*, 259–260.
58. On demands to reduce the minimum property qualifications in Pennsylvania, see Williamson, *American Suffrage*, 86–88, and Pole, *Political Representation*, 260.
59. Douglass, *Rebels and Democrats*, 66.
60. Williamson, *American Suffrage*, 35, 108–109, also p. 81.
61. *Md. Gaz.*, Aug. 15, 1776.
62. Brown and Brown, *Virginia*, 146 and *passim*; Williamson, *American Suffrage*, 29–31, and Pole, *Political Representation*, 146, agree with the Browns.

propose the fifty-acre clause?[63] When Jefferson drafted a new constitution for Virginia in 1783, he again included a minimum property
clause but left the amount open. He wanted to allow militiamen to
vote for representatives without meeting any property qualifications.
In Jefferson's opinion, one of the six "capital defects" of the constitution passed in 1776 was that it left the majority of those "who pay and
fight" disenfranchised. As a rule, not even half the names carried
on the tax rolls and on militia rosters, Jefferson pointed out, were
included on the lists of voting freeholders.[64]

North Carolina. A study of property distribution in North Carolina
between 1777 and 1784 has shown that, in a number of counties,
between 62 and 83 percent of male white adults owned more than
fifty acres of land.[65]

South Carolina. In South Carolina, apparently more than half the
male white adults could meet the property qualification.[66]

Georgia. Even before the abolition of the fifty-acre qualification,
about 70 percent of the male white adults could vote.[67]

Justification and Criticism of Property Qualifications

In May 1776, John Adams spoke out strongly against changing the
suffrage qualifications in Massachusetts. The qualifications were not
strictly applied anyhow, Adams argued, and they would probably
not be in the future. It would be a mistake to put their fundamental
value in question. "There will be no end of it. New claims will arise;
women will demand a vote; lads from twelve to twenty-one will think
their rights not enough attended to; and every man who has not a
farthing, will demand an equal voice with any other, in all acts of
state. It tends to confound and destroy all distinctions, and prostrate
all ranks to one common level."[68] Adams maintained that the vote

63. "A Bill Concerning the Election of Members of the General Assembly,"
Boyd *et al.*, eds., *Jefferson Papers*, II, 337, 345; Pole, *Political Representation*,
143–148.
64. Boyd *et al.*, eds., *Jefferson Papers*, VI, 296; Jefferson, *Notes on Virginia*, ed.
Peden, 118.
65. Williamson, *American Suffrage*, 30–31.
66. *Ibid.*, 35.
67. *Ibid.*, 31.
68. John Adams to James Sullivan, May 26, 1776, Adams, ed., *Works of John
Adams*, IX, 375–378.

must be limited to landowners. Extending it to all taxpayers would give rise to corruption.[69] Adams based his argument on a philosophical appeal to the arbitrariness of the very principle of majority decisions. Why should the majority have the right to impose its will on the minority and expect the minority to subordinate itself? Only because there was no acceptable alternative. Adams asked rhetorically why women were not allowed to vote. The same arguments that applied there applied to denying the vote to those without property. "Is it not equally true, that men in general, in every society, who are wholly destitute of property, are also too little acquainted with public affairs to form a right judgment, and too dependent upon other men to have a will of their own?" Granting the vote to people who were not financially independent, Adams thought, was like writing into the constitution a provision that would invite corruption. "Such is the frailty of the human heart, that very few men who have no property, have any judgment of their own. They talk and vote as they are directed by some man of property, who has attached their minds to his interest. . . . [They are] to all intents and purposes as much dependent upon others, who will please to feed, clothe, and employ them, as women are upon their husbands, or children on their parents." Adams claimed that James Harrington's law governing the relationship of property to political power operated with the same inevitability as Newton's laws governing mechanics: "Power always follows property. . . . The balance of power in a society, accompanies the balance of property in land."[70] Granting political power to the unpropertied had to strike a Harringtonian as an interference in the delicate operations of a law that could not be upset with impunity. A broader distribution of property, which Adams favored in this same letter, was considered a process that could be guided to some extent and that would result in a broader distribution of political power. But for the sake of political stability, the sequence could not be reversed.

An analysis of the arguments for property qualifications reveals the following assumptions: (1) Owning property makes a person free; (2) Property—and real estate in particular—ties its owner to the well-being of the community; (3) Anyone who levies taxes must also be subject to them; (4) Property and power in the same hands means

---

69. *Thoughts on Government*, in Adams, ed., *Works of John Adams*, IV, 195; John Adams to James Warren, July 7, 1777, *Warren-Adams Letters*, I, 339.
70. Adams, ed., *Works of John Adams*, IX, 376–377.

political stability; (5) Property is subject to the majority decisions of property owners only.

The idea that property makes a man free had long been a basic tenet of Anglo-American constitutionalism. It had been reinforced by the English Whigs' experience in their struggle against the crown's claim to power and by the comparable experience of the American whigs in their struggle with Parliament. Protection of property from arbitrary acts of government had proved to be the material basis for all other civil liberties. Intellectual freedom, experience had shown, presupposed economic independence. Even the Levellers had therefore insisted on three basic freedoms: "Liberty of conscience in matters of Faith, and Divine worship; Liberty of the Person, and liberty of Estate: which consists properly in the propriety of their goods, and a disposing power of their possessions."[71] And Algernon Sidney had regarded the right to property as "an appendage to liberty"; only the unfree had no claim to it.[72] In the same vein, John Dickinson formulated the relationship of liberty to property as most colonists perceived it in 1768. "We cannot be Happy, without being Free. . . . We cannot be free, without being secure in our property."[73] In 1775 an anonymous pamphleteer in Philadelphia expressed the same ideas: "By the Happiness of Society is to be meant chiefly, the Security of every one's Rights and Properties."[74] In June 1776, the congress representing the revolutionary committees in Pennsylvania called for a new constitution to secure—in that order—"property, liberty and the sacred rights of conscience."[75]

The assumption that the propertyless have "no will of their own" was the other side of the coin, and it can be found in English social theory from Locke to Blackstone. Hamilton was paraphrasing Blackstone when he said: "The true reason of requiring any qualification, with regard to property in voters, is to exclude such persons, as are *in so mean a situation*, that they are esteemed to have *no will* of their own"; only demagogues profited from the vote of the unpropertied.[76]

71. [John Lilburne], *Englands Birth-right justified against all arbitrary usurpation* . . . (London, 1645), cited in Macpherson, *Possessive Individualism*, 137.

72. Sidney, *Discourses Concerning Government*, III, 73.

73. *Writings of John Dickinson*, I, 275.

74. *Essay upon Government*, 11.

75. "Address of the Deputies," June 22, 1776, *Journals of the House of Representatives of Pennsylvania*, I, 42.

76. *Farmer Refuted*, Feb. 1775, in Syrett and Cooke, eds., *Hamilton Papers*, I, 106. Hamilton is referring to Blackstone, *Commentaries*, Book I, chap. 2, 171.

The *Pennsylvania Evening Post* used the same argument to attack the absence of property qualifications in Pennsylvania's constitution. It was "not difficult" to acquire land valued at fifty pounds. Those who had not managed to acquire anything were usually the stupidest and least informed members of society and therefore particularly susceptible to deceptive arguments. "If they are invested with the rights of election, which in a commonwealth are always the rights of Sovereignty, their errors and the villanies of their deceivers are immediately clothed with the sanction of laws."[77] Even Thomas Paine, who in principle opposed property qualifications with the argument "Freedom and fortune have no natural relation," denied the vote to servants. He considered paid employees of the government to represent one category of servants, but he did not explain why he excluded this group from the vote. The ordinary type of bound laborers he considered as having voluntarily renounced the responsibilities and therefore the rights of a citizen. "Their interest is in their master, and depending on him in sickness and in health, and voluntarily withdrawing from taxation and public service of all kinds, they stand detached by choice from the common floor." As soon as a servant assumed responsibility for his own affairs again, he should be given back all his civil rights.[78]

The opponents of high property qualifications asked why the liberating effect of property started only with ownership of land valued at fifty pounds sterling. They felt that a small amount of property should confer the same rights as large fortunes. "Every poor man has a life, a personal liberty, and a right to his earnings; and is in danger of being injured by government in a variety of ways; therefore it is necessary that these people should enjoy the right of voting for representatives, to be protectors of their lives, personal liberty, and their little property, which, though small, is yet, upon the whole, a

77. "A Dialogue between Orator Puff and Peter Easy," *Pa. Evening Post*, Oct. 24, 1776.
78. "A Serious Address to the People of Pennsylvania," Foner, ed., *Writings of Paine*, II, 287. Paine's argument reads like a paraphrase of the one the Levellers used in 1647: "The reason why we would exclude apprentices, or servants, or those that take alms, is because they depend upon the will of other men and should be afraid to displease." Macpherson, *Possessive Individualism*, 123. By the term servants, the Levellers seem to have meant all dependent men who sell their labor. *Ibid.*, 107, 144, 282. Peter Laslett, "Market Society and Political Theory," *Historical Journal*, VII (1964), 150–154, calls this view into question.

very great object to them."[79] Small property holdings were even more in need of protection than large ones, because "rich men enjoy too great a share of power at all times, even without the addition of governmental powers."[80] Furthermore, the war was daily demonstrating the potential social value of unpropertied men who were nonetheless capable of bearing arms, and anyone who protected property with his own life should have the same rights as a property owner. "Shall we who hold property be content to see our brethren, who have done their full share in procuring that security . . . on election days, standing aloof and sneaking into corners and ashamed to show their heads, in the meetings of freemen?" asked the town meeting of Northampton, Massachusetts.[81] The soldiers in the militia and in the Continental army did not wait long to press their claim to the vote.[82]

The second assumption, that property ties its owner to the well-being of the community, became the standard justification of property qualifications in the state bills of rights and constitutions. Virginia provided the first formulation of this idea, and Delaware, Maryland, Pennsylvania, and Vermont picked up the same wording: "All men, having sufficient evidence of permanent common interest with, and attachment to, the community, have the right of suffrage."[83] As early as 1670, the House of Burgesses had justified property qualifications by citing English laws that limited the vote to men "as by their estates, real or personall have interest enough to tye them to the endeavour of the publique good."[84] This idea was based on a realistic assessment of

79. "Watchman," *Md. Gaz.*, Aug. 15, 1776.

80. "Whitlock," *Pa. Evening Post*, May 22, 1777.

81. Return from Northampton, May 22, 1780, Mass. Archives, CCLXXVI, fol. 58.

82. On the leveling effect the claims of the soldiers had on the extension of suffrage, see McCormick, *Voting in New Jersey*, 71; Pole, "Suffrage Reform," N.J. Hist. Soc., *Procs.*, LXXIV (1956), 189; Douglass, *Rebels and Democrats*, 251.

83. Thorpe, ed., *Constitutions*, VII, 3813; *Convention of the Delaware State*, 18; Thorpe, ed., *Constitutions*, III, 1687, V, 3083, VI, 3740. The phrase is equivalent to the one that became common in the 19th century—"a stake in society" —the commitment that involves the individual in whatever risks the enterprise "society" might take.

84. Bishop, *History of Elections*, 71, 79. In 1696, Gov. William Markham of Pennsylvania had welcomed the newly appointed members of his council as follows: "You are all men that are fastened to the country by visible estates . . . and that's a great security you will study the interest of the country." Pole, *Political Representation*, 261.

human nature that presumed that men will not lightly betray their major economic interests. It was this fundamental motivation that would commit those who enjoyed the special privilege of legislators to the common good. An oath of loyalty to the constitution was good; an interest in the commonweal was better; and the best token of such interest was a piece of land. The same principle applied to voters. The unpropertied had no firm attachment to the established order. "People, having nothing to lose and a prospect of gaining by public convulsions," according to a writer in the *Pennsylvania Evening Post*, "are always the most ready to engage in seditious, tumultous, factuous proceeding."[85]

The same logic served in arguments against proposed substitutes for the land qualification, such as the payment of taxes or possession of movable property. Jefferson and Edmund Pendleton clarified the issue in an exchange in August 1776. Pendleton defended the property qualifications incorporated in Virginia's new constitution. "Those of fixed Permanent property, who cannot suddenly remove without injury to that property or Substituting another proprietor . . . alone I consider as having Political Attachment. The persons who when they have produced burthens on the State, may move away and leave them to be born by others, I can by no means think should have the framing of Laws."[86] Jefferson countered that he could not consider any man with a family and household as having no binding ties to the society in which he lived. "Take what circumstances you please as evidence of this, either the having resided a certain time, or having a family, or having property, any or all of them. Whoever intends to live in a country must wish that country well."[87] But the majority of Virginia's constitution makers and lawmakers were not ready to accept Jefferson's plea for manhood suffrage for white Virginians.

Other critics of property qualifications were more radical than Jefferson. They argued that private property could make a person

85. "A Dialogue between Orator Puff and Peter Easy," *Pa. Evening Post*, Oct. 24, 1776. See, too, *Pa. Ledger*, Nov. 26, 1776; "An Independent Whig," *N.-Y. Jour.*, Feb. 29, 1776; *Pa. Ledger*, Nov. 2, 1776; and *Providence Gaz.*, Mar. 20, 1779.
86. Aug. 10, 1776, Boyd *et al.*, eds., *Jefferson Papers*, I, 489. The town of Northampton, Massachusetts, presented the same argument on May 22, 1780: "The case may be that a man may have 200 [pounds] value of estate and no real estate . . . [but] personal estate, especially of some sort, is very easily transferred from place to place." Mass. Archives, CCLXXVI, fol. 58.
87. Aug. 26, 1776, Boyd *et al.*, eds., *Jefferson Papers*, I, 504.

disregard the public good because it created a personal interest that might well run counter to the interests of the community. High property qualifications would fill public offices with men who were ambitious, shrewd, and mainly intent on their own private interests.[88] In 1775 the *Providence Gazette* published an excerpt from James Burgh's *Political Disquisitions* that broke a taboo by suggesting that a legal limit be put on the amount of property anyone could hold, "a *noplus ultra*, beyond which individuals could not go."[89] But an "agrarian law" providing for maximum landholdings for any individual, an idea frequently discussed among republicans and radical Whigs in seventeenth- and eighteenth-century England, found little support in the New World.[90] It showed up only sporadically in public debate, usually in connection with attempts to combat the decline in "public virtue." An agrarian law, the reasoning was, would prevent individuals from owning too much property and consequently from acquiring "too much power and influence, dangerous to the liberties of the people."[91] The attempt to write this idea into the Pennsylvania bill of rights failed.[92]

The principle that anyone who levies taxes must also be subject to them was a third major defense of property qualifications, especially for holding office. In 1776 this principle was more readily accepted than any other. It was simply a logical extension of the rallying cry that had been raised in the colonies for years, "No taxation without representation." In the words of a defender of property qualifications in Connecticut: "Common prudence most certainly will direct the freemen of every elective state, to make choice of men to govern and tax them, who have estates of their own to be taxed by the same rule that they tax others."[93]

88. Samuel Adams to Elbridge Gerry, Jan. 2, 1776, Cushing, ed., *Writings of Samuel Adams*, III, 247.
89. *Providence Gaz.*, Dec. 9, 1775. The quotation comes from Burgh, *Political Disquisitions*, III, 186.
90. Robbins, *Eighteenth-Century Commonwealthman*, 15–16 and *passim*, index, s.v. "Agrarian."
91. Samuel McClintock to William Whipple, Aug. 2, 1776, Whipple Papers, Force Transcripts, Library of Congress.
92. See p. 194 above.
93. "A.B.," *Conn. Jour.*, Oct. 23, 1776. Similarly, "A Farmer," *Providence Gaz.*, Mar. 20, 1779; "Watchman," *Md. Gaz.*, Aug. 15, 1776. Town meeting resolve from Weymouth, Massachusetts, May 22, 1780, Mass. Archives, CCLXXVII, fol. 80, and from Petersham, Massachusetts, June 1, 1780, *ibid.*, fol. 104.

The logical rebuttal to this principle was again the arbitrarily established amount and kind of property that qualified a man to vote or hold office. Those with considerable property claimed that the majority rule of the unpropertied could cost them the loss of their property while a majority rule of those with property could have no disadvantages for the unpropertied. Opponents of this view argued that landowners were clever enough to distinguish between a "tax on Estates" and a "tax on polls." They would levy taxes to leave real estate relatively unaffected and would raise revenues instead, for instance by imposing a high poll tax. They would also prefer to put high taxes on consumer goods rather than on land. England constituted a case in point. Under Queen Anne, the vote had been placed in the hands of "the opulent." The result was that today the people had to pay high taxes on even the most basic necessities.[94]

Harrington's thesis that political power went hand in hand with land ownership—the fourth assumption—lost its force under the circumstances prevailing in America.[95] Since there was an overabundance of land, a parcel of land did not have the value it had in the British Isles. Paine had this point in mind when, in defending Pennsylvania's constitution, he put a far greater value on labor and population than on property. Wealth in America, he claimed, differed from wealth in Europe. "In the latter it only shifts hands, without either increasing or diminishing; but in the former there is a real addition of riches by population and cultivation."[96] By emphasizing the value of workers, even of those who owned nothing, Paine singled out a feature of the American situation that was no less characteristic than the relative ease with which land could be acquired. But in the eighteenth century, this insight gained political significance only in

94. Resolutions from Northampton, May 22, 1780, in Mass. Archives, CCLXXVI, fol. 58, and from Dorchester, in Handlin and Handlin, eds., *Popular Sources*, 778. "An Elector," *Pa. Packet*, Apr. 29, 1776.

95. This argument was seldom used in public discussion. Pole, *Political Representation*, 214, 216, 223, refers only to John Adams. Joseph Galloway outlined Harrington's basic argument for the First Continental Congress on Sept. 8, 1774. John Adams's note on Galloway's speech reads: "Power results from the real property of the society." Burnett, ed., *Letters of the Continental Congress*, I, 22; [Joseph Galloway], *A Candid Examination Of The Mutual Claims of Great-Britain, And The Colonies . . .* (New York, 1775), 35, 36.

96. "A Serious Address to the People of Pennsylvania," *Pa. Packet*, Dec. 1, 1778, also in Foner, ed., *Writings of Paine*, II, 283.

connection with measures to attract immigrants and with granting them citizenship.

The principle that property should be subject to the majority decisions of property owners only, a fifth assumption, could claim as its provenance the theory of social contract as handed down by the English Whigs of the seventeenth century. In terms of social theory, property qualifications and the postulate of equality could easily be reconciled by asserting that the distribution of property preceded the social contract, that "the Determination of Property must necessarily have been before the settlement of Government; this being only a Means for the securing of Property."[97] Everyone had an identical claim to retain in society what he brought with him when he entered it. If any restrictions at all were to be put on the individual's right to dispose of his property, then only a majority of those directly concerned could authorize such restrictions. Defenders of property qualifications also thought of the future, when in America, "as it has happened in all states, as their people and manufactures increase, . . . the numbers of those without property will bear a greater proportion to those who have property, than they do at present."[98]

Critics of property qualifications found the idea of the social contract no less useful to their side of the argument. Once the magic triad of life, liberty, and property was dissolved, property seemed to take a subordinate role. The protection of property could no longer be regarded as the sole purpose for the existence of a political community. (The replacement of "property" in the Declaration of Independence with the phrase "the pursuit of happiness" could be read to support this view.) If securing liberty and happiness was the prime purpose of the social contract and if the sign of a citizen's freedom was his right to have a voice in the community's affairs, then the vote was not a privilege but a right, "not only a civil; but . . . a natural right, which ought to be considered as a principle cornerstone in the foundation for the frame of government to stand on."[99] The denial of

97. *Essay upon Government*, 20. The Essex Result contains a similar statement. Taylor, ed., *Massachusetts*, 78–79.
98. "A Dialogue between Orator Puff and Peter Easy," *Pa. Evening Post*, Oct. 24, 1776. See, too, "Ludlow," *Pa. Jour.*, May 28, 1777; the message of the Massachusetts constitutional convention of 1780 to the towns, in Taylor, ed., *Massachusetts*, 125; and "Roundhead," *Boston Gaz.*, July 7, 1777.
99. Town meeting resolve of Stoughton, May 24, 1780, in Handlin and Handlin, eds., *Popular Sources*, 795.

the vote to those who cannot meet property qualifications is therefore a violation of the terms of social contract articulated in the bills of rights. In the words of the town meeting of Northampton, Massachusetts: "Will not such persons be in a state of absolute slavery to such a legislative, while they shall continue without the quantum of property prescribed . . . ? If they are to be subject to the jurisdiction and legislation of your legislature with regard to life, liberty and their day wages, or whatever small property they may acquire, and yet have no voice in the appointment of that legislature."[100] How many Americans in 1780 shared these doubts about the justness of property qualifications we will never know. What we know is that the question was publicly debated and that property qualifications had ceased to be an unquestioned feature of American politics. It took decades to abolish them throughout the Union, but the process started in 1776.

The leaders of republican political theory in 1776 hoped for the opposite solution. They expected all male adults to become voters because they would become property owners. The central role that they envisioned for the yeoman farmer in the stable development of American society rested on this belief. Jefferson suggested in his draft of the Virginia constitution that fifty acres of land be given to every landless grown man.[101] The proposal was not adopted but it also did not seem utopian in a society where the headright system was within living memory. The reasoning behind suggestions such as Jefferson's was summed up in John Adams's defense of property qualifications:

The only possible way, then, of preserving the balance of power on the side of equal liberty and public virtue, is to make the acquisition of land easy to every member of society; to make a division of the land into small quantities, so that the multitude may be possessed of landed estates. If the multitude is possessed of the balance of real estate, the multitude will have the balance of power, and in that case the multitude will take care of the liberty, virtue, and interest of the multitude, in all acts of government.[102]

100. Resolve of the Northampton town meeting, May 22, 1780, Mass. Archives, CCLXXVI, fol. 58.
101. Boyd *et al.*, eds., *Jefferson Papers*, I, 362.
102. John Adams to James Sullivan, May 26, 1776, Adams, ed., *Works of John Adams*, IX, 376–377.

In the decades after Independence, proponents of an active, interventionist federal and state land policy could have built their case on solid republican social philosophy of the first hour. But the distribution of property in the new nation was to be left to less rational forces.[103]

103. The framers of the Federal Constitution at first ignored property related issues. They left the regulation of the right to vote in federal elections to the states, not because they considered the issue unimportant but because, as Madison explained in *The Federalist*, "One uniform rule would probably have been as dissatisfactory to some of the States as it would have been difficult to the convention." Rossiter, ed., *Federalist Papers*, 326. The Fifth Amendment, too, dealt with property, guaranteeing that "No person shall . . . be deprived of life, liberty, or property, without due process of law; nor shall private property be taken for public use, without just compensation." But this amendment did little more than sum up the confiscation clauses of the state constitutions. Nevertheless, the sanctity of private property was central to the new American social and political order, and it was only consistent for a justice of the Supreme Court of the United States in 1795 to assume that he did not need a clause in the Constitution in order to base a verdict on that norm. "The right of acquiring and possessing property, and having it protected," Justice William Paterson declared, "is one of the natural, inherent, and unalienable rights of man. Men have a sense of property. Property is necessary to their subsistence, wants and desires; its security was one of the objects that induced them to unite in society." Vanhorne's Lessee v. Dorrance, 2 Dallas 304.

CHAPTER X

The Common Good

Public good is, as it were, a common bank, in which every individual has his respective share; and consequently whatever damage that sustains, the individuals unavoidably partake of the calamity.

John Hurt, *The Love of Our Country*, Philadelphia, 1777

The Common Good versus Colonial Rule

From 1775 on, the military situation prompted repeated calls for sacrifice, unity, and the subordination of private interests. Only a collective effort could bring victory to the colonists. Indeed, resistance against England could not have led to independence and the founding of a nation in defiance of the major sea power of the world if nothing more than individual greed and blind competition among individuals, communities, or regions had motivated the colonists. Almost daily during the Revolutionary years the common good was invoked under various names—"the public good," "the public weal," "the common interest," "the Good of the Whole," "common benefit," "general Utility," or "the general Happiness of the People."[1]

The very existence and development of colonial society had been the product of both collective and individual effort, of devotion to the common good as well as of the pursuit of private interests. In New England, the Puritan tradition had kept alive knowledge of the tension between the claims of the community and those of the individual. As late as 1774, a Connecticut preacher rejected the claim that unequal distribution of property predated the social contract and was therefore justified, arguing that God did not bring human beings together in a society solely for the sake of the individual's interests: "Every one must be required to do all he can that tends to the highest

1. Thorpe, ed., *Constitutions*, VII, 3813, V, 3081–3083; *Convention of the Delaware State*, 17–18; Taylor, ed., *Massachusetts*, 124.

good of the state."[2] With increasing secularization the idea of the common good acquired new significance. Even in mid-eighteenth-century New England, the invocation by the authorities of divine sanctions would have been insufficient; their decisions could only be regarded as legitimate if they served the common good. "Pursuing the true and common interests of the nation or people they govern" had to be the guiding principle of their actions.[3] "The Good, Safety and Happiness of the People, is the great End of civil Government; and must be considered as the only rational Object, in all original Compacts, and political Institutions."[4]

If this was the standard used for judging public officials whom the colonists themselves had elected, then it applied all the more to representatives of the crown. Between 1764 and 1776, the colonists repeatedly questioned the legitimacy of decisions made by Parliament, ministers, and governors, arguing that these decisions did not serve the well-being of the entire empire but only the interests of one part of it or, indeed, only the interests of a corrupt ministry. In a 1764 pamphlet directed against England's new colonial policy, James Otis expressed the colonists' claims in general terms valid for any political authority. "The end of government being the *good* of mankind, points out its great duties: It is above all things to provide for the security, the quiet, and happy enjoyment of life, liberty and property. There is no one act which a government can have a *right* to make, that does not tend to the advancement of the security, tranquility and prosperity of the people."[5] Otis's concise formulation also reflects the ambiguity that has characterized appeals to the common good in American society ever since. He defined the good of "mankind" as the guaranteed enjoyment of life, liberty, and property, that is, claims made by the individual, not by the collective. The political apparatus is seen as an instrument subservient not to the interests of

2. Nathaniel Niles, *Two Discourses on Liberty* . . . (Newburyport, Mass., 1774), 9, 12–13n, cited in Alan Heimert, *Religion and the American Mind from the Great Awakening to the Revolution* (Cambridge, Mass., 1966), 516.

3. *Conn. Courant*, Sept. 9, 1765, cited in Richard L. Bushman, *From Puritan to Yankee: Character and the Social Order in Connecticut, 1690–1765* (Cambridge, Mass., 1967), 283. See pp. 282–286 on the reconciliation of self-interest with the public good.

4. Town meeting resolution of the town of Mendon, Massachusetts, *Boston Gaz.*, June 7, 1773.

5. Otis, *Rights of the British Colonies*, 10–11.

"the state" as a collective but to the individual citizen. This point of view was a natural consequence of the colonists' political and economic situation. They suffered political and economic restrictions because of their status as colonists. To fight their second-class position, they had to deny their inferior collective character as colonists and simply demand equal treatment as individual subjects living in the mother country.

In these same years, the common good was also invoked by social critics in Britain and the colonies, who claimed that the growing desire for material gain was undermining allegedly traditional civic virtues. Their prophecies borrowed from antiquity the idea—and many of the supporting examples—that the decline of states was mainly attributable to the declining virtue of the citizenry. John Dickinson, for example, complained in his *Farmer's Letters* of 1768 that too many of his countrymen thought only of their own advantage and wanted only "to increase their own wealth, power, and credit, without the least regard for the society under the protection of which they live." But history has shown, Dickinson argued, that a nation hastens its own downfall "when individuals consider their interests as distinct from those of the public."[6] Even if this was a conventional theme of Anglo-American social criticism in the eighteenth century and not solely a direct response to the crisis of the empire it is a fact that in American public life of the 1770s and 1780s, innumerable cautionary and importunate appeals were made to the common good. There were several reasons that prompted pamphleteers and politicians to do so.

First of all, the military effort had to be strengthened against divisive regional interests and the desire for personal profit. In addition, the political cohesion of the thirteen rebelling colonies demanded increased recognition of the connecting common good. From 1774 on, colonial leaders had to deal with the question of whether the mere consciousness of an all-embracing common good was strong enough to hold together a loose confederation without one region or one clique, or even a military junta, dominating. Political theorists of the eighteenth century associated the republican form of government with an incessant clash of parties and factions that would lead to anarchy because the symbols of unity and permanence a hereditary

6. *Writings of John Dickinson*, I, 271, letter 12. Further examples and interpretations of the political aspect of this argument are in Bailyn, *Ideological Origins*, 60–66.

monarchy could provide were lacking. "Where many rule," an English opponent of republicanism declared, "each is a rival to the rest, and therefore has a distinct interest from the public; . . . the strength and spirit of the state is spent in countermining and opposition."[7] A writer using the pseudonym "Semper Eadem" (always the same) warned readers of the *Boston Gazette* that "party spirit" had destroyed the commonwealth of the Israelites.[8] Other newspapers reminded the colonists that the decline of a state was imminent whenever individuals saw their interests as divided from those of the public, and that a nation was like a body in which "concord" represented health, "discord," disease, and civil war, death.[9]

But this metaphor could serve just as convincingly to encourage the colonists to press on toward independence. The argument ran that the English constitution was doomed to fail because it did not subordinate the "distinct classes" of the monarch, the lords, and the commons to an idea of the common good that was binding for all. Thus, an irreconcilable conflict of interests would destroy England, just as the continuing conflict between patricians and plebians had brought about the downfall of the Roman republic. By contrast, the new American state would be solidly based on a community of interests in which all citizens shared. "Having no rank above that of freemen, she has but one interest to consult, and that interest, (blessed be *God* for it,) is the true and only interest of men as members of society."[10]

Another compelling reason for the significant role that the idea of the common good played in the political rhetoric of 1776 was that it was an integral part of social contract thinking. No one writing in 1776 and using the theory of social contract as his point of departure for explaining the purpose of the new state and of its governmental form could avoid reference to the common good. The Declaration of Independence enumerated as the king's first violation of his duties the refusal to assent to colonial laws, "the most wholesome and necessary for the public good." The state constitutions, naturally,

---

7. Usher, *Republican Letters*, 121; compare chap. 4, pp. 100–101 above.
8. *Boston Gaz.*, June 10, 1776.
9. "Thoughts on Different Subjects," *Pa. Ledger*, June 15, 1776; "An American Whig," *Providence Gaz.*, Apr. 3, 1779. Further examples are cited in Wood, *Creation of the American Republic*, 53–65.
10. "To The People Of North-America On The Different Kinds Of Government," *New York Packet. And The American Advertiser*, Mar. 28, 1776, also in *American Archives*, 4th Ser., V, 181–183.

incorporated the common good as the guiding value for the exercise of legitimate government.

The Common Good in the State Constitutions

The first three articles of Virginia's bill of rights recapitulated the tenets of the theory of social contract. The third named the common good as the highest consideration guiding governmental action and a justification for resistance against the abuse of governmental power. "Government is, or ought to be, instituted for the common benefit, protection, and security of the people, nation, or community; of all the various modes and forms of government, that is best which is capable of producing the greatest degree of happiness and safety." The sixth article added that the legislature's highest obligation was to serve the common good. This same article made the right to vote dependent on a "permanent common interest with, and attachment to the community." A male adult was expected to prove such attachment by acquiring property.[11]

The first article in Delaware's bill of rights established the sovereignty of the people and declared that governmental power existed "solely for the Good of the Whole." Any infringements on "public Liberty" would indicate the misuse of governmental power.[12]

Pennsylvania's bill of rights followed Virginia's wording and defined the criteria of good government as the "common benefit, protection and security of the people, nation or community." Good government was inconsistent with "the particular emolument or advantage of any single man, family, or set of men, who are a part only of that community."[13] The draft for the bill of rights included an article, later rejected by the constitutional convention, that would have set an upper limit on the acquisition of property and that justified this measure with "the general happiness of the people."[14]

Maryland adopted Delaware's bill of rights. Georgia did not draw up a bill of rights, but it did include the phrase *pro bono publico* in its state seal.[15]

11. Thorpe, ed., *Constitutions*, VII, 3813.
12. *Convention of the Delaware State*, 17–18.
13. Thorpe, ed., *Constitutions*, V, 3082–3083.
14. "Essay of a Declaration of Rights," Hist. Soc. Pa.
15. Thorpe, ed., *Constitutions*, III, 1686–1688, II, 784.

Massachusetts's bill of rights followed Virginia and Pennsylvania's wording and reinforced it by adding: "Government is instituted . . . not for the profit, honor, or private interest of any one man, family, or class of men." The constitution of Massachusetts went further than earlier ones in suggesting that defending the very existence of the political structure ("the body politic") might be part of securing the common good. The sequence in which the opening sentence of the preamble listed the duties of government was unusual in emphasizing the dependence of the individual on government for the enjoyment of his rights: "The end of the institution, maintenance, and administration of government, is to secure the existence of the body politic, to protect it, and to furnish the individuals who compose it with the power of enjoying in safety and tranquillity their natural rights, and the blessings of life."[16]

The bills of rights and the constitutions failed in one important respect. They did not reach a definition of the common good that resolved the ambiguities inherent in the concept as it was developed in the decade prior to 1776. The common good and the sum of private interests were seen as synonymous, and the possibility of conflict between them was belittled. In its preamble to the constitutional draft of 1779–1780, the constitutional convention of Massachusetts indulged in the following tautology: "The Interest of the Society is common to all its Members. The great Enquiry is, wherein this Common Interest consists."[17] The founding generation dealt with this question inductively. They did not see any point in trying to deduce an answer to it from a doctrine such as that of popular sovereignty. And they refused to take refuge in a metaphysical definition of the common good that provided the desired theoretical consistency, was free of all inner contradictions, and could be applied to all situations. Despite their penchant for the image of the state as a body, they did not go so far as to invest this body with a life and with interests of its own that would justify the ruthless subordination of the individual's interests.

"Public good is, as it were, a common bank."

In addition to the legally relevant constitutional texts, the idea of a common or public good was publicly discussed in metaphorical lan-

16. *Ibid.*, III, 1890, 1888–1889.
17. Taylor, ed., *Massachusetts*, 124.

guage, particularly in images taken from the world of commerce. A Philadelphia pamphlet of 1777 explained: "Public good is, as it were, a common bank, in which every individual has his respective share; and consequently whatever damage that sustains, the individuals unavoidably partake of the calamity."[18] The image was sufficiently ambiguous to reflect American reality accurately. It did not exclude a fundamental community of interests, a subordination of the individual customer to the general terms of doing business, any more than it excluded conflicting interests among the customers themselves. In the discussion that took place during the framing of the constitutions, conflict between different interest groups was not denied, but the conviction that these groups could exist in harmony dominated.

The comparison of the state to a corporation reflected this same assumption. "The case is similar to that of a trading company, possessed of a common stock, into which every one hath given his proportion," a Connecticut pamphlet of 1775 explicated. "The interest of this common stock is now the property of the whole body, and each individual is benefited in proportion to the good of the whole, and is a good or bad member in proportion as he uniteth to, or counteracteth the interest of the body." The analogies to a bank and to a corporation are at least as revealing of the founding generation's actual expectations as the abstract deductions from the theory of social contract with which this same writer, a clergyman, introduced his pamphlet: "As society evidently originates from mutual compact or agreement, so it is equally evident, that the members who compose it, unite in one common interest; each individual gives up all private interest that is not consistent with the general good, the interest of the whole body: And, considered as a member of society, he hath no other interest but that of the whole body, of which he is a member."[19]

The frequent invocation of the common good between 1776 and 1780 went together with a full awareness of the existing conflicts of interests among Americans. Conflicts between the interests of the coastal cities and the inland rural areas had been mounting for decades as trade increased. Political rhetoric had rather misleadingly labeled the groups involved as the "mercantile interest" and the "landed interest." The terms were misleading in the sense that the mercantile interest included more than the regular commercial activities of the merchants. Real estate in the urban areas as well as the

18. John Hurt, *The Love of Our Country* (Philadelphia, 1777), 10.
19. Levi Hart, *Liberty Described and Recommended* (Hartford, Conn., 1775), 11.

interests of artisans and of the professional classes indirectly dependent on commerce also came under the heading of the mercantile interest.[20] But these two terms were permanent fixtures in the debates
of the time. To cite only one especially articulate example, Petersham,
a small town in western Massachusetts, saw an almost irreconcilable
conflict of interests between the "mercantile towns" and the "freehold interest of the country" in 1776. The Petersham town meeting
felt the stability of the whole country could be maintained only if the
representatives of rural landholding interests were in the majority
in the legislature.

The mercantile interest being put on a par with the free-hold, cannot be safe,
more especially in a community where the balance of trade is against us, and
likely so to continue for a considerable time yet to come; which must be
where raw materials are exported, and manufactured ones imported. In such
case the merchant's interest will lead him to keep the people dependent on
the channel of his trade, and of consequence use every means to discourage
manufactures among us, as trade will lessen in proportion to their being carried on, and must very near come to a stand at the time when our manufactures are sufficient for our own consumption; and until such time as we
change the situation of our exports and imports to our advantage, as is
the case of *England*, the merchant's interest must ever operate against the
prosperity of his country.[21]

The debate on the relative merits of agriculture or commerce for
the development of American society also produced early forms of
the utilitarian definition of the common good, usually identified with
the nineteenth century. During the election campaign for the revolutionary assembly of Massachusetts in May 1776, an advocate of commercial interests urged readers of the *Massachusetts Spy* to vote only
for highly qualified candidates, for patriots, for rational men of integrity,

20. Pole, *Political Representation*, 177, see also pp. 63–65, and Michael Kammen, *Empire and Interest* (Philadelphia, 1970).
21. Resolution of the town meeting, Sept. 27, 1776, *American Archives*, 5th
Ser., II, 577. Further examples in Massachusetts newspapers were furnished
by the county convention of Worcester. *Mass. Spy*, Apr. 24, 1777, and William
Gordon, "To the Freemen of Massachusetts-Bay, Letter III," *Cont. Jour.*,
Apr. 16, 1778. The same economic situation gave rise to similar conflicts
between Philadelphia and rural western Pennsylvania. See Pole, *Political
Representation*, 115, 169, 260–270.

who will . . . promote the greatest happiness of the greatest numbers—who will not devote their time, their abilities and the powers with which they are vested, in advancing their personal profits and honors, and those of their respective families and friends.—Who will not do every thing in their power to destroy the commercial part of the community, without considering that the value of our lands is enhanced in proportion to the demand, which an extensive commerce, the opulence of the merchant, and the number of mechanics necessarily occasion.[22]

A premise of the utilitarian concept that many Americans fully shared was the firm belief that individual interests, clearly recognized and openly promoted, could be reconciled in the context of an expanding economy. The town delegates of Essex County typically deplored that too many had "fancied a clashing of interests amongst the various classes of men" and that they had forgotten that "our interests when candidly considered are one."[23] Practical suggestions put forth by the Essex whigs for the constitution of Massachusetts showed, however, that they identified the public good largely with the interests of the propertied classes. A law affecting private property, they claimed, is just only when it clearly advances "the good of the whole, which is to be determined by a majority of the members, and that majority should include those, who possess a major part of the property in the state."[24]

The reconcilability of conflicting interests and the necessity to protect the landed interest against the unmitigated application of the majority principle were also at issue in the debate over the unicameral legislature of Pennsylvania. The advocates of a single house took conflicting interests for granted and feared only that in a bicameral legislature one house would be dominated by "landed interests" and the other by "commercial interests." "To say, there ought to be two

22. *Mass. Spy*, May 18, 1776, also in Taylor, ed., *Massachusetts*, 29–30. Joseph Priestley wrote in 1768: "The good and happiness of the members, that is the majority of the members of any state, is the great standard by which everything relating to that state must finally be determined." *First Principles of Government*, 17. Francis Hutcheson, writing about 1737, had called "the general happiness" the "supreme end of all political union." *A System Of Moral Philosophy, In Three Books* (London, 1755), I, 226. Hutcheson discussed this question in regard to the desire of colonies for independence.
23. Essex Result, Taylor, ed., *Massachusetts*, 75–76.
24. *Ibid.*, 79. Calhoun's concept of "concurring majorities" was to be an elaboration of the same principle.

houses, because there are two sorts of interest, is the very reason why there ought to be but one, and *that one* to consist of every sort."[25] Even Pennsylvania's radical whigs, to whom the unknown author of this demand surely belonged, did not speculate about the existence of a latent general will or will of all that would manifest itself in the unicameral legislature; Rousseau had not been their teacher. For them, sufficient proof of a successfully functioning political system was the general acceptance of decisions arrived at by due political process. They demanded submission to the new popular government, not belief in a transpersonal general will: "No man is a true republican, or worthy of the name, that will not give up his single voice to that of the public: his private opinion he may retain; it is obedience only that is his duty."[26]

Closer than Rousseau to the founders' thinking about the common good and private interests was Hume's pessimistic view of human nature. Hamilton, for one, subscribed fully to Hume's idea that private interest was man's dominant motivation. In 1775 he quoted Hume verbatim: "In contriving any system of government, and fixing the several checks and controuls of the constitution, *every man* ought to be supposed a *knave*; and to have no other end in all his actions, but *private interest*. By this interest, we must govern him, and by means of it, *make him co-operate to public good*, notwithstanding his insatiable avarice and ambition."[27]

The constitutions of 1776 were to take the weakness of man as he is into account and not be based on the idea of a new man yet to evolve.

Parties, Representation, and the Common Good

It would take several decades of practical political experience before Americans would take the next step and institutionalize conflicts of interest groups in the form of political parties. In the eighteenth century, any sharpening of factional tendencies or of regional interests had evoked prophecies of total corruption and the end of popular

25. *Four Letters on Interesting Subjects* (Philadelphia, 1776), 20.
26. *Ibid*.
27. Syrett and Cooke, eds., *Hamilton Papers*, I, 95. Stourzh, *Hamilton and Republican Government*, chap. 3, discusses the pessimistic view of human nature in relation to the political theory of the founding generation.

government.[28] A constitution was by definition designed to reconcile conflicting interests and make the organization of interest groups superfluous. In this sense, the first constitutions as well as the Federal Constitution were "against parties."[29]

In the 1770s few Americans considered the possibility that parties might perform a useful function. A "Democraticus" suggested organizing the three branches of government in such a way that there would be different "orders of men, who, like parties in the State, will mutually watch and restrain the partialities to which any particular party or interest may incline."[30]

The Constitutional Society of Philadelphia, founded to defend Pennsylvania's unicameral legislature, in 1779 stated one of its principles as follows: "We will, as a 'party' support men and measures which will promise happiness and prosperity to the state, no matter who originates them."[31] The quotation marks around "party" indicated a shift in the use of the word. The Constitutionalists acknowledged their function as a party, but only as a good party that worked for the benefit of the community as a whole. Even a preacher speaking before the house of representatives and the council of Massachusetts in 1778 thought that parties could conceivably have a useful function in a republic. He only warned against the "parties and factions" that fed on false ambition and hatred, such as those that had contributed to the downfall of the Roman republic. He com-

28. Examples are given in Wood, *Creation of the American Republic*, chap. 10. See also Stephen E. Patterson, *Political Parties in Revolutionary Massachusetts* (Madison, Wis., 1973); Van Beck Hall, *Politics without Parties: Massachusetts, 1780–1791* (Pittsburgh, Pa., 1972); and Jackson Turner Main's *Political Parties before the Constitution* (Chapel Hill, N.C., 1973).
29. Richard Hofstadter, *The Idea of a Party System: The Rise of Legitimate Opposition in the United States, 1780–1840* (Berkeley, Calif., 1969), 40.
30. Purdie's *Va. Gaz.*, June 7, 1776, also in *American Archives*, 4th Ser., VI, 731. On the recognition of parties in England and America, see Caroline Robbins, "'Discordant Parties': A Study of the Acceptance of Party by Englishmen," *Pol. Sci. Qtly.*, LXXIII (1958), 505–529; Harvey C. Mansfield, Jr., *Statesmanship and Party Government: A Study of Burke and Bolingbroke* (Chicago, 1965); and Stourzh, *Hamilton and Republican Government*, 110–120. Bailyn, *Origins of American Politics*, 125–128, cites from the colonial press of 1733 and 1749 two favorable views of "parties," after discussing the fear, prevalent in Walpole's time, that parties could be destructive of the social order.
31. *Pa. Gaz.*, Apr. 28, 1779, also in Eugene Perry Link, *Democratic-Republican Societies, 1790–1800* (New York, 1942), 28.

mended "parties in a free state" that were intent on "the public liberty and welfare."[32]

This faith that opposing interests could be reconciled characterized the constitutionalism of 1776. The republican ideals of popular sovereignty, freedom, and equality acted as a permanent challenge to clarify the relationship between public and private interests, and the minorities that were calling for a greater realization of these principles kept the challenge alive. The crucial point is, however, that in no phase of the American Revolution did naive and doctrinaire belief in the supremacy of the public good lead to the establishment of one center of political power with supreme authority to assert the ideal, if need be with the help of the guillotine. The experience the Americans had in organizing their resistance against England and the difficulties of the war years discouraged naive faith in the day-to-day effectiveness of the common good as an ideal.

The constitutionalism of 1776 presupposed not the uniformity of private interests but only the possibility of resolving conflicts within the framework of the new political system. Consequently, the realists of 1776, as representatives of their interest groups, did not veil the existence of conflicts behind a cloud of rhetoric proclaiming the public good. Instead, they identified different interests and institutionalized them in graduated property qualifications for voting and office holding, in the system of checks and balances, and in the establishment of bicameral legislatures. At the heart of their solution for resolving conflict was the principle of representation. They assumed that with the help of a fair system of representation, conflicts could be resolved and the common good achieved.

32. Phillips Payson, *A Sermon Preached before the Honorable Council, and the Honorable House of Representatives, of the State of Massachusetts-Bay, in New-England, at Boston, May 27, 1778* (Boston, 1778), in John Wingate Thornton, ed., *The Pulpit of the American Revolution: or, The Political Sermons of the Period of 1776* (Boston, 1860), 342.

CHAPTER XI

Representation

A representative democracy, where the right of elections is well secured and regulated and the exercise of the legislative, executive and judiciary authorities, is vested in select persons, chosen really and not nominally by the people, will in my opinion be most likely to be happy, regular and durable.

Alexander Hamilton, 1777

"Virtual" Representation and the Colonial Assemblies

Distance from England and the administrative form of the first settlement companies had encouraged the early development of a system of representation within the British colonies in North America. As early as 1640, eight colonies had assemblies that represented the interests of the settlers in their dealings with the companies, the king's governors, or the proprietors. Between 1686 and 1689, the colonists in the Northeast successfully resisted an attempt to consolidate them into a Dominion of New England and place them under the rule of a viceroy and his privy council.[1] From the 1690s on, the assemblies regarded themselves more and more as comparable to the House of Commons and followed the rituals of Parliament as closely as they could.[2] In countless struggles with the governors and their councils,

1. Michael Kammen, *Deputyes and Libertyes: The Origins of Representative Government in Colonial America* (New York, 1969). See also, George L. Haskins, "Representative Government in Early New England: The Corporate and the Parliamentary Traditions," in *Liber Memorialis Sir Maurice Powicke* (Louvain, 1965), 83–98; J. R. Pole, *The Seventeenth Century: The Sources of Legislative Power* (Charlottesville, Va., 1969); and Pole's *Political Representation*, 54–63 (on Massachusetts); 94–108 (on Pennsylvania); 125–135 (on Virginia).
2. Jack P. Greene, "Political Mimesis: A Consideration of the Historical and Cultural Roots of Legislative Behavior in the British Colonies in the Eighteenth Century," *AHR*, LXXV (1969–1970), 337–363, esp. 343, 348. See also

the assemblies won increasing influence over legislation and administration in the colonies. After 1776 they became the most powerful
political institutions in the states. In the period following the Revolution, they tried to retain their position of strength. In the metaphorical
language of the day, the legislature was "the soul, the source of life
and movement" in the body of the state.[3] To persuade the state
legislatures to give up part of their power was the major task of the
supporters of the Federal Constitution of 1787.

The conflict between the assemblies and Parliament over the
Stamp Act resulted in the articulation of two mutually exclusive
theories of representation. The colonial assemblies had a fair claim to
truly reflecting the interests of their constituencies; voters and representatives were united by residence and land ownership in the same
district, and the property qualifications for voting permitted probably
three-fourths of the male white adults to vote.[4] The parliament at
Westminster did not even pretend to be directly representative in this
sense. In a pamphlet defending the Stamp Act, Secretary of the Treasury Thomas Whately argued in 1765 that nine-tenths of the English
population could not elect representatives either; all the inhabitants
of Leeds, Halifax, Birmingham, and Manchester, for example, a population exceeding that of even the largest colony, did not have the right
to send a single representative to Westminster. But this was not
insufferable, Whately said, because according to the principles of
the English constitution, they were "virtually" represented in Parliament, as indeed he thought the colonists were. Years before Edmund
Burke's much noted speech on the nature of representation, Whately
formulated the constitutional theory of the elected representative as
the guardian of the common good in contrast to the lobbyist for some
particular interest:

None are actually, all are virtually represented in Parliament; for every Member of Parliament sits in the House, not as Representative of his own Constituents, but as one of that august Assembly by which all the Commons of
Great Britain are represented. Their Rights and their Interests, however his
own Borough may be affected by general Dispositions, ought to be the great
Objects of his Attention, and the only Rules for his Conduct; and to sacrifice
these to a partial Advantage in favour of the Place where he was chosen,

Greene's *The Quest for Power: The Lower Houses of Assembly in the Southern
Royal Colonies, 1689–1776* (Chapel Hill, N.C., 1963).
3. "American Whig," Letter III, *Providence Gaz.*, Apr. 3, 1779.
4. See chap. 9, pp. 198–207 above.

would be a Departure from his Duty; if it were otherwise, *Old Sarum* would enjoy Privileges essential to Liberty, which are denied to *Birmingham* and to *Manchester*; but as it is, they and the Colonies and all *British* Subjects whatever, have an equal Share in the general Representation of the Commons of *Great Britain*, and are bound by the Consent of the Majority of that House, whether their own particular Representatives consented to or opposed the Measures there taken, or whether they had or had not particular Representatives there.

Whately considered the colonial assemblies comparable only to the city council of London. They could make some decisions independently, but they were clearly subordinate to Parliament.[5]

Given the concept of actual representation that had developed in the colonies, it was clear what their response to Whately would be: if the new concept of virtual representation had meaning in England, it was only to the degree that there was a community of interests between the enfranchised and the unenfranchised. The colonists, however—perhaps with the overwhelming approval of the English population—could be so exploited economically that they could no longer claim their property as their own. "The relation between the *British Americans* and the *English* electors is a knot too infirm to be relied on as a competent security," replied Maryland lawyer Daniel Dulany. "A total *dissimilarity* of situation, infers that their representation is *different*."[6] And James Otis of Boston turned Whately's argument around in one sentence. If Manchester, Birmingham, and Sheffield were not represented in Parliament, "they ought to be."[7]

In defending the competence of their assemblies, the colonists insisted that representatives and their constituencies share identical interests. And therefore, with few exceptions, they rejected the idea of sending representatives across the Atlantic for seven-year terms as insufficient and impractical. In a newspaper article of 1766 opposing the Stamp Act, John Adams saw representatives as strictly analogous

5. Thomas Whately, *The Regulations lately Made concerning the Colonies and the Taxes Imposed upon Them, Considered* (London, 1765), in Morgan, ed., *Prologue to Revolution*, 21–22.
6. Daniel Dulany, *Considerations On The Propriety of Imposing Taxes In The British Colonies, For the Purpose of raising a Revenue, by Act of Parliament* (Annapolis, Md., 1765), in Bailyn, ed., *Pamphlets of the American Revolution*, I, 615.
7. [James Otis], *Considerations On Behalf of the Colonists* (London, 1765), 9, quoted in Bailyn, *Ideological Origins*, 169.

to attorneys. Representation, he wrote, was simply a substitute for the decisions of all concerned. "It is in reality nothing more than this, the people choose attorneys to vote for them in the great council of the nation, reserving always the fundamentals of the government, reserving also a right to give their attorneys instructions how to vote, and a right at certain, stated intervals, of choosing a-new. . . . It is this reservation of fundamentals, of the right of giving instructions, and of new elections, which creates a popular check upon the whole government."[8] The notion that representatives were like attorneys with instructions had the great advantage for the colonists at this point that it avoided the issue of whether there was also an objective common interest that representatives must heed—an interest that Whately and Burke thought ought to be preeminent—without denying the existence of such an interest. Even if Parliament had allocated a seat or two to each colony, the attorney concept of representation could have been used to demonstrate the continuing necessity for colonial assemblies and the impracticability of sending elected representatives to Westminster for a term of seven years.

Representative Democracy

In 1776 representative assemblies assumed the power that king and Parliament had lost. Government by revolutionary committees had been only an interim solution.[9] During the two-year transitional period and in the following years, few doubts were expressed about the legitimacy or usefulness of the principle of representation. Even the enacting of constitutions was left to a representative assembly in all states except Massachusetts.[10]

Any newspaper article that dealt with the basic issues of government included in the first paragraph, after a brief summary of the theory of social contract and a nostalgic glance at the happy past when laws were worked out by all on the village green, the statement that representative government was a necessity of modern times. Only loyalist polemics against independence argued that the govern-

8. "The Earl of Clarendon to William Pym," *Boston Gaz.*, Jan. 27, 1766, in Adams, ed., *Works of John Adams*, III, 481.
9. See chap. 1, pp. 42–48.
10. See chap. 3, pp. 86–93.

mental form that would descend on the country after independence would no longer respect any system of responsible representation.[11] In reality, representation became the organizational principle, along with the system of checks and balances, that gave structure to the entire political process in the new states.

The American system of representation did not, however, exclude elements of what Max Weber has called "direct democracy." Among these elements were rotation in office, instructions from voters to their elected representatives, and the avocational character of public office. Representation was combined with plebiscitary elements.[12] Alexander Hamilton was therefore quite correct when in 1777 he characterized the New York constitution as "representative democracy" and rejected the stereotyped concept of "unstable democracy." "Popular governments" were unstable, he thought, only when the legislative or judicial powers were completely or even partially left to "the collective body of the people. But a representative democracy, where the right of elections is well secured and regulated and the exercise of the legislative, executive and judiciary authorities, is vested in select persons, chosen *really* and not *nominally* by the people, will in my opinion be most likely to be happy, regular and durable."[13]

Public discussion of the issue of representation between 1776 and 1780 was notably free of ideological rigidity. Debate was no longer based on theoretical projections, as it had been when the colonies were still part of the empire, but on traditional practice. The concept of representatives as attorneys, a concept that had appeared logical and binding to John Adams ten years earlier, now struck him as inadequate. Legislative authority, he thought, ought to be transferred "from the many to a few of the most wise and good." The rule of the best for the benefit of all was his intellectual ideal. But as a politician, he could not ignore the predominant view of representatives as advocates for specific interests. He therefore postulated that a legislature

11. See chap. 4, pp. 100–101.
12. Max Weber, *Wirtschaft und Gesellschaft: Grundriss der verstehenden Soziologie,* ed. Johannes Winckelmann (Cologne, 1964), I, 215. See also Ernst Fraenkel, *Deutschland und die westlichen Demokratien* (Stuttgart, 1964), 71–109.
13. May 19, 1777, Syrett and Cooke, eds., *Hamilton Papers,* I, 255. Hamilton also used this concept when he spoke in favor of the draft of the Federal Constitution before the ratifying convention of New York in 1788. *Ibid.,* V, 150. For an interpretation of this speech, see Stourzh, *Hamilton and Republican Government,* 48–51.

should "be in miniature an exact portrait of the people at large. It should think, feel, reason and act like them. That it may be the interest of this assembly to do strict justice at all times, it should be an equal representation, or, in other words, equal interests among the people should have equal interests in it."[14] The idea of the legislature representing in miniature the constellation of interests in the society at large was a product of the entire American political evolution up to that point.

But at the same time, the ideal of rule by the best also retained its appeal. Most whig leaders probably preferred to have a combination of both forms of representation. In 1778, the whigs of Essex County, Massachusetts, followed Adams almost word for word in their demand that the legislature be a miniature replica of the society. The representatives, they demanded, should reflect "the whole body politic, with all it's property, rights, and priviledges, reduced to a smaller scale." But the Essex delegates also believed that insight into the collective interests of society could best be expected from men of their own class, "men of education and fortune" whose experience and way of life could be assumed to qualify them for furthering the good of the whole. They were in a position to survey the various interest groups in their state and to compare them with those of neighboring states. They were familiar with agriculture, trade, and industry in their own state. Only persons with this kind of knowledge could evaluate the real interests of a state and the usefulness of individual bills. The Essex delegates further diluted their demand for a replica of societal interest groups true to scale by presenting an argument drawn from group psychology. An atmosphere of rational deliberation, they said, was possible only in an assembly of no more than one hundred persons. In a larger house of representatives "the variety of opinions and oppositions would irritate the passions. Parties would be formed and factions engendered. The members would list under the banners of their respective leaders: address and intrigue would conduct the debates, and the result would tend only to promote the ambition or interest of a particular party."[15]

The Essex whigs, also called the Essex Junto, knew what they deplored. The colonial assemblies had long functioned as a battling ground for spokesmen of interest groups and factions, and there was no reason to expect this to change drastically after independence.

14. Adams, ed., *Works of John Adams*, IV, 194, 195.
15. Essex Result, in Taylor, ed., *Massachusetts*, 81–83, 77.

And yet they piously expressed their hope that somehow future legislatures might mitigate the clash of parties and compel recognition of the common interest and the good of the whole.

Equal Representation

Incorporating new rules of representation into the state constitutions was seen as an opportunity to correct injustices that had been under discussion for a long time. For decades, the phrase "equal representation" had been used to demand a more equitable distribution of seats in the colonial assemblies. Since 1752 Pennsylvania's heavily populated towns near the coast had been demanding representation proportional to taxes paid and to number of inhabitants. Philadelphia, with a population of forty thousand, had only two representatives. In March 1776, the old assembly finally agreed on a redistribution.[16] In Virginia, the tidewater counties continued to insist on the old territorial principle of two representatives per county in order to retain their political influence against the increasing power of the growing western counties. Jefferson deplored the injustice of this system.[17] In Massachusetts, the royal governors had incorporated new towns without granting them any representation. In August 1775, the General Court reverted to the Charter of 1691 and allowed all towns and districts with at least thirty qualified voters to elect one representative. Towns with more than 120 voters were entitled to two representatives; Boston had four. The merchants of the urban areas who paid the most in tax revenues saw this measure as a threat to their influence. They objected to the use of an unmodified territorial principle and demanded that population size be taken into account. A bill that, for all practical purposes, was virtually railroaded through in May 1776 assured dominance to the larger towns. Communities with 220 freeholders would have three representatives. Every additional one hundred voters entitled a town to another representative. This law gave Boston twelve representatives, and the new house now had 266 members.[18]

16. Pole, *Political Representation*, 262–264, 253.
17. *Ibid.*, 187–289; Jefferson, *Notes on Virginia*, ed. Peden, 118–119.
18. Pole, *Political Representation*, 173–176. For other demands for reform of the representative system before 1776, see Belknap, *History of New-Hampshire*, III, 192; *American Archives*, 4th Ser., II, 159–160, 521, 1678–1679 (on New Hampshire); Brooke Hindle, "The March of the Paxton Boys," *WMQ*, 3d Ser., III

Strong adherence to the territorial principle—in New England the term "corporate principle" would be more accurate—stood in the way of other rational solutions. The concept of artificial electoral districts with a comparable number of voters only gradually came to replace the claim of natural, permanent units like towns and counties to equal representation. Analogous to this struggle on the state level was the one between large and small states on the federal level. The strong position of the small states in the conflict over the distribution of power as it was to be codified in the Federal Constitution derived to a great extent from the integrity granted to any constituted territorial unit.

The small towns in rural Massachusetts fought with persistence against the new idea that any other entities besides those of the incorporated towns might be used as a basis for a new system of representation. They held fast to the tried and true: "Each Town has rights, Liberties and Priviledges peculiar to the same, and as dear to them as those to any other, and which they have as just a right as any others to have guarded and protected. If larger Towns have more to represent them and more Voices in the General Court than the smaller, they will have the Advantage of the smaller; the smaller will not have their Rights equally guarded and protected." The town of Sunderland, Massachusetts, used this argument in its rejection of the terms of representation laid out in the constitution of 1780.[19] Northampton wanted to see the "principle of corporation equality" prevail over the "principle of personal equality."[20] The Lincoln town meeting declared, "Corporations are the Immediate Constituant part of the State and the Individuals are only the Remote parts in many respects."[21] The anonymous pamphlet entitled *The People the Best Governors* rejected the proposal that seats be distributed in proportion to the tax revenues of the counties on the grounds that it was a threat to freedom. Since all men had the same claim to freedom, the pamphlet argued, the distribution of power according to property could not be justified.

The pamphlet also noted that representation according to popu-

---

(1946), 462–463; and Douglass, *Rebels and Democrats*, 221 (on Pennsylvania). Jensen, *Articles of Confederation*, chap. 2, surveys the tension between East and West in all thirteen colonies before 1776.

19. May 15, 1780, Handlin and Handlin, eds., *Popular Sources*, 610.

20. May 22, 1780, *ibid.*, 577.

21. May 22, 1780, *ibid.*, 663.

lation brought considerable technical difficulties with it. Large towns would have to be divided and small ones combined. Since the populations of towns could change quickly, a single reapportionment would not solve the problem. Changes would continue to be necessary, and dissatisfaction would be constant. Yet it is an ancient truth "that *political bodies should be immortal.*" The author of this pamphlet turned to Blackstone as an authority. He could just as well have cited the arguments for virtual representation presented in 1765: "Though every member is chosen by a particular county or borough, yet, as is justly observed by Lord Cooke and others, when in parliament he serves for the whole nation." He thought taking taxes and population together as a basis for representation was "intirely capricious." The only reliable yardstick that could be used for distributing the seats in the legislature was land, "the most solid estate that can be taxed, and . . . the only permanent thing."[22]

In April 1776 the town delegates of the wealthy and heavily populated county of Essex formulated the opposing view. They warned against a rigid adherence to traditional forms and against a refusal to take changing circumstances into account. The rotten boroughs in England provided them with a ready example. The present situation in Massachusetts was so disastrous, they pointed out, that those who contributed only one-fourth of the tax revenues could elect a majority in the house of representatives. Essex, on the other hand, paid one-sixth of all taxes collected but was represented by only one-tenth of the legislature. It struck the Essex delegates as particularly paradoxical that additional seats could be created simply by dividing single towns into several new towns while the populations of the areas affected remained unchanged. For the future, they demanded representation according to numbers, to property, or to a combination of both.[23]

22. *People the Best Governors*, in Chase, *History of Dartmouth College*, ed. Lord, I, quotation on pp. 658–659. On Oct. 22, 1776, the town of Topsfield had argued similarly. Taylor, ed., *Massachusetts*, 42.
23. Apr. 25, 1776, Taylor, ed., *Massachusetts*, 38–39. Pole, *Political Representation*, 174, believes that this was the first publicly announced move away from the traditional mode of representation for the towns of New England. A similar statement occurs in "An Address to the Good Inhabitants of the State of Massachusetts Bay," *Boston Gaz.*, July 12, 1779. The town of Roxbury was particularly disturbed by the violation of the principles of equality and majority rule.

No one asked that the electoral districts be redrawn so that each had equal populations. The way to the twentieth-century principle of one man, one vote, began instead with the alliance of the mercantile interest and the urban population against the small rural towns that still wanted to determine representation solely on the basis of land ownership and traditional political entities. The compromise that presented itself was to divide the legislature into two chambers. The number of inhabitants or voters would determine the composition of one chamber, land ownership or territorial units the makeup of the other. The Essex delegates made just such a proposal. But none of the new state constitutions applied this solution with any consistency.

Composition of Houses of Representatives and Senates

None of the houses of representatives formed after the Declaration of Independence were organized according to a completely new scheme of representation. In New England, the town continued to be the unit represented. In the mid-Atlantic and southern states, it was the county or parish, in addition to the few incorporated cities. Every town in Connecticut could send one or two representatives to the lower house; Rhode Island towns could send two, four, or six. But by 1775 this system no longer reflected the actual distribution of population. In 1776 and 1778, the parish of Charleston, with thirty seats in the assembly, was assured a controlling influence in South Carolina. Other parishes in South Carolina had an average of six representatives. The constitution provided that from 1783 on, seats would be reapportioned every fourteen years according to the "strength" and "taxable property" of the parishes. In Virginia, because of the influence of the tidewater counties as has already been mentioned, the system of two representatives from each county was retained. Williamsburg and Norfolk were each allowed one representative, but they were to lose this privilege if their voting population numbered less than half the voters of any county for seven consecutive years. In New Jersey, every county could elect three delegates, in Delaware, seven. Philadelphia and every Pennsylvania county were each allowed six representatives. The Pennsylvania constitution provided that the distribution of seats in the future would be according to number of taxpayers. Seats would be reapportioned after a tax levy in

1778 and at seven-year intervals thereafter. Maryland granted every county four delegates, regardless of distribution of property and population; Annapolis and Baltimore could each elect two. North Carolina prescribed two representatives for each county and one each for the six largest urban settlements.

Georgia was the first state to incorporate into its constitution a graduated system that allowed for expansion. Each county received ten representatives, except for Liberty County, which was larger than the others and therefore received fourteen. The cities of Savannah and Sunbury could choose four and two delegates respectively "to represent their trade." Two small counties had only one delegate apiece. The constitution also established a scale to be applied to newly formed counties:

10	voters were entitled to	1	representative
30	"	2	representatives
40	"	3	"
50	"	4	"
80	"	6	"
100	"	10	"

There were no provisions for further expansion. New York had a graduated system, too, allowing each county and certain towns from two to ten representatives. A "census of the electors" was to be taken every seven years and the seats reapportioned accordingly.[24]

The constitutional convention of Massachusetts also adopted a graduated system but warned against striving for perfection in these matters. In its preamble to the constitutional draft, the convention favored distributing seats in accordance with the principle of equality. But what, the convention asked, did that really mean? The equality of all self-governing units, of all taxpayers, or of all inhabitants? "It cannot be understood thereby that each Town in the Commonwealth shall have Weight and importance in a just proportion to its Numbers and property. An exact Representation would be unpracticable even in a System of Government arising from the State of Nature, and much more so in a state already divided into nearly three hundred Corporations."[25] The plan that was presented and accepted

24. Purcell, *Connecticut in Transition*, 122; Lovejoy, *Rhode Island Politics*, 15; Thorpe, ed., *Constitutions*, VI, 3245, 3250, 3252, VII, 3816, V, 2595, I, 562, V, 3086, III, 1691–1692, V, 2790, II, 779, V, 2629.
25. Taylor, ed., *Massachusetts*, 126.

granted new towns one representative for the first 150 "rateable polls," i.e., taxpaying males over sixteen years old. The number of representatives would then increase according to the following scale:

1 representative for	150	"rateable polls"
2 representatives for	375	"
3 "	600	"
4 "	825	"

In other words, a representative would be added for every additional 225 taxpaying males. No upper limit was set. The ruling that all already incorporated towns, even with less than 150 taxpayers, could elect one representative clearly was a concession to the principle of corporation equality.[26]

In the process of constituting the upper houses, the principles of representation and balanced government overlapped. These houses were established to act as checks on the houses of representatives. But the problem of representation had a bearing on their further development. How was America's aristocracy of the successful to be represented? Property qualifications determined only who could vote and who could run for office, not the allocation of seats.[27] Strict construction of whig constitutional theory would have required senatorial election districts containing equal amounts of property, real as well as personal. But this was obviously too difficult to put into practice. Instead, the constitutions adopted interim solutions that used the counties as units to be represented, but nowhere near as much care was taken in differentiating between the counties as had been taken in establishing the rules for electing representatives. Only Virginia, New York, and Massachusetts took the trouble to create artificial districts of equal land area for the sole purpose of electing senators.

Virginia's twenty-four senators were to represent twenty-four districts to be created by law. Within these new senatorial districts the old counties would continue to exist as local electoral districts. The New York constitution was more precise. It divided the state's counties into four blocks that would elect nine, six, six, and three senators respectively for a total of twenty-four. New York adhered to constitutional theory more rigorously than any other state by prescribing that a census be taken in seven years and the senatorial seats redistrib-

26. *Ibid.*, 135.
27. See chap. 9, pp. 196–207.

uted, if necessary, in proportion to the number of freeholders. The size of freeholds was apparently not taken into consideration. In Massachusetts, however, the merchants and urban residents made their influence felt. There, forty senators were to represent districts yet to be created. These districts would be established on the basis of tax revenues and could be changed if necessary. During a transitional period the counties would function as districts. The largest, Essex and Suffolk counties, each had six senators; the islands of Nantucket and Dukes County shared one.[28]

New Hampshire simply weighted the existing counties and distributed the twelve councillor seats among them in the proportion five, two, two, two, one, moving from east to west. South Carolina's provisional constitution of 1776 permitted the provincial congress to simply draft thirteen councillors from its own ranks. The constitution of 1778 began to differentiate and granted the parishes and districts anywhere from one to three senators; and provision was made for the reapportionment of seats in both the senate and the house of representatives after seven years.

The distribution of senators in Delaware, Maryland, and North Carolina was not dependent on property distribution. Delaware's three counties each had three councillors for a total of nine. Maryland's fifteen senators, chosen by an electoral college, represented the west and east banks of the Potomac in the proportion nine to six. North Carolina allowed one senator per county.

The strength of the demand for equal representation of unequal territorial units showed itself even in the states that considered a second legislative chamber superfluous. Pennsylvania's constitution required that the eleven counties and the city of Philadelphia each have one representative in the executive council. Despite its name, the council was obviously not considered a purely executive institution. Georgia's constitution demanded that the executive council consist of two councillors per county. Vermont copied most of Pennsylvania's constitution but not this clause; Vermont's twelve councillors had no territorial qualification to meet.

Thus the first efforts to represent property interests in a separate chamber revealed the artificiality of this concept under American conditions. In political practice, the state senates did not represent "different" interests but soon became second, additional legislative

28. Thorpe, ed., *Constitutions, passim*. The following paragraphs also rest on the various constitutional provisions.

bodies, serving an essential function in the system of the division of the powers of government between several institutions.

Short Terms of Office

Belief in the system of representation and mistrust of representatives themselves were not mutually exclusive. The colonists had had considerable experience with the misuse of power, not in the form of an absolute monarch overstepping his limits but in the form of an unresponsive colonial administration supported by the British legislature. When Parliament closed Boston harbor in 1774 and introduced other coercive measures, Jefferson commented that "bodies of men as well as of individuals, are susceptible of the spirit of tyranny."[29] Shortly before the outbreak of war in 1775, Alexander Hamilton warned his fellow citizens that they could not expect justice from a parliament over which they had no control because "a fondness for power is implanted, in most men, and it is natural to abuse it, when acquired." The experience of the ages taught that it was folly to give men power without at the same time devising all possible means of controlling them.[30] Samuel Adams stated in December 1775 that controls were more effective than trust; even the august Greek Areopagus, which was so renowned for its wisdom and discretion that foreign states brought their disagreements before it for peaceful settlement, was subject to the control of a popular assembly.[31] For years English radical Whigs had bewailed the lack of control that the voters exerted over Parliament. The colonists now took over their arguments word for word.[32]

In light of colonial tradition as well as their recent experience, the provincial congresses that framed constitutions in 1776 were prepared to impose limits on themselves and on their successors in office. The limiting of governmental powers took several forms. The two most fundamental of these were the bills of rights and the fixed procedures

29. Boyd *et al.*, eds., *Jefferson Papers*, I, 124.
30. Syrett and Cooke, eds., *Hamilton Papers*, I, 126.
31. Samuel Adams to James Warren, Dec. 25, 1775, Cushing, ed., *Writings of Samuel Adams*, III, 245.
32. For example, see "Cassandra to Cato," *Pa. Packet*, Apr. 29, 1776, also in *American Archives*, 4th Ser., V, 1093 ("Cassandra" quotes Obadiah Hulme); "Eudoxus," *Pa. Packet*, Apr. 22, 1776.

for ratifying and amending constitutions. The third consisted of a number of technical measures: limited terms of office, instructions for representatives, restrictions on reelection, and the system of checks and balances, including the controls the two legislative chambers exert over each other.[33]

None of the constitutions provided for the recall of legislative or executive officials during their terms of office. A few towns in Massachusetts had favored such recall, and one of them wanted to include in the bill of rights that all public officials could be recalled at any time, but to most, short terms of office seemed to provide sufficient control.[34] In contrast to their counterparts in the English parliament, who were elected for seven-year terms, all representatives in the new states followed the tradition established in most assemblies of the colonial period and ran for reelection each year. The only exception to this rule was in South Carolina, where representatives were elected for two years. "Where annual elections end, there slavery begins," had been part of the political folklore of the colonial period. The new constitutions applied the maxim and extended it to senators, governors, and governors' councillors as well, as the table on the opposite page shows. The average term of office laid down for senators by the constitutions was about two and a half years. For governors, it was one and a half years and for councillors, three years. Maryland had the longest term of office for senators, five years. Delaware and New York set the longest term of office for governors, three years. The potentially longest term granted any public official, apart from judges, was given to councillors in Virginia. The constitutional provision was so unclear that it permitted indefinite terms for privy councillors. It only required the house and the senate to replace, by joint resolution, two of the eight members every three years, and it prohibited the councillors thus voted out from running for the same office again for a period of three years. If the two most senior councillors would leave office after each three-year period, then all privy

33. Checks and balances will be discussed in the next chapter.
34. June 1, 1780, Mass. Archives, CCLXXVI, fol. 104. The town of Westminster expressed a similar view, June 9, 1778, Taylor, ed., *Massachusetts*, 69–70. Compare, too, Warwick, Oct. 4, 1776, Handlin and Handlin, eds., *Popular Sources*, 113–114, and Kenneth Colegrove, "New England Town Mandates: Instructions to the Deputies in Colonial Legislatures," Colonial Society of Massachusetts, *Transactions*, XXI (1919), 425–427.

Terms of Office for Representatives,
Senators, Governors, and Councillors

	Repre-sentatives	Senators	Governors	Councillors
New Hampshire	1	1	1	
Massachusetts	1	1	1	1
Connecticut	1		1	1
Rhode Island	1		1	1
New York	1	4	3	
New Jersey	1	1	1	
Pennsylvania	1		1	3
Delaware	1	3	3	2
Maryland	1	5	1	1
Virginia	1	4	1	3 to indefinite
North Carolina	1	1	1	1
South Carolina	2	2	2	2
Georgia	1		1	

councillors automatically served a term of twelve years. However, the constitution did not specifically prohibit longer terms for six of the eight councillors.[35] No other state copied this singular combination of the principle of rotation in office with a rare form of "congressional" confirmation or dismissal of executive officers.

35. Thorpe, ed., *Constitutions*, VII, 3817.

Instructions: Direct Popular Influence on Legislation

The electorate's instructions to its representative on specific issues combined a plebiscitary element with the principle of representation. This combination was not a controversial point in constitutional debates between 1776 and 1780. In New England, instructions had been regarded as a basic part of the representational system from the outset. In 1640 Plymouth provided by law for instructions, and in 1641 the General Court of Massachusetts asked the towns to give their delegates instructions on two controversial issues. In the House of Burgesses the right to give instructions was defended at length in 1754.[36]

In England, the question of whether or not members of Parliament could receive instructions had been debated for years. Edmund Burke's Bristol speech of 1774 against the binding mandate was a response to the opposing view of a preceding speaker who also proved to be a successful candidate for a seat in Parliament. This speaker's party had made the right of instruction a major point in its platform.[37] James Burgh's radical Whig reader, published in the following year, shows that the right of instruction had been a goal of parliamentary reformers for over a century.[38]

Americans made use of instructions in such a flexible way, however, that Europeans might not have thought the practice amounted to instruction at all. In any case, Americans avoided the disadvantages that Burke foresaw. The instructing bodies, the town meetings, and the county conventions knew how counterproductive it could be to tie their representatives' hands with detailed and rigid instructions. They sent strict instructions only on crucial questions, such as the decision for independence or for a new constitution. Mecklenburg County's five delegates to the provincial congress of North Carolina,

36. Colegrove, "New England Town Mandates," Col. Soc. Mass., *Trans.*, XXI (1919), 414–416. Bailyn cites a number of comparable cases, *Pamphlets of the American Revolution*, I, 93n, as does Pole, *Political Representation*, 541–542.

37. P. T. Underdown, "Henry Cruger and Edmund Burke: Colleagues and Rivals at the Bristol Election of 1774," WMQ, 3d Ser., XV (1958), 31. Underdown points out that the right to instruct was "one of the major items" held by the party in opposition to Burke. In addition to Burke, other political thinkers in Britain had rejected instructions of members of Parliament. See Pole, *Political Representation*, 16, 419, 441.

38. Burgh, *Political Disquisitions*, I, book 4, chaps. 1–3, presents a survey of the arguments for and against instruction in 1775.

for instance, received the following instructions in November 1776: "Gentlemen: You are chosen by the inhabitants of this county to serve them in Congress or General Assembly for one year and they have agreed to the following Instructions which you are to observe with the strictest regard. . . ."[39] The instructions the reputedly stubborn Massachusetts town of Pittsfield sent its representative in reaction to the constitutional draft of 1778 provide a vivid example of the more flexible way in which instructions were used. The framing of a new constitution, the Pittsfielders let their representative know, was of such consequence that he surely would want to know what his constituents' expectations were. "You are therefore hereby instructed to unite with said convention in drawing up a Bill of Rights and in forming a new Constitution. . . . We wish you to oppose all unnecessary delay. . . . The said Bill of Rights and Constitution you will move to be printed. . . . You are not to dissolve the convention, but to adjourn from time to time." If his instructions had ended here, the Pittsfield representative would indeed have had little opportunity to use his own judgment. He was even commissioned to make specific motions. All that was left to his discretion was when he would make them. But despite what had gone before, the concluding lines of these instructions granted the representative considerable freedom after all. "On the whole, we empower you to act agreeable to the dictates of your own judgment after you have heard all the reasonings upon the various subjects of disquisition, having an invariable respect to the true liberty and real happiness of this State throughout all generations, any instructions herein contained to the contrary notwithstanding."[40] Thus the Pittsfielders wrote into their instructions a section empowering their representative to disregard parts of those same instructions, but they would never have considered this as giving up their right to instruct. They had no sense of having tested the limits of this institution but had simply made restrained use of a sharp weapon.

39. Saunders, ed., *N.C. Col. Recs.*, X, 870a. Orange County issued comparable instructions.
40. Undated town meeting resolve, 1779, in Taylor, ed., *Massachusetts*, 118–119. For other examples of town meeting returns in the form of instructions, see *ibid.*, 71, 72, and Mass. Archives, CLVI, fol. 115 (Topsfield), fol. 132 (Warwick), CCLXXVI, fol. 29 (Dartmouth), fol. 72 (Medway). An example of a different nature: "We offer to your Consideration the Following Remarks . . . ," Petersham, *ibid.*, fol. 104.

Three of the eleven constitutions explicitly guaranteed the right of instruction. Pennsylvania's declaration of rights was the first to enumerate "the right . . . to instruct their representatives' among the citizens' liberties." North Carolina's bill of rights took over this resolution. The Massachusetts bill of rights followed Pennsylvania's example closely on this point, and listed, after the right to assemble peacefully, the people's right to "give instructions to their representatives, and to request of the legislative body, by the way of addresses, petitions, or remonstrances, redress of the wrongs done them, and of the grievances they suffer."[41]

An attempt to go beyond instructions and institutionalize yet another kind of popular participation in lawmaking failed. Pennsylvania's constitution was the only one to venture the following legislative procedure:

To the end that laws before they are enacted may be more maturely considered, and the inconvenience of hasty determinations as much as possible prevented, all bills of public nature shall be printed for the consideration of the people, before they are read in general assembly the last time for debate and amendment; and, except on occasions of sudden necessity, shall not be passed into laws until the next session of assembly; and for the more perfect satisfaction of the public, the reasons and motives for making such laws shall be fully and clearly expressed in the preambles.[42]

The idea soon proved to be impracticable. What were "bills of public nature"? What should be considered a "sudden necessity"? How were the views of the public to be gathered? The whole clause was an easy target for opponents of the Pennsylvania constitution.[43]

The logical place for guaranteeing the right to instruct on the federal level would have been the First Amendment to the Constitution. On August 15, 1789, in the course of debate on this amendment, the House of Representatives of the United States did discuss a motion that not only would have denied the federal legislature the right to limit the freedoms of speech, assembly, petition, and press but also would have secured voters "the right . . . to instruct their

41. Thorpe, ed., *Constitutions*, V, 3048 (Articles XIV and XVI), 2788 (Article XVIII), III, 1892 (Article XIX).
42. *Ibid.*, V, 3086 (Article XV).
43. "K.," *Pa. Packet*, Sept. 24, 1776; *Pa. Ledger*, Nov. 2, 1776; "C.," *Pa. Jour.*, Mar. 27, 1777; "Phocion," *ibid.*, Mar. 12, 1777.

representatives."[44] The motion was not adopted. There would be no right of instruction at the federal level. But the decision might well have gone the other way, and it would be wrong to consider instructions to a congressman by the voters of his district as alien to the American system.

The Public Eye

Several state constitutions ruled that the doors of the legislative chambers be open to anyone, unless there were particular reasons for a secret session, and that an official record of proceedings should be published. This was a great step forward in the development of legislative procedure and the creation of a politically relevant public opinion.

Since 1688 the mother of parliaments had asserted absolute freedom of speech for its members, but only behind closed doors. Keeping out spies in the pay of the monarch was one of the original motivations for secrecy. Privacy of debate was one of the privileges of Parliament. In 1770 the Commons and the Lords reasserted the exclusion of "strangers" from their chambers. In 1771 the House of Commons reluctantly gave up enforcement of the prohibition against publishing parliamentary speeches, and the London newspapers were free to report fully on the controversial debates of the 1770s.[45]

Practices in the colonial assemblies varied. In Massachusetts, the records of meetings of the General Court had been published since 1685.[46] In Pennsylvania, debates in the assembly had been considered confidential as late as 1764. From 1770 on, voters were granted ad-

44. *The Debates and Proceedings in the Congress of the United States, 1789–1824* . . . (Washington, D.C., 1834–1856), 1st Congress, 1st session, 761. Compare Rufus King's suggestion, made during debate on ratification in Massachusetts, that the senators in the new federal congress be instructed by the General Court. Elliott, ed., *Debates on the Adoption of the Constitution*, II, 47.
45. Dudley Julius Medley, *A Student's Manual of English Constitutional History*, 5th ed. (Oxford, 1913), 287–288; K. R. MacKenzie, *The English Parliament*, rev. ed. (Harmondsworth, Eng., 1959), 58–62; Pole, *Political Representation*, 402–404.
46. Colegrove, "New England Town Mandates," Col. Soc. Mass., *Trans.*, XXI (1919), 432.

mission.[47] Then in July 1776, Pennsylvania's constitutional convention resolved that its records should be published weekly in English and German.[48] The new constitution demanded that "the doors of the house in which the representatives of the freemen of this state shall sit in general assembly, shall be and remain open for the admission of all persons who behave decently, except only when the welfare of this state may require the doors to be shut."[49] The constitution also obliged the assembly to publish its votes and proceedings twice a week while it was in session. At the request of only two members, the clerk had to record how each member voted in any voice vote; and any representative would have the chance to add an explanation of why he voted as he did. In North Carolina, too, the request of only two representatives could force the house to record how each member voted on an issue. Also, the records, including the roll calls, had to be published immediately after the close of the legislative session.[50]

New York's constitution prescribed daily publication of the legislative records, provided the pressure of business permitted it; and the lawmakers were allowed to strike whole passages before publication.[51] The constitutional convention itself, however, preferred to complete its work in private meetings. A motion to open the constitutional debates to the public was defeated by a large majority.[52] The provincial congress of Virginia, too, excluded the public during those weeks in May 1776 when it discussed the bill of rights. At other times visitors could enter the gallery and lobby with the permission of a member of the house.[53] New Jersey's provincial congress of June 1776 voted on the first day of its session to exclude the public, a decision soon attacked in a petition asking "that the doors of Congress be kept open except in cases where secrecy is necessary."[54]

In 1787 the Federal Constitution was drafted behind closed doors. Its ratification, however, was an orgy of public debate. The Constitution enjoined the national legislature to publish its proceedings, "excepting such Parts as may in their Judgment require Secrecy," and to include the yeas and nays on any question if one-fifth of those present

47. Pole, *Political Representation*, 277–278.
48. *American Archives*, 5th Ser., II, 11.
49. Thorpe, ed., *Constitutions*, V, 3085.
50. *Ibid.*, 2794 (Articles XLV and XLVI).
51. *Ibid.*, 2632 (Article XV).
52. *Journals of the Provincial Congress of New York*, I, 856.
53. Resolution of May 29, 1776, in *American Archives*, 4th Ser., VI, 1542.
54. *Ibid.*, 1616, 1623.

desired to do so. Verbatim records of debates were, however, not officially published until 1873. The Constitution did not compel House and Senate to open their doors to the public. But at least the House of Representatives normally conducted its sessions in public from the beginning, and the Senate did so from 1793 on.[55]

On the federal as well as on the state level the publicness of legislative debate contributed to the formation of public opinion as an essential part of the political system. From the Revolutionary period on, political practice thus combined two elements of modern parliamentary government, representation and plebiscite, that in theory seemed to exclude one another.[56]

Rotation in Office

During the colonial period, short terms of office had not prevented the recurrent reelection of individuals, some of whom retained certain offices for decades at a time, nor had it prevented the growth of dynasties that laid claim to public offices.[57] The new constitutions, therefore, set limits on reelection to offices that were considered either potential positions of power or potential sinecures. There was less concern about the office of representative than about senatorial seats, council seats, and the governorship.

Rotation in offices—also called "rotation of civil offices" and "rotation of power"—was an old republican ideal based on a belief in the capability of many citizens to assume public office.[58] The advocates of rotation cited the authority of the English radical Whigs and

55. Frederic A. Ogg and P. Orman Ray, *Introduction to American Government: The National Government*, 7th rev. ed. (New York, 1942), 316–317. A monograph on the slow development of the "publicness" of political life in 17th- and 18th-century America, with a comparative look at European conditions, is one of the desiderata in American history.

56. Ernst Fraenkel, *Das amerikanische Regierungssystem: Eine politologische Analyse*, 2d ed. (Cologne, 1962), 297.

57. Despite annual elections, terms of office as high as 19, 33, and 50 years were recorded in Massachusetts and Connecticut. Benjamin F. Wright, Jr., "The Origins of the Separation of Powers in America," *Economica*, XIII (1933), 173; Dirk Hoerder, *Society and Government, 1760–1780: The Power Structure in Massachusetts Townships* (Berlin, 1972), investigates patterns of officeholding in five Massachusetts towns.

58. "Hints for a Form of Government," *Pa. Evening Post*, July 16, 1776; "To the

of Harrington's model state.[59] The radical Whigs believed that the corrupting influence of the court was so great that even a member of Parliament of the greatest integrity should not be exposed to it for more than a year. Therefore, the reformers had made it their goal to prevent bribes by constantly changing the members of Parliament. Advocates of rotation in America based their case in part on the corrupting influence of political power and on a general mistrust of professional politicians. Also, frequent changeover in officeholders would spur on a large number of able men to prepare to serve the country for a time. Excessively long periods of office would, on the contrary, discourage potential candidates from acquiring the knowledge necessary for public office. This argument obviously assumed a good education to be a precondition for a successful officeholder. (One newspaper writer specifically mentioned a knowledge of history, the law, government, economics, and "humanity" as essential.)[60] John Adams explicitly applied the idea of encouraging competition among the elite for public office when he drafted the constitution of Massachusetts. He suggested that no governor should serve for more than five out of any seven consecutive years. Not only would this time limit prevent him from accumulating power over an extended period of time in office, but also at the same time the possibility of achieving the high office of governor would induce a number of men to devote their energies to public affairs.[61] This idea,

Electors of Councillors," signed "Alociapt," *Boston Gaz.*, May 25, 1778; "An American," *Md. Gaz.*, June 27, 1776.

59. On Nov. 23, 1775, the *Pa. Evening Post* printed an excerpt entitled, "Of Exclusion by Rotation," from James Burgh's *Political Disquisitions*. In this passage, Burgh cited Harrington's suggestions that an incumbent in a public office not be allowed to run for that office again for one term, and that a third of the legislature be replaced every year. *The Oceana of James Harrington, Esq., and his other works* (London, 1771 [orig. publ. 1656]), book 1, chap. 12, 282–300. On Harrington's use of Venice as a model, see Zera S. Fink, *The Classical Republicans: An Essay in the Recovery of a Pattern of Thought in Seventeenth-Century England*, 2d ed. (Evanston, Ill., 1962), 65, 139, and *passim*. On the favor that the principle of rotation enjoyed among radical Whigs in Britain, see Robbins, *Eighteenth-Century Commonwealthman*, index, s.v. "Constitutional safeguards."

60. "Alociapt," *Boston Gaz.*, May 25, 1778. Also, "Loose Thoughts on Government," by "Democraticus," Purdie's *Va. Gaz.*, June 7, 1776, also in *American Archives*, 4th Ser., VI, 731.

61. Adams, ed., *Works of John Adams*, IV, 250–251.

however, failed to convince the convention, and the constitution left the governor's eligibility for reelection open.

The rotation principle also seemed useful to those who feared the increasing influence of demagogues in the aftermath of the Revolution. With their cries for freedom, demagogues could mislead "the generality" and harm "the public." The hope was also expressed that rotation could prevent a ruling clique or "party" from forming.[62] Some bills of rights used the image of an officeholder's "return" to the ranks of his equals to justify short terms and rotation. It was thought that these same measures in the Pennsylvania constitution would preclude an "unwelcome aristocracy" from developing.[63]

Virginia's constitution was the first to include detailed prohibitions against reelection. After a four-year term, a senator could not be reelected for another four years; and every year, one-fourth of the senators would be newly elected. The governor, after serving one year, could be reelected twice but would then have to wait four years before running for governor again. Privy councillors, as has already been mentioned, could not hold office for three years after they had been voted out by joint resolution of house and senate.

Pennsylvania was the only state to restrict the reelection of members to the lower house. Only three states regulated the reelection of senators, but six limited that of sheriffs, coroners, and governors. Massachusetts and New Hampshire—as well as South Carolina in its constitution of 1776—prescribed no rules for rotation in office. The table on pp. 310–311 summarizes the rules for rotation contained in the state constitutions passed between 1776 and 1780.

A Comparative Outlook

In revolutionary France of 1789 conflicting ideas of representation were advanced, which were no more compatible than the concepts of virtual and actual representation in the American colonies. The monarch claimed to represent the nation. The plurality of estate and

---

62. "Political Observations," *Pa. Packet*, Nov. 14, 1774, Jensen, ed., *American Colonial Documents*, 818; "An Independent Whig," *N.-Y. Jour.*, Feb. 29, 1776.
63. "They should, at fixed periods, be reduced to a private station, return into that body from which they were originally taken." Virginia bill of rights, Thorpe, ed., *Constitutions*, VII, 3813. The Massachusetts bill of rights contains a similar stipulation, *ibid.*, III, 1890–1891, V, 3087.

corporate interests related to the crown and to each other in a completely dysfunctional way, and it was impossible to deal with the needs of the society harmoniously and efficiently. With the third estate's proclamation, on June 17, 1789, of an "Assemblée nationale," the old regime of a nation divided into and represented by the crown and the estates of clergy, nobility, and commons—the *Ständestaat*—came to an end, and the modern system of national representation began to spread in continental Europe. As the revolution progressed, two alternative modern concepts of representation were proposed. The followers of Abbé Sieyès wanted to see the representatives, once elected, free from instructions by their particular constituencies, free to form a true "représentation nationale." The more radical disciples of Rousseau, on the other hand, wanted a "représentation populaire," that is, permanent control of the delegate by his electorate. Both groups believed in a preexisting common good and refused to determine in an empirical way what the actual needs of the society were. They were not prepared to work out a "practical balance of interests, a reconciliation between the different groups that make up the state, whether those groups be political, social, economic, professional, or religious in nature, whether their orientation be cultural or ethnic."[64]

Americans in 1776 and 1787 did not have to deal with such sharply opposed alternatives or such dogmatic demands. America had not been obliged to throw off a monarch who claimed, solely in himself, to represent the nation. George III officiated as "king in parliament." English colonial policy had created and encouraged a highly successful system of representation, one that was soon ready to exist independently of the mother country. The assemblies, representing a relatively large constituency in a relatively homogeneous population, had accurately reflected the interests of the society. The colonies and the counties, and the parishes and towns within them, had long been functioning political entities that were now ready to be

64. This whole paragraph is based on Eberhard Schmitt, "Repraesentatio in toto und Repraesentatio Singulariter: Zur Frage nach dem Zusammenbruch des französischen Ancien régime und der Durchsetzung moderner parlamentarischer Theorie und Praxis im Jahr 1789," *Historische Zeitschrift*, CCXIII (1971), 529–576; quotation from 574, my translation. See, too, Schmitt's *Repräsentation und Revolution: Eine Untersuchung zur Genesis der kontinentalen Theorie und Praxis parlamentarischer Repräsentation aus der Herrschaftspraxis des Ançien régime in Frankreich, 1760–1789* (Munich, 1969). See also Jean Roels, *Le Concept de représentation politique au 18ᵉ siècle français* . . . (Louvain, 1950), and Pole, *Political Representation*, 526–539.

represented at a higher level. As a consequence, delegates from the thirteen states were able to peacefully and easily construct a durable "national representation" within a decade after Independence. No established republican ideology had obliged the founding generation of 1776 to develop completely new political institutions or modes of representation. On the contrary, established forms of representation partially determined the shape American republican government would take.

CHAPTER XII

The Separation of Powers

Q. Why would you have your government so mixed?

A. Because the experience of ages has proved that mixed governments are the best.

Q. Simplicity is amiable and convenient in most things, why not
in government?

A. Human nature is such, that it renders simple government
destructive, and makes it necessary to place one power over
against another to ballance its weight.

Pennsylvania Evening Post, March 16, 1776

Colonial Origins

One of the means to overcome the inferior status of the colonies was
to ignore it and to regard each colony as a complete political entity
within which the same principles of government applied as in Britain.
This was particularly true for the idea of preventing arbitrary and
oppressive government by having several persons or institutions participate in the exercise of governmental powers. Since 1688 the idea
had been part of the much praised "mixed" and "balanced" British
constitution.[1] It was used in numerous conflicts between the colonial

---

[1]. See Vile, *Constitutionalism*; W. B. Gwyn, *The Meaning of the Separation of
Powers: An Analysis of the Doctrine from Its Origin to the Adoption of the United
States Constitution* (New Orleans, La., 1965); Corinne Comstock Weston,
"Beginnings of the Classical Theory of the English Constitution," Am. Phil.
Soc., Procs., C (1956), 133–144, and Weston, *English Constitutional Theory and
the House of Lords, 1556–1832* (London and New York, 1965); Francis Dunham
Wormuth, *The Origins of Modern Constitutionalism* (New York, 1949); Fink,
Classical Republicans; Stanley Pargellis, "The Theory of Balanced Govern-
ment," in Conyers Read, ed., *The Constitution Reconsidered* (New York, 1938);
Malcolm P. Sharp, "The Classical American Doctrine of 'the Separation of
Powers,'" *University of Chicago Law Review*, II (1934–1935), 385–436.

assemblies and governors. When the governor of Massachusetts attempted in 1742 to raise his own salary without seeking the annual approval of the house of representatives, the house objected and claimed that this action "would greatly tend to lessen the just weight of the other two branches of the government."[2] To calm fears that the colonies were moving toward independence, a Philadelphia pamphlet declared in 1759 that increasing "the People's Power" in Pennsylvania had not undermined the authority of the governor. Pennsylvania had developed neither a "popular" nor a "monarchical" government, the pamphlet went on, but a "mix'd Form."[3] A London compendium of 1755 was pleased to find that the colonial governments were uniform despite differences in their origins. All of them resembled the government of Britain: "By the governor, representing the King, the colonies are monarchical; by a Council they are aristocratical; by a house of representatives, or delegates from the people, they are democratical: these three are distinct and independent of one another, and the colonies enjoy the conveniences of each of these forms of government, without their inconveniencies, the several negatives being checks upon one another."[4] The implication conveyed to the reader was that the provincial governments in North America were miniature replicas of the British system, and not a threateningly new and alien development.

In reality, however, it proved to be impossible to transfer to the colonies a governmental system based on legally defined estates; a *Ständestaat* could not be recreated in the New World. In the American social and political environment, application of the English concepts of mixed government and separation of powers led to the modern system of a functional division of powers among several institutions with constitutionally prescribed forms of cooperation. Public debate in the colonies ignored this fundamental transformation. Colonial writers simply went on repeating that the colonists were merely imitating the mother country in a most natural way. A preacher speaking before the Massachusetts General Court in 1770, for example, reminded his listeners that "the whole power cannot with

2. Reply from the Massachusetts house of representatives to Gov. William Shirley, 1742, quoted in William Seal Carpenter, "The Separation of Powers in the Eighteenth Century," *American Political Science Review*, XXII (1928), 37.
3. Benjamin Franklin [?], *True and Impartial State Of the Province of Pennsylvania* (Philadelphia, 1759), 9.
4. William Douglass, *A Summary, Historical and Political, of the British Settlements in North-America* (London, 1755), I, 213–215.

safety be entrusted with a single person; nor with many, acting jointly in the same public capacity," and that "various branches of power, concentring in the community from which they originally derive their authority, are a mutual check to each other in their several departments, and jointly secure the common interest."[5] By using the vague phrase "concentring in the community," the speaker circumvented the issue of precisely how the English system of king, lords, and commons applied to colonial society. Similarly, when George Mason, writing in 1773, needed to explain the split that took place between the governor's council and the representatives of Virginia in 1680, he viewed it quite naturally as a logical step in American political evolution, yet at the same time he saw this development as a recreation of the English example. As the population had grown, Mason wrote, so the number of representatives had grown too. In joint votes the councillors always found themselves in a minority. In order to preserve their independent voice, they were finally forced to meet separately. "The Gentlemen of the Council, of their own mere Notion, thought proper to Walk upstairs, and formed in Imitation of the English House of Peers, a separate and distinct Branch of the Legislature."[6]

Between 1774 and 1776, in the acute phase of debate with crown and Parliament, the Continental Congress also drew on the principle of checks and balances. In its statement of principles of October 1774, the Congress objected to the crown's appointment of governors' councillors for indefinite terms in several colonies. The dependence of the councillors on the crown, the Congress argued, eroded legislative freedom in the colonies, because "it is indispensably necessary to good government, and rendered essential by the English constitution, that the constituent branches of the legislature be independent of each other."[7] The incident showed clearly that the colonists did not worry about the lack of a social base for an independent upper house; all they considered necessary was a functionally independent third institution.

Opponents of independence did not accept functional separation of powers as sufficient and warned that there could be no balanced government in a republic.[8] The *Encyclopedia Britannica* of 1773 re-

5. Sermon by Samuel Cook, in Thornton, ed., *Pulpit of the American Revolution*, 159.
6. George Mason, "Extracts from the Virginia Charters with some Remarks on Them," Bancroft Transcripts, fol. 91, New York Public Library.
7. Declaration of Oct. 14, 1774, Commager, ed., *Documents*, 83.
8. On Apr. 6, 1776, the *Pa. Ledger*, for example, printed an excerpt from

flected this same opinion. Under the heading "Government," the encyclopedia explained that republics were always "unmixed" (no distinction was made between modern republics and those of antiquity) and that the English constitution, by contrast, was a mixed government that enjoyed "the main advantages of an aristocracy and a democracy, and yet is free from the disadvantages and evils of either of them." The article also contained a brief summary of the allegedly Gothic origins of the British mixed form of government.[9]

Simple Government Rejected

Once the royal governor, the monarchical element in the colonial system, had been removed, the way was clear for organizing the legislative process in a purely functional way that would involve a republican governor, an executive council, a house of representatives, and an upper house. Some, however, asked why it was necessary to

---

Blackstone's *Commentaries* on the system of balances in the English constitution.

9. "The Roman and most of the Grecian States were built upon the *republican plan*; but when the Goths, and other northern nations destroyed the Roman empire and extended their conquests into far distant countries, they established wherever they came, a *mixed form* of government. The preservation of this constitution depending upon the balance between the king, nobility and people, the legislative power was lodged in these three estates, called by different names in different countries; in the north *diets*, in Spain *cortes*, in France *estates*, and in Britain *parliaments*. . . . This mixed form of government is, however, now driven almost out of Europe, in some parts of which we can hardly find the shadow of liberty left, and in many there is no more than the name remaining. France, Spain, Portugal, Denmark and part of Germany were all an age or two ago limited monarchies, governed by princes, well advised by parliaments or courts, and not by the absolute will of one man. But now all their valuable rights and liberties are swallowed up by the arbitrary power of their princes: whilst we in Great Britain have still happily preserved this noble and ancient *Gothic constitution*, which all our neighbours once enjoyed. There is such a due balance of property, power and dominion in our constitution, that, like the ancient government of Sparta, it may be called an empire of laws, and not of men; being the most excellent plan of limited monarchy in the world." *Encyclopedia Britannica* (1773), s.v. "Government." On the 18th-century revival of interest in the Goths, see Samuel Kliger, *The Goths in England: A Study in Seventeenth and Eighteenth Century Thought* (Cambridge, Mass., 1952), esp. 112–209.

let the interaction of several artificially constructed governmental agencies interfere with the rule of the elected representatives of the people. In America there was only one estate whose interests the government was to serve. Was not a "simple" form of government called for under these conditions?

In conscious opposition to the much praised balanced English constitution, a minority called for a "simple" constitution in 1776. They sought to substitute the ideal of simplicity for that of divided and balanced government. Thomas Paine was the first effective advocate of simple government in the colonies. He argued in *Common Sense* that the balance obtained in the English constitution by the separation of powers was a farce because it was obvious for all to see that the three components involved did not enjoy equal status. The monarch had gained too much power. Paine claimed that his plan was in keeping with "a principle in nature which no art can overturn, viz. that the more simple any thing is, the less liable it is to be disordered, and the easier repaired when disordered."[10] Such a statement may seem surprisingly naive in the context of political theory at the time, but in some intellectual circles simplicity had been a popular topic of salon conversation and cultural criticism for years. Eskimos and South Sea Islanders had been exhibited in London as representatives of the simple life.[11] Once the connection between living primitive people and one's own tribal past was established, the observation followed naturally that the "ancient Saxon constitution" had once been "just as simple" as the Pennsylvania constitution, which was now under attack because of its simplicity.[12]

A small town in New England picked up the idea of simplicity and declared that with "a mode of goverment the more simple, the less Danger of the loss of Liberty."[13] *The People the Best Governors*, a pamphlet written to defend the rights of rural towns in New England, appealed to the same ideal. The people, the pamphlet stated, were the best guardians of their own freedom. "The more simple, and the more immediately dependent . . . the authority is upon the people the better."[14] Even an article calling for reforms in the army in 1778

10. Foner, ed., *Writings of Paine*, I, 7, 6.

11. Chauncey Brewster Tinker, *Nature's Simple Plan: A Phase of Radical Thought in the Mid-Eighteenth Century* (Princeton, N.J., 1922), 1–5, 6–9.

12. "Demophilus," *Pa. Packet*, Oct. 22, 1776.

13. Resolution of Oct. 1779, in Handlin and Handlin, eds., *Popular Sources*, 430.

14. *People the Best Governors*, in Chase, *History of Dartmouth College*, ed. Lord, I, 656.

used a mechanical analogy that applied both to military and civil organization: "In mechanics, simplicity and efficacy are certain and concomitant. . . . Too great a combination of powers impedes the motion, and eventually destroys the use of the machine or structure."[15]

The opponents of Pennsylvania's unbalanced constitution ridiculed the idea of simplicity by defining it as "notions . . . common or natural, or simple, or easy, or not troubled with much thought."[16] Benjamin Rush stated tersely in the same debate that despotism was the simplest form of government and urged that "simplicity in principles" not be confused with "simplicity in the application of principles to practice."[17] But even the Pennsylvania constitution, which was repeatedly attacked for lacking separated and balanced branches of government, was not an instrument of direct democracy. One of its defenders listed the elements of separation and institutional checks it contained. Judges of the higher courts were independent of the legislature by virtue of their fixed salaries and seven-year appointments, and since they could not hold a second public office at the same time, there was also no danger that the legislature could offer them other lucrative posts as tokens of favor. Because the governor's council was directly elected by the people, it, too, was independent and could not be arbitrarily recalled by a majority of the voters.[18]

The advocates of simplicity were not able to achieve any lasting political influence. Simple plans for government organization were rejected as reflecting an idyllic view of society that no longer applied, not even in America. An opponent of the unicameral legislature in Pennsylvania went so far as to say that even in America the unequal distribution of property had already produced a "monarchical spirit" that "a mixed government" (to which, moreover, the population was accustomed) would help overcome. He proposed "a supreme executive magistrate (with a necessary check) and two orders in the body of legislation." He added that these orders would, of course, derive their authority from the people.[19]

A pessimistic view of human nature was part of the argument

---

15. "A Lieutenant Colonel," *Cont. Jour.*, Jan. 29, 1778.
16. *Pa. Ledger*, Oct. 12, 1776.
17. Rush, *Observations upon the Government of Pennsylvania*, 7.
18. "Remarks on the Resolves published against the Plan of Government," *Pa. Evening Post*, Nov. 9, 1776.
19. "Farmer," Nov. 5, 1776, *American Archives*, 5th Ser., III, 518. The newspaper in which this article appeared is not cited *ibid*.

for a system of checks and balances. A carefully thought out scheme of opposing and cooperating institutions could, perhaps, counteract the ill effects of human weakness. Stated crassly, the argument ran as follows:

Q. Why would you have your government so mixed?
A. Because the experience of ages has proved that mixed governments are the best.
Q. Simplicity is amiable and convenient in most things, why not in government?
A. Human nature is such, that it renders simple government destructive, and makes it necessary to place one power over against another to ballance its weight.[20]

Unicameral versus Bicameral Legislature

If anything was considered incompatible with the idea of simplicity, it was an institution comparable to the House of Lords that could prevent a majority of the representatives from enacting a law. Without rejecting the separation of powers in principle, the advocates of simplicity opposed dividing the legislature into two chambers with mutual veto power. In the winter of 1775/1776, sympathy for unicameral legislatures had been strong enough in the Continental Congress to prevent John Adams from recommending a uniform constitutional draft for all the states.[21] Between 1776 and 1780, there were numerous advocates of a unicameral legislature in both Massachusetts and Pennsylvania.[22]

Constantly recurrent points in the case for unicameral legislatures were: (1) The English constitution was a failure. The upper house had proved to be useless, and the councils established by the

---

20. *Pa. Evening Post*, Mar. 16, 1776.
21. See chap. 2, p. 56.
22. When James Warren wrote to John Adams in Feb. 1777 and reported to him how slowly the framing of the Massachusetts constitution was progressing, he stated regretfully: "Various are the opinions both as to the manner of doing it, as to the thing itself. Many are for having it done by a Convention, and many are for one Branch only." *Warren-Adams Letters*, I, 296. For other statements in favor of a unicameral legislature in Massachusetts, aside from those that will be cited later in this chapter, see Taylor, ed., *Massachusetts*, 43, 119; Handlin and Handlin, eds., *Popular Sources*, 113, 528, 731–732.

colonial constitutions had taken sides with the crown or the proprietor.[23] (2) No minority should be able to prevent a majority of popular representatives from passing a law. (3) The existence of two houses would give institutional form to a clash of interests that was incompatible with the common good.[24] An anonymous pamphleteer expressed this argument in its most succinct form: "The more houses, the more parties." Mutual veto powers would bring government to a standstill.[25] (4) Unicameral legislatures had proved their value. The town meetings were unicameral legislatures; the Continental Congress was a unicameral legislature; and as far as Pennsylvania was concerned, it had had a unicameral legislature ever since William Penn enacted the Charter of Privileges in 1701. This legislature was empowered, of course, only to draw up bills; the governor alone could actually enact them.[26] (5) A senatorial chamber would encourage the formation of a new kind of aristocracy and become a political arena for the ambitious. Who, given the choice, would prefer to remain in the lower house, where he would have to put up with passionate speeches characterized by ignorance and prejudice? The upper house would naturally try to become as independent as possible from the ignorant masses and would soon press for a three-year,

23. "One of the People," *Pa. Evening Post*, Nov. 23, 1776; "Massachusettensis," *N.-E. Chron.*, May 2, 1776; "Eudoxus," *Pa. Packet*, Apr. 22, 1776. In the *Md. Gaz.* of Nov. 26, 1779, "A.B.C." urged that the justified mistrust the people had felt toward the council before Independence not be transferred to the new senate: "It is sincerely to be lamented, that the same prejudices should prevail under the new constitution."

24. "Massachusettensis," *N.-E. Chron.*, May 2, 1776; "Eudoxus," *Pa. Packet*, Apr. 22, 1776; "One of the People," *Pa. Evening Post*, Nov. 23, 1776; "Remarks on the Resolves," *ibid.*, Nov. 19, 1776; John Sullivan to Meshech Weare, Dec. 12, 1775, in Hammond, ed., *Papers of John Sullivan*, I, 147; [Thomas Paine], "A Serious Address," no. 3, *Pa. Packet*, Dec. 1778, also in Foner, ed., *Writings of Paine*, II, 294.

25. *Four Letters on Interesting Subjects*, 20.

26. Thorpe, ed., *Constitutions*, V, 3078–3079. In the charter, a council is mentioned only in the phrase "the Governor and Council for the Time being." However, the council had no part in the formal procedures of legislation. It was nothing more than an executive council, a purely advisory body to assist the governor. Selsam, *Pennsylvania Constitution*, 9. On bicameral legislatures before 1701 and on the influence the executive councils exercised on legislation even after 1701, see Thomas Francis Moran, *The Rise and Development of the Bicameral System in America* (Baltimore, 1895), 38–42.

then a seven-year term.[27] The "gentry who seem most dissatisfied with a single legislature" were referred to Montesquieu's *Spirit of the Laws*, Book 5, where they could read that "equality is the soul of a republic."[28]

John Adams wrote the first and most influential defense of the bicameral legislature in the spring of 1776. In the proposals he had made for the Virginia constitution in November 1775, he had argued only for a balance of power between the legislative, executive, and judicial branches.[29] Now he argued primarily against unicameral legislatures. He focused his attack on the all-powerful congresses and conventions that had united legislative, executive, and judicial functions in themselves and represented an even greater concentration of powers than unicameral legislatures. His two main arguments against the continuing existence of these congresses and conventions also applied to unicameral legislatures. He was convinced that an assembly, like an individual, would always be intent on its own interest, and that it would lack essential executive and judicial knowledge and skills.[30]

Adams had neither theoretical nor practical difficulty in reconciling the concept of a functional separation of powers into legislative, executive, and judicial with a balance of power between a governor and an upper and lower house. Speaking from the perspective of colonial experience, he took as given the separation of the executive and the legislature and the competition between them. A third power was needed to mediate. Because of its dependence on the legislature, the judicial branch was too weak to perform this function. The only solution was to divide the legislature: "Let a distinct assembly

27. "One of the People," *Pa. Evening Post*, Nov. 23, 1776.
28. "Remarks on the Resolves," *ibid.*, Nov. 19, 1776. A full contemporary critique of Pennsylvania's unicameral system is to be found in the report of the council of censors of 1783, reprinted in *Proceedings relative to calling the Conventions*, 66–128. In 1789, Benjamin Franklin summarized the arguments for unicameral legislatures in his unsuccessful defense of the Pennsylvania constitution. He made no contributions to public debate on this question between 1776 and 1780, unless he did so under an as yet unidentified pseudonym. "Queries and Remarks respecting Alterations in the Constitution of Pennsylvania," in Albert Henry Smyth, ed., *The Writings of Benjamin Franklin*, X (New York, 1907), 56–58.
29. Letter to Richard Henry Lee, Nov. 1775, Adams, ed., *Works of John Adams*, IV, 186.
30. Adams, *Thoughts on Government, ibid.*, 196–197.

be constituted, as a mediator between the two extreme branches of the legislature, that which represents the people, and that which is vested with the executive power."[31] Adams based his argument on the inevitability of conflict at the level of delegated power. He did not, in this connection, justify senates as representatives of special property interests.

The arguments that were brought forth in public debate against unicameral legislatures can be summarized as follows. (1) A single chamber, like a person functioning alone, tends to react rashly and will be motivated only by self-interest. The Essex whigs suspected that it might legislate tax advantages for its members and prolong the terms of office to the point that representatives, like those in Holland, could stay in office for life.[32] (2) The English system had indeed failed, but only because the constitution was not really balanced. The new republican constitutions, however, could now introduce a perfected system of checks and balances. Richard Henry Lee saw the development of just such a system as the primary task of the Virginia constitutional convention.[33] (3) In America there were no artificial distinctions between noblemen and commoners, as in Europe, but even here there were at least two classes, the outgrowth of "natural distinctions of rank" based on "superior degrees of industry and capacity." In order to protect themselves against the power of these natural aristocrats, Benjamin Rush argued, the "men of middling fortunes" had to unite their strength in a separate legislative chamber.[34] What Rush's friend John Adams had seen as a council of sages mediating between the executive and a popular assembly, Rush himself saw as a council of aristocrats against which both the executive branch and the representatives of the mass of voters would have to form a defensive barrier.

Other proponents of a bicameral legislature did not emphasize this class division as much as Rush had. They accepted the model of an upper and lower house but thought that in America it would have

31. *Ibid.*, 195–196.
32. Massachusetts constitutional convention's preamble to the constitutional draft of 1780, Taylor, ed., *Massachusetts*, 125. Also, *Pa. Evening Post*, Mar. 16, 1776; Essex Result in Handlin and Handlin, eds., *Popular Sources*, 343–344.
33. R. H. Lee to Edmund Pendleton [?], May 12, 1776, Ballagh, ed., *Letters of R. H. Lee*, I, 190–191; Rush, *Observations upon the Government of Pennsylvania*, 8.
34. Rush, *Observations upon the Government of Pennsylvania*, 9.

to be justified in terms of function rather than in terms of social strati-fication. William Hooper, who represented North Carolina for many years in the Continental Congress, spoke in his proposals of a combi-nation of "virtue," "wisdom," and "power." Virtue should charac-terize the political behavior of the people and their representatives; wisdom, that of the few who, because of their talents or better educa-tion, constituted "a second Class." Extensive power to act decisively should be delegated to one trustworthy individual. Like Adams, Hooper assigned the role of mediator between the people and the executive branch to the senatorial class.[35] A writer in the *Virginia Gazette* added that the essential qualifications senators had to have to fill this mediating role were education, experience, and wisdom. They should be "the ablest men in the nation" and thus combine the virtues of a natural aristocracy with those of democracy.[36] The special need to protect property, a need that had been cited in support of special property requirements for the constituency of senators, played an astonishingly small role in arguments for bicameral legislatures.

Separation Clauses in the State Constitutions

All the state constitutions reflected the principles of the separation of powers and of checks and balances. None proclaimed or applied Paine's principle of simplicity. The constitutions of New Hampshire, South Carolina, and New Jersey, which were all adopted before the Declaration of Independence and which all had provisional status, were rather incomplete models of the separation as well as the bal-ance of powers. New Hampshire's provincial congress in January 1776 empowered itself to assume the duties of a house of representa-tives and to elect a council of twelve to be "a distinct and separate branch of the Legislature." The council would be chaired by a presi-dent appointed by the council.[37] In March 1776 South Carolina ac-quired a legislative council in a similar fashion, and both chambers then elected a president jointly. As a successor to the governor's council of the colonial period, South Carolina instituted a privy coun-

35. William Hooper to the congress of the state of North Carolina, Oct. 26, 1776, Saunders, ed., *N.C. Col. Recs.*, X, 867.
36. "Loose Thoughts on Government," signed "Democraticus," Purdie's *Va. Gaz.*, June 7, 1776, also in *American Archives*, 4th Ser., VI, 731.
37. Thorpe, ed., *Constitutions*, IV, 2452. The following paragraphs are also based on the constitutional texts in Thorpe.

cil that was made up of members of both chambers. Its task was to advise and control the president. The regulation that a representative or councillor would lose his seat if he were elected president or vice-president shows a clear step in the direction away from the parliamentary system and toward separating executive from legislative functions. The South Carolina constitution was explicit in denying the executive a traditional monarchical prerogative: "The president and commander-in-chief shall have no power to make war or peace, or enter into any final treaty, without the consent of the general assembly and legislative council." This ruling prefigured the provisions for ratifying treaties incorporated in the Federal Constitution of 1787. The judiciary was not granted the status of an autonomous and independent third branch. The privy council acted as a court of chancery, and justices of the peace stayed in office "during pleasure" of the executive. The legislature appointed the superior court judges, however, and they could be recalled only for misconduct in office.[38]

New Jersey's constitution called for a division of government into three branches but also did not include the judiciary among them. The borderlines between the governor, the general assembly, and the "Legislative Council" remained fluid. Three or more members of the legislative council could at any time form a privy council that was empowered to elect a vice-president who could, if necessary, represent the governor. The privy council, presided over by the governor, could also function as a final judicial authority.[39]

Virginia's constitution of June 1776 was the first constitutional document since the *Instrument of Government*, under which Britain had been governed from 1653 to 1657, to include the principle of the separation of powers in express terms. It did so with a clarity that no previous statement of either theory or practice had achieved: "The legislative, executive and judiciary departments shall be separate and distinct, so that neither exercise the powers properly belonging to the other: nor shall any person exercise the powers of more than one of them at the same time."[40]

Virginia was also first in defining the judiciary as a distinct third branch of government. Justices of the county courts were, however, eligible to run for house or senate. Since Virginia's senators were elected directly by the counties, they were the first to be truly inde-

38. *Ibid.*, VI, 3247, 3246; constitution of 1776, Articles XXVI, XVI, XX.
39. *Ibid.*, V, 2596; Articles VIII, IX.
40. This is Vile's judgment. *Constitutionalism*, 119.

pendent of the lower house. The executive did not have a similarly independent base of power. The governor was elected by separate votes in both houses, and he was to act "with the advice" of a council of state appointed by both chambers. At the conclusion of his term the house of representatives could call him to account for his actions in office by impeachment. Superior court judges were elected by the house and senate but were not held accountable to the legislature. They could stay in office indefinitely "during good behaviour." Like clergymen or anyone holding a lucrative public office, they were excluded from sitting in the house or senate. The Virginia constitution also established the incompatibility of an executive office (especially membership in the council of state) and either chamber of the legislature.

Pennsylvania's controversial constitution did not concentrate all governmental power in a single representative assembly either. It distinguished and separated "the supreme executive power" of the president and his council from legislative power. The direct election by the counties of the twelve members of the council for three-year terms made the president and the councillors relatively independent of the legislature. Candidates for president were chosen from the council, and the president was elected by a joint vote of the council and the house of representatives. Pennsylvania's constitution limited the terms of high court judges to seven years and prohibited them from holding seats in either the legislature or the executive.[41]

The New York constitution was the first to have the governor elected by a direct popular vote. This was another step away from the parliamentary toward the American presidential system. He was not, however, given the power to veto legislation. Instead, the supreme court judges, along with the governor and the chancellor, formed the "council to revise," which had the novel task of reviewing the constitutionality of all new bills. Their decision could be overruled only by a two-thirds majority in both houses. Impeachment proceedings could be initiated by the lower house, but neither the upper house nor the executive branch could pass judgment on them. A novel "court for the trial of impeachments" was to be composed of senators, the chancellor, and the judges of the supreme court, or the major part of them. No other early constitution gave so much power to the judiciary.[42]

Massachusetts adopted Virginia's clear position on the separation

---

41. Thorpe, ed., *Constitutions*, V, 3084, 3086–3087; sections 3, 19, 23.
42. *Ibid.*, 2628, 2632–2633, 2635; Articles III, XVII, XXXII.

of powers and on the independent status awarded the judiciary as the third branch of government: "The legislative department shall never exercise the executive and judicial powers, or either of them: The executive shall never exercise the legislative and judicial powers, or either of them: The judicial shall never exercise the legislative and executive powers or either of them: To the end it may be a government of laws and not of men." As in New York, the governor of Massachusetts was elected directly by the people and was therefore more independent of the legislature than governors in the remaining states were. Contrary to John Adams's wishes, he did not receive full veto power but only a veto that could be overruled by a two-thirds majority in both houses. The primary task of an advisory executive council elected by the legislature was to prevent favoritism and arbitrary decisions in appointing judges and military and administrative officers. Judges, most of whom were appointed by the executive, would retain their offices indefinitely "during good behaviour."[43]

With the constitution of Massachusetts, which clearly built on the constitutions of other states and was itself soon to be copied by New Hampshire's second constitution of 1784, we thus have the fully developed model of the American type of separated and balanced government.

None of the constitutions specified procedures of mediation between the two chambers of the legislature. South Carolina's constitution of 1776 said only that a bill passed by one house and rejected by the other could not be reintroduced until three days had passed. Maryland's senators were prohibited from exerting pressure on the house of representatives by adding what have since become known as "riders" to tax bills. Massachusetts and South Carolina in 1778 obliged both houses to schedule their sessions for the same period.

The judiciary was not yet seen as guardian of the constitutional order. The question of what later came to be called judicial review, i.e., the reviewing of laws for their constitutionality, was left completely open.[44] The authors of the early constitutions were fully aware that unconstitutional laws might well win the approval of the

43. *Ibid.*, III, 1893, 1899–1903, 1905–1906; Article XXX of the declaration of rights, and chap. 2, section 1, and chap. 3 of the frame of government.
44. For some early instances of "judicial review" dating from 1778 on and for the discussion in Philadelphia, see Charles Grove Haines, *The American Doctrine of Judicial Supremacy* (New York, 1959), 88–143, and Stourzh, "American Revolution," in *Truth and Tragedy*, 169–173.

legislature, even if it were bicameral. But the two methods they devised for meeting this danger were not based on faith that the judiciary would have the ability, integrity, and authority to recognize
such laws and annul them. The methods were based instead on belief
in the value of a delaying veto, if not of an absolute one, and in the
necessity for periodic review and revision of the constitution. New
York's council of revision arose from the first of these beliefs, Pennsylvania's and Vermont's councils of censors from the second. The
composition of the New York council of revision suggests a move
toward commissioning the judiciary with this task. A simple majority
ruled in the council, which consisted of the governor, the chancellor,
and at least two supreme court judges.

Although the principle of the separation of powers and the
system of checks and balances obviously required that judges be
appointed for life, some New England towns protested against such
encroachment on popular rights, arguing that such judges would not
only be independent of the legislature, but also of the people, "which
is making the delegated Power greater than the Constituent . . . the
Creature greater than the Creator."[45] Thomas Paine added a pessimistic view of human nature to his argument for limiting the term
of justices of the peace in Pennsylvania to seven years and for empowering the legislature to recall them in cases of "misbehaviour."
A judge who could not be recalled, Paine contended, had "power
absolute," and until men were created anew, such power would
remain dangerous.[46]

But, once more, republican ideologues had to cede to experience.
In England, judges held office *quam diu se bene gesserint*, "during good
behaviour." In the colonies, however, judges had been denied this
independence, at least in the colonies administered directly by the
crown; and in 1753, it was once again reaffirmed that judges in the
colonies would hold office *durante bene placito*, "during the pleasure of
the crown." These measures had evoked protest from the colonists
and unceasing demands that colonial judges also stay in office "during good behaviour."[47] After Independence, therefore, only one state

45. The town of Lenox, Massachusetts, in its rejection of the constitution of
1778, May 20, 1778, Taylor, ed., *Massachusetts*, 61.
46. "A Serious Address to the People of Pennsylvania on the Present Situation of their Affairs," *Pa. Packet*, Dec. 1, 1778; Foner, ed., *Writings of Paine*,
II, 295.
47. Bailyn, ed., *Pamphlets of the American Revolution*, I, 66–67, and Greene,

(South Carolina) retained the objectionable formula "during plea-sure." The other states appointed judges at their higher courts either practically for life or for clearly fixed terms such as five or seven years. Little ink was spilled in attempts to explore the contradictory ele-ments inherent in an independent judiciary as part of a form of government based on popular sovereignty. Nor was that issue solved when an independent national judiciary was established in 1787.

Beginnings of the Presidential System

The conventional wisdom is that the state governments under the first constitutions were characterized by a strong legislature and a weak executive branch; the conventional explanation for this is that in the past the governors, royal or proprietary, had been the enemy and that it was only natural for the republicans of 1776 to free themselves from strong executives. But this observation is only one segment of a larger picture, and, viewed in a comparative and long-range perspec-tive, it is not even the most significant element in the founding situa-tion of the American political system. The striking fact of historical dimension is that the reaction against the colonial governor was so weak that it did not lead to parliamentary government with an execu-tive committee of members of the legislature, but rather that within a decade the American system of presidential government evolved with full clarity and permanence.

There were, it is true, opponents of a separate executive branch of government who feared that the powers of this office would be abused as they had been in the past. A commentator on the rejected Massachusetts constitution of 1778 considered the office of governor and the executive council superfluous. Freedom was usually lost, he thought, through the delegation of too much power to one person or one small group. He made the suggestion, which was never picked up again, that legislation be enacted on the state level, as it had been in the past, but that the executive function be left to the counties: at a

---

Quest for Power, 330–332, 343. Compare Leonard Woods Labaree, *Conservatism in Early American History* (New York, 1948), 373, 388–391. As early as Jan. 12, 1640, the House of Lords had resolved to urge the king to designate fewer judges' terms *durante bene placito* and more *quam diu se bene gesserint*. Ernst Klimowsky, *Die englische Gewaltenteilungslehre bis zu Montesquieu* (Berlin, 1927), 18.

county convention, delegates from the towns could elect their own public officials from among the capable men known personally to everyone. For similar reasons the idea of a governor and senate was also rejected by a few Massachusetts towns.[48]

Those who, on the contrary, thought the new executives were much too weak in comparison to the royal governors, were particularly concerned about the efficient conduct of the war. An extremist in this group suggested that a "dictator" be installed for three or six months.[49] Others pointed out that "such large Bodies as Conventions, or committees where Party, Caprice, Ignorance, and Convictions too often prevail are by no means calculated to pursue measures which require Vigour, Secrecy, and Dispatch." Vigor, secrecy, and dispatch soon became the catchwords of the proponents of efficient independent executive branches.[50]

Most of the constitutions adopted the system that had proved its worth in the corporative colonies of Connecticut and Rhode Island and had the legislatures elect a "governor" or "president," usually for a one-year term. New York and Massachusetts were the first states to deviate from this pattern. They held direct popular elections for governor. In New York, the governor's term was three years, in Massachusetts, one year.[51]

None of the constitutions attempted to limit the powers of the executive solely to carrying out the laws passed by the legislature. The controversial points were the role of the governor in the lawmaking process and his power over appointments to lucrative offices. A vestige of the royal prerogative remained only in the form of extensive powers the governor could exercise in emergencies such as war or an epidemic, and in his power to pardon criminals.[52] Only one state instituted the role of the executive as an initiator of legislation,

48. "Occolampadius," in *Indpt. Chron.*, Mar. 26, 1778; Handlin and Handlin, eds., *Popular Sources*, 528, 212–213, 859; *N.-E. Chron.*, May 2, 1776.
49. "To the Assembly of Pennsylvania," by "A Citizen," *Pa. Evening Post*, Dec. 7, 1776. In the *Pa. Packet* of Sept. 24, 1776, a writer who signed himself "K" ridiculed Pennsylvania's powerless executive.
50. William Duer to Tench Tilgham, Sept. 28, 1776, William Duer Papers, Correspondence, 1752–1786, Box 1, New-York Historical Society, New York City. See, too, the Essex Result, Handlin and Handlin, eds., *Popular Sources*, 344–345.
51. See the table of terms of office in chap. 11.
52. Compare the lists of governors' duties in Thorpe, ed., *Constitutions*, III, 1696 (Maryland); V, 3087–3088 (Pennsylvania); 2792 (North Carolina); 2633 (New York).

a role that is taken for granted today. The New York constitution obliged the governor to present a report on "the condition of the State" once during each legislative session, and this report was to contain suggestions for legislation.[53] The precedent for the state of the Union message required from the president of the United States was thus set.

John Adams was convinced that the executive needed the veto as a defense against the legislature's persistent attempts to arrogate all power to itself. Abuse of the veto was unlikely, he argued, because the governor was in office for only one year and could act on important questions only with the approval of the executive council.[54] By 1779, Adams was no longer claiming that the veto was needed against the legislature but against influential "men of wealth, of ambitious spirits, of intrigue, of luxury and corruption" who would form "factions" to oppose the governor. "The executive, which ought to be the reservoir of wisdom, as the legislature is of liberty, without this weapon of defense, will be run down like a hare before the hunters."[55]

Adams found no support for his idea of a republican philosopher-king for a limited term in Massachusetts.[56] The constitutional convention rejected the absolute veto and followed New York's example by instituting a veto that could be overruled by a two-thirds majority in the legislature. The convention's preamble to the constitution explained that the governor could just as well be entrusted with a delaying veto as he could be with the role of supreme military commander because he was "emphatically the Representative of the whole People."[57] Some towns were not convinced by this argument and rejected even the delaying veto as a violation of the principle of separation of powers contained in the bill of rights.[58]

53. *Ibid.*, VI, 3244, 3253, III, 1687, V, 2787, 2633.
54. Adams, ed., *Works of John Adams*, IV, 186, 196–197, 231.
55. John Adams to Elbridge Gerry, Nov. 4, 1779, *ibid.*, IX, 506. Compare Walsh, *Political Science of John Adams*, 81–87.
56. Other statements opposing an executive veto may be found in Randolph's *History of Virginia*, ed. Shaffer, 255–256; "Democraticus," Purdie's *Va. Gaz.*, June 7, 1776, also in *American Archives*, 4th Ser., VI, 732; "Whitlock," *Pa. Evening Post*, May 24, 1777; William Hooper, Oct. 26, 1776, Saunders, ed., *N.C. Col. Recs.*, X, 868.
57. Taylor, ed., *Massachusetts*, 125–126.
58. The towns of Middleborough and Richmond were among those objecting. Handlin and Handlin, eds., *Popular Sources*, 694, 487.

New York devised what would remain a unique institution to give the governor a part in making political appointments. Just as the convention had objected to a purely executive veto and had granted veto power only to the council of revision that could be overruled only by a two-thirds majority in both houses, so it created a council for appointments, consisting of the governor and one senator—to be elected for one year by the house of representatives—from each of the four senatorial districts.[59]

But whatever reservations there may have been about a powerful executive, all the constitutions made the governor or the president of the executive council commander-in-chief of the military. The usual practice was that the governor could call out the militia only with the approval of the executive council, and the army only with the approval of the legislature. Once military forces were mobilized, however, the governor was given supreme command over them.[60] Several constitutions contained a declaration of principle that "in all cases and at all Times the Military ought to be under strict Subordination to and governed by the Civil Power."[61] The colonists' traditional suspicion of military rule, even of standing armies, was strong enough to prevent any realistic chance for a Cromwellian regime to emerge during the War of Independence.

All the states, with the exception of New Hampshire and New York, provided their governors with executive councils. It was the task of these councils as one constitution simply put it, "to advise the Governor in the execution of his office."[62] But the executive councils never developed any political power of their own and remained little more than committees appointed by the legislature to watch over the activities of the executive branch. They were less powerful than the

59. Thorpe, ed., *Constitutions*, V, 2633. Compare *Journals of the Provincial Congress of New York*, I, 836, 843, 853, 857, 860; Thorpe, ed., *Constitutions*, V, 2628.

60. Thorpe, ed., *Constitutions*, VII, 3817, I, 564, VI, 3088, III, 1695–1696, I, 279, II, 782, III, 1901.

61. Delaware declaration of rights in *Convention of the Delaware State*, 20. See too, Thorpe, ed., *Constitutions*, VI, 3257, III, 1688, and the complaint against George III, contained in the preamble to the Virginia constitution, that he had tried "to render the military independent of, and superior to, the civil power."

62. Thorpe, ed., *Constitutions*, V, 2791 (North Carolina); for similarly comprehensive definitions, see *ibid.*, VII, 3817 (Virginia) and III, 1904 (Massachusetts).

governors' councils of the colonial period, because most of the former councils' powers were transferred to the senates. The Federal Constitution of 1787 dropped the institution altogether and gave to the Senate the power to "advise" the president in matters of appointment and to approve of treaties he had negotiated with other governments.

Looking back from New Hampshire's constitution of 1784, closely modeled as it was on that of Massachusetts, to New Hampshire's provisional constitution of January 1776, we can clearly see the evolution of an increasingly clear division of governmental powers. The English system, based on a balance of the three estates, had been replaced by a balance among three institutions, none of which could claim supremacy over the other two.

When in 1787 and 1788 the proposed Federal Constitution was attacked for violating "the political maxim that the legislative, executive, and judiciary departments ought to be separate and distinct," Madison could easily demonstrate the irrelevance of the charge. Montesquieu, the authority used by the critics, had not advocated a separation of powers pure and simple. His much praised model, the British constitution, permitted several functions to be exercised jointly or in a partially overlapping manner by the several branches. For example, the crown was an integral part of the lawmaking process, judges were appointed by the monarch but could be removed on address of both Houses of Parliament, and the House of Lords could sit as a judicial tribunal. Similarly, among the American state constitutions, Madison went on to argue, there was "not a single instance in which the several departments of power have been kept absolutely separate and distinct."[63] If we accept Madison as representative of the highest level of political thinking among the American founders, we have to conclude that in their thinking the ideals of separation of powers and of mixed and balanced government had merged into one concept of limited government. By 1787 separation and balance were considered as complementary elements that only together ensured free government.

63. Rossiter, ed., *Federalist Papers*, no. 47, 301–308, quotations on 301, 304. Compare throughout, Conkin, *Self-Evident Truths*, chaps. 7 and 8.

CHAPTER XIII

Federalism

We shall remain weak, distracted, and divided in our councils; our strength will decrease; we shall be open to all the arts of the insidious Court of Britain, and no foreign Court will attend to our applications for assistance before we are confederated. What contract will a foreign state make with us, when we cannot agree among ourselves?

Samuel Chase to Richard Henry Lee, July 30, 1776

The peace treaties of 1783 confirmed the existence of a nation that reached from the Atlantic coast to the Mississippi and from the Great Lakes to the Spanish Floridas, a state with a claim to sovereignty comparable to that of any European power. The political struggle over how government was to be organized in this territory that dwarfed the land area of European nations lasted twice as long as the military and diplomatic one for independence. It took fourteen years to resolve this political struggle, which began with the first Continental Congress in September 1774 and ended when New York, the last of the major states, ratified the Federal Constitution on July 26, 1788. Only a temporary resolution of the battle over the division of power between the states and the Confederation had been reached on March 1, 1781, when Maryland, the last of the thirteen states, signed the Articles of Confederation.

Independence and Federation

The federal power structure of the new nation did not reflect a special quality of republican government. It evolved almost naturally from the complexity of the situation the War of Independence imposed on the colonies. There was no preexisting monolithic idea of sovereignty to which centralist-minded politicians could have appealed.

The framing of a formal constitution for the Confederation proceeded analogously to the proclaiming of independence. In both cases, existing conditions were simply formally acknowledged. Long before the Declaration of Independence was signed, the Continental Congress had acted like the legislature and executive of an independent state; and long before the Articles of Confederation were ratified, the thirteen colonies acted like a confederation in their conduct of the war. And in both cases, the Congress acted on the specific instructions its members had received from the legislatures of their home states.

A number of political leaders had hoped to proclaim the Confederation almost at the same time that they proclaimed independence, but the formal sanction of the Confederation had to wait another five years, partly because in July 1776 the delegates to the Continental Congress had no mandate to frame a federal constitution. By July 1776, the Congress had already proved its value and viability to such a degree that most of its members felt it was far more important to declare independence at that time than to write a constitution defining their own powers.

The representative assemblies of the colonies had been struggling for some eighty years to expand their authority and to assume responsibility for all domestic decisions, including the levying of taxes. They were, understandably, in no great hurry to replace the crown with another centralized government, even if it were of their own devising. But by December 1775, when the king declared the colonies to be in a state of rebellion, the need to present a united front was clear to the members of the Continental Congress. A few weeks after the Declaration of Independence had been signed, Samuel Chase of Maryland pointed out how detrimental the conflict over the Articles of Confederation was. Too few delegates, Chase claimed, were aware of the pressing needs and "the real interests" of America. "We shall remain weak, distracted, and divided in our councils," he argued. "Our strength will decrease; we shall be open to all the arts of the insidious Court of Britain, and no foreign Court will attend to our applications for assistance before we are confederated. What contract will a foreign state make with us, when we cannot agree among ourselves?"[1] The politicians who saw independence as the only ac-

---

1. Samuel Chase to Richard Henry Lee, July 30, 1776, Burnett, ed., *Letters of the Continental Congress*, II, 32.

ceptable and lasting solution to the conflict with Britain regarded a federal constitution, along with the state constitutions, as a further step in the process of national liberation. The opponents of independence warned that without a new arbitrating power to replace the authority of the crown, nothing would prevent civil war from breaking out among the selfish and land-hungry colonists.[2]

The Continental Congress in 1774 and 1775

The assemblies of twelve of the mainland colonies—Georgia and the Canadian colonies did not participate—sent delegates to the First Continental Congress in Philadelphia because they did not want to take independent measures to aid occupied Massachusetts. On the first day of its session, the Congress unpretentiously called itself "a number of the Delegates chosen and appointed by the Several Colonies and Provinces in North America to meet and hold a Congress at Philadelphia."[3] The task of the delegates was defined in their credentials. None of the delegations had precise instructions, and no mention was made of independence or confederation.[4] The first motion made on the first day of the session was that the Congress should appoint a committee to devise rules of conduct to govern debate and decision making.[5] This motion was the first step toward the framing of a constitution, for within a few hours the assembly was obliged to deal with the basic question every confederation must face, that of the division of power among its member units. The form the problem took was how much weight each delegation should have. Conflict arose immediately between the large colonies and the small ones. The small colonies invoked the integrity of each colony and insisted on one vote per delegation. The large colonies called for equal representation that reflected the size of population.

A lack of information decided the issue. Since no statistics were available, the large colonies agreed not to take the "importance" of

2. W. P. Adams, "Republicanism," *Pol. Sci. Qtly.*, LXXXV (1970), 410–411.

3. Ford *et al.*, eds., *Journals of the Continental Congress*, I, 13.

4. For credentials, see *ibid.*, 15–24. The credentials of the Connecticut delegation read, for example: "To consult and advise with the Commissioners or committees of the several English Colonies in America, on proper measures for advancing the best good of the Colonies." *Ibid.*, 18.

5. Motion made by James Duane, *ibid.*, 24.

each colony into account and accepted the small colonies' suggestion as an interim solution. Each colony received one vote, and each delegation decided internally how that vote would be cast. If there was a tie within a delegation, that delegation was forced to abstain.[6] This method of procedure, to which the large states continued to object, remained in force until 1789.

When the Second Continental Congress met in Philadelphia in May 1775, the War of Independence had already begun. The war presented the confederation with pressing tasks even before the form of the confederation itself had been determined. An army that the Congress had not mobilized had laid British-occupied Boston under siege and the Congress now had to assume control of military operations in Massachusetts and appoint a commander-in-chief.

Three drafts for articles of confederation—Benjamin Franklin's of July 1775, John Dickinson's of July 1776, and the final draft of November 1777—show the degree of consensus and conflict that existed on the issue of constituting the confederation. Franklin's draft for "Articles of Confederation and Perpetual Union" was presented to the Congress in July 1775 in hopes of clarifying the undefined status —"neither dependent nor independent"—of the colonies.[7] Most of Franklin's colleagues were not ready to act on his proposals. He was the first to raise and suggest clear solutions to problems of confederation that most members of the Congress were still reluctant to approach at all. A number of his formulations would, however, eventually be incorporated into the Articles of Confederation.

Franklin's "United Colonies of North America" were to be a "firm League of Friendship" formed to defend the freedom, property, security, and general well-being of its people. Within its own borders, each colony was to be granted the competences it possessed at that time, including the right to frame a constitution. The Congress, which was to meet annually, was to have broad powers. It could declare war, receive and appoint ambassadors, form alliances, establish

6. *Ibid.*, 25.
7. See John Adams on Franklin's position, in a letter of July 23, 1775, to Abigail Adams, Burnett, ed., *Letters of the Continental Congress*, I, 175. Franklin's draft of July 21, 1775, is in Ford *et al.*, eds., *Journals of the Continental Congress*, II, 195–199. For an interpretation, see Gerald Stourzh, *Benjamin Franklin and American Foreign Policy*, 2d ed. (Chicago, 1969), chaps. 3 and 4. On earlier forms of cooperation among the colonies in the 17th and 18th centuries, see Harry M. Ward, *"Unite or Die": Intercolony Relations, 1690–1763* (Port Washington, N.Y., 1971).

new colonies in the West, arbitrate border disputes, and settle other conflicts between the colonies. It was in charge of the military forces and was responsible for establishing a postal system and a currency valid in all the colonies. Franklin felt strongly that the Congress should be given full authority to protect "the General Welfare" and to regulate "our general Commerce." Every colony should contribute to the federal treasury in proportion to the number of male inhabitants between the ages of sixteen and sixty. Franklin also thought the issue of representation should be settled in terms of population. Colonies would be allowed one delegate for every five thousand males between sixteen and sixty; this delegate could vote independently and would not be bound by the collective decision of his delegation. Franklin did not envision an independent executive. When the Congress was not in session, an executive council with twelve members would exercise extensive powers. It could conduct foreign policy, appoint public officials, make payments, and even make legislative proposals to the Congress. Amendments to the "Constitution" would be possible with the approval of a majority of the assemblies or provincial congresses. The members of the Congress would vote to ratify this draft at its next session after they had received instructions from their home assemblies. Franklin did not prescribe whether this decision should be unanimous or not.

After brief debate, Franklin's plan was tabled for a year, probably because two groups objected to it. The opponents of independence were against it because its adoption would have been a *de facto* declaration of independence, and some advocates of independence were against it because they wanted the states to reserve more powers for themselves. Franklin's draft shows, however, that the demand for a viable federal government, for obvious pragmatic reasons, had been voiced from the beginning of the war and that a scheme for such a government did not have to be developed anew in the 1780s.

The Articles of Confederation, 1776–1778

In the months preceding the Declaration of Independence, the problem of forming foreign alliances became more and more pressing. The reluctance of potential allies like France, Spain, and the Netherlands to enter into agreements with dependent colonies forced the Americans to make a formal break with England and to so organize themselves that they at least appeared to be a firmly established political entity worthy of political, military, and financial aid. Logically, the motion in favor of independence made on June 7 in the Continental Congress called for the conclusion of alliances and for a "plan of confederation."[8] Two weeks after the Declaration of Independence, a committee of thirteen, consisting of one delegate per colony, presented, in a closed session of the Congress, a draft written by John Dickinson of Pennsylvania. This draft had much in common with Franklin's. The "Confederacy" was to be called "The United States of America" and was to be a "firm League of Friendship" for defending the confederacy's freedoms and promoting its "general Welfare." The states, still referred to as "colonies" in the draft, would continue to be solely responsible for matters of "internal police," provided they did not fall under the jurisdiction of the confederation. Dickinson defined the powers of the confederation in as broad terms as Franklin had. Foreign policy and the conduct of war were its clear prerogatives. Treaties with Indians also belonged to the exclusive province of the confederation. Trade agreements made by the confederation had precedence over state customs regulations. The confederation would set up a postal system, a national currency, and a national standard of weights. The Congress would settle all conflicts between the states, including territorial disputes. Like Franklin, Dickinson wanted to make contributions to the federal treasury proportional to population but without consideration of age or sex. Only Indians, who paid no taxes, would not be counted. In the matter of representation, Dickinson capitulated before the status quo. Every colony would, as in the past, have one vote in the annual meeting of delegates. Individuals could not vote independently of their delegation. At least nine votes would be required for all important decisions, such as declarations of war, formations of alliances, currency valuations, the issuing of paper money, the raising of credit, and the acceptance of new states into the Union. Dickinson also followed Franklin in wanting to appoint an executive committee—a council of state—to which each state would send one delegate and which would conduct the business of government, including command of the military, between sessions of the Congress. Dickinson suggested further that the regulations governing the exercise of trades and crafts in any state should not discriminate against migrants from other states. Dickinson's articles of confedera-

---

8. Ford *et al.*, eds., *Journals of the Continental Congress*, V, 425. See, too, John Penn's report of Feb. 14, 1776, on the mood of the Congress. Burnett, ed., *Letters of the Continental Congress*, I, 349.

tion could be ratified only with the approval of all the state legislatures, and, contrary to Franklin's draft, amendments also had to be passed unanimously.[9]

In two major debates—one in July and August 1776, the other from April to November 1777—the Congress shifted the balance of power in favor of the states. The version of the articles presented to the state legislatures in November 1777 and approved by them more than three years later guaranteed the states far more than control over their own "internal police." The second article read: "Each State retains its sovereignty, freedom and independence, and every power, jurisdiction, and right, which is not, by this confederation expressly delegated to the United States in Congress assembled."[10] The Congress of the confederation, made up of delegations with one vote each, was granted only a few specific powers, not any overriding, broadly defined ones. Furthermore, most of its powers could only be exercised, as Dickinson had suggested, with the approval of nine delegations. Among these powers were the rights to declare war, to enter into alliances, and to make trade agreements. In this last point, the draft of November 1777 differed sharply from Franklin's and Dickinson's versions. Here the federal government could make no commercial treaties that infringed on the different customs regulations of the individual states. But the Congress was empowered to set the value of coins and paper money, to raise credit, to equip the military, to make treaties with the Indians, and to maintain postal stations at cost. The Congress could also appoint commissions with full powers of arbitration to settle territorial disputes or other conflicts between states. These "commissioners or judges to constitute a court" represented a first step toward establishing the judiciary power the federal government would later develop. When the Congress was not in session, a Committee of the States, to which each state would send one delegate, would conduct business, collect duties, and supervise the military. An attempt to make this committee into a second legislative chamber with veto power failed.[11]

The Congress could not levy taxes. Instead, the states agreed to make voluntary contributions proportional to the value of their surveyed land. New Jersey and four southern states pushed through this

9. Text in Ford *et al.*, eds., *Journals of the Continental Congress*, V, 546–554.
10. *Ibid.*, IX, 908.
11. Suggestion made by Thomas Burke of North Carolina on May 5, 1777, *ibid.*, VII, 328–329.

solution. Since land in the northern states had a much higher value, this measure attempted to force the North to provide most of the financing for the war. But the lack of accurate statistics soon made this solution unworkable in practice.[12]

Ratification of the articles and any subsequent amendments to them would have to be accomplished by a unanimous vote. This rigid stipulation finally forced the advocates of a stronger national government in 1787 to violate a clear constitutional command.

The draft of the articles was sent to the state legislatures with an accompanying letter dated November 15, 1777. The letter apologized for the long and complex process involved in framing and ratifying a constitution. But the successful conclusion of this process would establish the authority of the American governmental system both at home and in Europe: "It will confound our foreign enemies, defeat the flagitious practices of the disaffected, strengthen and confirm our friends, support our public credit, restore the value of our money, enable us to maintain our fleets and armies, and add weight and respect to our councils at home, and to our treaties abroad."[13] The Congress hoped the delegates would return in the spring of 1778 with positive instructions to put the first federal constitution into effect.

The Classic Issues: Representation and Regionalism

One reason why the Articles of Confederation never became more than an interim solution was that they failed to reconcile major divergent interests and in particular left the question of representation unsolved. A constitutional system that was essentially an agreement on how decisions would be reached could last only if existing interest groups were sufficiently involved in the decision-making process to have a large stake in maintaining the established order. Interest groups would have to be able to pursue their goals openly, and genuine compromises between groups would have to be reached if the Confederation was to achieve permanence. Ever since the debates on representation and voting methods in the first meetings of the Continental Congress in 1774, giving divergent interests their due had been the key issue in the development of American federalism.

12. *Ibid.*, IX, 801. E. James Ferguson, *The Power of the Purse: A History of American Public Finance, 1776–1790* (Chapel Hill, N.C., 1961), 209.
13. Ford *et al.*, eds., *Journals of the Continental Congress*, IX, 933–934.

In the tenth number of *The Federalist*, Madison did no more than articulate an assumption implicit in public debate for over ten years.

In the struggle over the division of power at the federal level, three overlapping interest groups played particularly important parts. They were the slaveholders in the South, the large and small states, and the states with claims to land in the West.

The slaveholding states refused to allow their black populations to be counted as part of their total populations for purposes of determining troop contributions or assessing their contributions to the federal treasury. The conflict between regional interest groups became vividly clear in this issue. "The eastern Colonies have a great advantage in trade," Samuel Chase of Maryland stated. "This will give them a superiority. We shall be governed by our interests, and ought to be." Edward Rutledge of South Carolina added, "The Eastern Colonies will become the carriers for the Southern; they will obtain wealth for which they will not be taxed."[14] Thomas Lynch of South Carolina threatened to use the South's ultimate weapon: "If it is debated, whether their slaves are their property, there is an end of the confederation." According to his logic, slaves should not be counted any more than sheep or cattle because slaves, too, were property.[15] Benjamin Franklin's response to Lynch indicates how sharp the debate had become. The difference between slaves and sheep, Franklin said, was that the latter strengthened the economy and that "sheep will never make any insurrections."[16]

The populous states with over 300,000 inhabitants (Virginia had about 400,000, Massachusetts about 350,000, and Pennsylvania about 300,000) felt that their interests could not be adequately represented as long as the small and medium-sized states formed a majority.[17] Benjamin Franklin, ever realistic, warned that a confederation based "upon such iniquitous principles will never last long."[18]

14. Debate of July 30, 1776, *ibid*., VI, 1080.

15. *Ibid*.

16. *Ibid*.

17. The estimated populations of the other states around the year 1775 were: Georgia, 25,000 (1783); Delaware, 30,000; Rhode Island, 58,000; New Hampshire, 100,000; New Jersey, 130,000; Connecticut, 200,000; New York, 200,000; North Carolina, 200,000; South Carolina, 200,000; Maryland, 250,000. Evarts B. Greene and Virginia D. Harrington, *American Population before the Federal Census of 1790* (New York, 1932), 7.

18. During discussion in the Congress, July 30, 1776, Ford *et al*., eds., *Journals of the Continental Congress*, VI, 1079.

The same confrontation between the principles of territorial representation and numerical representation (and majority rule) that had taken place over the distribution of seats in the state legislatures now took place at the federal level. In the states, the argument had been that every last little town on the frontier was just as much a legal corporate entity as the largest coastal port and therefore should be equally represented in the legislature. In the Continental Congress, John Witherspoon of New Jersey declared on behalf of the small states: "Every Colony is a distinct person." Consequently, one vote per state was the only just solution.[19] The small states refused to be moved by the argument that their interests would be represented in the regional blocks—northeastern, middle Atlantic, and southern— to which they belonged.

In August 1776, when John Adams spoke for proportional representation and the interests of the larger states, he argued that men were not motivated by reason and a sense of justice. "It is interest alone which can be trusted. . . . Therefore the interests within doors should be the mathematical representatives of the interests without doors." In his argument, Adams also cited the variety of regional interests, a point that Madison later emphasized in the tenth number of *The Federalist*. Virginia, Pennsylvania, and Massachusetts, Adams claimed, had so many divergent interests that they could never cooperate enough to suppress the small states.[20] Benjamin Rush supported Adams and reminded the delegates of the neighborhood relations that bound large states to small states. Massachusetts lay between the small states of New Hampshire and Rhode Island; Pennsylvania, adjacent to New Jersey and Delaware; and Virginia, between Maryland and North Carolina. He also appealed to the new national consciousness. "We are now a new nation. . . . When I entered that door, I considered myself a citizen of America."[21]

Speakers for the small states were not convinced. They argued that "the safety of the whole depends upon the distinctions of Colonies."[22] "We are representatives of States, not individuals."[23] Suggestions for compromise, such as giving Rhode Island, Delaware,

---

19. July 30, 1776, *ibid*.
20. *Ibid.*, 1104.
21. John Adams's notes on the debate of Aug. 1, 1776, Adams, ed., *Works of John Adams*, II, 499–500.
22. Hopkins of Rhode Island, *ibid.*, 501.
23. Roger Sherman of Connecticut, speaking in the same debate, *ibid.*, 499.

and Georgia one delegate each and the rest of the states one delegate per fifty thousand inhabitants, could not win a majority. Representation proportional to contributions to the federal treasury was also rejected for similar reasons.[24]

The small states did not give up their resistance until 1787, when the Senate, with two representatives from each state, regardless of its size, was formed to satisfy their demands. At the same time, the slaveholding states agreed to the compromise that five blacks would count as the equivalent of three whites in the allocation of seats in the House of Representatives and the levying of direct taxes.

Another conflict that the draft of the Articles of Confederation left unresolved delayed ratification by three years. Several states had charters that left their western borders undefined, and these states claimed territories extending to the Mississippi. In some cases, their claims overlapped. The "landless" states of New Hampshire, Rhode Island, New Jersey, Pennsylvania, Delaware, and Maryland proposed, without success, that the federation as represented by the Congress become the proprietor of the territory west of the Appalachians. A larger part of the Congress's financial needs could then be met by the sale of federal lands in the West. In addition, speculators from the landless states had bought land from the Indians without considering the claims of some of the states to sovereignty over it, and the lobbyists representing these speculators vigorously supported federal control over the western lands, anticipating that the Congress would not contest their previous purchase.

By February 1779, twelve states had empowered their delegates to ratify the Articles, but Maryland remained adamant and insisted categorically that the territory north of the Ohio be ceded to the Union. Maryland's stubbornness encouraged resistance on the part of the other landless states, and in the winter of 1779/1780, a majority in its favor began to take shape.[25] Diplomatic pressure from France and a major British offensive in the South that had begun in 1779 and forced Governor Jefferson to seek refuge in the backcountry contributed to the motives for reaching an agreement. Virginia's house of representatives finally agreed to cede Virginia's western territories to the Union if the purchases that land speculators from Maryland and

24. Motions made on Oct. 7, 1777, Ford *et al.*, eds., *Journals of the Continental Congress*, IX, 780–781.
25. Jensen, *Articles of Confederation*, 226–228.

elsewhere had made from the Indians were declared void. On the same day that the New York delegation formally relinquished that state's claims to western territories, Maryland's delegates signed the Articles of Confederation. The city of Philadelphia celebrated March 1, 1781, with a thirteen-gun salute, bell ringing at noon, and fireworks on water and on land at night.[26] The liaison between the thirteen states had finally been made constitutionally legitimate.

As part of the compromise finally achieved, the Congress had pledged to use the land ceded to it for the common good of all the states and in due time to organize it into "distinct republican states."[27] This decision was the first step toward the expansionist federalism that provided the constitutional basis for the settlement of the entire continent in the course of the following century.

Since this first federal constitution remained subject to amendment, the advocates of a stronger national government could accept it as a transitional solution while continuing to work toward their final goal. In January 1781, when ratification of the Articles was in sight, James Duane, a delegate from New York, wrote to General Washington that the formal completion of the Confederation could not but have consequences for the new nation's dealings with Europe. Now the Americans' resolve to stand and fight together could no longer be doubted. The "Federal Union" would find it easier to raise credit; loans from France, Spain, and Holland, together with the contributions of the states themselves, would make an effective war effort possible. The psychological effect on American national consciousness, Duane thought, was as important as military advantages. "By the accomplishment of our Federal Union," he declared, "we are become a Nation. In a political view it is of more real Importance than a Victory over all our Enemies." At the same time, he predicted that the effort to strengthen the central government would continue, and further articles "as will give vigour and authority to Government" would soon be proposed.[28]

26. Report in the *Pa. Gaz.*, Burnett, ed., *Letters of the Continental Congress*, VI, 1–2.
27. Resolution of Oct. 10, 1780, in Ford *et al.*, eds., *Journals of the Continental Congress*, XVIII, 915.
28. Jan. 29, 1781, Burnett, ed., *Letters of the Continental Congress*, V, 551–552.

The State Constitutions and
the Powers of the Confederation

The Declaration of Independence, the state constitutions, and the Articles of Confederation all failed to clarify the controversial issue of ultimate sovereignty.[29] The state constitutions did not themselves list the powers that they denied or granted to the Congress. The only explicit ruling they made concerning their ties to the Confederation was about the election of delegates by the state legislatures.

Some states tried to clarify their relationship to the Confederation by means of the concept of "internal police." The English lexicographer Samuel Johnson defined this rather vague term in his dictionary of 1755 as the "regulation and government of a city or country so far as regards the inhabitants." In his first American dictionary, published in 1806, Noah Webster defined "police" as "the government of a city or place."[30] Some states, in instructions to their delegates in the Continental Congress, claimed for themselves the right to regulate "internal police." Rhode Island, for example, instructed its delegates in May 1776 to ensure that no measures enacted by the Continental Congress infringe on Rhode Island's sovereignty, that is, on "all the Powers of Government, so far as relates to its internal Police and Conduct of our own Affairs, civil and religious."[31] Five state bills of rights contained the phrase "internal police" without elaborating on its meaning. Delaware's bill of rights was the first to declare: "The people of this State have the sole exclusive and inherent Right of governing and regulating the internal Police of the same." Pennsylvania used the same wording. Maryland expanded it to read "regulating the internal government and police," and North Carolina adopted the same phrase. Massachusetts reserved to itself all powers not "explicitly delegated" to the Congress.[32] The states, in other words, were no more able to solve individually the question of the exact distribution of power between them and the Congress than their delegates could collectively.

29. See chap. 6, pp. 133–137.
30. Samuel Johnson, cited in *Encyclopaedia of the Social Sciences*, s.v. "Police Power"; Noah Webster, *A Compendious Dictionary of the English Language* (Hartford, Conn., 1806).
31. Ford *et al.*, eds., *Journals of the Continental Congress*, IV, 353–354. Further citations in Jensen, *Articles of Confederation*, 119.
32. *Convention of the Delaware State*, 18.

Prospects for a New National Constitution

Government under the Articles of Confederation proved inadequate to solving postwar economic problems, and those who envisaged the United States as a major economic power soon prompted the movement toward a government with broader powers.[33] Why, they asked, should the thirteen American republics be satisfied with their existence as medium-sized agrarian states? If they really joined forces, they could become a prosperous "American Empire" able to settle and exploit the entire North American continent and to develop trade with all the nations of the world. As long as an impotent congress, dependent on the good will of Amsterdam bankers in all major financial matters, stood as the only unifying element between competing state governments, there was little chance of fulfilling this ambitious vision. But in a few more years political leaders who were concerned with the economic development of the entire nation and with its political status in the eyes of the major European powers could make a reality of their concept of federal government. The victory they won in 1788 was possible because in the end their opponents in the upper class and throughout the middle class, oriented as they were to regional interests and to states' rights, were receptive nonetheless to the vision of a growing American commercial empire.

It is not surprising that Washington, more than anyone else, linked the struggle for independence to the vision of America as a powerful nation; for as the commander-in-chief of an inadequately supplied army, he had experienced, to a point approaching despair, the limits of cooperation possible between federated states. In February 1781 he issued a plea that the "ablest and best men" be sent to the Continental Congress and that the political power of that assembly be expanded. He believed these measures essential to America's independence, status, and "consequence" in Europe, indeed, to her future as a nation. And his comment on the peace treaty of 1783 was that the system of "State politics" in force up to that time could not assure America's future as a great, respected, and happy people or ward off the dangers that threatened from the European powers "who may be jealous of our greatness."[34] Businessman and journalist

33. Merrill Jensen, *The New Nation: A History of the United States during the Confederation, 1781–1789* (New York, 1950), defends the system.
34. John C. Fitzpatrick, ed., *The Writings of George Washington* (Washington, D.C., 1931–1944), XXI, 320, XXVI, 276.

Peletiah Webster argued in a 1783 pamphlet for a closer union of the thirteen states. If they joined together and settled on an effective national government, Webster argued, they would be strong enough to discourage any potential enemy. They would become an increasingly desirable trade partner for every "manufacturing nation" in Europe because they had raw materials and foodstuffs to offer and would buy manufactured goods. The same kind of trade would develop between the North and the South, and every additional trade link would further contribute to the security of the Confederation.[35]

The constitution that replaced the Articles of Confederation in 1788 did not represent a counterrevolution or a restoration, as is sometimes claimed, but simply the extension of centralizing tendencies that had existed since the beginning of the war for independence. The Federal Constitution not only enlarged considerably the power and authority of the federal government, but also changed its organization drastically to that of the three distinct branches of a bicameral legislature, a president, and a judiciary. The office of the president was comparable to that of a governor and also provided for his participation in lawmaking, and the judicial system used in the states served as a model for a relatively independent federal judiciary that was headed by the Supreme Court.

The presidential system did not develop in America because Americans wanted a substitute for the king. If that is what they had wanted, a more exact copy of the British system with a prime minister, a cabinet responsible to the legislature, and a head of state elected for life would have served them better. The presidential system at the federal level can be ascribed much more to the beliefs of the authors of the first state constitutions that free government, stability, and efficiency were most likely to be found with the combination of governor, assembly, and courts to which they were accustomed from colonial times, and to the fact that the architects of the Federal Constitution of 1787 adhered to the outline of the familiar building plan. Madison therefore attempted to win over New York anti-Federalists

35. [Pelatiah Webster], *A Dissertation On The Political Union And Constitution Of The Thirteen United States of North-America . . .* (Philadelphia, 1783), 4. On the ideas of national greatness, of expansion, and of commercial growth, see Arthur Burr Darling, *Our Rising Empire, 1763–1803* (New Haven, Conn., 1940); Richard Warner Van Alstyne, *The Rising American Empire* (Oxford, 1960); William Appleman Williams, *The Contours of American History* (Cleveland, Ohio, 1961); Stourzh, *Hamilton and Republican Government*, chap. 5.

by demonstrating the structural similarities of the republican state constitutions and the equally republican Federal Constitution.[36]

The Federalists of 1787 created political institutions on the national level that were firmly based on a pattern already existing on the state level. The combination of government on both levels, the American variant of federal government, largely fulfilled their idea of a modern nation-state founded on the principles of free republican government or, as Hamilton had called it, representative democracy. They were convinced that this political system permitted the realization of their vision of a great commercial "empire." The vision has undoubtedly come true. The norms for legitimate political action proclaimed in 1776, the protection of every person's life and liberty, equality and pursuit of happiness, have not been superseded. What remains in question is the capability of political institutions to adapt to changing circumstances and to put into practice the ideals of liberty and social justice that have been proclaimed for so long.

36. Rossiter, ed., *Federalist Papers*, no. 39, 242.

APPENDIXES

Property Qualifications in First
State Constitutions and Election Laws

New Hampshire

	1727 election law	Nov. 15, 1775, election law	1784 constitution
HOUSE			
electors	fr. worth £50	taxpayer	taxpayer
candidates	fr. worth £300	£200 fr.	pers. est. worth £100 including fr. worth £50
SENATE			
electors			taxpayer
candidates			fr. worth £200
GOVERNOR			
electors			taxpayer
candidates			pers. est. worth £500 including fr. worth £250
EXECUTIVE COUNCIL			
electors			The council is chosen by joint ballot from among the members of the legislature.
candidates			

SOURCES: No exhaustive and reliable summary of all aspects of colonial election laws has yet been compiled. The table is based on data in the constitutional texts and in the following monographs: Cortlandt F. Bishop, *History of Elections in the American Colonies* (New York, 1893); Albert Edward McKinley,

The Suffrage Franchise in the Thirteen English Colonies in America (Philadelphia, 1905); Chilton Williamson, *American Suffrage: From Property to Democracy, 1760–1860* (Princeton, N.J., 1960); Francis Newton Thorpe, *A Constitutional History of the American People, 1776–1850* (New York, 1898); and Frank Hayden Miller, "Legal Qualifications for Office in America, 1619–1899," American Historical Association, *Annual Report . . . for the Year 1899* (Washington, D.C., 1900), I, 89–153, table between pp. 106 and 107.

ABBREVIATIONS:
fr. = freehold; pers. est. = personal estate; real est. = real estate

Massachusetts

	1691 charter	1778 draft constitution	1780 constitution
HOUSE			
electors	fr. worth 40s. per year, or pers. est. worth £40	taxpayer	est. worth £60, or fr. worth £3 per year
candidates		pers. est. worth £200 including real est. worth £100	est. worth £200, or fr. worth £100
SENATE			
electors		pers. est. worth £60 "clear of all charges"	est. worth £60, or fr. worth £3 per year
candidates		pers. est. worth £400 including real est. worth £200	pers. est. worth £600, or fr. worth £300, or both to the amount of £600
GOVERNOR			
electors	The governor is appointed by the crown.	pers. est. worth £60 "clear of all charges"	pers. est. worth £60, or fr. worth £3 per year
candidates		pers. est. worth £1,000 including real est. worth £500	fr. worth £1,000
EXECUTIVE COUNCIL			
electors candidates	The councillors or assistants are chosen by the assembly.		The councillors are chosen from among the senators by the house and senate meeting in joint session.

Connecticut

1715 election law
(valid throughout the 18th century)

HOUSE
electors   fr. worth 40s. per year, or pers. est. worth £40

candidates   same as electors

SENATE
electors
candidates

GOVERNOR
electors   fr. worth 40s. per year, or pers. est. worth £40

candidates   same as electors

EXECUTIVE
COUNCIL
electors   fr. worth 40s. per year, or pers. est. worth £40
candidates
("assistants") same as electors

Rhode Island

	1762 election law	1798 election law
HOUSE		
electors	fr. worth £40 or 40s. per year *The eldest son of a qualified freeholder could also vote.*	fr. worth $134
candidates	fr. worth £40 or 40s. per year	
SENATE electors candidates		
GOVERNOR electors	fr. worth £40 or 40s. per year	
candidates	same as electors	
EXECUTIVE COUNCIL electors candidates ("assistants")	fr. worth £40 or 40s. per year same as electors	

New York

	1699 election law	1701 election law	1777 constitution
HOUSE electors	fr. worth £40 free of debts, or being a freeman of the corporation of Albany or the city of New York	fr. worth £40 regardless of mortgages	fr. worth £20, or rented real est. worth 40s. per year
candidates	fr. worth £40 free of debts	fr. worth £40 regardless of mortgages	
SENATE electors			fr. worth £100 clear of debts
candidates			fr.
GOVERNOR electors			fr. worth £100 clear of debts
candidates			fr.
EXECUTIVE COUNCIL electors candidates			

New Jersey

	1709 election law	1776 election law and constitution
HOUSE electors	fr. of 100 acres, or pers. and real est. worth £50. *Inhabitants of the towns of Perth Amboy and Burlington could vote if they were "householders."*	pers. est. worth £50 proclamation money clear of debts
candidates	fr. of 1,000 acres, or pers. and real est. worth £500	pers. and real est. worth £500 proclamation money
SENATE electors		pers. est. worth £50 proclamation money clear of debts
candidates		pers. and real est. worth £1,000 proclamation money
GOVERNOR electors		The governor is elected by joint ballot of both chambers of the legislature.
candidates		
EXECUTIVE COUNCIL electors candidates		

Pennsylvania

	1706 election law	1776 constitution
HOUSE		
electors	fr. of 50 acres, 12 acres thereof "seated and cleared," or pers. est. worth £50 clear of debts	taxpayer, or son of freeholder
candidates	same as electors	
SENATE		
electors		
candidates		
GOVERNOR		
electors		
candidates		
EXECUTIVE COUNCIL		
electors		
candidates		

Delaware

	1734 election law	1776 constitution
HOUSE		
electors	fr. of 50 acres, 12 acres thereof "cleared and improved," or pers. est. worth £50 lawful money	fr. of 50 acres, 12 acres thereof "cleared and improved," or pers. est. worth £50
candidates		fr.
SENATE		
electors		fr. of 50 acres, 12 acres thereof "cleared and improved," or pers. est. worth £50
candidates		fr.
GOVERNOR		
electors		The "president" is elected by joint ballot of both houses of the legislature.
candidates		fr.
EXECUTIVE COUNCIL		
electors		
candidates		

Maryland

	1715 election law	1776 constitution
HOUSE		
electors	fr. of 50 acres, or "visible estate" worth £40. *Inhabitants of Annapolis could vote if they owned a town lot with a house, or "a visible estate" worth £20, or were housekeepers who had served for 5 years as apprentice to a trade.*	fr. of 50 acres, or pers. est. worth £30
candidates		real or pers. property worth £500
SENATE		
electors		2 specially elected electors per county, owning real or pers. property worth £500
candidates		real and pers. property worth £1,000
GOVERNOR		
electors		The governor is elected by joint ballot of both chambers of the legislature.
candidates		real and pers. property worth £5,000, £1,000 thereof to be fr. est.
EXECUTIVE COUNCIL		
electors		The governor's council is elected by joint ballot of both chambers of the legislature.
candidates		fr. of lands and tenements worth £1,000

Virginia

	1762 election law, reaffirmed in 1769	1776 constitution
HOUSE electors	fr. of 25 acres with 12′ × 12′ house; or fr. of 50 acres unsettled; or town lot with 12′ × 12′ house *Housekeepers in Williamsburg and Norfolk could also vote if they had served to any trade for 5 years.*	"the right of suffrage . . . shall remain as exercised at present"
candidates		freeholder, or otherwise "duly qualified according to law"
SENATE electors		"the right of suffrage . . . shall remain as exercised at present"
candidates		freeholder, or otherwise "duly qualified according to law"
GOVERNOR electors		The governor is elected by joint ballot of both chambers of the legislature.
candidates		
EXECUTIVE COUNCIL electors candidates		The council of state is chosen by joint ballot of both chambers of the legislature.

North Carolina

	1760 election law	1776 constitution
HOUSE		
electors	fr. of 50 acres *In several towns taxpaying* *tenants of houses also* *could vote.*	taxpayer
candidates	fr. of 100 acres	fr. of 100 acres
SENATE		
electors		fr. of 50 acres
candidates		fr. of 300 acres
GOVERNOR		
electors		The governor is elected by joint ballot of both chambers of the legislature.
candidates		fr. of 1,000 acres
EXECUTIVE COUNCIL		
electors		The council of state is elected by joint ballot of both chambers of the legislature.
candidates		

South Carolina

	1759 election law	1776 constitution	1778 constitution
HOUSE electors	fr. in a settled plantation; or 100 acres of unsettled but taxed land; or town lot or house worth £60 proclamation money; or tax of 10s. proclamation money	same as 1759	fr. of 50 acres; or a town lot; or having paid taxes the preceding year; or being "taxable the present year . . . in a sum equal to the tax on 50 acres"
candidates	same as electors	same as 1759	same as 1759 except that general residence requirement is dropped if fr. exceeds £3,500
SENATE electors		The legislative council is elected by the first chamber of the legislature.	fr. of 50 acres; or a town lot; or having paid taxes the preceding year; or being "taxable the present year . . . in a sum equal to the tax on 50 acres"
candidates			settled fr. worth 2,000 "pounds currency clear of debts" The general residence requirement is dropped if fr. exceeds £7,000

GOVERNOR		
electors	The "president" is elected by joint ballot of both chambers of the legislature.	The governor is elected by joint ballot of both houses of the legislature.
candidates		settled fr. worth 10,000 "pounds currency clear of debts"
EXECUTIVE COUNCIL		
electors	One half of the privy council is elected by each chamber of the legislature.	The privy council is elected by joint ballot of both houses of the legislature.
candidates		settled fr. worth 10,000 "pounds currency clear of debts"

Georgia

	1761 election law	1777 constitution
HOUSE		
electors	fr. of 50 acres	taxpayer "possessed in his own right of 10 pounds value," or "being of any mechanic trade"
candidates	fr. of 500 acres	fr. of 250 acres, or "some property to the amount of 250 pounds"
SENATE		
electors		
candidates		
GOVERNOR		
electors		The governor is elected by the one-chamber legislature.
candidates		Candidates for governor must be members of the legislature.
EXECUTIVE COUNCIL		
electors		The executive council is elected by the one-chamber legislature.
candidates		Candidates for the executive council must be members of the legislature.

Rotation in Office as Stipulated in Constitutions from 1776 to 1780

States	Representative	Senator	Governor
New England States	No rotation requirements		
New York		4 yr. term; re-election possible; term of ¼ of senators expires each yr.	
New Jersey			
Pennsylvania	1 yr. term; re-election possible for a total of 3 yrs. within a 7 yr. period		1 yr. term; after 3 continuous terms in office reelection after 4 yr. pause
Delaware		3 yr. term; reelection after 3 yr. pause; term of ⅓ of senators expires each yr.	3 yr. term; reelection after 3 yr. pause
Maryland			1 yr. term; after 3 continuous terms in office reelection after 4 yr. pause
Virginia		4 yr. term; reelection after 4 yr. pause; term of ¼ of senators expires each yr.	1 yr. term; after 3 continuous terms in office reelection after 4 yr. pause

Council	Sheriff and Coroner	Others
	1 yr. term; after 4 continuous terms in office reelection after 1 yr. pause	
	1 yr. term; after 3 continuous terms in office reelection after 3 yr. pause	
3 yr. term; re-election after 4 yr. pause; term of ⅓ of councillors expires each yr.	1 yr. term; after 3 continuous terms in office reelection after 4 yr. pause	
2 yr. term; reelection after 3 yr. pause	1 yr. term; after 3 continuous terms in office reelection after 3 yr. pause	
	1 yr. term; after 3 continuous terms in office reelection after 4 yr. pause	delegates to Continental Congress: 1 yr. term; reelection possible for a total of 3 yrs. within a 6 yr. period. 2 delegates are replaced each yr.

States	Representative	Senator	Governor
North Carolina			1 yr. term; re-election possible for a total of 3 yrs. within a 6 yr. period
South Carolina (1778)			
Georgia			1 yr. term; reelection after 2 yr. pause

Council	Sheriff and Coroner	Others
		delegates to Continental Congress: 1 yr. term; after 3 continuous terms in office reelection after 1 yr. pause
2 yr. term; reelection after 4 yr. pause; term of ½ of councillors expires each yr.	2 yr. term; reelection after 4 yr. pause	commissioner of the treasury, secretary of state, attorney general, and others: 2 yr. term; after 4 yrs. in office re-election possible after 4 yr. pause

BIBLIOGRAPHY

Primary Sources

PRINTED SOURCES

Acherley, Roger. *The Britannic Constitution: or, The fundamental form of government in Britain.* . . . London, 1727.

Adams, Charles Francis, ed. *The Works of John Adams.* Boston, 1850–1856.

Adams, John, and Leonard, Daniel. *Novanglus, and Massachusettensis; or, Political Essays . . . on the Principal Points of Controversy between Great Britain and her Colonies.* Boston, 1819.

Aristotle. *Politics.*

Bailyn, Bernard, ed. *Pamphlets of the American Revolution, 1750–1776.* Cambridge, Mass., 1965.

Ballagh, James Curtis, ed. *The Letters of Richard Henry Lee.* New York, 1911.

Belknap, Jeremy. *The History of New-Hampshire.* Philadelphia, 1784; Boston, 1791–1792.

Bennett, George, ed. *The Concept of Empire: Burke to Attlee, 1774–1947.* London, 1953.

Blackstone, William. *Commentaries on the Laws of England.* Philadelphia, 1771.

Bland, Richard. *An Inquiry into the Rights of the British Colonies.* . . . Williamsburg, Va., 1766.

Bolingbroke, Henry Saint John, Viscount. *A Dissertation upon Parties.* . . . 2d ed. London, 1735.

Boucher, Jonathan. *A View of the Causes and Consequences of the American Revolution.* New York, 1967; orig. publ. London, 1797.

Bouton, Nathaniel *et al.*, eds. *The Provincial and State Papers of New Hampshire.* Concord, N.H., 1867–1943.

Boyd, Julian P. *et al.*, eds. *The Papers of Thomas Jefferson.* Princeton, N.J., 1950–   .

Bradford, Alden, ed. *Speeches of the governors of Massachusetts, from 1765 to 1775.* . . . Boston, 1818.

Brunhouse, Robert L., ed. *David Ramsay, 1749–1815: Selections from His Writings.* American Philosophical Society, *Transactions*, N.S., LV, pt. iv (1965).

Burgh, James. *Political Disquisitions; or An Enquiry into public errors, defects, and abuses.* Philadelphia, 1775.

Burnett, Edmund C., ed. *Letters of Members of the Continental Congress.* Washington, D.C., 1921–1936.

Butterfield, L. H. *et al.*, eds. *Diary and Autobiography of John Adams.* Cambridge, Mass., 1961.

Candler, Allen D., comp. *The Colonial Records of the State of Georgia.* Atlanta, Ga., 1904–1916.

Cartwright, John. *The Legislative Rights of the Commonalty Vindicated; or, Take your choice.* . . . 2d ed. London, 1777.

Catterall, Helen Tunnicliff, ed. *Judicial Cases concerning American Slavery and the Negro.* Washington, D.C., 1926–1936.

Chafee, Zechariah, Jr., comp. and ed. *Documents on Fundamental Human Rights: The Anglo-American Tradition.* Cambridge, Mass., 1951–1952.

[Chalmers, James]. *Plain Truth; Addressed To The Inhabitants of America.* . . . Philadelphia, 1776.

Chastellux, marquis de. *Travels in North-America, in the Years 1780, 1781, and 1782.* London, 1787.

Commager, Henry Steele, ed. *Documents of American History.* 7th ed. New York, 1963.

The Congressional Register; Or, History Of The Proceedings And Debates Of The first House of Representatives of The United States of America. . . . New York, 1789–1790.

[Cooper, David]. *A serious address to the rulers of America, on the inconsistency of their conduct respecting slavery.* . . . Trenton, N.J., 1783.

Cushing, Harry Alonzo, ed. *The Writings of Samuel Adams.* New York, 1904–1908.

The Debates and Proceedings in the Congress of the United States, 1789–1824. . . . Washington, D.C., 1834–1856.

The Political Writings of John Dickinson. . . . Wilmington, Del., 1801.

Douglass, William. *A Summary, Historical and Political, of the British Settlements in North-America.* London, 1755.

Drayton, John. *Memoirs of the American Revolution.* . . . Charleston, S.C., 1821.

Elliot, Jonathan, ed. *The Debates in the Several State Conventions on the Adoption of the Federal Constitution, as Recommended by the General Convention at Philadelphia, in 1787.* Washington, D.C., 1836–1845.

An Essay upon Government, Adopted by the Americans. . . . Philadelphia, 1775.

Farrand, Max, ed. *The Records of the Federal Convention of 1787.* Rev. ed. New Haven, Conn., 1937.

Filmer, Robert. *Patriarcha, or the Natural Power of Kings.* London, 1680.

Fitzpatrick, John C., ed. *The Writings of George Washington.* Washington, D.C., 1931–1944.

Foner, Philip S., ed. *The Complete Writings of Thomas Paine.* New York, 1945.

Force, Peter, ed. *American Archives* . . . , 4th Ser. and 5th Ser. Washington, D.C., 1837–1853.

Ford, Worthington Chauncey et al., eds. *Journals of the Continental Congress, 1774–1789.* Washington, D.C., 1904–1937.

Four Letters on Interesting Subjects. Philadelphia, 1776.

Franklin, Benjamin [?]. *A True and Impartial State Of the Province of Pennsylvania.* Philadelphia, 1759.

The Freeholder's Political Catechism. Very necessary to be studied by every Freeman in America. London and New York, 1769.

[Galloway, Joseph]. *A Candid Examination of the Mutual Claims Of Great-Britain, And The Colonies.* . . . New York, 1775.

The Genuine Principles of the ancient Saxon, or English Constitution. Philadelphia, 1776.

Greene, Jack P., ed. *The Diary of Colonel Landon Carter of Sabine Hall, 1752–1778.* Charlottesville, Va., 1965.

Hamilton, Alexander. *The Farmer Refuted: or, A more impartial and comprehensive View of the Dispute between Great-Britain and the Colonies.* . . . New York, 1775.

Hammond, Isaac W., comp. *Town Papers. Documents Relating to Towns in New Hampshire.* . . . Concord, N.H., 1882–1884.

Hammond, Otis G., ed. *Letters and Papers of Major-General John Sullivan.* Concord, N.H., 1930.

Handlin, Oscar, and Handlin, Mary, eds. *The Popular Sources of Political Authority: Documents on the Massachusetts Constitution of 1780.* Cambridge, Mass., 1966.

The Oceana of James Harrington, Esq., and his other works. London, 1771; orig. publ. 1656.

Hart, Levi. *Liberty Described and Recommended.* Hartford, Conn., 1775.

Hemphill, William Edwin, ed. *Extracts from the Journals of the Provincial Congresses of South Carolina, 1775–1776.* Columbia, S.C., 1960.

Hendel, Charles W., ed. *David Hume's Political Essays.* Indianapolis, Ind., 1953.

Hertzberg, Ewald Friedrich, Graf von. *Huit dissertations qui M. le Comte de Hertzberg, Ministre d'Etat, Membre et actuellement Curateur de l'Académie de Berlin, a lues dans les assemblées publiques de l'Académie Royale des Sciences et Belles Lettres de Berlin, Tenue pour l'anniversaire du Roi Frédéric II dans les Années 1780–1787.* Berlin, 1787.

[Hollis, Thomas]. *The True Sentiments of America.* . . . London, 1768.

[Howard, Martin]. *A Letter From A Gentleman at Halifax.* . . . Newport, R.I., 1765.

Hurt, John. *The Love of Our Country.* Philadelphia, 1777.

Hutcheson, Francis. *A System Of Moral Philosophy, In Three Books.* London, 1755.

Hutchinson, Thomas. *The History of the Province of Massachusetts Bay, from the Year 1750 until June 1774.* London, 1828.

——. *Strictures upon the Declaration of the Congress at Philadelphia,* ed. Malcolm Freiberg. Old South Leaflets, no. 227. Boston, 1958; orig. publ. London, 1776.

[Inglis, Charles]. *The True Interest of America Impartially Stated, in Certain st[r]ictures on a Pamphlet Intitled Common Sense.* Philadelphia, 1776.

Jacobson, David L., ed. *The English Libertarian Heritage: From the Writings of John Trenchard and Thomas Gordon in* The Independent Whig *and* Cato's Letters. Indianapolis, Ind., 1965.

Jefferson, Thomas. *Notes on the State of Virginia*, ed. William Peden. Chapel Hill, N.C., 1955.
_____. *A Summary View of the Rights of British America*. Williamsburg, Va., 1774.
Jensen, Merrill, ed. *American Colonial Documents to 1776*. In David C. Douglas, ed., *English Historical Documents*, IX. New York, 1955.
_____, comp. *Tracts of the American Revolution, 1763–1776*. Indianapolis, Ind., 1967.
Johnston, Henry P., ed. *The Correspondence and Public Papers of John Jay*. New York, 1890–1893.
Journal of the Convention for framing a Constitution of Government for the State of Massachusetts Bay, from . . . September 1, 1779, to . . . June 16, 1780. Boston, 1832.
A Journal Of The Honorable House of Representatives, Of The Colony Of The Massachusetts-Bay, in New-England [*May 29 to June 27, 1776*]. Boston, 1776.
Journals of the House of Representatives of the Commonwealth of Pennsylvania. Philadelphia, 1782.
The Journal of the Proceedings of the Provincial Congress of North-Carolina, held at Halifax the 12th day of November, 1776. Newbern, N.C., 1777.
Journals of the Provincial Congress, Provincial Convention, Committee of Safety and Council of Safety . . . of New-York. 1775–1776–1777. . . . Albany, N.Y., 1842.
Koch, Adrienne, and Peden, William, eds. *The Life and Selected Writings of Thomas Jefferson*. New York, 1944.
Lee, Arthur. *An Appeal To The Justice And Interests Of The People Of Great Britain, In The Present Dispute With America*. 4th ed. New York, 1775.
Levy, Leonard W., ed. *Freedom of the Press from Zenger to Jefferson: Early American Libertarian Theories*. Indianapolis, Ind., 1966.
[Lilburne, John]. *Englands Birth-right justified against all arbitrary usurpation . . . .* London, 1645.
Locke, John. *The Second Treatise of Government*, ed. Thomas P. Peardon. Indianapolis, Ind., 1952.
McCloskey, Robert Green, ed. *The Works of James Wilson*. Cambridge, Mass., 1967.
Machiavelli, Niccolò. *The Prince and the Discourses*, ed. Max Lerner. New York, 1940.
Massachusetts Historical Society, *Collections*, 5th Ser., IV. Boston, 1878.
The Memorial and Petition of a Numerous Body of the Inhabitants of Said Colony, Known by the Name of the United Company. N.p., [Apr. or May 1776].
Montesquieu, baron de. *De l'Esprit des lois*, ed. Gonzague Truc. Paris, 1961.
_____. *The Spirit of the Laws*, trans. Thomas Nugent. New York, 1949.
Moore, Frank, ed. *Materials for History Printed from Original Manuscripts*. New York, 1861.
_____, ed. *The Patriot Preachers of the American Revolution. . . .* New York, 1862.

Morgan, Edmund S., ed. *The New York Declaration of 1764*. Old South Leaflets, no. 224. Boston, 1948.

———, ed. *Prologue to Revolution: Sources and Documents on the Stamp Act Crisis, 1764–1766*. Chapel Hill, N.C., 1959.

Morris, Richard B. *et al.*, eds. *John Jay: The Making of a Revolutionary*. New York, 1975– .

Moultrie, William. *Memoirs of the American Revolution, So Far as It Related to the States of North and South Carolina, and Georgia*. New York, 1802.

Niles, Hezekiah, ed. *Principles and Acts of the Revolution in America*. New York, 1876; orig. publ. Baltimore, 1822.

Niles, Nathaniel. *Two Discourses on Liberty*. . . . Newburyport, Mass., 1774.

[Otis, James]. *Considerations On Behalf of the Colonists*. London, 1765.

Otis, James. *The Rights Of The British Colonies Asserted and proved*. Boston, 1764.

———. *A Vindication of the Conduct of the House of Representatives of the Province of the Massachusetts-Bay*. Boston, 1762.

The People The Best Governors: Or A Plan Of Government Founded On The Just Principles Of Natural Freedom. N.p., 1776.

Price, Richard. *Observations on the Nature of Civil Liberty, the Principles of Government, and the Justice and Policy of the War with America*. London, 1776.

Priestley, Joseph. *An Essay on the First Principles of Government, and on the Nature of Political, Civil, and Religious Liberty*. London, 1768.

Proceedings of the Convention of the Delaware State, Held at New-Castle On Tuesday the Twenty-seventh of August, 1776. Wilmington, Del., 1927; orig. publ. 1776.

The Proceedings relative to calling the Conventions of 1776 and 1790. Harrisburg, Pa., 1825.

Ramsay, David. *The History of the Revolution of South-Carolina, from a British Province to an Independent State*. Trenton, 1785.

Randolph, Edmund. *History of Virginia*, ed. Arthur H. Shaffer. Charlottesville, Va., 1970.

Richardson, James D., ed. *A Compilation of the Messages and Papers of the Presidents, 1789–1897*. Washington, D.C., 1897.

Rossiter, Clinton, ed. *The Federalist Papers*. New York, 1961.

Rousseau, Jean Jacques. *Du Contrat social; ou, principes du droit politique*. . . . Éditions Garnier Frères. Paris, 1960.

Rush, Benjamin. *Observations Upon The Present Government of Pennsylvania*. . . . Philadelphia, 1777.

Saunders, William L., ed. *The Colonial Records of North Carolina*. Raleigh, N.C., 1886–1890.

[Serle, Ambrose]. *Americans against Liberty: Or, An Essay on the Nature and Principles of True Freedom, Shewing that the Designs and Conduct of the Americans tend only to Tyranny and Slavery*. London, 1775.

Sidney, Algernon. *Discourses Concerning Government*. Philadelphia, 1805; orig. publ. London, 1698.

Smith, Adam. *The Wealth of Nations*. London and New York, 1954; orig. publ. 1776.

Smyth, Albert Henry, ed. *The Writings of Benjamin Franklin*. New York, 1907.

Syrett, Harold C., and Cooke, Jacob E., eds. *The Papers of Alexander Hamilton*. New York, 1961– .

Taylor, Robert J., ed. *Massachusetts, Colony to Commonwealth: Documents on the Formation of Its Constitution, 1775–1780*. Chapel Hill, N.C., 1961.

Thornton, John Wingate, ed. *The Pulpit of the American Revolution: or, The Political Sermons of the Period of 1776*. Boston, 1860.

Thorpe, Francis Newton, comp. and ed. *The Federal and State Constitutions, Colonial Charters, and Other Organic Laws of the States, Territories, and Colonies Now or Heretofore Forming the United States of America*. Washington, D.C., 1909.

Trenchard, John, and Gordon, Thomas. *Cato's Letters; or, Essays on Liberty, Civil and Religious, And other important Subjects*. 3d ed. London, 1733.

Usher, G. *Republican Letters; or, An Essay, Shewing the Evil Tendency of the Popular Principle*. . . . London, 1778.

Van Schreeven, William J., comp., and Scribner, Robert L., ed. *Revolutionary Virginia: The Road to Independence*, I. Charlottesville, Va., 1973.

Vaughan, Alden T., ed. *Chronicles of the American Revolution*. New York, 1965.

Warren-Adams Letters: Being Chiefly a Correspondence among John Adams, Samuel Adams, and James Warren. Massachusetts Historical Society, *Collections*, LXXII. Boston, 1917.

[Webster, Pelatiah]. *A Dissertation On The Political Union And Constitution Of The Thirteen United States Of North-America*. . . . Philadelphia, 1783.

Williams, Samuel. *A Discourse on the Love of Our Country*. . . . Salem, Mass., 1775.

[Wilson, James]. *Considerations On The Nature And The Extent Of The Legislative Authority Of The British Parliament*. Philadelphia, 1774.

Wright, John, ed. *The Parliamentary History of England, from the Earliest Period to the Year 1803*. London, 1812–1820.

Wroth, L. Kinvin *et al.*, eds. *Province in Rebellion: A Documentary History of the Founding of the Commonwealth of Massachusetts, 1774–1775*. Cambridge, Mass., 1975.

Young, Thomas. *To the Inhabitants of Vermont, a Free and Independent State, bounding on the River Connecticut and Lake Champlain*. Bound together with the broadside, *In Congress, May 15, 1776. Whereas His Britannic Majesty*. . . . Philadelphia, 1777.

Zubly, John Joachim. *Eine Kurzgefasste Historische Nachricht von Den Kämpfen Der Schweitzer für Die Freyheit*. Translated as *The Law of Liberty: A Sermon on American Affairs*. Philadelphia, 1775.

NEWSPAPERS

Boston-Gazette, and Country Journal.
Connecticut Courant, and Hartford Weekly Intelligencer.
Connecticut Journal (New Haven).
Continental Journal, and Weekly Advertiser (Boston).
Dunlap's Pennsylvania Packet, or, the General Advertiser (Philadelphia).
Freeman's Journal, or New-Hampshire Gazette (Portsmouth).
Independent Chronicle. And the Universal Advertiser (Boston).
Maryland Gazette (Annapolis).
Massachusetts Gazette; and the Boston Weekly News-Letter.
Massachusetts Spy Or, American Oracle of Liberty (Worcester).
New-England Chronicle (Boston).
New-Hampshire Gazette (Portsmouth).
New-Jersey Gazette (Trenton).
New-York Gazette: and the Weekly Mercury.
New-York Journal; or, the General Advertiser.
New York Packet. And the American Advertiser.
Pennsylvania Evening Post (Philadelphia).
Pennsylvania Gazette (Philadelphia).
Pennsylvania Journal; and the Weekly Advertiser (Philadelphia).
Pennsylvania Ledger: or the Virginia, Maryland, Pennsylvania, and New-Jersey Weekly Advertiser (Philadelphia).
Providence Gazette; and Country Journal (R.I.).
Rivington's New York Loyal Gazette.
Virginia Gazette (Williamsburg).

SPECIAL COLLECTIONS

Boston. State House. Massachusetts Archives.
New York. New-York Historical Society. William Duer Papers.
New York. New York Public Library. Bancroft Transcripts.
Philadelphia. Historical Society of Pennsylvania. Broadsides.
Philadelphia. Historical Society of Pennsylvania. Shippen Family Papers.
Washington, D.C. Library of Congress. Weare Papers.
Washington, D.C. Library of Congress. Whipple Papers, Force Transcripts.

Secondary Sources

Abernethy, Thomas Perkins. *Western Lands and the American Revolution*. New York, 1937.

Adair, Douglass. "Rumbold's Dying Speech, 1685, and Jefferson's Last Words on Democracy, 1826." In Trevor Colbourn, ed., *Fame and the Founding Fathers*. New York, 1974.

Adams, Randolph G. *Political Ideas of the American Revolution: Britannic-American Contributions to the Problem of Imperial Organization, 1765 to 1775*. 3d ed. New York, 1958.

Adams, Willi Paul. "Republicanism in Political Rhetoric before 1776." *Political Science Quarterly*, LXXXV (1970), 397–421.

———. " 'The Spirit of Commerce Requires That Property Be Sacred': Gouverneur Morris and the American Revolution." *Amerikastudien/American Studies*, XXI (1976), 309–334.

Ahlstrom, Sydney E. *A Religious History of the American People*. New Haven, Conn., 1972.

Alden, George Henry. *New Governments West of the Alleghenies before 1780*. Madison, Wis., 1897.

Allen, David Grayson. "The Zuckerman Thesis and the Process of Legal Rationalization in Provincial Massachusetts." *William and Mary Quarterly*, 3d Ser., XXIX (1972), 443–460. With "Michael Zuckerman's Reply." *William and Mary Quarterly*, 3d Ser., XXIX (1972), 461–468.

Amann, Peter, ed. *The Eighteenth-Century Revolution: French or Western?* Boston, 1963.

Ammerman, David. *In the Common Cause: American Response to the Coercive Acts of 1774*. Charlottesville, Va., 1974.

Angermann, Erich *et al.*, eds. *New Wine in Old Skins: A Comparative View of Socio-Political Structures and Values Affecting the American Revolution*. Stuttgart, 1976.

———. "Ständische Rechtstraditionen in der amerikanischen Unabhängigkeitserklärung." *Historische Zeitschrift*, CC (1965), 61–91.

Arendt, Hannah. *On Revolution*. London, 1963.

Bailyn, Bernard. *The Ideological Origins of the American Revolution*. Cambridge, Mass., 1967.

———. *The Origins of American Politics*. New York, 1968.

Barnhart, John D. *Valley of Democracy: The Frontier versus the Plantation in the Ohio Valley, 1775–1818*. Bloomington, Ind., 1953.

Becker, Carl. *The Declaration of Independence: A Study in the History of Political Ideas*. New York, 1942.

———. *The Heavenly City of the Eighteenth-Century Philosophers*. New Haven, Conn., 1932.

———. *The History of Political Parties in the Province of New York, 1760–1776*. Madison, Wis., 1960; orig. publ. 1909.

Bergman, Peter M., and McCarroll, Jean, comps. *The Negro in the Continental Congress*. New York, 1969.

Berkhofer, Robert F., Jr. "Jefferson, the Ordinance of 1784, and the Origins of the American Territorial System." *William and Mary Quarterly*, 3d Ser., XXIX (1972), 231–262.

Bernstein, David Alan. "New Jersey in the American Revolution: The Establishment of a Government amid Civil and Military Disorder, 1770–1781." Ph.D. dissertation, Rutgers University, 1970.

Bishop, Cortlandt F. *History of Elections in the American Colonies*. New York, 1893.

Bonno, Gabriel. *La Constitution britannique devant l'opinion française de Montesquieu à Bonaparte*. Paris, 1931.

Bonomi, Patricia U. *A Factious People: Politics and Society in Colonial New York*. New York, 1971.

Bowman, Larry. "The Virginia County Committees of Safety, 1774–1776." *Virginia Magazine of History and Biography*, LXXIX (1971), 322–337.

Breen, Timothy H. "John Adams' Fight against Innovation in the New England Constitution: 1776." *New England Quarterly*, XL (1967), 510–520.

Bridenbaugh, Carl. *Mitre and Sceptre: Transatlantic Faiths, Ideas, Personalities, and Politics, 1689–1775*. New York, 1962.

Brown, Richard D. "The Massachusetts Convention of Towns, 1768." *William and Mary Quarterly*, 3d Ser., XXVI (1969), 94–104.

————. *Revolutionary Politics in Massachusetts: The Boston Committee of Correspondence and the Towns, 1772–1774*. Cambridge, Mass., 1970.

Brown, Robert E. "Democracy in Colonial Massachusetts." *New England Quarterly*, XXV (1952), 291–313.

————. *Middle-Class Democracy and the Revolution in Massachusetts, 1691–1780*. Ithaca, N.Y., 1955.

————. *Reinterpretation of the Formation of the American Constitution*. Boston, 1963.

————, and Brown, B. Katherine. *Virginia, 1705–1786: Democracy or Aristocracy?* East Lansing, Mich., 1964.

Brunhouse, Robert L. *The Counter-Revolution in Pennsylvania, 1776–1790*. Harrisburg, Pa., 1942.

Burnett, Edmund Cody. *The Continental Congress*. New York, 1941.

Burrows, Edwin G., and Wallace, Michael. "The American Revolution: The Ideology and Psychology of National Liberation." *Perspectives in American History*, VI (1972), 167–306.

Bushman, Richard L. *From Puritan to Yankee: Character and the Social Order in Connecticut, 1690–1765*. Cambridge, Mass., 1967.

Cannon, Walter Faw. "Four Interpretations of the History of the State of Franklin." East Tennessee Historical Society, *Publications*, No. 22 (1950), 3–18.

Carpenter, William Seal. "The Separation of Powers in the Eighteenth Century." *American Political Science Review*, XXII (1928), 32–44.

Cary, John. "Statistical Method and the Brown Thesis on Colonial Democracy." *William and Mary Quarterly*, 3d Ser., XX (1963), 251–276.

Cecil, Evelyn. *Primogeniture: A Short History of Its Development in Various Countries and Its Practical Effects*. London, 1895.

Colbourn, H. Trevor. *The Lamp of Experience: Whig History and the Intellectual Origins of the American Revolution*. Chapel Hill, N.C., 1965.

Colegrove, Kenneth. "New England Town Mandates: Instructions to the Deputies in Colonial Legislatures." Colonial Society of Massachusetts, *Transactions*, XXI (1919), 411–449.

Coleman, Kenneth. *The American Revolution in Georgia, 1763–1789*. Athens, Ga., 1958.

Collins, Edward D. "Committees of Correspondence of the American Revolution." American Historical Association, *Annual Report . . . for the Year 1901*. Washington, D.C., 1902.

Conkin, Paul K. *Self-Evident Truths*. Bloomington, Ind., 1974.

Corwin, Edward S., and Peltason, Jack W. *Understanding the Constitution*. 3d ed. New York, 1964.

Crowl, Philip A. *Maryland during and after the Revolution: A Political and Economic Study*. Baltimore, 1943.

Cushing, Harry A. *History of the Transition from Provincial to Commonwealth Government in Massachusetts*. New York, 1896.

Cushing, John D. "The Cushing Court and the Abolition of Slavery in Massachusetts: More Notes on the 'Quock Walker Case.'" *American Journal of Legal History*, V (1961), 118–144.

Dangerfield, George. *Chancellor Robert R. Livingston of New York, 1746–1813*. New York, 1960.

Daniell, Jere R. *Experiment in Republicanism: New Hampshire Politics and the American Revolution, 1741–1794*. Cambridge, Mass., 1970.

Darling, Arthur Burr. *Our Rising Empire, 1763–1803*. New Haven, Conn., 1940.

Davis, David Brion. *The Problem of Slavery in the Age of Revolution, 1770–1823*. Ithaca, N.Y., 1975.

Delmage, Rutherford E. "The American Idea of Progress, 1750–1800." American Philosophical Society, *Proceedings*, XCI (1947), 307–314.

Detweiler, Philip F. "Congressional Debate on Slavery and the Declaration of Independence, 1819–1821." *American Historical Review*, LXIII (1957–1958), 598–616.

Dickerson, Oliver Morton. *American Colonial Government, 1696–1765: A Study of the British Board of Trade in Its Relation to the American Colonies, Political, Industrial, Administrative*. New York, 1962; orig. publ. Cleveland, Ohio, 1912.

Dippel, Horst. *Germany and the American Revolution, 1770–1800: A Sociohistorical Investigation of Late Eighteenth-Century Political Thinking*, trans. Bernhard A. Uhlendorf. Chapel Hill, N.C., 1977.

Dodd, Walter Fairleigh. *The Revision and Amendment of State Constitutions*. Baltimore, 1910.

Douglass, Elisha P. "German Intellectuals and the American Revolution." *William and Mary Quarterly*, 3d Ser., XVII (1960), 200–218.

———. *Rebels and Democrats: The Struggle for Equal Political Rights and Majority Rule during the American Revolution*. Chapel Hill, N.C., 1955.

Duff, Stella F. "The Case against the King: The *Virginia Gazettes* Indict George III." *William and Mary Quarterly*, 3d Ser., VI (1949), 383–397.

Dunbar, Louise Burnham. *A Study of "Monarchical" Tendencies in the United States from 1776 to 1801*. Urbana, Ill., 1923.

Echeverria, Durand. *Mirage in the West: A History of the French Image of American Society to 1815*. Princeton, N.J., 1957.

Eckenrode, H. J. *The Revolution in Virginia*. Boston, 1916.

Erdman, Charles R., Jr. *The New Jersey Constitution of 1776*. Princeton, N.J., 1929.

Farrand, Max. "The Delaware Bill of Rights of 1776." *American Historical Review*, III (1897–1898), 641–650.

Fay, Bernard. *The Revolutionary Spirit in France and America: A Study of Moral and Intellectual Relations between France and the United States at the End of the Eighteenth Century*. New York, 1927.

Ferguson, E. James. *The Power of the Purse: A History of American Public Finance, 1776–1790*. Chapel Hill, N.C., 1961.

Fink, Z. S. *The Classical Republicans: An Essay in the Recovery of a Pattern of Thought in Seventeenth-Century England*. 2d ed. Evanston, Ill., 1962.

Fletcher, F. T. H. *Montesquieu and English Politics (1750–1800)*. London, 1939.

Flick, Alexander C., ed. *The American Revolution in New York: Its Political, Social and Economic Significance*. Albany, N.Y., 1926.

———, ed. *History of the State of New York*. New York, 1933–1937.

Fraenkel, Ernst. *Das amerikanische Regierungssystem: Eine politologische Analyse*. 2d ed. Cologne, 1962.

———. *Deutschland und die westlichen Demokratien*. Stuttgart, 1964.

France Amérique, 1776–1789–1917: Déclaration d'indépendance, Déclaration des droits de l'homme et du citoyen . . ., trans. P.-H. Loyson and J. H. Woods. Paris, 1918.

Friedrich, Carl J. *Constitutional Government and Democracy: Theory and Practice in Europe and America*. Boston, 1941.

Frothingham, Richard. *Life and Times of Joseph Warren*. Boston, 1865.

———. *The Rise of the Republic of the United States*. Boston, 1872.

Fry, William Henry. *New Hampshire as a Royal Province*. New York, 1908.

Fuhlbruegge, Edward A. "New Jersey Finances during the American Revolution." New Jersey Historical Society, *Proceedings*, LV (1937), 167–190.

Ganyard, Robert L. "North Carolina during the American Revolution: The First Phase, 1774–1777." Ph.D. dissertation, Duke University, 1963.

Gay, Peter. *The Enlightenment: An Interpretation*. New York, 1969.

Ghelfi, Gerald John. "European Opinions of American Republicanism during the 'Critical Period,' 1781–1789." Ph.D. dissertation, Claremont Graduate School and University Center, 1968.

Gibson, James E. "The Pennsylvania Provincial Congress of [June 18 to 25] 1776." *Pennsylvania Magazine of History and Biography*, LVIII (1934), 312–341.

Gipson, Lawrence Henry. *The British Empire before the American Revolution*. New York, 1936–1969.

Godechot, Jacques. *France and the Atlantic Revolution of the Eighteenth Century, 1770–1799*, trans. Herbert H. Rowen. New York, 1965.

Grant, Charles S. *Democracy in the Connecticut Frontier Town of Kent*. New York, 1961.

Green, Fletcher M. *Constitutional Development in the South Atlantic States, 1776–1860: A Study in the Evolution of Democracy*. Chapel Hill, N.C., 1930.

Greene, Evarts B., and Harrington, Virginia D. *American Population before the Federal Census of 1790*. New York, 1932.

Greene, Jack P. *All Men Are Created Equal*. Oxford, 1976.

————."Political Mimesis: A Consideration of the Historical and Cultural Roots of Legislative Behavior in the British Colonies in the Eighteenth Century." *American Historical Review*, LXXV (1969–1970), 337–367.

————. *The Quest for Power: The Lower Houses of Assembly in the Southern Royal Colonies, 1689–1776*. Chapel Hill, N.C., 1963.

Grimm, Dieter. "Europäisches Naturrecht und amerikanische Revolution: Die Verwandlung politischer Philosophie in politische Techne." *Ius Commune*, III (1970), 120–151.

Gwyn, W. B. *The Meaning of the Separation of Powers: An Analysis of the Doctrine from Its Origin to the Adoption of the United States Constitution*. New Orleans, La., 1965.

Haines, Charles Grove. *The American Doctrine of Judicial Supremacy*. New York, 1959.

Hall, Van Beck. *Politics without Parties: Massachusetts, 1780–1791*. Pittsburgh, Pa., 1972.

Hancock, Harold. "The Kent County Loyalists." *Delaware History*, VI (1954–1955), 3–24, 92–139.

————. "Thomas Robinson: Delaware's Most Prominent Loyalist." *Delaware History*, IV (1950–1951), 1–36.

Handlin, Oscar, and Handlin, Mary F. "Radicals and Conservatives in Massachusetts after Independence." *New England Quarterly*, XVII (1944), 343–355.

Haskins, George L. "Representative Government in Early New England: The Corporate and the Parliamentary Traditions." In *Liber Memorialis Sir Maurice Powicke*, 83–98. Louvain, 1965.

Hawke, David. *In the Midst of a Revolution*. Philadelphia, 1961.

Haynes, Fred E. "Struggle for the Constitution in Massachusetts." M.A. thesis, Harvard University, 1891.

Henderson, H. James. *Party Politics in the Continental Congress*. New York, 1974.

Hendricks, Nathaniel. "A New Look at the Ratification of the Vermont Constitution of 1777." *Vermont History*, XXXIV (1966), 136–140.

Hilldrup, Robert L. "The Virginia Convention of 1776." Ph.D. dissertation, University of Virginia, 1935.

Hindle, Brooke. "The March of the Paxton Boys." *William and Mary Quarterly*, 3d Ser., III (1946), 461–486.

Hoar, R. S. "When Concord Invented the Constitutional Convention." *Boston Transcript*, July 3, 1917.

Hoerder, Dirk. *Crowd Action in Revolutionary Massachusetts, 1765–1780*. New York, 1977.

———. *Society and Government, 1760–1780: The Power Structure in Massachusetts Townships*. Berlin, 1972.

———. "Vom korporativen zum liberalen Eigentumsbegriff: Ein Element der amerikanischen Revolution." In Hans-Ulrich Wehler, ed., *200 Jahre amerikanische Revolution und moderne Revolutionsforschung*, 76–100. Göttingen, 1976.

Hoffman, Ronald. *A Spirit of Dissension: Economics, Politics, and the Revolution in Maryland*. Baltimore, 1973.

Hofstadter, Richard. *America at 1750: A Social Portrait*. New York, 1971.

———. *The Idea of a Party System: The Rise of Legitimate Opposition in the United States, 1780–1840*. Berkeley, Calif., 1969.

Holdsworth, William. *A History of English Law*. 6th rev. ed. London, 1938– .

Humphreys, R. A. "The Rule of Law and the American Revolution." *Law Quarterly Review*, LIII (1937), 80–98.

Hutson, James H. "An Investigation of the Inarticulate: Philadelphia's White Oaks." *William and Mary Quarterly*, 3d Ser., XXVIII (1971), 3–25.

Jameson, John Alexander. *The Constitutional Convention: Its History, Power and Modes of Proceeding*. 3d ed. Chicago, 1873.

Jensen, Merrill. *The Articles of Confederation: An Interpretation of the Social-Constitutional History of the American Revolution, 1774–1781*. Madison, Wis., 1940.

———. *The Founding of a Nation: A History of the American Revolution, 1763–1776*. New York, 1968.

———. *The New Nation: A History of the United States during the Confederation, 1781–1789*. New York, 1950.

Jezierski, John V. "Parliament or People: James Wilson and Blackstone on the Nature and Location of Sovereignty." *Journal of the History of Ideas*, XXXII (1971), 95–106.

Jones, Matt Bushnell. *Vermont in the Making, 1750–1777*. Cambridge, Mass., 1939.

Jordan, Winthrop D. *White over Black: American Attitudes toward the Negro, 1550–1812*. Chapel Hill, N.C., 1968.

Kammen, Michael. *Deputyes and Libertyes: The Origins of Representative Government in Colonial America*. New York, 1969.

Keim, C. Ray. "Primogeniture and Entail in Colonial Virginia." *William and Mary Quarterly*, 3d Ser., XXV (1968), 545–586.

Keir, David Lindsay. *The Constitutional History of Modern Britain since 1485*. 7th ed. London, 1964.

Kelly, Alfred H., and Harbison, Winfred A. *The American Constitution: Its Origins and Development*. 3d ed. New York, 1963.

Kemmerer, Donald L. *Path to Freedom: The Struggle for Self-Government in Colonial New Jersey, 1703–1776*. Princeton, N.J., 1940.

Kenyon, Cecelia M. "Republicanism and Radicalism in the American Revolution: An Old-Fashioned Interpretation." *William and Mary Quarterly*, 3d Ser., XIX (1962), 153–182.

Kläy, Heinz. *Zensuswahlrecht und Gleichheitsprinzip*. Bern, 1956.

Klein, Milton M. "Democracy and Politics in Colonial New York." *New York History*, XL (1959), 221–246.

Kliger, Samuel. *The Goths in England: A Study in Seventeenth and Eighteenth Century Thought*. Cambridge, Mass., 1952.

Klimowsky, Ernst. *Die englische Gewaltenteilungslehre bis zu Montesquieu*. Berlin, 1927.

Labaree, Benjamin Woods. *The Boston Tea Party*. New York, 1964.

Labaree, Leonard Woods. *Conservatism in Early American History*. New York, 1948.

Lanctot, Gustave. *Canada and the American Revolution, 1774–1783*. Cambridge, Mass., 1967.

Laslett, Peter. "Market Society and Political Theory." *Historical Journal*, VII (1964), 150–154.

———. *The World We Have Lost*. New York, 1965.

Lemisch, Jesse. "Jack Tar in the Streets: Merchant Seamen in the Politics of Revolutionary America." *William and Mary Quarterly*, 3d Ser., XXV (1968), 371–407.

Lester, William S. *The Transylvania Colony*. Spencer, Ind., 1935.

Levy, Leonard W. *Legacy of Suppression: Freedom of Speech and Press in Early American History*. Cambridge, Mass., 1960.

Lincoln, Charles H. *The Revolutionary Movement in Pennsylvania, 1760–1776*. Philadelphia, 1901.

Lincoln, Charles Z. *The Constitutional History of New York. . . .* Rochester, N.Y., 1906.

Link, Eugene Perry. *Democratic-Republican Societies, 1790–1800*. New York, 1942.

Loewenstein, Karl. *Political Power and the Governmental Process*. 2d ed. Chicago, 1965.

Lokken, Roy N. "The Concept of Democracy in Colonial Political Thought." *William and Mary Quarterly*, 3d Ser., XVI (1959), 568–580.

Lovejoy, David S. *Rhode Island Politics and the American Revolution, 1760–1776*. Providence, R.I., 1958.

————. "Rights Imply Equality: The Case against Admiralty Jurisdiction in America, 1764–1776." *William and Mary Quarterly*, 3d Ser., XVI (1959), 459–484.

Lundin, Leonard. *Cockpit of the Revolution: The War for Independence in New Jersey*. Princeton, N.J., 1940.

Lynd, Staughton. *Intellectual Origins of American Radicalism*. New York, 1968.

————. "The Mechanics in New York Politics, 1774–1788." *Labor History*, V (1964), 225–246.

————. "Who Should Rule at Home? Dutchess County, New York, in the American Revolution." *William and Mary Quarterly*, 3d Ser., XVIII (1961), 330–359.

McColley, Robert. *Slavery and Jeffersonian Virginia*. Urbana, Ill., 1964.

McCormick, Richard P. *Experiment in Independence: New Jersey in the Critical Period, 1781–1789*. New Brunswick, N.J., 1950.

————. *The History of Voting in New Jersey: A Study of the Development of Election Machinery, 1664–1911*. New Brunswick, N.J., 1953.

McCrady, Edward. *The History of South Carolina in the Revolution, 1775–1780*. New York, 1901.

MacKenzie, K. R. *The English Parliament*. Rev. ed. Harmondsworth, Eng., 1959.

McKinley, Albert Edward. *The Suffrage Franchise in the Thirteen English Colonies in America*. Philadelphia, 1905.

McLaughlin, Andrew C. *A Constitutional History of the United States*. New York, 1936.

————. *The Foundations of American Constitutionalism*. New York, 1932.

McLoughlin, William G. *New England Dissent, 1630–1833: The Baptists and the Separation of Church and State*. Cambridge, Mass., 1971.

Macpherson, C. B. *The Political Theory of Possessive Individualism: Hobbes to Locke*. Oxford, 1962.

McRee, Griffith J. *Life and Correspondence of James Iredell. . . .* New York, 1857–1858.

Maier, Pauline. *From Resistance to Revolution: Colonial Radicals and the Development of American Opposition to Britain, 1765–1776*. New York, 1972.

————. "Popular Uprisings and Civil Authority in Eighteenth-Century America." *William and Mary Quarterly*, 3d Ser., XXVII (1970), 3–35.

Main, Jackson T. "The One Hundred." *William and Mary Quarterly*, 3d Ser., XI (1954), 354–384.

————. *Political Parties before the Constitution*. Chapel Hill, N.C., 1973.

Mansfield, Harvey C., Jr. *Statesmanship and Party Government: A Study of Burke and Bolingbroke*. Chicago, 1965.

Mason, Bernard. *The Road to Independence: The Revolutionary Movement in New York, 1773–1777*. Lexington, Ky., 1966.

Meader, Lewis H. "The Council of Censors." *Pennsylvania Magazine of History and Biography*, XXII (1898), 265–300.

Medick, Hans. *Naturzustand und Naturgeschichte der bürgerlichen Gesellschaft: die Ursprünge der bürgerlichen Sozialtheorie als Geschichtsphilosophie und Sozialwissenschaft bei Samuel Pufendorf, John Locke und Adam Smith*. Göttingen, 1973.

Medley, Dudley Julius. *A Student's Manual of English Constitutional History*. 5th ed. Oxford, 1913.

Miller, Frank Hayden. "Legal Qualifications for Office in America, 1619–1899." American Historical Association, *Annual Report . . . for the Year 1899*, I, 89–153. Washington, D.C., 1900.

Miller, John C. "The Massachusetts Convention of 1768." *New England Quarterly*, VII (1934), 445–474.

———. *Sam Adams: Pioneer in Propaganda*. Boston, 1936.

Monaghan, Frank. *John Jay. . . .* New York, 1935.

Moran, Thomas Francis. *The Rise and Development of the Bicameral System in America*. Baltimore, 1895.

Morgan, Edmund S., and Morgan, Helen M. *The Stamp Act Crisis: Prologue to Revolution*. 2d ed. rev. New York, 1962.

Morison, Samuel Eliot. "The Struggle over the Adoption of the Constitution of Massachusetts, 1780." Massachusetts Historical Society, *Proceedings*, L (1916–1917), 353–412.

———. "The Vote of Massachusetts on Summoning a Constitutional Convention, 1776–1916." Massachusetts Historical Society, *Proceedings*, L (1916–1917), 241–249.

Morris, Richard B. *The American Revolution Reconsidered*. New York, 1967.

———. *The Emerging Nations and the American Revolution*. New York, 1970.

———. *Studies in the History of American Law, with Special Reference to the Seventeenth and Eighteenth Centuries*. 2d ed. New York, 1963.

Murrin, John M. "The Myths of Colonial Democracy and Royal Decline in Eighteenth-Century America: A Review Essay." *Cithara*, V (1965), 53–69.

———. Review essay in *History and Theory*, XI (1972), 226–275.

Nettels, Curtis Putnam. "The Origins of the Union and of the States." Massachusetts Historical Society, *Proceedings*, LXXII (1957–1960), 68–83.

Nevins, Allan. *The American States during and after the Revolution, 1775–1789*. New York, 1924.

O'Brien, William. "Did the Jennison Case Outlaw Slavery in Massachusetts?" *William and Mary Quarterly*, 3d Ser., XVII (1960), 219–241.

Ogg, Frederic A., and Ray, P. Orman. *Introduction to American Government: The National Government*. 7th ed. rev. New York, 1942.

Palmer, R. R. *The Age of the Democratic Revolution: A Political History of Europe and America, 1760–1800*. Princeton, N.J., 1959–1964.

———. "Notes on the Use of the Word 'Democracy,' 1789–1799." *Political Science Quarterly*, LXVIII (1953), 203–226.

Paltsits, Victor Hugo. *Washington's Farewell Address*. New York, 1935.

Pargellis, Stanley. "The Theory of Balanced Government." In Conyers Read, ed., *The Constitution Reconsidered*. New York, 1938.

Parrington, Vernon Louis. *Main Currents in American Thought: An Interpretation of American Literature from the Beginnings to 1920*, I. New York, 1927.

Parsons, J. E., Jr., "Locke's Doctrine of Property." *Social Research*, XXXVI (1969), 389–411.

Patterson, Stephen E. *Political Parties in Revolutionary Massachusetts*. Madison, Wis., 1973.

Persons, Stow. "The Cyclical Theory of History in Eighteenth Century America." *American Quarterly*, VI (1954), 147–163.

Pole, J. R. "Historians and the Problem of Early American Democracy." *Amerian Historical Review*, LXVII (1961–1962), 626–646.

––––––. *Political Representation in England and the Origins of the American Republic*. London, 1966.

––––––. *The Seventeenth Century: The Sources of Legislative Power*. Charlottesville, Va., 1969.

––––––. "Suffrage and Representation in Massachusetts: A Statistical Note." *William and Mary Quarterly*, 3d Ser., XIV (1957), 560–592.

––––––. "Suffrage Reform and the American Revolution in New Jersey." New Jersey Historical Society, *Proceedings*, LXXIV (1956), 173–194.

Purcell, Richard J. *Connecticut in Transition, 1775–1818*. Washington, D.C., 1918.

Quarles, Benjamin. *The Negro in the American Revolution*. Chapel Hill, N.C., 1961.

Ranke, Leopold von. *Über die Epochen der neueren Geschichte*, ed. Theodor Schieder and Helmut Berding. Munich, 1971.

Reed, H. Clay. "The Delaware Constitution of 1776." *Delaware Notes*, VI (1930), 7–42.

Robbins, Caroline. " 'Discordant Parties' : A Study of the Acceptance of Party by Englishmen." *Political Science Quarterly*, LXXIII (1958), 505–529.

––––––. *The Eighteenth-Century Commonwealthman: Studies in the Transmission, Development and Circumstance of English Liberal Thought from the Restoration of Charles II until the War with the Thirteen Colonies*. Cambridge, Mass., 1961.

Roels, Jean. *Le Concept de représentation politique au 18e siècle français. . . .* Louvain, 1950.

Rossiter, Clinton. *Seedtime of the Republic: The Origin of the American Tradition of Political Liberty*. New York, 1953.

Rowe, G. S. "Thomas McKean and the Coming of the Revolution." *Pennsylvania Magazine of History and Biography*, XCVI (1972), 3–47.

Rowland, Kate Mason. *The Life of George Mason, 1725–1792*, I. New York, 1892.

Rudé, George. *The Crowd in History: A Study of Popular Disturbances in France and England, 1730–1848*. New York, 1964.

Rutland, Robert Allen. *The Birth of the Bill of Rights, 1776–1791*. Chapel Hill, N.C., 1955.

Saye, Albert Berry. *A Constitutional History of Georgia, 1732–1945*. Athens, Ga., 1948.

Schlatter, Richard. *Private Property: The History of an Idea*. New Brunswick, N.J., 1951.

Schlesinger, Arthur Meier. *The Colonial Merchants and the American Revolution, 1763–1776*. New York, 1957.

Schmitt, Eberhard. "Repraesentatio in toto und Repraesentatio Singulariter: Zur Frage nach dem Zusammenbruch des französischen Ançien régime und der Durchsetzung moderner parlamentarischer Theorie und Praxis im Jahr 1789." *Historische Zeitschrift*, CCXIII (1971), 529–576.

————. *Repräsentation und Revolution: Eine Untersuchung zur Genesis der kontinentalen Theorie und Praxis parlamentarischer Repräsentation aus der Herrschaftspraxis des Ançien régime in Frankreich, 1760–1789*. Munich, 1969.

Schröder, Hans-Christoph. "Das Eigentumsproblem in den Auseinandersetzungen um die Verfassung von Massachusetts, 1775–1787." In Rudolf Vierhaus, ed., *Eigentum und Verfassung: zur Eigentumsdiskussion im ausgehenden 18. Jahrhundert*, 11–67. Göttingen, 1972.

Selsam, J. Paul. *The Pennsylvania Constitution of 1776: A Study in Revolutionary Democracy*. Philadelphia, 1936.

Shalhope, Robert E. "Toward a Republican Synthesis: The Emergence of an Understanding of Republicanism in American Historiography." *William and Mary Quarterly*, 3d Ser., XXIX (1972), 49–80.

Sharp, Malcolm P. "The Classical American Doctrine of 'the Separation of Powers.'" *University of Chicago Law Review*, II (1934–1935), 385–436.

Shoemaker, Robert W. "'Democracy' and 'Republic' as Understood in Late Eighteenth-Century America." *American Speech*, XLI (1966), 83–95.

Sparks, Jared. *The Life of Gouverneur Morris. . . .* Boston, 1832.

Spurlin, Paul Merrill. *Montesquieu in America, 1760–1801*. Baton Rouge, La., 1940.

————. "Rousseau in America, 1760–1809." *French-American Review*, I (1948), 8–20.

Stackpole, Everett S. *History of New Hampshire*, II. New York, 1916.

Stokes, Anson Phelps, and Pfeffer, Leo. *Church and State in the United States*. Rev. ed. New York, 1964.

Stourzh, Gerald. *Alexander Hamilton and the Idea of Republican Government*. Stanford, Calif., 1970.

————. "The American Revolution, Modern Constitutionalism, and the Protection of Human Rights." In Kenneth Thompson and Robert J. Myers, eds., *Truth and Tragedy: A Tribute to Hans J. Morganthau*. Washington, D.C., 1977.

————. *Benjamin Franklin and American Foreign Policy*. 2d ed. Chicago, 1969.

_____. "Die tugendhafte Republik: Montesquieus Begriff der 'vertu' und die Anfänge der Vereinigten Staaten von Amerika." In H. Fichtenau and H. Peichl, eds., *Österreich und Europa: Festgabe für Hugo Hantsch zum 70. Geburtstag*. Graz, 1965.

_____. "William Blackstone: Teacher of Revolution." *Jahrbuch für Amerika-studien*, XV (1970), 184–200.

Tate, Thad W. "The Social Contract in America, 1774–1787: Revolutionary Theory as a Conservative Instrument." *William and Mary Quarterly*, 3d Ser., XXII (1965), 375–391.

Taylor, Robert J. *Western Massachusetts in the Revolution*. Providence, R.I., 1954.

Thayer, Theodore. *Pennsylvania Politics and the Growth of Democracy, 1740–1776*. Harrisburg, Pa., 1953.

Thorpe, Francis Newton. *A Constitutional History of the American People, 1776–1850*. New York, 1898.

Tinker, Chauncey Brewster. *Nature's Simple Plan: A Phase of Radical Thought in the Mid-Eighteenth Century*. Princeton, N.J., 1922.

Trumbull, J. Hammond. *Historical Notes on the Constitutions of Connecticut, 1639–1818. . . .* Hartford, Conn., 1901.

Turner, Frederick Jackson. *The Significance of Sections in American History*. With an introduction by Max Farrand. New York, 1950.

Underdown, P. T. "Henry Cruger and Edmund Burke: Colleagues and Rivals at the Bristol Election of 1774." *William and Mary Quarterly*, 3d Ser., XV (1958), 14–34.

Uphouse, June E. "The Attitude of the Colonists toward the King and Royal Family during the Decade of Controversy." M.A. thesis, Indiana University, 1960.

Upton, Richard Francis. *Revolutionary New Hampshire: An Account of the Social and Political Forces Underlying the Transition from Royal Province to American Commonwealth*. Hanover, N.H., 1936.

Van Alstyne, Richard Warner. *The Rising American Empire*. Oxford, 1960.

Vile, M. J. C. *Constitutionalism and the Separation of Powers*. Oxford, 1967.

Wagar, W. Warren. "Modern Views of the Origins of the Idea of Progress." *Journal of the History of Ideas*, XXVIII (1967), 55–70.

Walsh, Correa Moylan. *The Political Science of John Adams: A Study in the Theory of Mixed Government and the Bicameral System*. New York and London, 1915.

Ward, Harry M. *"Unite or Die": Intercolony Relations, 1690–1763*. Port Washington, N.Y., 1971.

Warden, G. B. *Boston, 1689–1776*. Boston, 1970.

Ware, Ethel K. *A Constitutional History of Georgia*. New York, 1947.

Washburn, Emory. "Somerset's Case, and the Extinction of Villenage and Slavery in England." Massachusetts Historical Society, *Proceedings*, VII (1863–1864), 308–326.

Watlington, Patricia. *The Partisan Spirit: Kentucky Politics, 1779–1792*. New York, 1972.

Weber, Max. *Gesammelte Aufsätze zur Religionssoziologie*, I. Tübingen, 1920–1921.

———. *Wirtschaft und Gesellschaft: Grundriss der verstehenden Soziologie*, ed. Johannes Winckelmann, I. Cologne, 1964.

Wells, William V. *The Life and Public Services of Samuel Adams, Being a Narrative of His Acts and Opinions, and of His Agency in Producing and Forwarding the American Revolution . . .* , III. Boston, 1865.

Weston, Corinne Comstock. "Beginnings of the Classical Theory of the English Constitution." American Philosophical Society, *Proceedings*, C (1956), 133–144.

———. *English Constitutional Theory and the House of Lords, 1556–1832*. London and New York, 1965.

Williams, E. Neville. *The Eighteenth-Century Constitution, 1688–1815: Documents and Commentary*. Cambridge, 1960.

Williams, Samuel Cole. *History of the Lost State of Franklin*. Rev. ed. New York, 1933.

Williams, William Appleman. *The Contours of American History*. Cleveland, Ohio, 1961.

Williamson, Chilton. *American Suffrage: From Property to Democracy, 1760–1860*. Princeton, N.J., 1960.

———. *Vermont in Quandary: 1763–1825*. Montpelier, Vt., 1949.

Wolin, Sheldon S. *Politics and Vision: Continuity and Innovation in Western Political Thought*. Boston, 1960.

Wood, Gordon S. *The Creation of the American Republic, 1776–1787*. Chapel Hill, N.C., 1969.

Wormuth, Francis Dunham. *The Origins of Modern Constitutionalism*. New York, 1949.

Wright, Benjamin Fletcher, Jr. *American Interpretations of Natural Law: A Study in the History of Political Thought*. Cambridge, Mass., 1931.

———. "The Early History of Written Constitutions in America." In *Essays in History and Political Theory in Honor of Charles Howard McIlwain*. Cambridge, Mass., 1936.

———. "The Origins of the Separation of Powers in America." *Economica*, XIII (1933), 169–185.

Young, Alfred F. *The Democratic Republicans of New York: The Origins, 1763–1797*. Chapel Hill, N.C., 1967.

Zeichner, Oscar. *Connecticut's Years of Controversy, 1750–1776*. Chapel Hill, N.C., 1949.

Zilversmit, Arthur. *The First Emancipation: The Abolition of Slavery in the North*. Chicago, 1967.

———. "Quok Walker, Mumbet, and the Abolition of Slavery in Massachu-

setts." *William and Mary Quarterly*, 3d Ser., XXV (1968), 614–624.
Zuckerman, Michael. *Peaceable Kingdoms: New England Towns in the Eighteenth Century*. New York, 1970.
————. "The Social Context of Democracy in Massachusetts." *William and Mary Quarterly*, XXV (1968), 523–544.

INDEX

Abolitionism: among Quakers, 181; and gradual emancipation, 182; in Massachusetts, 184–185

Absolutism, 106, 108; and rule of law, 159

Acherley, Roger, 11

Act of Settlement (1701), 10

Act of Toleration (1689), 10

Adams, John: on liberty, 13, 157, 168; British constitution praised by, 13, 168; on Stamp Act, 19n; on founding spirit, 23; on consent of the governed, 26, 119; on Boston Tea Party, 31; on "continental Constitution," 50; plan of 1775 by, 51; on federal governments in Europe, 53; uniform state constitution opposed by, 56; unicameral legislature opposed by, 56, 264–265; on New Hampshire government, 57–58; on sovereignty of Parliament, 57–58; on independence, 60, 61; Massachusetts constitution drafted by, 92; favors veto for governor, 92, 124; on Thomas Paine, 104; on democracy and republic, 109, 115–116, 123; on mixed government, 116; on Turgot, 120; *Thoughts on Government* by, contrasted with *Common Sense*, 121–124; on virtue, 124; answers Daniel Leonard, 170; on equality, 170, 175; opposes law to abolish slavery, 183; defends property qualifications for voting, 207–208, 216; on representation, 232–233, 234–235; on function of senate, 264–265; on regional interests, 285

Adams, Samuel, 92; and committees of correspondence, 34; unicameral legislature favored by, 56; on gov-ernment in New Hampshire, 59; and use of "Democracy," 106; on misuse of power by legislatures, 243

Agrarian law, 213. *See also* Property, maximum holding of

Allegiance, 103

Allen, Thomas, 46

Alliances, 280–281

Amending procedure, 140–144. *See also* Constitution, right to alter

American Revolution: historiography of, xv; role of dissent in, xv; European interpretations of, xvi, 3, 127–128; and French Revolution, xvi, 7, 98, 121; significance of, in world history, 17; revolutionary quality of, 22, 27, 147, 176–177; social structure and political process in, 27, 177; violence in, 28; and democracy, 43; undoctrinaire quality of, 118, 124; European reactions to, 130–133

Arendt, Hannah: on founding mythology, xv; on American and French revolutions, 7; defines revolution, 22; on sovereignty and tyranny, 132

Aristocracy, 168; rejected, 26; proposed for Carolina by Locke, 100; and republics, 108–109; advantages of, 112, 259; as smear word, 152, 253; encouraged by bicameral legislature, 179, 263

Army: standing army, 10, 274; Continental Army, 52, 279

Articles of Confederation, 51, 276, 277, 288–289; and political ideas, 4; silence of, on right to resist, 138; Benjamin Franklin's draft of, 279–280; John Dickinson's draft of,